FACTOR ANALYSIS AT 100

Historical Developments and Future Directions

D1610412

FACTOR ANALYSIS AT 100

Historical Developments and Future Directions

Edited by

Robert Cudeck
The Ohio State University

and

Robert C. MacCallum
University of North Carolina at Chapel Hill

2007

LAWRENCE ERLBAUM ASSOCIATES, PUBLISHERS
Mahwah, New Jersey   London

Copyright © 2007 by Lawrence Erlbaum Associates, Inc.

Lawrence Erlbaum Associates, Inc., Publishers
10 Industrial Avenue
Mahwah, New Jersey 07430
www.erlbaum.com

Cover concept by FDS Graphics

Cover design Tomai Maridou

Library of Congress Cataloging-in-Publication Data:

Factor analysis at 100: historical developments and future directions / edited by Robert Cudeck and Robert C. MacCallum.
    p. cm.
  Includes bibliographical references and index.
ISBN 978-0-8058-5347-6 — 0-8058-5347-2 (cloth: acid-free paper)
ISBN 978-0-8058-6212-6 — 0-8058-6212-9 (pbk: acid free paper)
ISBN 978-1-4106-1580-0 — 1-4106-1580-4 (e book)
1. Factor analysis—History. I. Cudeck, Robert. II. MacCallum, Robert C. III. Title: Factor analysis at one hundred.

QA278.5.F32 2007
150.28'7–dc22

                                                        2006015919

Books published by Lawrence Erlbaum Associates are printed on acid-free paper, and their bindings are chosen for strength and durability.

Printed in the United States of America.

10 9 8 7 6 5 4 3 2 1

To Ledyard R Tucker

Beginning with his time as a student of L. L. Thurstone at the University of Chicago and throught his distinguished career at the Educational Testing Service in Princeton University and at the University of Illinois, Ledyard Tucker was a model scholar, scientist, and teacher. Directly or indirectly, he had a profound influence on many of the authors of the chapters in this volume. His contributions to the theory and methods of factor analysis are still clearly visible in modern methodological and applied research.

Contents

11 Understanding Human Intelligence Since Spearman   205
John L. Horn and John J. McArdle

12 Factoring at the Individual Level: Some Matters
for the Second Century of Factor Analysis   249
John R. Nesselroade

13 Developments in the Factor Analysis of Individual
Time Series   265
Michael W. Browne and Guangjian Zhang

14 Factor Analysis and Latent Structure of Categorical
and Metric Data   293
Irini Moustaki

15 Rotation Methods, Algorithms, and Standard Errors   315
Robert I. Jennrich

16 A Review of Nonlinear Factor Analysis
and Nonlinear Structural Equation Modeling   337
Melanie M. Wall and Yasuo Amemiya

Contributors   363

Author Index   369

Subject Index   377

Preface

Not so long ago a factor analysis of reasonable size, which today can be accomplished in seconds with a few mouse clicks, required a large investment in time and effort by an experienced investigator. Old-hand researchers tell stories from their days as graduate students when a factor analysis required weeks of work. Because of modern computers, complicated analyses such as factor analysis have become simple even as their usefulness has increased.

However, the real and substantial progress that has been made between our time and the first presentation of factor analysis by Charles Spearman in 1904 is not the improvement in calculation efficiency. The progress is rather in the impressive evolution of models and methods for the analysis of latent variables in the social sciences. Factor analysis is one of the great success stories of statistics in the social sciences because the primary focus of attention has always been on the relationships among fundamental traits such as intelligence, social class, or health status, that are unmeasurable. Factor analysis provided a way to go beyond empirical variables, such as tests and questionnaires, to the corresponding latent variables that underlie them. The great accomplishment of Spearman was in advancing a method to investigate fundamental factors. It has proven its utility in hundreds of scientific studies, across dozens of disciplines, and over a hundred years.

This book is the result of a conference that was held at the University of North Carolina in the spring of 2004 to commemorate the 100 year anniversary of Spearman's famous article. The purpose of the conference and of this book was to review the contributions of the last century that have produced the extensive body of knowledge associated with factor analysis and other latent variable models. The contributors also took the occasion to describe the main contemporary themes in statistical models for latent variables and to give an overview of how these ideas are being extended. Given the unique place that latent variable models have come to occupy in the study of individual differences, and the success of statistical models in advancing substantive knowledge in the social sciences, this review of the present state of practice is appropriate. The idea of a commemorative volume for a statistical method is unusual, to say the least. It goes without saying that the event being observed is not about abstract and artificial equations but rather the intellectual accomplishments of hard-headed researchers who work on important scientific problems of broad social relevance.

These contributions cover a wide range of topics. Several are focused on historical trends and the special contributions of Charles Spearman and L. L. Thurstone to factor thinking. Other chapters investigate the foundations of the exploratory model including the important issue of analytic rotation and the distinctive perspectives of the factor model compared to its much-confused alter ego principal components analysis. Karl Jöreskog presents a personal review of the development of structural equation modeling. Two fundamental theoretical problems are reviewed: the problem of factorial invariance and the problem of approximating models. Several contributions address developments that are currently popular, especially the analysis of categorical variables, the extension of latent variables to nonlinear models, and models for longitudinal and time series data. The collection of topics is eclectic, but each is scholarly and thoughtful. Together they address many of the main conceptual currents that correspond to current theoretical and applied work with latent variable models.

After some deliberation, it was decided not to include computer code for analyses that are described here even though some of the chapters illustrate new statistical concepts with interesting examples. This decision followed from the simple fact that we wanted the contributors to present the most timely ideas for data analysis. To also require that computer programs be written, although obviously desirable in general, would have diverted effort from the main task of reviewing the most interesting modern latent variable models. Many examples can be run on commercially available software. The authors indicate which are appropriate in each chapter. In other cases, a good strategy is to consult the individual web pages of particular authors for datasets and computer code. Because computing capabilities change constantly, there is something to be said for not presenting specialized code that is in danger of becoming dated sooner than anyone wishes.

This book can serve as a resource for researchers and students who are acquainted with factor analysis and other latent variable models and who want an up-to-date treatment of the major current themes. Several chapters would be ideal for a semester-long course dealing with intermediate topics in latent variable models. Although the level of mathematical detail is not high, we assume that readers will have a background in graduate-level statistics, factor analysis, and structural equation models. Every chapter contains additional literature for further reading.

Many talented people helped make this project a success, and we appreciate all these contributions. In particular, Michael Browne, Patrick Curran, Irini Moustaki, John Nesselroade, Kristopher Preacher, and Keith Widaman kept the project on track and provided welcome organizational direction. The graduate students in quantitative psychology and Ms. Ginny Maisch at the University of North Carolina assisted in a number of ways, both small and large. Rebecca Larsen, Tanya Policht, and Debra Riegert of Lawrence Erlbaum oversaw production of the book with patience and good humor, for which we are grateful.

—*Robert Cudeck*
—*Robert MacCallum*

Acknowledgments

This edited volume is based on presentations by the 15 chapter authors at a conference held at the University of North Carolina at Chapel Hill, May 13–15, 2004. The conference was organized to recognize the 100th anniversary of the publication of Charles Spearman's seminal article about the structure of intelligence, an article that presented foundational concepts and approaches to the methods that became known as *factor analysis*.

We wish to acknowledge generous financial support from several sources that made the conference, and, in turn, this book, possible: The National Science Foundation (Award #BCS-0350659), The Society of Multivariate Experimental Psychology, The College Board, the L. L. Thurstone Psychometric Laboratory at the University of North Carolina, and the Quantitative Psychology Program at the University of California Davis. Additional support in the form of staff assistance and facilities was provided by the Psychology Department at the University of North Carolina.

We also acknowledge the assistance of many people in organizing the conference. Members of the organizing committee were Robert MacCallum and Robert Cudeck (Chairs), and Michael Browne, Patrick Curran, Irini Moustaki, John Nesselroade, and Keith Widaman. Kristopher Preacher developed the conference Web site (www.fa100.info). Many graduate students in the Quantitative Psychology Program at the University of North Carolina participated in planning the conference and provided much assistance during the conference itself, including Li Cai, Donna Coffman, Cheryl Hill, Michael Edwards, Daniel Serrano, and R. J. Wirth. Ginny Maisch, Program Assistant at the L. L. Thurstone Psychometric Laboratory, provided valuable staff support in organizing and running the conference.

CHAPTER 1

Factor Analysis in the Year 2004: Still Spry at 100

Robert Cudeck
Ohio State University

In 1904, Charles Spearman published a capital idea. His celebrated article, "'General Intelligence' Objectivity Determined and Measured," (shown in Fig. 1-1) marks the beginning of the quantitative investigation of latent variables. It provided a theoretical underpinning and rationale to the measurement of individual differences in human ability, and in addressing the problem of many manifest variables that are resolved into more fundamental psychological constructs, Spearman introduced an important statistical tool: factor analysis.

Spearman's achievement is especially impressive in light of the statistical knowledge of the early 20th century (Stigler, 1986). The normal distribution, most completely developed by DeMoivre in 1733, was 175 years old. The multivariate normal distribution dates from Lagrange in 1776, and least squares, as presented by Legendre in 1805, had been in use for decades. But Yule outlined multiple correlation only in 1897. And Galton had introduced regression and the correlation coefficient only in 1889. Barely 15 years after Galton's pathbreaking insight, Spearman (1927), in attempting to "find out whether, as Galton has indicated, the abilities commonly taken to be intellectual had any correlation with each other or with sensory discrimination" (p. 322), exploited both regression and correlation in a new theory of human abilities.

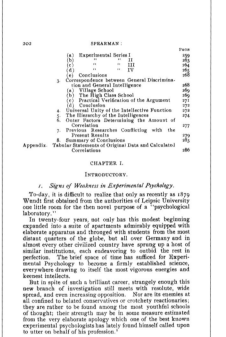

FIGURE 1–1. Spearman's (1904) article. From " 'General Intelligence,' Objectively Determined and Measured," by C. Spearman, 1904, *American Journal of Psychology, 15*, pp. 201–202. Reproduced with permission of the University of Illinois Press.

It was a singular accomplishment. From a modern perspective, the work has all the elements of excellent science: a substantive theory, interesting data, and a formal model based on the theory that accounted for empirical observations. Bartholomew (1995) summarized both the historical context and the scientific contribution. It is appropriate that the centenary of Spearman's birth was marked by a series of retrospective articles published by the *British Journal of Mathematical and Statistical Psychology* (Lovie, 1995). Another special issue appeared in the *Journal of Personality and Social Psychology* (Lubinski, 2004), devoted especially to the study of human abilities after Spearman. In May 2004, the authors of this book participated in a conference held at the University of North Carolina (UNC), titled, like this volume, "Factor Analysis at 100: Historical Developments and Future Directions." The purpose of FA100 was to review progress and prospects in the study of latent variables with statistical models in light of the many accomplishments of the previous century. Faculty at the Thurstone Psychometric Laboratory at UNC agreed to host the meeting. Financial support from the National Science Foundation, the College Board, the Society of Multivariate Experimental Psychology, the Psychology Departments of the University of North Carolina and the University of California, Davis, provided the wherewithal. A group of prominent researchers agreed to participate. Other knowledgeable colleagues joined in as conference attendees. The result was a truly engaging retrospective event; many thoughtful presentations, many stimulating exchanges.

A commemorative conference of this kind could have been designed around a number of different themes. The conference could have been devoted to substantive knowledge in scientific domains, such as ability, personality structure, occupational prestige or prejudice, where factor analysis has been an essential tool in understanding fundamental aspects of individual differences and social influences. Another possible theme of the conference could have been philosophical issues associated with the study of latent variables; issues that pertain both to philosophy of science and philosophy of measurement, fundamental problems of whether, wherefore, and existence in the study of basic human traits. Yet another possibility was a conference organized around historical developments, to review the principle themes and major players, and the connection between ideas over time. Still another suggestion for the conference theme was to assemble a practical list of latent variable procedures, the aim of which was to summarize modern techniques and to assemble an up-to-date resource for applied researchers. Finally, one nefarious member of the organizing committee thought it would be engaging if the conference basically encouraged a good fight—over factor scores, model fit, rotation strategies (oblique or die), or the nominalistic problem (give the factor a name and presto! It magically exists)—a theme that would be consistent with the sometimes contentious history of factors. Controversies serve an invaluable function and have been integral in the evolution of factor analysis. From Spearman's time to the present day, they point out limitations, sharpen concepts, stimulate further research, and occasionally force new directions.

In spite of the appeal of these alternative themes, FA100 was organized around methodological issues and mathematical models. This emphasis reflects our opinion that general statistical tools, which can be applied to diverse research objectives, have an important utility in their own right.

There are fads in science. Poor ideas sometimes persist a long time. But few scientific concepts last a century unless they represent an intellectual point of view or provide a frame of reference that helps organize the empirical facts and promote the research enterprise. Theories constructed around latent variables are commonplace today. The reason they have proliferated—the reason they are integral in the social sciences, health sciences, biological sciences, occasionally even the physical sciences—is first of all because of their irresistible face validity. The simple fact that manifest variables of seemingly quite different kinds correlate positively makes something like an underlying factor attractive. In many cases latent variables are unavoidable, perhaps even inevitable. In some substantive domains, it is simply not possible to even begin the discussion of basic human traits without resorting to latent variables.

This does not mean that factors have convincingly and often been shown to exist, for example, in a physical sense. In the best of situations, where the theoretical structure is carefully reasoned, the variables are high quality, and the sample large and representative, latent variables are elusive. Even less do they have anything like the expansive characteristics ascribed to them in breezy, prosaic analyses based on haphazard collections of variables and convenience samples. Over the years, blistering critiques have been leveled at latent variable models in general, at factor analysis specifically, and at Spearman's two-factor theory of intelligence especially. The most trenchant criticisms have undeniable merit, forcefully questioning fundamental assumptions if not the basic plausibility of the model. Limitations and criticisms notwithstanding, it is inarguable to assert that factor analysis has turned out to be one of the most successful of the multivariate statistical methods and one of the pillars of behavioral research. It has proven its worth in numerous substantive domains. The best investigations that feature factor-type structures are hardly mindless exercises. It is a truism that the ultimate value of any particular empirical study is always open to debate, including penetrating examination of sampling scheme, experimental design or statistical methodology, and especially of the theoretical model that is featured. But when did a mathematical model have to be literally true to be scientifically useful? A distinguishing characteristic of a useful model is that it can be extended to more general contexts. The original hope for the chapters of this book was that they would have a historical theme, and would relate various aspects of present-day latent variable models back to Spearman's two-factor structure. Considering that the contributors are scientists and not historians, the connections back to the earliest form of factor analysis came through admirably. But then again, most authors found the impulse to extend the humble two-factor model into new territory to be irrepressible. For a conference that purported to be a look back to the beginnings in 1904, and for a book that intended to show quiet reverence to the founding fathers, there is a lot of new material in this volume of which the founding fathers never dreamed.

It is easy to be enthusiastic about this book. There indeed are several chapters with a clear historical perspective. In a wonderful commentary, Bartholomew (chap. 2) reviews the major insights that underlie the thinking of the early factor analysts but then reformulates in more modern form, generalizes, and extends quite broadly. Spearman, as is universally known, proposed factor analysis only to learn almost immediately that such a simple model was inadequate to completely describe relevant data. It is not historically accurate to state that L. L. Thurstone single-handedly transformed factor analysis and gave it the completely modern complexion of the multiple factor model. On the other hand, Thurstone's contributions were pivotal on a number of grounds, and his broad approach and clear focus on rigor and practicality are as important as those of any single scientist. Bock (chap. 4) and Jones (chap. 3) present two distinct perspectives on the influence of Thurstone and his role in the development of factor analysis.

Latent variable models for the description of change have become hugely popular. Bollen (chap. 6) and McArdle (chap. 7) both review the basic statistical ideas as well as recent extensions of factor analysis to latent growth curve models. A fascinating subtext in this domain is the distinction between models that are designed to represent average growth in the population versus those focused on change of particular persons, as the history of individual differences in psychology has emphasized. Nesselroade (chap. 12) summarizes this tradition and includes a commentary on contemporary thinking. Browne and Zhang (chap. 13) present a very general framework for individual time series processes based on latent variables that can be specialized and generalized to several related alternatives.

The famous original motivating problem that led to factor analysis was the study of intelligence. Research in this domain has been vigorous—and contentious—since Spearman's time. There is no prospect that it will end soon. Horn and McArdle (chap. 11) summarize a century of scientific activity in the study of human abilities. The great majority of latent variable models assume continuous variables and linear regressions. This of course is Spearman's doing, for he approached the problem exactly this way. Everyone appreciates that most collections of realistic data are categorical, however, and that curvilinear relationships among variables are commonplace. Overviews and extensions of latent variable models to categorical data are provided by Moustaki (chap. 14) and to nonlinear functions and structures by Wall and Amemiya (chap. 16). These two contributions are especially welcome because they summarize important material that is already having an influence on practice.

In the present day as much as in the past, scientific developments are the accomplishments of individual scientists. Jöreskog (chap. 5) presents a personal account of factor analysis and the numerous extensions of latent variables to structural equation models. Jöreskog's influence has been enormous, both for theory as well as practice of latent variable models. This review is a noteworthy summary of his contributions. The exploratory factor model is replete with hard problems. The two most daunting are estimation and rotation, which is the same as saying that everything about the exploratory model is difficult. Jennrich (chap. 15) re-states the rotation problem, then shows that large classes of rotation algorithms can be treated in a unified fashion. He also shows that performing the rotation can be done simply and efficiently, and that standard errors of rotated loadings can be obtained routinely. It is a technical *tour de force*.

Factor analysis is an abstract statistical model, an idealized description of actual human behavior in accounting for experimental data. This is an obvious statement of fact, but it is underappreciated. MacCallum, Browne, and Cai (chap. 9) give a lucid presentation of the implications of factor analysis as an approximating model. They pay particular attention to the way this affects estimation, producing unexpected findings about the most popular estimators. Millsap and Meredith (chap. 8) have written the most cogent and authoritative accounts of factorial invariance available. Their chapter continues the tradition. According to theory, a *factor* is a fundamental kind of variable. It is supposed to characterize everyone in the population. It is supposed to display similar measurement properties across populations. When this is not true, the information in the factor differs for subpopulations, which is *prima facie* evidence that the factor is biased. In practical terms, the invariance problem is arguably the most important issue in the actual use of the model. Although there are no easy approaches that are guaranteed to help meet the standards of invariance, an unvarnished review of issues is valuable.

The *yin* and *yang* of dimension-reducing models are principal components and factor analysis. The algebraic structures are so dissimilar, the proper domains of application so conspicuous. Sharing a superficial similarity, the two methods have profoundly different theoretical makeup. Keith Widaman (chap. 10) has studied the respective histories and pedigrees in an attempt to again distinguish methods that are complementary but much confused.

One especially creative contribution to FA100 unfortunately could not be included in this book. The quantitative graduate students of the Thurstone Laboratory produced two beautiful exhibits: the Factor Analysis Timeline and the Factor Analysis Genealogy. They are available on the Web at http://www.fa100.info/timeline050504.pdf http://www.fa100.info/tree050504.pdf

Factor analysis and related latent variable models are one of the real success stories of statistics in the social sciences. It is fitting to mark the occasion of the centenary of Spearman's seminal article with an assembly of scientists of this caliber to reflect on past accomplishments and to consider future directions. Factor analysis, the first 100 years: It's been a good start.

REFERENCES

Bartholomew, D. J. (1995). Spearman and the origin and development of factor analysis. *British Journal of Mathematical and Statistical Psychology, 48*, 211–220.

Lovie, P. (1995). Charles Edward Spearman F.R.S. 1863–1945. A commemoration on the 50th anniversary of his death. *British Journal of Mathematical and Statistical Psychology, 48*, 209–210.

Lubinski, D. (2004). Introduction to the special section on cognitive abilities: 100 years after Spearman's (1904) "'General intelligence,' objectively determined and measured." *Journal of Personality and Social Psychology, 86*, 96–111.

Spearman, C. (1904). "General intelligence," objectively determined and measured. *American Journal of Psychology, 15*, 201–293.

Spearman, C. (1927). *The abilities of man.* London: MacMillan.

Stigler, S. M. (1986). *The history of statistics: The measurement of uncertainty before 1900.* Cambridge, MA: Harvard University Press.

CHAPTER 2

Three Faces of Factor Analysis

David J. Bartholomew
London School of Economics and Political Science

ORIGINS

Spearman's Idea[1]

The origin of *factor analysis* is to be found in Spearman (1904) but the details are tantalizingly brief. The paper is a very long one, 91 pages, but only a small part, notably the table on page 276, is concerned with something recognizable today as factor analysis and then almost as a side issue. The focus is more on the question of whether the common factor underlying a variety of branches of intellectual activity is the same as that which underlies tests of sensory discrimination. Thus, Spearman (1904) reaches the conclusion: "On the whole then, we reach the profoundly important conclusion that there really exists a something that we may provisionally term 'General Sensory Discrimination' and similarly a 'General Intelligence,' and further that the functional correspondence between these two is not appreciably less than absolute" (p. 272).

Of more immediate relevance to factor analysis, he states what he calls "our general theorem," which is "Whenever branches of intellectual activity are at all dissimilar, then their correlations with one another appear wholly due to their being all variants wholly saturated with some common fundamental Function (or group of Functions)" (p. 273). He distinguishes this central Function from "the specific

---

[1]Spearman's contribution to the origins of factor analysis was described in Bartholomew (1995). That paper has much in common with this but here the focus is not primarily on Spearman.

factor [which] seems in every instance new and wholly different from that in all the others" (p. 273). These ideas are translated into numbers in the table on page 271 with only the sketchiest justification for the calculations involved. Nevertheless it is a table of factor loadings (correlations of the test scores with the factor, *general intelligence*) and communalities. It is, then, the first example of a factor analysis.

The simplest way to justify this analysis, but not the one used by Spearman, (according to the remark at the bottom of page ii of the Appendix in Spearman, 1927/1932)) is to appeal to the theory of partial correlation. This had been introduced by Yule (1897) in some detail. The essence of what Spearman needed is contained in the formula for the partial correlation between two variables, i and j say, given a third variable which following Spearman we call G. Thus

$$r_{ij.G} = \frac{r_{ij} - r_{iG}r_{jG}}{\sqrt{(1 - r_{iG}^2)(1 - r_{jG}^2)}}. \qquad \text{(Equation 2.1)}$$

If the correlation between i and j is wholly explained by their common dependence on G, then $r_{ij.G}$ must be zero. This implies that

$$r_{ij} = r_{iG}\,r_{jG} \quad (i, j = 1, 2, \ldots, p). \qquad \text{(Equation 2.2)}$$

If the correlation matrix $\mathbf{R} = \{r_{ij}\}$ can be represented in this way, then we have evidence for an underlying common factor. Spearman found this to be so and gave estimates of $\{r_{iG}\}$ in his table on page 276.

In the beginning, factor analysis consisted in seeing whether the correlation matrix had the required structure. In particular, whether the "tetrad differences" given by

$$r_{ij}r_{hk} - r_{ik}r_{jh} \qquad \text{(Equation 2.3)}$$

are all zero. These are equivalent to (2) and the ratio r_{ij}/r_{ih} does not depend on i and hence is the same for all rows of the table (excluding the diagonal elements). A similar argument applies to the columns because the matrix is symmetrical. At this basic level, we see that the correlation matrix is the key to unearthing a common factor. Later it was shown that if there were two or more (independent) underlying factors, the correlation matrix would have a structure of the form

$$r_{ij} = \sum_{h=1}^{q} \lambda_{ih}\,\lambda_{jh} \quad (i \neq j). \qquad \text{(Equation 2.4)}$$

The first face of factor analysis thus starts from the correlation matrix. What can be learned about the factor structure is, therefore, contained in that matrix. Early factor analysis was dominated by the study of correlation matrices and mathematicians with skills in this field were enlisted to help (see, e.g., references to Ledermann on page 386 of Thomson, 1950).

There is more to this than meets the eye because a *correlation coefficient* is a measure of *linear* correlation. The decision to use product moment correlation, therefore, implies an assumption that item test scores are linearly related to any underlying factors. Although implicit from the beginning, it only became the central idea in the second phase of factor analysis's history—its second face. Before moving on to that, we digress to notice that the structure (3) does not imply that the observed correlations were generated from a common dependence on a single factor. There is at least one other explanation, associated with the name of Godfrey Thomson.

Thomson's Alternative Model

It is common in statistics to find that more than one model makes exactly the same observational predictions. We may describe this as a "lack of model identi-fication." Spearman's one-factor model, which provided a good fit to many data sets, supposed that individuals varied along a scale of what we will continue to call G. This led, naturally, to the supposition that this underlying factor was "real." Thomson (1950) pointed out that there was another model, capable of describing the data equally well, which did not involve such a common factor. At most, only one of these models could describe physical reality and hence there was no certain empirical evidence for the reality of Spearman's factor.

This matter was much debated in the psychological literature in the 1920s and, for good reasons, Spearman's model came out on top. Thomson's model is largely forgotten though it is worth noting that Mackintosh (1998) has recently pointed out that it corresponds, in part at least, with contemporary ideas on brain function. It is, therefore, worth taking another look at Thomson's "sampling model." The original debate was somewhat clouded by the lack of a clear notion of a random variable. Thomson, himself, used simple examples based on dice and such like to get the idea across but this seems to have engendered misunderstanding and comprehension in equal measure! The nearest and clearest exposition seems to be due to Dodd (1929), with whom Thomson (1950) said he agreed on a great deal if not on everything. The following account, in modern dress, is very similar to Dodd's treatment although it is not the most general form possible. However, it is sufficient to make the point that it is, empirically, indistinguishable from Spearman's one-factor model.

Suppose the brain contains N "bonds," which may be called into play when test items are attempted. (N is thought of as "large" but this is not necessary for the argument.) Some items will be more demanding than others and so more bonds will be used in their solution. The correlations between two test scores are supposed to result from the use of some bonds being common to both items. The term, *sampling theory model*, arises from the fact that the bonds used by any item are supposed to be selected at random from the N available.

Assume that item i requires Np_i (assumed to be an integer) bonds. The con-tribution that bond i makes to the score on that item, x_i, is a random variable e_i. The score may thus be expressed as

$$x_i = a_{i1}e_i + a_{i2}e_2 + \cdots + a_{iN}e_N \quad (i = 1, 2, \ldots n) \qquad \text{(Equation 2.5)}$$

or

$$\mathbf{x} = \mathbf{Ae}$$

where the coefficients $\{a_{ij}\}$ are indicator variables taking the value 1 if the bond is selected and 0 otherwise. The as are, therefore, also random variables with joint distribution determined by the method of sampling. It is convenient to suppose that the es are mutually independent and have zero means but we allow their variances to differ with $\mathrm{var}(e_i) = \sigma_j^2$ $(j = 1, 2, \ldots, N)$. We now have to find the structure of the covariance (or correlation) matrix. Given these assumptions

$$E(x_i) = 0 \quad (i = 1, 2, \ldots, n)$$

$$E(x_i x_j) = E\, E(x_i x_j | a_i, a_j)$$

$$= E \sum_{h=1}^{N} \sum_{k=1}^{N} a_{ih} a_{jk} E(e_h\, e_k)$$

$$= E \sum_{h=1}^{N} a_{ih} a_{jh} \sigma_h^2 \quad (i, j = 1, 2, \ldots, N;\ i \neq j).$$

If we assume that successive samplings are independent and that all bonds are equally likely to be selected then

$$E(a_{ih} a_{jh}) = p_i\, p_j.$$

Hence,

$$E(x_i x_j) = p_i\, p_j \sum_{h=1}^{N} \sigma_h^2 = \mathrm{cov}(x_i,\, x_j) \quad (i, j = 1, 2, \ldots, n).$$

When $i = j$,

$$\mathrm{var}(x_i) = \sum_{h=1}^{N} E a_{ih}^2 \sigma_h^2 = \sum_{h=1}^{N} E a_{ih} \sigma_h^2 = p_i \sum_{h=1}^{N} \sigma_h^2, \quad (i = 1, 2, \ldots, n).$$

Hence

$$\mathrm{corr}(x_i,\, x_j) = \sqrt{p_i\, p_j} \quad (i, j = 1, 2, \ldots, n;\ i \neq j).$$

This has exactly the same form as the correlation matrix of Spearman's one-factor model. Hence the two are not empirically distinguishable.

The parameters $\{\sqrt{p_i}\}$ in Thomson's model correspond to the factor loadings $\{r_{iG}\}$ in Spearman's model. Estimates of the factor loadings can, therefore, be translated into estimates of the proportions of bonds that are selected in attempting an item, by the fact that $p_i = r_{iG}^2$ $(i = 1, 2, \ldots, n)$. Typical values of r_{iG} are in the range (.5–1) so this would imply quite a high proportion of bonds being used.

Spearman criticized the sampling theory model on the grounds that it allowed no individual differences. Thomson denied this but he and Spearman may have been at cross purposes. Thomson pointed out that the sampling of bonds would be a separate operation for each individual and thus that the selection would not usually be the same for any two individuals. However, to estimate the correlations, it would be necessary to suppose that they had the same expectations for all individuals. One cannot estimate a correlation from a single pair of test scores from one individual. Only by assuming that the correlations are the same for every individual does one have the replication necessary to make an estimate. One has to assume, therefore, that the method of sampling and the parameters $\{p_i\}$ (and N) are the same for all individuals.

There is an inherent implausibility about assuming homogeneity in any human population even if one does not wish to attribute any heterogeneity to differences in innate ability. Whether or not the assumption of a fixed N, the number of bonds is plausible, or whether it is sensible to suppose that the number of bonds called into play by a given item is a fixed number is also questionable. Perhaps the fact that Spearman's model could be extended to several factors, and in that form, successfully fitted to a very wide range of data, gave it the advantage.

Thomson himself conceded that Spearman went a long way to meet his objections but his alternative model is worth recalling as a reminder that finding a good fitting model is not the same as finding the real mechanism underlying the data.

FACTOR ANALYSIS: LINEAR MODELS

The second face of factor analysis starts, not with a correlation matrix, but with a model. The use of models in statistics on a regular basis seems to date from the 1950s. A *statistical model* is a statement about the distribution of a set of random variables. A simple linear regression model, for example, says that the dependent variable y is normally distributed with mean $a + bx$ and variance σ^2, where a and b are unknown constants and x is an observable variable. In the case of factor analysis, the move to a model-based approach was gradual. The rudimentary concept was contained in the idea that an observed test score was composed of a common part and a specific part. This is made explicit, for example, in Spearman and Jones (1950) but was implicit, as we have already noted, in the use of product moment correlations. Hotelling's (1933) introduction of principal components analysis, which was concerned with expressing a set of variables $(x_1, x_2, \ldots, x_p)$ as a linear function of p orthogonal variables $(y_1, y_2, \ldots, y_p)$ doubtless encouraged factor analysts to think of factor analysis in similar terms. However, it was in Lawley and Maxwell (1963, 1971) that a linear model was made the starting point for developing the theory in a systematic way. Actually, this formulation was incomplete but, in its essentials, it still holds sway today. In modern notation, Lawley and Maxwell supposed that

$$x_i = \lambda_{i1} y_1 + \lambda_{i2} y_2 + \ldots + \lambda_{iq} y_q + e_i \quad (i = 1, 2, \ldots, p). \qquad \text{(Equation 2.6)}$$

In this equation, the λs are constants and the xs, ys, and es are *random variables*. Thus if one imagines that the y values for item i are drawn at random from some distribution and the es are drawn similarly, then the model postulates that, if they are combined according to (6), the resulting random variable will be x_i. It is usually assumed that the ys are independent with normal distribution and (without loss of generality) unit variances; e_i is assumed to be normal with variance ψ_i. Lawley and Maxwell (1963, 1971) state, like many since, that all the random variables in (6) may be assumed to have zero means without any loss of generality. This is not so. It is tantamount to assuming that the mean of x_i is known. In practice, this is seldom the case. It is more accurate to insert an unknown mean μ_i on the right hand side of (6). We then have the *standard linear normal factor model* in use today. The omission of μ_i does not have serious consequences but its inclusion makes for clarity.

Equations in random variables, like (6), need to be thought about very carefully. Much of the confusion that has surrounded the topic of *factor scores* stems from failing to distinguish between random variables and mathematical variables (see text to come).

An alternative way of writing the model, which is less prone to misunderstanding, is to write it in terms of probability distributions as in Bartholomew and Knott (1999). Thus we suppose

$$x_i \,|\, y_1 y_2 \ldots , y_q \sim N \left(\mu_i + \sum_{j=1}^{q} \lambda_{ij} y_i , \; \psi_i \right) \quad (i = 1, 2, \ldots , p). \qquad \text{(Equation 2.7)}$$

$$y_j \sim N(0, \; 1) \quad (j = 1, 2, \ldots , q) \qquad \text{(Equation 2.8)}$$

The first line in (7) is a regression model for x_i in terms of regressor variables $y_1, y_2, \ldots , y_q$. If the ys were known, factor analysis could be handled with the framework of regression theory. As it is, the ys are random variables and so their joint distribution must be specified, as in the second line of (7).

Once we have a probability model, as specified in (7), the whole field of inferential statistics is available to us. For example, the parameters $\{\mu_i\}$, $\{\lambda_{ij}\}$ and $\{\psi_i\}$ can be estimated by maximum likelihood. Hypotheses can be tested about the values of those parameters and so on. What can be known about any y, once the xs have been observed, is contained in the posterior distribution of y given $x_1, x_2, \ldots , x_p$.

It is worth pausing to ask the justification for regarding this as another way of looking at Spearman's factor analysis. The answer, of course, is that the correlation structure to which it leads is the same. If, for example, one writes down the likelihood function it turns out that the sample means, $\overline{x_1}, \overline{x_2}, \ldots , \overline{x_p}$ and the sample covariance matrix $\hat{\Sigma}$ are sufficient for the parameters. In particular, the covariance matrix Σ has the form

$$\Sigma = \Lambda \Lambda' + \Psi \qquad \text{(Equation 2.9)}$$

which is precisely what the correlation approach (4) leads to. If there is one factor, for example, the theoretical covariance between x_i and x_j is

$$\text{cov}(x_i, x_j) = \lambda_i \lambda_j \quad (i \neq j)$$

and it can easily be shown that λ_i is the correlation between y and x_i. The correlation between x_i and x_j is of the same form.

As in standard linear regression, much can be achieved without the assumptions of normality. The covariance structure has the same form if the distributional assumptions are dropped.

Once factor analysis is viewed in this way, it is easier to pose the *factor scores* problem. This is concerned with predictions, or estimating the unobserved values of y to be associated with and x. The problem had been recognized from the beginning, of course. Spearman had proposed an ad hoc method (Spearman, 1927/1932; Spearman & Jones, 1950). This involved obtaining p estimates of y by putting $e_i = 0$ in (6) and then taking an average. Thomson (1950) found the best linear regression of y on x, noting that this did not require knowledge of the individual values of the ys. For obvious reasons, these became known as regression scores. Other types of scores were proposed using various criteria but the subject became confused by attempts to interpret the linear equations of (6) or (7), by analogy with principal components analysis, as though they were equations in mathematical variables. The argument would usually go as follows.

If $q = p$ and if $e_i = 0$ for all i the equations of (6) are formally the same as in principal components analysis. The xs and ys are not then random variables but represent real numbers. The equations may then be invoked to give y in terms of x. If $q < p$, the argument goes, there are more unknowns than equations: p xs and q ys gives $p + q$ unknowns and only p equations. The factors are then said to be indeterminate. Thomson's regression method can the be regarded as one possible way of getting a "best fit" solution to the equations. This operation changes the random variables into mathematical variables and thus changes the question being asked.

It is clear that, once the model is formulated in terms of probability distributions, as in (7), that the question that the model is capable of answering is: What is the distribution of y *given* x? The answer follows inexorably from the laws of probability and is given by the posterior distribution of y given x. Point predictions of y can then be found as measures of location of that distribution. Posterior measures of spread then give an indication of the imprecision of those predictions.

The model-based approach thus enables us to provide rigorous methods for answering the traditional questions addressed by factor analysis.

THE THIRD FACE OF FACTOR ANALYSIS

It is a curious fact of statistical history that there has been a strong focus on methods for continuous data. Regression and correlation analysis and then the analysis of variance have, for the most part, presupposed that the variables involved were continuous. Other multivariate methods introduced along the way, such as discriminant analysis, principal-components analysis, and canonical correlation fall into the same mold. It is interesting to speculate how far this can be attributed to the fact that the data on crop yields that confronted Sir Ronald Fisher at Rothamsted were continuous. It is unsurprising that factor analysis should have started from the same supposition and concentrated on correlation.

Of course, these methods have been widely used on data that were not continuous. Coarsely grouped variables, ordered categorical variables—even binary variables—have been grist to the analysts' mill. Indeed, much ingenuity has been exercised to treat categorical data as if it were continuous by introducing, for example, pseudocorrelation coefficients of one sort or another.

In practice, and especially in the social sciences, much of the data we encounter is not continuous but categorical. Sometimes the categories are ordered and sometimes not. Often they are binary, being derived from true–false or yes–no questions in sample surveys. In fact, sample surveys are a common source of data for which continuous methods are not appropriate. Matters are often made more difficult by the fact that a survey is likely to lead to a mixture of types of variables thus calling for hybrid methods capable of coping with all sorts of variables.

In turning to the third face of factor analysis, we are looking below the surface to identify the essential questions that factor analysis is intended to answer.

In factor analysis, we are asking whether the dependencies among a set of variables can be explained by their common dependence on one or more unobserved latent variables (or factors). There is nothing in this statement that refers to the level of measurement of the variables involved. If, therefore, we formulate the problem in sufficiently general terms, we should have a general enough framework to include variables of all sorts. The essential elements of the problem are the interdependence of a set of observable variables and the notion of conditional independence.

Suppose we have p observable random variables $\mathbf{x}' = (x_1, x_2, \ldots, x_p)$ with joint probability distribution $f(\mathbf{x})$. This may be a joint probability density if the xs are all continuous, a joint probability function if they are all discrete; otherwise it is a mixed function.

The question is: Do there exist factors $y_1, y_2, \ldots, y_q \ (= \mathbf{y}')$ such that the xs are conditionally independent? That is, can we find a q and variables $y_1, y_2, \ldots, y_q$ such that

$$f(\mathbf{x}|\mathbf{y}) = \prod_{i=1}^{p} f(x_i|\mathbf{y}). \qquad \text{(Equation 2.10)}$$

In the case of the normal linear model, this question is answered by finding a q such that an adequate fit is obtained with the linear model. With other kinds of variable (nonnormal as well as as noncontinuous), different methods will be required but, conceptually, the problem is the same.

This insight seems to have escaped factor analysts until quite recently. In fact, this more general way of looking at the problem had an independent origin in what seemed to be a quite different problem—in sociology, not psychology. This disciplinary divide probably accentuated the gulf and prolonged the separate existence of a distinct body of theory.

Lazarsfeld was the pioneer of this distinct kind of factor analysis and he called it *latent structure analysis* (see, e.g., Lazarsfeld & Henry, 1968). Essentially, he allowed one or both of the sets of variables x and y to be categorical. Factor analysis was thus excluded because both x and y are then continuous. In retrospect, this seems to be a curious development but, although Lazarsfeld recognized that there were similarities with factor analysis, he thought that the differences were more significant. The differences were, in fact, in matters of computation and in the appearance of the formulae. These things are not fundamental. The similarities were in the nature of the questions asked. This family likeness becomes more apparent when we adopt a sufficiently general notation as in (10).

The closeness of latent structure analysis and factor analysis is even more obvious when we discover that all the variants in common use can be subsumed under a linear model called, in Bartholomew and Knott (1999), the *General Linear Latent Variable Model (GLLVM)*. This may be seen as a generalization of the normal linear factor model in almost exactly the same way as the generalized linear model generalizes the general linear model of statistics. In the normal linear factor model, it is assumed that each x_i has a linear regression on the factors with normal residuals. All other standard latent structure models emerge as special cases if we suppose that each x_i comes from a one-parameter, exponential family distribution. In this case, it is the canonical parameter that is a linear function of the factors rather than the mean. In the standard linear model, there is nothing that requires the regression variables (the factors in a factor model) to be continuous. Categorical variables can be represented by indicator variables, or vectors. Viewed in this way, factor analysis is simply the attempt to explain the interdependence of a set of variables in terms of their dependence on a small set of underlying variables that may be categorical or continuous.

There is one important class of problem that does not fit neatly into this framework. This occurs when some of the variables, the manifest variables in particular, are ordered categorical. These can be accommodated in one of two ways. One is to put order constraints on the parameters of the model in a way calculated to reflect the fact that the "higher" effect on the response probability increases monotonically as we move through the categories. The other way is to regard the ordered categories as a grouped form of a continuous variable. The latter is often the most realistic but the choice, ideally, should be guided by what gives rise to the ordering in the first place. For a fuller discussion of this matter, see Bartholomew, Steele, Moustaki, and Galbraith (2002), especially chapter 9.

The unifying effect of adopting this way of looking at factor analysis has some interesting consequences for dealing with the problem of factor scores. (A first look at this problem from the point of view of the linear model was given in section 2.) The problem, we recall, was to locate an individual in the factor space on the basis of the observed value of their x. Within the general framework, the way we do this is obvious. If x and y are random variables then, when x is known, all of the information about y is conveyed by its posterior distribution $f(y|x)$. This simple fact shows that there is no single value of y to be associated with any x. There is a probability distribution over the y space and any "score" must, therefore, be a summary measure of the distribution. Measures of location are the natural measures to use. A posterior measure of dispersion is then appropriate to show how imprecise the score is—how reliable, in other words.

Is is curious how, in the latent structure tradition, this is exactly the approach that has been used. To take the simplest case, suppose that we have fitted a model in which a single y is supposed to be binary—meaning that there are just two latent classes. The posterior distribution of y is thus a two-point distribution. If, without loss of generality, we take the two values of y to be 0 and 1, the expectation, for example, is $E(y|x) = \Pr\{y = 1 \mid x\}$. A *posteriori*, therefore, we calculate the probability that the individual falls into category 1.

In the factor model, by contrast, this route has not been followed, although Thomson's "regression" estimate is a distribution-free implementation of the same idea.

A BROADER PERSPECTIVE

The unified approach seen in the third face of factor analysis does more than simplify our understanding and make for economy of thought. It also gives a deeper insight into the nature of certain familiar features of individual techniques.

We have seen that the existence of q continuous factors $y_1, y_2, \ldots, y_q$ means that the joint distribution can be expressed in the form

$$f(x) = \int_y \prod_{i=1}^{p} f(x_i|y)\, f(y)\, dy. \qquad \text{(Equation 2.11)}$$

The xs may be continuous or categorical. It is immediately clear that this has the form of a mixture with $f(y)$ as the mixing distribution. Mixtures occur in many branches of statistics and a great deal is known about them and their properties.

A second important feature is that any transformation $y \to z$ in (11) leaves $f(x)$ unchanged because if is merely a change of variable in the integral. There are thus infinitely many pairs $\{f(y), f(x_i|y)\}$ leading to the same $f(x)$. Since the only distribution we can directly learn about is $f(x)$ there is no empirical way of distinguishing among this infinite set of possible models. In practice, of course, we narrow the set down by fixing $f(y)$ or requiring $f(x_i|y)$ to belong to some convenient family but these choices are, essentially, arbitrary. There is thus an inevitable indeterminacy in all factor models.

A special case of this indeterminacy is very familiar in the linear factor model where it lies behind the concept of *rotation*. In that case the transformation to $z = My$, where M is an orthogonal matrix, leads to the same covariance matrix and hence, (under the usual normal assumptions) to the same joint distribution. The general formulation shows this to be a special case of a more fundamental indeterminacy.

Rotation by a linear transformation is not peculiar to the linear factor model. All members of the class of GLLVMs with continuous ys have the canonical parameter as a linear combination of the factors. Thus if

$$\theta_i = \alpha_{i0} + \alpha_{i1}y_1 + \alpha_{i2}y_2 + \ldots + \alpha_{iq}y_q \qquad \text{(Equation 2.12)}$$

or

$$\theta = A\,y, \ \text{say,}$$

then

$$\theta = AM^{-1}z \qquad \text{(Equation 2.13)}$$

where $z = My$. The zs have the same independent standard normal distributions as the ys but their coefficients are transformed from A to AM^{-1}. The two versions of the model are thus indistinguishable because the distribution $f(x)$ is unaffected. This is the usual account of rotation but it is now revealed as characteristic of a much wider class of models.

The indistinguishability of models extends to what we might term *near indistinguishability*, which is just as important practically. The best known example, perhaps, has been known for some time but has been investigated most thoroughly by Molenaar and von Eye (1994). Thus it is known that the covariance structure of the linear factor model is the same as that of a latent profile model with one more latent class than there are factors. On the basis of the covariance matrix alone, one cannot distinguish between the two models. Only by looking at other aspects of the joint distribution would it, in principle, be possible to discriminate. The full practical implication of this result for the vast number of factor analyses that have been carried out seems to have been scarcely noticed.

A further example is provided by the latent class model with two classes and the latent trait model. Empirically, it is very difficult to distinguish these, yet they say radically different things about the prior distribution of the latent variable. In the former case, it is a two-point distribution and, in the latter, it is usually taken as a standard normal distribution. Further discussion and an example will be found in Bartholomew et al. (2002, section 9.4).

Another way of characterising results of this kind is to say, as the title of Molenaar and von Eye's paper implies, that latent variables are very poorly determined. This result has far-reaching implications for all work on the relationships among latent variables.

A final result, with practical implications, takes us back to the factor score question. For the family of models of the GLLVM class, the joint distribution of

x can be expressed in the form

$$f(x) = \int_{\mathbf{y}} f(X|\mathbf{y})\, f(\mathbf{y})\, d\mathbf{y} \qquad \text{(Equation 2.14)}$$

where X is a q vector with elements of the form

$$X_j = \sum_{i=1}^{p} a_i x_i \quad (j = 1, 2, \ldots, q). \qquad \text{(Equation 2.15)}$$

This shows that $f(x)$ depends on x only through q linear combinations of the xs. Any factor score, for any member of this family, should therefore be a function of these "sufficient" statistics, as they are called in Bartholomew and Knott (1999).

Many purely empirical attempts at scaling have proposed to use linear combinations of the observed scores—whether in educational testing or other fields. It is interesting to observe that the third face of factor analysis provides theoretical underpinning for the use of linear combinations. In a sense, therefore, we have come full circle to a point where we see that Spearman's original attempt to find a method of constructing a measure of general intelligence eventually leads to the same kind of measure as his more empirically minded successors proposed on intuitive grounds.

CONCLUDING OVERVIEW

It is commonly thought, especially among social scientists, that mathematical abstraction makes understanding more difficult. In reality, it often makes things simpler. Abstraction makes for economy of thought by focusing on what is essential and ignoring what is peripheral.

This chapter has moved from the specific, in the shape of Spearman's original problem, to a very general framework, within which many methods having the same basic structure appear. This shows that it is not essential to worry about whether variables are continuous, discrete, or categorical; this is a secondary matter. The notion of the conditional independence of the manifest variables, given the latent variables, on the other hand is central. This distinction often comes across more clearly when computing. The E–M algorithm, for example, is no respecter of the level of measurement of the variables with which it deals.

The general approach with which we have concluded may seem entirely foreign to those who work in one specific field of latent variable analysis—like factor analysis. The formulae used in different fields look very different and the terminologies are, virtually, foreign languages. This chapter has, unashamedly, presented an abstract approach as the way of seeing the significance of Spearman's original contribution and its implications, which go far beyond what he could have imagined 100 years ago.

REFERENCES

Bartholomew, D. J. (1995). Spearman and the origin and development of factor analysis. *British Journal of Mathematical and Statistical Psychology, 48*, 211–220.

Bartholomew, D. J., & Knott, M. (1999). *Latent variable models and factor analysis* (2nd ed.). London: Arnold.

Bartholomew, D. J., Steele, F., Moustaki, I., & Galbraith, J. I. (2002). *The analysis and interpretation of multivariate data for social scientists.* Boca Raton, FL: Chapman & Hall/CRC.

Dodd, S. C. (1929). The sampling theory of intelligence. *The British Journal of Psychology, 19*, 306–327.

Hotelling, H. (1933). Analysis of a complex of statistical variables into principal components. *Journal of Educational Psychology, 24*, 417–441, 498–520.

Lawley, D. N., & Maxwell, A. E. (1963), *Factor analysis as a statistical method.* London: Butterworth.

Lawley, D. N., & Maxwell, A. E. (1971). *Factor analysis as a statistical method* (2nd ed.). New York: American Elsevier.

Lazarsfeld, P. F., & Henry, N. W. (1968). *Latent structure analysis.* New York: Houghton-Mifflin.

Mackintosh, N. J. (1998), *IQ and human intelligence.* Oxford: Oxford University Press.

Molenaar, P. C. M., & von Eye, A. (1994). On the arbitrary nature of random variables. In A. von Eye & C. C. Clogg (Eds.), *Latent variables analysis* (pp. 226–242). Thousand Oakes, CA: Sage.

Spearman, C. (1904). General intelligence objectively determined and measured. *American Journal of Psychology, 15*, 201–293.

Spearman, C. (1932). *The abilities of man.* London: Macmillan. (Original work published 1927)

Spearman, C., & Jones, L. W. (1950). *Human abilities: A continuation of "The abilities of man."* London: Macmillan.

Thomson, G. (1950). *The factorial analysis of human ability* (4th ed.). London: University of London Press.

Yule, G. U. (1897). On the theory of correlation. *Journal of the Royal Statistical Society, 60*, 812–851.

CHAPTER 3

Remembering L. L. Thurstone

Lyle V. Jones[1]

L. L. Thurstone Psychometric Laboratory, The University of North Carolina at Chapel Hill

No one other than Charles Spearman exerted a stronger influence on the development of factor analysis than Louis Leon Thurstone. Here, I trace events in Thurstone's life, from childhood in the United States and in Sweden, back again to high school in New York, an engineering degree at Cornell, his affiliation with Thomas A. Edison, an instructorship in engineering at Minnesota, and then becoming a psychologist with a PhD degree from The University of Chicago. He chaired a department at the Carnegie Institute of Technology before joining the faculty at Chicago, where he produced his major contributions to factor analysis, scaling, test theory, and other aspects of quantitative psychology. Following his faculty retirement from Chicago, he then founded a new psychometric laboratory at the University of North Carolina that still today remains an active center for research and graduate education.

THURSTONE'S CHILDHOOD

Thurstone's unusual childhood quite certainly influenced not only his personal characteristics, but the nature of his scientific contributions as well.

He was born Louis Leon Thunström in Chicago in May, 1887, of parents who had emigrated from Sweden. His father was a Lutheran minister. His schooling

---

[1]In addition to sources cited from L. L. Thurstone, some of the content here is taken from Adkins Wood (1962), Jones (1998), and from private communications with Paul Horst in 1985 and from Thelma Thurstone in 1980 and other times.

began in Berwyn, Illinois. After 1 year, his family moved to Centerville, Mississippi, and then the family moved again, this time to Stockholm, Sweden, where from age 8 he attended Swedish schools, a public school, and then a private boys' school. Sensitive to his inadequate linguistic knowledge, he focused on learning Swedish.

After 6 years, his family again prepared to emmigrate to the United States. Fourteen-year-old Leon told his parents that he would not accompany them unless he could take his favorite books with him. Being unwilling to bear the cost of adding books to their luggage, his mother said he could take three books if he carried them on board the ship. He collected his Euclid geometry, a world atlas, and an encyclopedia of philosophic essays, and carried them aboard the ship in Stockholm.

Leon attended high school in Jamestown, New York. As a sophomore he won a $30 dollar prize in a geometry contest with which he purchased a Kodak camera (photography then became a lifelong hobby) and a bicycle. At about that time, his first publication appeared as a letter to the editor in the *Scientific American* (Thunström, 1905). It proposed a method of diverting the Niagara River for several hours each day in order to provide a source of power but without disrupting the beauty of Niagara Falls.

While he still attended high school, his parents changed the family surname from Thunström to Thurstone, designed to make social life easier for their son and his younger sister. However, the relearning of English remained a serious challenge for him. In his high school, every graduating senior was required to give a 5-minute talk to an audience of several hundred students. Leon met with the principal to declare that he would not be able to graduate if required to give that talk. He was excused from the requirement and he did graduate.

ENGINEERING (AND THOMAS A. EDISON)

Thurstone enrolled in the School of Engineering at Cornell University. While still a student there, he invented and patented a movie camera and projector that, with the use of rotating mirrors, avoided the flicker that was characteristic of movies in the early decades of the 20th century. Thomas A. Edison agreed to view a demonstration of the invention. Edison was impressed, but Edison's laboratory in New Jersey already had been designed to build Edison cameras, so Thurstone was complimented with thanks. He earned his Master of Engineering degree at Cornell in 1912. Then for the summer, he accepted the offer to be Thomas Edison's full-time laboratory assistant. He later wrote of Edison:

> He displayed a startling fluency of ideas, which often ranged far from the immediate problem. He seemed to have an absolutely endless array of stories; very few of them were fit for publication. If problem-solving ability is to be studied scientifically and experimentally, it will be advisable to include studies of different kinds of fluency. (Thurstone, 1952, p. 299)

Edison was known for hastily discarding ideas that had not borne fruit. Without hesitation, he simply tried something else. It is reported that after 10,000 unsuccessful efforts to develop a storage battery, a friend expressed sympathy for his failure. "I have not failed," replied Edison. "I just have discovered 10,000 ways that don't work." Thurstone displayed similar work habits. When dissatisfied with a draft manuscript, he did not try to revise it, but discarded it and started afresh.

In the fall of 1912, Thurstone became an instructor of geometry at the School of Engineering at the University of Minnesota. As at Cornell, where he had taken courses from E. B. Titchener and Madison Bentley, he also attended psychology classes at Minnesota. His motivation was to understand the interface between tools developed by engineers and the users of those tools. He wondered, can the ways by which people learn to use engineering devices be expressed as mathematical functions? Minnesota psychology professors, Herbert Woodrow and J. B. Miner, fostered his interests and in 1914 helped him to become a graduate student at The University of Chicago.

THE UNIVERSITY OF CHICAGO (I)

At Chicago, Thurstone first enrolled in the College of Education with Professor Charles Judd, at that time chair of the Department of Educational Psychology. Thurstone wrote this about that experience:

> I recall one of my first impressions of graduate students of psychology. When they were asked a question, they would start to talk fluently, even when they obviously knew nothing about the subject. I was sure that engineers had higher standards of intellectual honesty. One of my first courses was called Advanced Educational Psychology and it was taught by Professor Judd. I used to wonder what the elementary course could be like if the course I was taking was called advanced. I soon became accustomed to the fact that prerequisites did not mean anything and that there was no real sequence of courses in psychology, even though they were listed by number and title to give the appearance of a sequence, in which one course was supposed to build on another. I never had an elementary course in psychology or in statistics. My first degree was M.E. and I was never flattered when it was interpreted at Chicago as a master's degree in Education. (Thurstone, 1952, p. 300)

After only one term, he shifted to psychology from educational psychology and was sponsored by James Rowland Angell,[2] chair of the Psychology Department at that time.

---

[2] Angell later became dean of the faculties and then acting president at Chicago, president of the Carnegie Corporation of New York, and then president of Yale University from 1921 until his retirement in 1937.

CARNEGIE INSTITUTE OF TECHNOLOGY AND WASHINGTON, DC

Walter Bingham was the head of the Division of Applied Psychology at the Carnegie Institute of Technology and earlier had earned a PhD at Chicago. He visited the Psychology Department seeking to recruit an assistant. He selected Thurstone who, after 1 year of graduate study, moved to Pittsburg to become Bingham's assistant and to write his PhD dissertation on mathematical learning functions, later published as a *Psychological Monograph* (Thurstone, 1919).

When awarded his PhD in 1917, Thurstone became an instructor at Carnegie Tech. Also that year he served with Edward L. Thorndike and Arthur S. Otis as the Statistical Unit appointed by Robert M. Yerkes[3] to evaluate the pilot testing of the Army Alpha, which then was immediately adopted by the Army Surgeon General to test nearly 2 million soldiers in the following 18 months. In 1918, Thurstone became assistant professor, the next year associate professor, the next year professor and chair of the Department of Applied Psychology.[4] From 1919 to 1923, he developed a series of tests of intelligence, clerical skills, engineering aptitude, and ingenuity, often to meet needs in both the military and the civil service.

In 1923, the department of applied psychology at Carnegie Tech was abolished. Funded by the Carnegie Corporation of New York, Thurstone spent 1923 to 1924 in Washington, DC at the Institute for Governmental Research. His charge was to recommend ways to improve U.S. civil service examinations.

Thelma Gwinn had come from Missouri as a graduate student in Thurstone's department at Carnegie Tech in 1920. Thelma earned a bachelor's degree in Germanic language from the University of Missouri and had aspired to teach high school German. World War I had sharply reduced the number of German classes in U.S. high schools, and Thelma was unemployed. A professor at the University of Missouri knew of the applied psychology graduate program at Carnegie Tech, and suggested that, given Thelma's strong interest and background in mathematics, she investigate that program. She became one of a very few women to enroll there, earned a master's degree in Thurstone's department in 1923, and became his assistant in Washington, DC for the following year.

The Institute for Governmental Research happened to share its office building on Dupont Circle with the American Council on Education (ACE). The ACE had begun to develop aptitude tests for high school students and college freshman to

---

[3]Yerkes, in 1917, as president of the American Psychological Association, received endorsements first from the APA Board of Directors, next from the National Research Council, and finally from the Surgeon General of the United States Army, to organize within the Department of the Army a psychology unit to develop tests to aid in the classification of soldiers. Among others engaged in that effort were Harold C. Bingham, Edwin G. Boring, Carl C. Brigham, Lewis M. Terman, and George M. Whipple (see Yerkes, 1921).

[4]Because Thurstone was underweight, he was exempt from the draft of World War I.

guide students about selecting a college major. During their year there, Gwinn and Thurstone often discussed that program with ACE personnel.

In the summer of 1924 Leon and Thelma married and he accepted a position on the psychology faculty at The University of Chicago.

THE UNIVERSITY OF CHICAGO (II)

The contact with the ACE proved to be of considerable importance to the Thurstones because from 1924 to 1945, they were continuously supported to manage the ACE tests for high school seniors and college freshman. Every year they produced a new edition with new norms, an activity that maintained their interests in testing practice and theory. Without the challenges from that project, their subsequent pioneering contributions to factor analysis and test theory were unlikely to have emerged.

The period 1925 to 1930 was one in which Thurstone produced and published a remarkable series of creative articles on psychological and educational scaling based upon assuming a normal distribution of some trait and characterizing a person's level on that trait as a deviation from the mean in standard deviation units. These contributions formed a foundation for educational and psychological measurement that has continued to stimulate new developments over the ensuing 80 years.

In 1929, the new president at the University of Chicago was 29-year-old Robert Hutchins.[5] One of Hutchins's many innovations at Chicago allowed for course credit by examination as an alternative to student enrollment in required courses. Thurstone became the chief examiner for that program. Among the many examiners who worked with him were Dorothy Adkins, Harold Gulliksen, Paul Horst, Marion Richardson, John Stalnecker, Dael Wolfle, and others who later made substantial contributions to psychometrics.

Thurstone's faculty appointment was in psychology, but his office was two blocks distant from the psychology department. Charles Merriam, chair of the Political Science Department, had provided Thurstone an office and adjoining work rooms in the Social Science Research building. One evening in the 1930s, he told Thelma, "I think I will establish a psychometric laboratory and I will be its director." Thelma said, "You can't do that. The chairman would not approve of that, the dean would not approve." Thurstone said, "I know. That's why I put the sign on the door this afternoon." That sign, The Psychometric Laboratory, remained as a plaque on the door of a spacious work room until the time of Thurstone's faculty retirement in 1952.

In the 1930s a representative from the Works Progress Administration (WPA) contacted the Thurstones. The WPA granted federal funds for the hiring of the

---

[5]Thurstone at that time was 42.

unemployed. The agent from its higher education section asked if they could use some assistance in the laboratory and might they be willing to hire 100 helpers? Thurstone said "No, not 100, but maybe as many as 20," and funding became available for as many as 20 assistants,[6] highly talented young men and women, victims of the depression in the mid-1930s.[7] The assistants helped to construct, administer, score, and analyze results from the 57-test battery that provided data for the publication of *Psychometric Monograph Number 1*, entitled "Primary Mental Abilities" (Thurstone, 1938). The project was based on data from about 300 subjects, all University of Chicago freshmen who engaged in 15 hours of testing during a vacation week. They were paid for their time, and 92% of them finished all of the tests.

Near the end of *Psychometric Monograph Number 1*, Thurstone discusses the relation between students' ability profiles and students' expressed vocational interests. He reported that high verbal, high word fluency, and low number abilities characterize people with interests in advertising, journalism, and other writing professions. Some students with high verbal ability, high perceptual ability, but low reasoning scores expressed an interest in acting. He found that people with engineering interests were high in deduction, space, and number, while interests in chemistry or geology also were associated with high spatial skills. These appear to be cited as suggestions for further research on how ability profiles might provide useful academic and/or vocational guidance to students.[8]

Thurstone believed that rotation to simple structure was his greatest contribution to factor analysis. He also recognized the importance for *common* factor analysis of a related innovation, using "communalities" rather than "ones" (or total variance) in the diagonal elements of the correlation matrix.

---

[6]Among those helpers, Thelma Thurstone said that three were PhDs in mathematics.

[7]Ledyard Tucker had earned an engineering degree at Colorado and was among those hired by the Thurstones.

[8]Paul Horst was well aware of this work. Paul finished his PhD with Thurstone in 1935. He told Thurstone, "I am going to take a job at Proctor and Gamble in Cincinnati, Ohio." Thurstone said "But, Paul, you are an academic type." Paul said, "Yes I know it. I am going to get rich and then I am going to retire to a university professorship." That is precisely what he did. From 1935 to 1947, Paul saved his money as a well-paid industrial psychologist. He then retired from Proctor and Gamble to join the faculty at the University of Washington where I was an M.S. student, and I took his courses the first year he was there. As director of the counseling center at the University of Washington, in the tradition of Thurstone, he developed a test battery designed to predict success in college courses differentially by course subject area. By 1955, the tests were taken by high school seniors who intended to apply for admission to the University of Washington. With the program's success, it later was expanded and offered to high school seniors intending to apply to any college or community college in the state. For budgetary reasons, the program was terminated in 1993. Some believe that its demise constituted a disservice to graduating high school students in the state, and that such a program is needed today not only in Washington but in other states as well (see Clemans, Lunneborg, & Raju, 2004).

Thurstone was not always gentle with his critics, and he could become somewhat defensive. He wrote,

> ... it has been a mystery to me why the fundamentally simple notion which I call simple structure, has been twisted around by some critics as the most inconceivable nonsense. ... Factor analysis has not been generally accepted by mathematical statisticians. When the statistician turns his attention to the multiple factor problem, he must deal with the communality concept and its effect on the rank of the correlation matrix. If he denies this problem, he not only admits his inadequacy but also his failure to understand the problem. ... he will not solve the problem by laughing it out of court. (Thurstone, 1947, p. v)

Harold Hotelling developed the principal components method for reducing variance–covariance matrices. A failure to recognize the different goals of the "competing" methods had created some antagonism between Hotelling and Thurstone. However, by the time Thurstone came to Chapel Hill in 1952, Hotelling already was a professor there and strongly supported the Thurstones' faculty appointments. As colleagues at The University of North Carolina (UNC), Hotelling and Thurstone were friendly and mutually respectful.

Thurstone also could be generous with his praise. Citing again from Thurstone (1947),

> A special acknowledgment is due Mr. Ledyard Tucker, who was my chief assistant for a number of years. His thorough mastery of the theory and computational methods of multiple-factor analysis has been of the greatest aid not only in preparing the present manuscript but also in the numerous factorial experiments that have been made here in recent years. ... My principal acknowledgment is to my wife, who has been a partner in the formulation of each problem, as well as in all the experimental studies of this laboratory. (p. xiii)

Thurstone received many honors. He was elected president of the Midwestern Psychological Association in 1930 and president of the American Psychological Association in 1932. The Psychometric Society was founded in 1935–1936, and he was its first president. He was elected a member of the National Academy of Sciences in 1938, then a fellow of the American Academy of Arts and Sciences. He was a fellow as well of the American Statistical Association, and an honorary fellow of the British Psychological Society.

John B. Carroll was a student of B. F. Skinner in the University of Minnesota's Psychology Department and visited Chicago to work with Thurstone in 1940, where Carroll wrote his doctoral dissertation. He was Skinner's first PhD. Carroll's contributions not only to psychometrics but to psycholinguistics and language learning were very much influenced by his work with Thurstone.[9]

---

[9]This early contact with Thurstone probably influenced Carroll's decision in 1974 when he agreed to become William R. Kenan, Jr. Professor and Director of the L.L. Thurstone Psychometric Laboratory

THURSTONE AND SPEARMAN

What did Thurstone really think about Spearman's contribution? In 1933, Thurstone wrote:

> The student who begins his study of factor analysis should read Spearman's early papers. His book, *The Abilities of Man*, has its main content in the appendix that should have been expanded to be the book itself. . . . We must distinguish between Spearman's method of analyzing the intercorrelations of a set of variables for a single common factor and his theory that intelligence is such a common factor which he calls "g." (Thurstone, 1933, p. iii)

The appendix in Spearman's book provides the tetrad equations, the mathematics underlying factor analysis, while the much longer text is intended to justify the theory of general intelligence. Thurstone endorsed the equations but not Spearman's theory of g. He agreed with Godfrey Thompson who had shown that even when the tetrad differences are essentially zero, there are legitimate alternative explanations that involve multiple factors instead of g.[10]

> By 1947 Thurstone seems to have become friendlier to Spearman's theory: "It seems likely that a second-order general factor, determined from correlated primaries, may turn out to be Spearman's general intellective factor '**g**.'" (Thurstone, 1947, p. viii)

Thus, while appearing initially to have questioned the construct of general intelligence—or certainly the evidence for it—he later became more accepting of g if it was conceived to be divisible into oblique primary factors.

MY ASSOCIATION WITH THURSTONE

As a PhD student at Stanford, I wrote to Thurstone in 1949 to ask whether, were I to be awarded a National Research Council (NRC) postdoctoral fellowship, I could spend a year working with him at Chicago. He wrote back saying "yes," thereby allowing me to propose that activity in my application to the NRC. In the spring of 1950, I was completing my dissertation and was pondering job offers from Harvard

---

at The University of North Carolina. Carroll earlier had moved through the faculty ranks at Harvard and then was senior research psychologist at the Educational Testing Service.

[10]Paul Horst recalled a conversation from the 1930s with Professor Thurstone, who said, "Paul, we have to do something about Spearman's general factor theory." He had remained skeptical about the evidence for g. Spearman had treated disturbance factors as negligible if their size was not greater than two probable errors away from zero, and had interpreted that as substantiating the existence of the general factor Because Spearman's studies involved small numbers both of tests and subjects, that criterion for accepting g was overly lenient. The risk of what we now know as a Type II error was extremely high.

as an instructor, and from both Kansas and Hawaii as assistant professor. Although each of these differed distinctly from the others, I had little enthusiasm for any of them. A letter finally arrived from the NRC offering a fellowship award. Gratefully I accepted and moved to Chicago to study with Thurstone in the company of several other postdoctoral fellows.[11]

My plan at Chicago was to analyze data from the standardization of the 1937 Stanford-Binet intelligence test, intending to develop oblique factor solutions, based on graphical transformations.[12] Thurstone and I met weekly to review results from the graphs that I created during the prior week, so that he could advise me about fruitful next steps. I learned that he could anticipate far better than I the likely influences of a two-dimensional transformation on the simple structure for the other (hidden) dimensions. His spatial-thinking skills were exceptional, as one would expect from his lifelong interests and competence in geometry.

In early 1951, Karl Holzinger offered a course on factor analysis in the College of Education. I intended to enroll in his course, but at the last moment decided to ask Professor Thurstone if, as the sponsor of my postdoctoral activities, that would be acceptable to him. With a look of disbelief, he said, "Certainly, Jones, if you want to, but you'll find it to be a total waste of time."[13]

Toward the end of the postdoctoral year, I was weighing faculty offers from Cornell, Johns Hopkins, and Michigan. Each was attractive and while puzzling over which to accept, I was startled when Thurstone asked me, "Would you like to join the faculty here?" I said, "Oh, yes indeed!" He and I then became faculty colleagues in 1951–1952. A year later, I again was surprised when I learned that faculty members at The University of Chicago could not be employed after age 65, that he was 65, and that he was about to depart. He considered offers from the Universities of Washington, California at Berkeley, and North Carolina.

THE UNIVERSITY OF NORTH CAROLINA

The selection of UNC was based largely on the simultaneous award of professorships to both Leon and Thelma Thurstone, something not possible at Chicago because of antinepotism policies (and something missing from the offers from Berkeley and Seattle). At Chapel Hill, Thelma became a professor of education as

---

[11] Allen Edwards, a University of Washington professor who taught me my first psychological statistics course, was among those, as were James Birren, gerontologist from the University of Southern California, Jean Cardinet from Paris, Per Saugsted from Norway, and Horace Rimoldi from Argentina. We all attended Thurstone's class on factor analysis and we also become close friends.

[12] The project was an extension of my master's thesis under Lloyd G. Humphreys at the University of Washington (Jones, 1949), that had served to motivate me to study with Thurstone. Results from the postdoctoral project later were published as Jones (1954).

[13] I did attend the class, but only for the first few meetings.

well as research associate in the Psychometric Laboratory, and Leon was appointed professor of psychology and laboratory director.

The Psychometric Laboratory occupied a separate two-story building, Nash Hall, near the Carolina Inn, two blocks from the psychology department. The Thurstones built a home near campus with a seminar room similar to the one in their home in Chicago that was famous for its Wednesday evening seminars, led usually by visitors, with an invited guest list of about 30 people. Thelma served coffee and pastry after the talk, at Chapel Hill as had been the case also at Chicago.

From 1952 to 1955, Thurstone and I continued to engage in joint research, mostly with support from grants and contracts that he generously had left with me and that I had successfully renewed at Chicago.

In July of 1955, I received a letter from Thurstone inviting me to visit the Thurstone family for a few days in August at their lakeshore summer home near Traverse City, Upper Michigan. I accepted, and dates were agreed upon. The three Thurstone sons[14] tried their best to teach me to water ski. I didn't master that challenge, but did have good fun and good companionship.

Unexpectedly, during the visit, Thurstone took me aside for a "fatherly" talk. Among other things, he said "Lyle, take good care of your research grants and contracts. Never give anyone, a chairman, a dean, or any one else the authorization to spend money from those accounts."[15] He also told me, "At Chapel Hill, I had the chance to affiliate either with the department of psychology where Dorothy Adkins was chair or with the Institute of Statistics, where Gertrude Cox was the director and where Harold Hotelling was an active participant. Perhaps I should have chosen the latter."[16]

Several weeks after my visit came news that L. L. Thurstone had died in September of 1955. In due course, I learned that Thelma Gwinn Thurstone had agreed to serve as acting director of the Psychometric Lab, but only until the completion of obligations under existing grants and contracts. In early 1957, Dorothy Adkins still served as chair of psychology and invited me to visit UNC to consider becoming the director of the Psychometric Laboratory. I did visit, accepted the offer, and remain there today.

To honor its founder, the lab later was named the L. L. Thurstone Psychometric Laboratory. Over its history of 50-plus years, it has hosted more than 50 postdoctoral visitors and granted more than 100 PhDs to recipients who occupy prominent

---

[14]Robert, born in 1927, is emeritus professor at the School of Engineering, University of Alabama at Huntsville. Conrad (1930–1997) was professor of surgery at Stanford. Frederick (Fritz; 1932–2005) was professor of biomedical engineering at Duke.

[15]I learned later that his department chairman at Chicago had "tithed" Thurstone's research accounts, spending 10% of their total funds on departmental expenses that Thurstone considered to be unrelated to the purpose of the awards.

[16]He may have learned that salary levels and other forms of university support were more generous in statistics than in psychology, so that the alternate affiliation might have proven to be more rewarding.

positions at universities and corporate and governmental research agencies. It is still a lively center for research and graduate education.

REFERENCES

Adkins Wood, D. (1962). *Louis Leon Thurstone, creative thinker, dedicated teacher, emminent psychologist.* Princeton, NJ: Educational Testing Service.

Clemans, W. V., Lunneborg, C. E., & Raju, N. S. (2004). Professor Horst's legacy: A differential prediction model for effective guidance in course selection. *Educational Measurement: Issues and Practice, 23*(3), 23–30.

Jones, L. V. (1949). A factor analysis of the Stanford–Binet at four age levels. *Psychometrika, 14*, 299–331.

Jones, L. V. (1954). Primary abilities in the Stanford–Binet, age 13. *Journal of Genetic Psychology, 84*, 125–147.

Jones, L. V. (1998). L. L. Thurstone's vision of psychology as a quantitative rational science. In G. A. Kimble & M. Wertheimer (Eds.), *Portraits of pioneers in psychology* (Vol. 3, pp. 85–102). Mahwah, NJ: Lawrence Erlbaum Associates.

Thunström, L. L. (1905). How to save Niagara. *Scientific American, 93*, 27.

Thurstone, L. L. (1919). The learning curve equation. *Psychological Monographs, 26*(114), 1–51.

Thurstone, L. L. (1933). *The theory of multiple factors.* Ann Arbor, MI: Edwards Brothers, Inc.

Thurstone, L.L. (1938). Primary mental abilities. *Psychometric Monographs, 1*, 1–121.

Thurstone, L. L. (1947). *Multiple-factor analysis.* Chicago: University of Chicago Press.

Thurstone, L. L. (1952). L. L. Thurstone. In E. G. Boring, H. S. Langfeld, H. Werner, & R. M. Yerkes (Eds.), *A history of psychology in autobiography* (Vol. 4, pp. 295–321). Worcester, MA: Clark University Press.

Yerkes, R. M. (1921). Psychological testing in the U.S. Army. *Memoirs of the National Academy of Sciences, 15*, 1–890.

CHAPTER 4

Rethinking Thurstone

R. Darrell Bock
University of Chicago

From the evidence in the published record, the centroid method of factor analysis did not spring full-blown from Louis Leon Thurstone's creative mind. Rather, it grew in his thinking over a period of several years. In this chapter, I attempt to retrace the path of his thought after it first came to light in the paper, "Multiple Factor Analysis," published in the September 1931 issue of *Psychological Review*. By that time, Spearman had admitted that tests that can be considered measures of intelligence might contain group factors in addition to the general factor and factors specific to each test. Citing only Spearman's contributions to the subject, Thurstone proposed to cut through the dissention over group factors by positing an unrestricted multiple-factor model in which the test scores are expressed as linear functions of unobservable factor scores that account for the pairwise correlations among the tests. The coefficients of these functions, the *factor loadings*, would serve to describe general and group factors without distinction between them. The role of multiple factor analysis in psychology would be to find primary sources of individual differences in intelligence and identify tests by which they could be measured. Thurstone's goal was to describe intelligence as a profile of abilities rather than a single test composed of, in his words, "a hodgepodge of tasks combined with unknown weights."

In this first formulation of the multiple factor model, Thurstone acknowledged the existence of specific factors and measurement error but did not include them explicitly. Also, as customary at the time, he assumed that the scales of all variables, observable and unobservable, were in standard form. Introducing the further restriction that the factor scores should be uncorrelated, he arrived at the familiar expressions for the test score variances and correlations in terms of factor loadings.

These results brought him to what came to be called the *fundamental formula* of the centroid method—that in the one-factor case, the factor loading of each test is estimated by the sum of the corresponding row or column of the correlation matrix divided by the square root of the sum of all entries in the table (which at this point in his thinking included unities in the diagonal). In present-day statistical terminology, we would say that these ratios are consistent estimators of one-factor loadings.

Next came the hard part: how to generalize this formula to multiple factors. His solution to this problem involved locating the most strongly related group of tests in the correlation table and applying the fundamental formula summing only over those tests in each column, then dividing by the square root of the sum of all correlations between variables in that group. For later factors, similar groups were identified and used in the same way, except that the formulas were modified to subtract the contribution of the previously estimated factors; at his point, Thurstone did not make use of tables of residual correlations. Uncharacteristically, he did not present computing examples or numerical results in this paper. He states only that he had applied the method to intercorrelations of responses to the Strong Vocational Interest Inventory and found factors of interest in science, language, people, and business.

That Thurstone did not cite earlier attempts of others to devise a multiple-factor analysis is understandable. Truman Kelley made such an attempt in his 1928 book, *Crossroads in the Mind of Man*, and expressed the test scores as linear combinations of uncorrelated latent variables. But he retained the distinction between general and group factors, made use of Spearman's tetrad differences, and did not arrive at a satisfactory general method of estimating the factor loadings. Kelley himself described the treatment as "clumsy" in his more successful 1935 work, *The Essential Traits of Mental Life*. The other source, a thin book by Cyril Burt entitled *The Distribution and Relations of Educational Abilities*, published in 1917 by the Education Officer of the London County Council, is more enlightening, but it was undoubtedly unknown to either Thurstone or Kelly at the time. It was however known to Holzinger (who had studied with Spearman in England) and was referred to by Holzinger and Harman in their 1941 text on factor analysis. Burt's book is historically interesting because it presents for the first time the fundamental centroid formula as an estimator of the general factor loadings. It also introduces the residual correlation table and employs rearrangement of rows and columns of the table to identify the tests loading of group factors. The work foreshadows Thurstone's test grouping procedure in the 1931 paper but does not explicitly define a multiple factor model. Burt did not, however, present his ideas along these lines in an organized way until his 1941 book, *The Factors of Mind*, and he had relatively little influence on the subsequent development of factor analysis.

In the preface to *The Vectors of Mind*, published in 1935, Thurstone tells of the event that stimulated his thinking on how to estimate of factor loadings without grouping the tests. Sometime late in 1931, while having lunch at the University of Chicago Quadrangle Club, with Professors Bliss from the Department of Mathematics and Bartky from the Department of Astronomy, he showed them a table of test intercorrelations and explained what he was trying to accomplish. He does not quote them, but one can imagine the good professors replying along the lines of "What you have there is a real symmetric matrix, and what you are looking for is a preferred basis such as its principal vectors. Some study of matrix algebra may be of help to you." They may also have referred Thurstone to an accessible treatment of this subject in the introductory textbook, *Introduction to Higher Algebra*, written originally in 1907 by Maxime Bôcher, a professor of mathematics at Harvard. The book was not in the University of Chicago library in 1931, but it had been kept in print by Macmillan and was available in technical book stores. Thurstone referred to it as a source he used in subsequent work. He also took the professors' advice seriously and hired a graduate student in mathematics to tutor him on matrix algebra.

Thurstone's undergraduate education in electrical engineering, absent matrix algebra, would have included instruction in calculus, differential equations, and determinants as they appear in multiple integration and the solution of simultaneous linear equations. With this background and his capacity for concentrated study, he quickly mastered the essentials of matrix algebra and applied them in work reported in a monograph entitled *The Theory of Multiple Factors* reproduced from the typescript in January, 1933, and distributed by the University of Chicago Bookstore. A considerable advance from the 1931 paper, it contains for the first time the terms, *communality*, designating the common factor variance and, *uniqueness*, designating the sum of specific and measurement error variance. Rotation of axes is introduced for the first time, the principal axes are defined, and the derivatives are obtained for locating principal axes when maximizing the sum of squared of projections of the test vectors on the axes. Set equal to zero, these derivatives comprise a set of homogeneous linear equations, the determinant of which is a function of undetermined multipliers. That function is the characteristic equation of the matrix, its roots are the values of the multipliers, and the solutions of homogeneous equations with those values substituted are the invariant, or principal, vectors of the matrix.

Thurstone does not designate the vectors as such, or anywhere use the term *matrix*, but refers to them as the coordinates of principal axes—the factor loadings. He notes that the sum of squares of the loadings indicates the importance of each axis in accounting for variation of in the test scores, but he does not identify them as the latent roots of the matrix. There follows an artificial example of factor loadings for seven tests and three factors contrived so that the third factor loadings are linear combination of the first and second factor loadings. Thurstone laboriously grinds through the calculation and solution of the characteristic equation of the corresponding correlation matrix. One of the three roots is of course, zero, which shows the number of nonzero roots to be the number of factors required to account for the correlations. Finally, substituting the roots for the undetermined multipliers,

TABLE 4–1

Factor Loadings for Thurstone's Nine-Variable Problem by Three Methods

	Centroid Factor				Thurstone's Iterative Principal Factor				Modern MINRES Principal Factor			
Test	I	II	III	h^2	I	II	III	h^2	I	II	III	h^2
1	.774	−.069	.115	.617	.783	−.006	.044	.615	.773	−.022	.094	.607
2	.650	.367	−.207	.600	.613	.411	−.124	.560	.640	.412	−.184	.613
3	.731	−.167	.191	.599	.752	−.099	.066	.550	.727	−.116	.152	.566
4	.665	.118	.220	.505	.652	.102	.164	.462	.654	.101	.233	.492
5	.804	−.306	−.083	.747	.805	−.235	−.172	.733	.813	−.290	−.057	.749
6	.593	.485	−.019	.587	.545	.584	−.025	.635	.577	.518	−.053	.604
7	.738	−.124	.211	.605	.744	−.064	.132	.575	.745	−.078	.241	.619
8	.725	−.038	−.117	.591	.760	.035	−.105	.590	.751	.004	−.062	.568
9	.772	−.291	−.314	.779	.765	−.171	−.467	.829	.796	−.297	−.344	.840
Root	4.718	.597	.313		4.608	.620	.326		4.710	.641	.306	

he solves the homogeneous equations and obtains the factor loadings on the two nondegenerate axes.

Regrettably, Thurstone found that the labor of computing the coefficients of the characteristic equation, even with an electrical rotary calculator, would be prohibitive with larger numbers of tests. Always resourceful, he then devised an ad hoc iterative procedure for approximating a principal factors solution in larger problems. He applied the procedures to correlations of nine intelligence tests administered by the College Entrance Examination Board to a sample of 4,175 examinees in 1928. The proportions of variance accounted for by the first three principal factors were .512, .069, and .036, showing that the test space was essentially one-dimensional. Working from Thurstone's three-decimal-point correlations for this problem, I have verified that his results are in reasonably good agreement with a MINRES principal factor analysis with six iterations of communality (see Table 4–1). He could have taken little pleasure in this, however, for the amount of computation was still beyond the technology of the time; he reported later that these calculations took him several weeks to complete. To apply the procedure to the large test batteries he envisioned for a comprehensive study of intelligence would have been hopeless. At this point, I think we can assume that Thurstone must have felt thoroughly discouraged; not only he was unhappy with the original formulation of the centroid solution that required grouping of tests, but the rigorous principal factor solution, optimal in the sense of accounting for maximum variance with any given number of factors, was not feasible with existing computing machinery.

Let us leave Thurstone at this impasse for the moment and look at what Harold Hotelling was doing in 1932. His background was quite different than Thurstone's. He received a BA degree at the University of Washington in journalism with minors in economics and mathematics. A period of work for a local paper was not successful because, as he said later, "I wrote too slowly." He then applied for an economics fellowship at Columbia but was rejected. Princeton was more receptive, however, accepted him for the graduate program mathematics, and eventually awarded him the PhD. On the evidence of his subsequent publications in econometrics, Columbia recognized their previous error and in 1931 appointed him to a post in its Department of Economics. As he had become interested in statistics, he spent a semester leave at Harpenden with R. A. Fisher. In 1930, Truman Kelley had moved from Stanford to Harvard and had occasion to be in New York attending meetings of the Unitary Traits Committee of the Carnegie Corporation, which included Karl Holzinger, Charles Spearman, and E. L. Thorndike, among others. Hotelling must have met Kelley then, for he acknowledges his role in initiating the study supported in part by the Carnegie Corporation that led to his seminal paper, "Analysis of a Complex of Statistical Variables into Principal Components." The final version of the paper was published in the September and October, 1933, issues of the *Journal of Educational Psychology*. In that paper, Hotelling presents an iterative method much simpler and faster than that of Thurstone for computing the roots and vectors of a real symmetric matrix. He acknowledges in a footnote that in June, 1932, "Professor Thurstone presented at the Syracuse meeting of the American Association for the Advancement of Science certain of the considerations which have served as a point of departure for this paper" (p. 428). Obviously Thurstone was reporting the results of his iterative procedure as it appeared in *Theory of Multiple Factors*. Sitting in the audience, Hotelling must have been thinking, "There must be an easier way!" In the same footnote, Hotelling states "Since this [paper] was written professor Thurstone has kindly sent me a pamphlet he has prepared for class use [i.e., the *Theory* monograph] ... His iterative procedure appears to have no relation to that of [my paper]" (p. 428).

My conjecture is that Hotelling had sent Thurstone a draft version of his paper on principal components early in 1933. I base the conjecture on the fact that in the published version of the paper, he expresses his indebtedness "to Professors L. L. Thurstone, Clark V. Hull, C. Spearman, and E. L. Thorndike, who raised some further questions treated" (p. 417). It is easy to understand as follows why seeing the draft version would have helped Thurstone overcome the impasse in his thinking.

The iterations of Hotelling's method consist of two steps: (a) starting from some choice of elements of an initial trial vector, treated as a $1 \times n$ matrix, the $n \times n$ correlation matrix is premultiplied by that vector (row by column cumulative multiplication); (b) the elements of the resulting vector are divided by the absolute value of their largest element, and the next iteration uses the result as the new trial vector. Iterations continued in this way converge geometrically to a vector proportional to the first principal vector of the matrix. The largest element of the converged vector is the characteristic root; setting the sum of squares of the vector elements equal to the root yields the first-component loadings (see the computing example in chap. 2 of my textbook *Multivariate Statistical Methods in Behavioral Research*; 1975). The second root and vector are obtained by first computing the residual correlation matrix in the usual way—subtracting from each element of the product of the first-component loadings of the corresponding row and column. New values for the initial trial vector are chosen and the iterative process repeated for that factor.

When working with scores for intelligence tests, all correlations in the initial matrix will be positive. For that reason the conventional choice of the initial trial vector for the first component has all elements equal to 1; the result of the first iteration is then simply the column sums of the matrix. For second principal component, however, the residual correlation matrix will contain both positive and negative elements and the columns will sum to zero. Therefore, the convention for choosing the initial values of the new trial vector is to set values corresponding to columns with a majority of negative elements to -1 and the remainder to $+1$. The same applies initial trial values for residual matrices of subsequent components. Iterations from these trial values will in general converge to the respective principal vectors.

It would not have been lost on Thurstone that the result of the initial iteration for the first component is precisely the centroid estimate of the first factor loadings when applied to the correlation matrix without alteration of the diagonal elements. The same would apply if communalities were in the diagonal. He would have also been well aware that as a number of variables increases, sums weighted by more or less homogeneous positive quantities will approach proportionality with unweighted sums. First centroid factor loadings will therefore be in reasonably good approximation to first principal factor loadings. Similarly for subsequent factors, the column sums of elements residual matrices weighted by $+1$s and -1s of the trial vectors, after corresponding changes of sign, will result in centroid factor in good approximation to their principal factor loadings.

So there he has it!—a noniterative procedure that will approximate the principal factor solution but requires no time-consuming, cumulative multiplications. To facilitate summation when working with the residual matrices, where the signs of both the trial value and the residual correlation have to be taken into account, he would simply reflect the signs in rows and columns corresponding to negative trial values. Because he had already obtained good approximations to the characteristic roots and vectors for the nine-test computing example in *The Theory of Multiple Factors*, he could assess the accuracy of a centroid solution when the number of variables is relatively small. As we see in Table 4–1 of this chapter, the centroid and principal axes solution for that example are in reasonably good agreement.

With these results in hand, Thurstone (1933a) immediately prepared a brief supplement to the *Theory* monograph under the title, *A Simplified Multiple Factor Method and an Outline of the Computations*, and he had the typescript reproduced for distribution by the University of Chicago Bookstore. In later writings, he gives the date of distribution as May 1933. In this supplement, he refers for the first time to the table of correlations as a correlation matrix and the table of factor loadings as a factor matrix. Also for the first time, he uses symbol h^2 for the communality and substitutes the absolute value of the largest correlation in each column of the correlation matrix as a provisional value for the communality.

While preparing this chapter, I discovered that I am not the first to notice the connection between Hotelling's procedure and the centroid method. In a footnote of their 1941 book *Factor Analysis: A Synthesis of Factorial Methods*, Holzinger and Harman comment, "A further analogy between the centroid and principal factor methods may be noted. Each centroid factor is actually the first approximation, in [Hotelling's] iterative scheme, to the principal factor" (p. 184). They do not delve into the matter further.

Thurstone moved quickly to apply this fast and objective method of factor analysis to a number of large data sets. These included ratings of personality traits described by 60 different adjectives; the analysis resulted in five factors characterized by the adjective with highest loading trait, namely, *friendly, patient, persevering, capable, and self-important*. Along similar lines, an analysis of ratings of patients psychotic symptoms yielded clusters of symptoms identified as *catatonic, cognitive, manic, hallucinatory*, and *depressive*. A study of attitudes toward disputed social issues identified the radicalism–conservatism dimension for the first time. In September of 1933 he presented these results in his presidential address to the American Psychological Association, subsequently published in the January, 1934, issue of *The Psychological Review*. In this address, he took the opportunity to introduce a large audience to the terms *correlation matrix* and *factor matrix*, and to show schematically that the matrix product of the factor matrix times its transpose yields a correlation matrix with communalities in the diagonal. He refers to the number of factors as the *rank* of this matrix.

The year 1934 and part of 1935 was a period of intense work for Thurstone. In 1935, the University of Chicago Press published *The Vectors of Mind*, his extended treatise on multiple factor analysis. It expands greatly on results in the *Theory* monograph and includes a new section on the *simple structure* concept and the numerical procedures for transforming a factor solution to simple structure. It introduces the concepts of *bounding hyperplanes*, *oblique rotations*, and *second-order factors*. It also includes, for the first time in the psychological or statistical literature, an introductory section containing definitions and results of matrix algebra and their geometrical interpretations. In this, he set a precedent that many others have followed, including Holzinger and Harman in their 1941 text on factor analysis, Roy's 1957 text, *Some Aspects of Multivariate Analysis*, Harman's 1960 text, *Modern Factor Analysis*, my own 1975 multivariate text, and as recently as 1983, for the benefit of the numerical analysis field, Golub and Van Loan's text *Matrix Computations*.

As a matter of interest, I reviewed both the *Journal of the American Statistical Association* (JASA) and the *Annals of Mathematical Statistics* (AMS) looking for applications of matrix algebra before 1935. Even as late as 1940, JASA contained not only no matrix algebra, but hardly any algebra at all; it was still largely a journal of statistics in the old sense—the presentation and analysis of tables of economic and social indicators. The earliest instance of matrix algebra I could find was in the AMS, Volume 6, 1935, in an article by Y. K Wong entitled "Application of

Orthogonalization Processes to the Theory of Least-Squares." Although AMS was a self-proclaimed mathematical journal, the author felt obliged to include tutorial material on vectors, inner products, linear dependence, and matrices and their reciprocals. (Members of the Psychometric Society will be interested to know that this volume also contains an article by Paul Horst entitled "A Method for Determining the Coefficients of a Characteristic Equation." It is 25 lines long and contains some of the most cryptic notation I have ever encountered. It must have been written after Horst had seen either Thurstone's *Theory of Multiple Factors*, or a draft of *The Vectors of Mind*.)

Speaking of notation, I add that although Hotelling may have derived his iterative procedure for latent roots and vectors in matrix terms, in consideration of the audience, he confined his presentation to scalar algebra. Curiously, however, he introduces a notational convention from tensor calculus—namely, that when an equation is written as say, $b_i = a_{ij}$, it denotes the summation of the right-hand member with respect to the j subscript. This device is somewhat unsettling to anyone accustomed to seeing the summation sign in these equations. Surely, this is the only paper containing tensor notation in the entire psychological literature and perhaps the statistical literature.

To return to Thurstone's accomplishments, in the space of 4 years, he had (a) fully specified the multiple-factor model, (b) established that the number of factors required to account for pairwise correlation of variables is the rank of the correlation matrix with communalities in the diagonal, (c) found a computationally feasible method of estimating the factor loadings, (d) defined the oblique factor model, (e) dealt with the rotation problem, and (f) introduced matrix algebra to the field of psychometrics. He lacked only a rigorous method for estimating the communalities; that had to await the contributions of Lawley in 1940, Joreskog in 1963, and the coming of electronic computers. But for practical work with large numbers of tests, rough estimates of the communalities were quite satisfactory and were productively used in many factor studies in the intervening years. Thurstone further elaborated his concepts and methods in his textbook *Multiple Factor Analysis*, published in 1947, but the essential results were already in *The Vectors of Mind*.

Thurstone also pursued with equal vigor his larger goal of clarifying the nature of intelligence. By 1938, he had carried out the empirical studies and factor analyses by which he identified seven primary factors of mental ability. Among these, as I pointed out in my 1973 *Psychometrika* paper, "Word and Image," the verbal and spatial factors turned out to be of fundamental importance. They ultimately found an explanation as effects of individual differences in hemispheric dominance in the processing verbal and spatial information in left and right brain. These differences had first been inferred from studies of left- and right-brain damage on language impairment. There were also indications that the degree of specialization is greater in men than in women, a credible explanation for the marked sex differences typically seen in performance on spatial tests. These findings have been amply confirmed by functional magnetic resonance imaging (fMRI) of neural activity during cognitive task performance (see the references to Vikingstad, George, Johnson, Cao (2000) and Smith & Jonides (1999) in the list that follows). These studies also show pronounced individual differences in all these effects. The presence of these differences gives factor analysis with the power to detect features of cognitive tasks that an a common functional effect in brain activity. In this way, factor analytic studies can help identify cognitive tasks likely to show specific localization in fMRI studies. Direct factor analysis of *item responses* is more promising in this role than analysis of test scores because many more task features can be investigated simultaneously. Recent computational advances have made high-dimensional, full-information item factor analysis available for this purpose.

The following is an example of how item factor analysis can reveal communalities of task performance that have implications for cognitive functioning. In her 1985 dissertation, *Attributes of Spatial Test Items That Influence Cognitive Processing*, at the University of Chicago, Michele Zimowski applied item factor analysis to the Space Relations subtest of an obsolete version of Bennett's (1947) *Differential Aptitude Tests* (DAT). Analyzing individual item responses of 391 twelfth-grade students, she found a surprising result. The analysis revealed four factors associated with common features of certain of the test items. As described by Zimowski (1985), three of the items primarily defining Factor 1 contained square objects, all presented in identical format in their unfolded form. Factor 2, on the other hand, was largely defined by two groups of items all containing rectangular forms or cube-based pyramids. Factor 4 was defined by octahedrons and squares with one side divided into equal fourths in their unfolded versions, and Factor 3 was defined by at least three distinct subsets of similar items. Apparently to save effort in the original construction of the test, variations of the same basic figures were used several times among the 48 items.

If all such recurring figures appeared in a single factor, we might attribute the factor to individual differences in strength of a visual memory trait. But it is inconceivable that, in the population of examinees, there could be separate and independent traits for each type of recurring figure. The types are merely arbitrary artifacts of the test construction. A more plausible explanation would be that when a person engages the item cognitively and responds correctly to the first occurrence of a figure, there is a conscious or unconscious perception that the response is in fact correct. There is an internal "aha" experience, so to speak. If that experience acts as reward in reinforcing the cognitive process, there will be an increase in probability of success when the figure recurs in a later item. Suppose then that fMRI shows some specific area of the brain light up for a correct response but not for a wrong response. That would imply a neural basis for the increased association of responses to items of similar type. The corresponding item factor would be one of process rather than of trait. Such an observation would be evidence of both the validity of the factor analytic result and the role of reinforcement in shaping cognition.

We could also think of designing test items in the light of fMRI results. Spatial items, for example, could be constructed so as to show greatest right-hemisphere specialization of brain function. Indirectly, to the extent that sex differences reflect hemispheric specialization, Zimowski did this experimentally for certain spatial tests in her study that were presented by individually timed slide projection. Using data from an pilot study with varying item projection times, she chose for the main study the times expected to maximize sex differences in probability of correct response.

This conjoining of cognitive psychology and neuroscience has created a new domain of application for item factor analysis. Exploratory factor studies of responses to a variety of information processing tasks will point to those that best represent performance variation to be investigated in subsequent fMRI studies. Complementary use of these techniques has the potential for new directions of progress in Thurstone's still uncompleted program of finding the primary sources of intelligent behavior.

REFERENCES

Bennett, G. K. (1947). *Differential Aptitude Tests*. New York, Psychological Corporation.
Bôcher, M. (1931). *Introduction to higher algebra*. New York: Macmillan.
Bock, R. D. (1975). *Multivariate statistical methods in behavioral research*. New York: McGraw-Hill.
Bock, R. D. (1973). Word and image: sources of the verbal and spatial factors in mental test scores. *Psychometrika, 38*, 437–457.
Burt, C. (1917). *The distribution and relations of educational abilities*. London: P. S. King & Son.
Burt, C. (1941). *The factors of mind: An introduction to factor analysis in psychology*. New York: MacMillan.
Golub, G. H., & Van Loan, C. F. (1983). *Matrix computations*. Baltimore: The Johns Hopkins University Press.
Harman, H. H. (1960). *Modern factor analysis*. Chicago: University of Chicago Press.
Holzinger, K. J. & Harman, H. H. (1941). *Factor analysis: A synthesis of factorial methods*. Chicago: University of Chicago Press.
Horst, P. (1935). A method for determining the coefficients of a characteristic equation. *Annals of Mathematical Statistics, 6*, 83–84.
Hotelling, H. (1933). Analysis of a complex of statistical variables into principal components. *Journal of Educational Psychology, 24*, 417–441, 498–520.
Jöreskog, K. G. (1963). *Statistical estimation in factor analysis*. Stockholm: Almquist & Wiksell.
Kelley, T. L. (1928). *Crossroads in the mind and man*. Stanford, CA: Stanford University Press.
Kelley, T. L. (1935). *The essential traits of mental life*. Cambridge, MA: Harvard University Press.
Lawley, D. N. (1940). The estimation of factor loadings by the method of maximum likelihood. *Proceedings of the Royal Society of Edinburgh, 60*, 64–82.
Roy, S. N. (1957). *Some aspects of multivariate analysis*. New York:Wiley.
Smith, E. E. & Jonides, J. (1999). Storage and executive processes in the frontal lobes. *Science. 283*, 1657–1661.
Thurstone, L. L. (1931). Multiple factor analysis. *Psychological Review, 38*, 406–427.

Thurstone, L. L. (1933a) *A simplified multiple factor method and an outline of the computations*. Chicago: University of Chicago Bookstore.

Thurstone, L. L. (1933b). *The theory of multiple factors*. Chicago: University of Chicago Bookstore.

Thurstone, L. L. (1934). The vectors of mind. *Psychological Review, 41*, 1–32.

Thurstone, L. L. (1935). *The vectors of mind*. Chicago: University of Chicago Press.

Thurstone, L. L. (1947). *Multiple factor analysis*. Chicago: University of Chicago Press.

Vikingstad, E. M., George, K. P., Johnson, A. F., & Cao, Y. (2000). Cortical language lateralization in right-handed normal subjects using functional magnetic resonance imaging. *Journal of Neurological Science, 175*, 17–27.

Wong, Y. K. (1935). Application of orthogonalization processes to the theory of least-squares. *Annals of Mathematical Statistics, 6*, 53–75.

Zimowski, M. F. (1985). *Attributes of spatial test items that influence cognitive processing*. Unpublished doctoral dissertation, The University of Chicago.

CHAPTER 5

Factor Analysis and Its Extensions

Karl G Jöreskog
Uppsala University

Although its roots can be traced back to the work of Francis Galton, it is generally considered that factor analysis began with the celebrated article by Spearman (1904). In the first half of the 20th century, factor analysis was mainly developed by psychologists for the purpose of identifying mental abilities by means of psychological testing. Various theories of mental abilities and various procedures for analyzing the correlations among psychological tests emerged. The most prominent factor analysts in the first half of the 20th century seem to be Godfrey Thomson, Cyril Burt, Raymond Cattell, Karl Holzinger, Louis Thurstone, and Louis Guttman. A later generation of psychological factor analysts that played important roles are Ledyard Tucker, Henry Kaiser, and Chester Harris. For the early history of factor analysis, see the articles by Bartholomew (1995) and Hägglund (2001), the text books by Harman (1967) and Mulaik (1972) and the review article by Mulaik (1986).

Factor analysis was found to be quite useful in the early stages of experimentation and test development. Thurstone's (1938) primary mental abilities, French's (1951) factors in aptitude and achievement tests, Guilford's (1956) structure of intelligence, and the structure of personal characteristics of Romney and Bynner (1992) are good examples of this.

In the 1950s, there seem to be two schools of factor analysis: the psychometric school and the statistical school. The *psychometric school* regarded the battery of tests as a selection from a large domain of tests that could be developed for the same psychological phenomenon and focused on the factors in this domain. By contrast, the *statistical school* regarded the number of tests as fixed and focused on the inference from the individuals being tested to a hypothetical population of individuals. The distinction between the two perspectives is particularly contrasted with regard to the number of factors. In the psychometric perspective, it was assumed that there are a small number of major factors and possibly a large number of minor factors; whereas in the statistical perspective, the number of factors is assumed to be small relative to the number of tests.

Whereas the factor analysis literature in the first half of the 20th century was dominated by psychologists, the literature of the second half of the century was dominated by statisticians. In fact, there has been an enormous development of the statistical methodology for factor analysis in the last 50 years. This has been accompanied by an equally enormous development of computational methods for factor analysis. During this period, the applications of factor analysis spread from psychology to many other disciplines, for example, international relations, economics, sociology, communications, taxonomy, biology, physiology, medicine, geology, and meteorology.

This chapter is an attempt to give an account of the developments of factor analysis as a statistical method in the last 50 years and its extensions from classical exploratory factor analysis to confirmatory factor analysis, multiple-group factor analysis, structural equation models, and general covariance structures.

EXPLORATORY FACTOR ANALYSIS

The basic idea of factor analysis is the following. For a given set of manifest response variables $x_1, \ldots, x_p$ one wants to find a set of underlying latent factors $\xi_1, \ldots, \xi_k$, fewer in number than the observed variables. These latent factors are supposed to account for the intercorrelations of the response variables in the sense that when the factors are partialed out from the observed variables, there should no longer remain any correlations between these. If both the observed response variables and the latent factors are measured in deviations from their means, this leads to the linear factor analysis model:

$$x_i = \lambda_{i1}\xi_1 + \lambda_{i2}\xi_2 + \cdots + \lambda_{ik}\xi_k + \delta_i, \quad i = 1, 2, \ldots, p, \qquad \text{(Equation 5.1)}$$

where δ_i, the unique part of x_i, is uncorrelated with $\xi_1, \xi_2, \ldots, \xi_k$ and with δ_j for $j \neq i$. In matrix notation, Equation 5.1 is

$$\mathbf{x} = \mathbf{\Lambda}\xi + \delta, \qquad \text{(Equation 5.2)}$$

where $\mathbf{x} = (x_1, x_2, \ldots, x_p)'$, $\xi = (\xi_1, \xi_2, \ldots, \xi_k)'$ and $\delta = (\delta_1, \delta_2, \ldots, \delta_p)'$ are random vectors and $\mathbf{\Lambda}$ is a matrix of order $p \times k$ of parameters called factor loadings. The objective of factor analysis is to determine the number of factors k and estimate the factor loadings λ_{ij}.

Through the 1950s, factor analysis was characterized by a set of procedures for analyzing the correlation matrix $\mathbf{R}$ of the manifest variables. Four problems of factor analysis emerged:

- Number of factors.
- Communalities.

- Factor extraction.
- Factor rotation.

These four problems are highly interrelated.

Number of Factors

There is no unique way to determine the number of factors. This is best done by the investigator who knows what the variables [are supposed to] measure. Then the number of factors can be specified a priori at least tentatively. Many procedures have been suggested in the literature to determine the number of factors analytically. One that was widely used was "Kaiser's little jiffy" which says that the number of factors should be equal to the number of eigenvalues of the correlation matrix **R** which are greater than 1.[1] A similar ad hoc rule, also based on the eigenvalues of **R**, is Cattell's (1966) scree-plot, where the eigenvalues are plotted against their rank and the number of factors is indicated by the "elbow" of the curve. Other procedures for deciding on the number of factors are based on statistical fit. For example, with the maximum likelihood method, one can test the hypothesis that $k = k_0$ where k_0 is a specified number of factors. This can be developed into a sequential procedure to estimate the number of factors.

Communalities

The communalities problem is as follows. What numbers should be put in the diagonal of the correlation matrix **R** to make this approximately equal to $\mathbf{\Lambda\Lambda'}$, where $\mathbf{\Lambda}$ is a $p \times k$ matrix of factor loadings? Such numbers are called communalities and the correlation matrix with communalities in the diagonal is denoted $\mathbf{R}_c$. Thus, the communalities should be chosen such that $\mathbf{R}_c$ is Gramian and of rank k. Then $\mathbf{\Lambda}$ could be determined such that

$$\mathbf{R}_c \approx \mathbf{\Lambda\Lambda'} \,. \qquad \text{(Equation 5.3)}$$

The problem of communalities was involved in much discussion of factor analysis in the 1950s. For example, in Harman's (1967) book, a whole chapter is devoted to this problem. The communality problem is highly related to the factor extraction problem. The most important papers on these problems are those by Guttman (1944, 1954b, 1956, 1957, 1958).

Guttman (1956) showed that the squared multiple correlation R_i^2 in the regression of the ith manifest variable on all the other manifest variables is a lower bound

---

[1]Henry Kaiser gave this rule in his dissertation 1956, see Kaiser (1970). Actually, this is the first part of the little jiffy; the second part says that the factors should be rotated by Varimax.

for the communality c_i^2 of the ith variable:

$$c_i^2 \geq R_i^2 \ , i = 1, 2, \ldots, p \ . \tag{Equation 5.4}$$

Factor Extraction

Once the communalities have been determined, there are various methods for deter-mining Λ in Equation 5.3. The most common method in the early literature is one that chooses the columns of Λ proportional to the eigenvectors of R_c corresponding to the k largest eigenvalues. This is in fact a least squares solution in the sense that it minimizes

$$tr(R_c - \Lambda\Lambda')^2 \ . \tag{Equation 5.5}$$

Rotation

The matrix Λ in Equation 5.3 is only determined up to an orthogonal rotation. If Λ in 5.3 is replaced by $\Lambda^* = \Lambda U$, where U is an arbitrary orthogonal matrix of order $k \times k$, then

$$\Lambda^*\Lambda^{*'} = \Lambda\Lambda' \ .$$

This is a special case of a more general formula for factor transformation given in the Factor Transformation section and further discussion of the rotation problem is postponed until that section.

A Simple Solution

Much of the discussion in the 1950s were procedures for choosing communalities and extracting factor loadings. There was a need for a statistical formulation. In particular, one needed to get away from the use of the sample correlation matrix R. A simple solution to all four problems of factor analysis is as follows.

The counterpart of the communality c_i^2 is the uniqueness $u_i^2 = 1 - c_i^2$. Hence, Equation 5.4 is equivalent to

$$u_i^2 \leq 1 - R_i^2 = 1/r^{ii} \ , \tag{Equation 5.6}$$

where r^{ii} is the ith diagonal element of R^{-1}. The last step in Equation 5.6 follows from Equation (23.3.4) in Cramér (1957).

Jöreskog (1963) suggested to take

$$u_i^2 = \theta r^{ii} \ , \tag{Equation 5.7}$$

where $\theta < 1$ is a parameter to be estimated.

In terms of the population covariance matrix Σ this model is

$$\Sigma = \Lambda\Lambda' + \theta(diag\Sigma^{-1})^{-1} \ , \tag{Equation 5.8}$$

which is to be interpreted as an implicit equation defining $\boldsymbol{\Sigma}$ as a function of $\boldsymbol{\Lambda}$ and θ. Jöreskog (1963) developed a simple noniterative method for estimating $\boldsymbol{\Lambda}$ and θ from the sample covariance matrix S.

Pre- and postmultiplying Equation 5.8 by $(diag\,\boldsymbol{\Sigma}^{-1})^{\frac{1}{2}}$ and defining

$$\boldsymbol{\Sigma}^* = (diag\,\boldsymbol{\Sigma}^{-1})^{\frac{1}{2}}\boldsymbol{\Sigma}(diag\,\boldsymbol{\Sigma}^{-1})^{\frac{1}{2}},$$

and

$$\boldsymbol{\Lambda}^* = (diag\,\boldsymbol{\Sigma}^{-1})^{\frac{1}{2}}\boldsymbol{\Lambda}$$

gives

$$\boldsymbol{\Sigma}^* = \boldsymbol{\Lambda}^*\boldsymbol{\Lambda}^{*'} + \theta\mathbf{I},$$

which shows that $p - k$ of the eigenvalues of $\boldsymbol{\Sigma}^*$ are equal to θ. Since S is a consistent estimate of $\boldsymbol{\Sigma}$,

$$\mathbf{S}^* = (diag\,\mathbf{S}^{-1})^{\frac{1}{2}}\mathbf{S}(diag\,\mathbf{S}^{-1})^{\frac{1}{2}},$$

is a consistent estimate of $\boldsymbol{\Sigma}^*$. Let $\hat{\gamma}_1, \hat{\gamma}_2, \ldots, \hat{\gamma}_p$ be the eigenvalues of $\mathbf{S}^*$ in descending order and let $\omega_1, \omega_2, \ldots, \omega_k$ be unit-length eigenvectors corresponding to the k largest eigenvalues. Furthermore, let

$$\boldsymbol{\Gamma}_k = diag(\hat{\gamma}_1, \hat{\gamma}_2, \ldots, \hat{\gamma}_k),$$

and

$$\boldsymbol{\Omega}_k = (\omega_1, \omega_2, \ldots, \omega_k).$$

Then the simple solution is

$$\hat{\theta} = \frac{1}{p - k}(\hat{\gamma}_{k+1} + \hat{\gamma}_{k+2} + \cdots + \hat{\gamma}_p),$$

$$\boldsymbol{\Lambda} = (diag\,\mathbf{S}^{-1})^{-\frac{1}{2}}\boldsymbol{\Omega}_k(\boldsymbol{\Gamma}_k - \hat{\theta}\mathbf{I})^{\frac{1}{2}}\mathbf{U},$$

where U is an arbitrary orthogonal matrix of order $k \times k$. This solution also offers a solution to the number of factors problem. Choose the smallest k such that $\hat{\theta} < 1$.

This simple solution has several obvious advantages:

- It is noniterative and very fast to compute.
- It does not require estimates of communalities.
- Heywood cases cannot occur, that is, the estimates of uniquenesses that are the diagonal elements in $\hat{\theta}\,diag\,\mathbf{S}^{-1}$ are always positive.
- It is scale-free in the sense that if $\mathbf{x}$ is replaced by $\mathbf{Dx}$, where $\mathbf{D}$ is a diagonal matrix of scale factors, then $\boldsymbol{\Lambda}$ will be replaced by $\mathbf{D\Lambda}$ while $\hat{\theta}$ is unchanged.

Note that the matrix $\mathbf{S}^*$ is independent of $\mathbf{D}$, yet it is not a correlation matrix. The part $\mathbf{\Omega}_k(\mathbf{\Gamma}_k - \hat{\theta}\mathbf{I})^{\frac{1}{2}}\mathbf{U}$ of the solution is also independent of $\mathbf{D}$.

Furthermore the simple solution has the following psychometric interpretation. If $p \to \infty$ in such a way that $k/p \to 0$ (note that k can also increase when p increases), then $\theta \to 1$ and in the limit the factors become determinate in the sense that they become linear functions of the manifest variables.

Jöreskog (1969a) called model 5.8 *image factor analysis* after Guttman (1953). Assuming multivariate normality of $\mathbf{x}$, Jöreskog (1969a) developed a maximum likelihood method for this model and Browne (1985) obtained the information matrix. Hayashi & Bentler (2000) compared it with other scaling models.

One can only speculate why image factor analysis did not become widely used. One reason may be that computers became faster and iterative methods became computationally feasible (see later sections). Another reason may be that the restrictions on uniqueness in the form 5.7 were considered unnecessary.

An Iterative Solution

The least squares solution in 5.5 lends itself to an iterative solution. After $\mathbf{\Lambda}$ has been determined, the communalities can be reestimated as the sum of squares of each row in $\mathbf{\Lambda}$. Putting these new communalities in the diagonal of $\mathbf{R}$ gives a new matrix $\mathbf{R}_c$ from which a new $\mathbf{\Lambda}$ can be obtained. This process can be repeated. In this process, it can happen that one or more of the communalities exceed 1, so called *Heywood cases*. Such Heywood cases occurred quite often in practice and caused considerable problems.

This kind of factor analysis solution, called *Minres*, by Harman (1967) was commonly discussed in the literature in the 1950s and 1960s but few writers seemed to realize the this is the solution to a more general least squares problem, namely one that minimizes the *Unweighted Least Squares* (ULS) fit function

$$F_{\text{ULS}}(\mathbf{\Lambda}, \mathbf{\Psi}) = \frac{1}{2}tr[(\mathbf{R} - \mathbf{\Lambda}\mathbf{\Lambda}' - \mathbf{\Psi})^2], \qquad \text{(Equation 5.9)}$$

with respect to both $\mathbf{\Lambda}$ and $\mathbf{\Psi}$, where $\mathbf{\Psi}$ is a diagonal matrix of unique variances. Jöreskog (1977) showed that the ULS solution can be obtained by minimizing the concentrated fit function

$$f_{\text{ULS}}(\mathbf{\Psi}) = \min_{\mathbf{\Lambda}} F(\mathbf{\Lambda}, \mathbf{\Psi}). \qquad \text{(Equation 5.10)}$$

MAXIMUM LIKELIHOOD FACTOR ANALYSIS

In the first half of the 20th century, factor analysts used the model without regard for the distribution of the data. No distributional assumptions were made. One just computed correlations and factor-analyzed these. An exception is the early paper by Lawley (1940), who made the assumption that the data represents a random sample of observations from a multivariate normal distribution with covariance matrix

$$\mathbf{\Sigma} = \mathbf{\Lambda}\mathbf{\Lambda}' + \mathbf{\Psi} .$$ (Equation 5.11)

Assuming that the mean vector of the manifest variables is unconstrained, he showed that the logarithm of the likelihood function is

$$\log L = -\frac{1}{2}n[\log |\mathbf{\Sigma}| + tr(\mathbf{S}\mathbf{\Sigma}^{-1})] ,$$

where n is the sample size minus 1. This leads to the problem of minimizing the fit function, see, for example, Jöreskog (1967),

$$F_{\mathrm{ML}}(\mathbf{\Lambda}, \mathbf{\Psi}) = \log |\mathbf{\Sigma}| + tr(\mathbf{S}\mathbf{\Sigma}^{-1}) - \log |S| - p .$$ (Equation 5.12)

At the minimum F_{ML} equals $-2/n$ times the logarithm of the likelihood ratio for testing the hypothesis that $\mathbf{\Sigma}$ is of the form 5.11 against the alternative that $\mathbf{\Sigma}$ is an unconstrained positive definite matrix, see, for example, Jöreskog (1967). Hence, F_{ML} is always nonnegative and n times the minimum value of F_{ML} can be used as a test statistic for testing the model.

The assumption of normality is used in much of the factor analysis literature in the second half of 20th century and the maximum likelihood method has become the most common method of factor analysis. However, as late as the mid 1960s, there was no good way for computing the estimates. An exception is Howe (1955), who developed a Gauss-Seidel algorithm. Browne (1968) discussed the computational problems of factor analysis and compared several analytic techniques. Jöreskog (1967) approached the computational problem by focusing on the concentrated fit function

$$f(\mathbf{\Psi}) = \min_{\mathbf{\Lambda}} F(\mathbf{\Lambda}, \mathbf{\Psi}) ,$$ (Equation 5.13)

which could be minimized numerically. If one or more of the ψ_i gets close to zero, this procedure becomes unstable, a problem that can be circumvented by reparameterizing

$$\theta_i = \ln \psi_i , \quad \psi_i = +e^{\theta_i} ,$$ (Equation 5.14)

(see Jöreskog, 1977). This leads to a very fast and efficient algorithm.[2] Heywood cases can still occur in the sense that $\hat{\psi}_i$ becomes practically 0 when $\theta_i \to -\infty$. Other fast algorithms have been developed by Jennrich & Robinson (1969) and by Jennrich (1986).

---

[2]The FORTRAN program for the Jöreskog–1967 method was called UMLFA. It was later revised by Sörbom to include the Jöreskog–1977 methods. This version called EFAP was distributed by Scientific Software, Inc (now Scientific Software International) in Chicago. Exploratory factor analysis is now available in LISREL; see Jöreskog, Sörbom, du Toit, and du Toit (2003).

In practice, the assumption of multivariate normality seldom holds but the maximum likelihood (ML) method has been found to be very robust to departures from normality at least as far as parameter estimates is concerned, see, for example, Boomsma & Hoogland (2001). However, certain adjustments are needed to obtain correct standard errors and test statistics under nonnormality; see Satorra & Bentler (1988). A more general treatment that avoids the assumption of multivariate normality is outlined in the General Covariance Structures section.

Generalized Least Squares

A generalized least squares fit function

$$F_{\text{GLS}}(\mathbf{\Lambda}, \mathbf{\Psi}) = \frac{1}{2}tr[(\mathbf{I} - \mathbf{S}^{-1}\mathbf{\Sigma})^2] \qquad \text{(Equation 5.15)}$$

was formulated by Jöreskog & Goldberger (1972) and was further developed by Browne (1977). The GLS estimates can also be obtained by minimizing the corresponding concentrated fit function in Equation 5.13, see Jöreskog (1977).

Weighted Least Squares

The three fit functions for ULS, GLS, and ML described earlier can be seen to be special cases of one general family of fit function for weighted least squares:

$$F_V(\mathbf{\Lambda}, \mathbf{\Psi}) = \frac{1}{2}tr[(\mathbf{S} - \mathbf{\Sigma})\mathbf{V}]^2 \qquad \text{(Equation 5.16)}$$

where $\mathbf{V}$ is any positive definite weight matrix. The special cases are

$$\text{ULS}: \ \mathbf{V} = \mathbf{I} \qquad \text{(Equation 5.17)}$$

$$\text{GLS}: \ \mathbf{V} = \mathbf{S}^{-1} \qquad \text{(Equation 5.18)}$$

$$\text{ML}: \ \mathbf{V} = \hat{\mathbf{\Sigma}}^{-1} \qquad \text{(Equation 5.19)}$$

In particular, it can be shown that the ML estimates can be obtained as iteratively reweighted least squares, see, for example, Browne (1977).

Factor Transformation

As stated previously, when $k > 1$, the factor loadings in $\mathbf{\Lambda}$ are not uniquely defined. Geometrically the factor loadings may be viewed as p points in a k-dimensional space. In this space, the points are fixed but their coordinates can be referred to different factor axes. If the factor axes are orthogonal, we say we have an *orthogonal solution*; if they are oblique we say that we have an *oblique solution* where the cosine of the angles between the factor axes are interpreted as correlations between the factors. In statistical terminology, an orthogonal solution corresponds to *uncorrelated factors* and an oblique solution corresponds to *correlated factors*. One can also have solutions in which some factors are uncorrelated and some are correlated, see, for example, Jöreskog (1969b).

To facilitate the interpretation of the factors, one makes an orthogonal or oblique rotation of the factor axes. This rotation is usually guided by Thurstone's *principle of simple structure*, which essentially states that only a small fraction of the loadings in each row and column should be large. Geometrically, this means that the factor axes pass through or near as many points as possible.

In early times, the rotation was done by hand, which could be very tedious. A real breakthrough came when Carroll (1953) and Kaiser (1958) developed procedures for analytic rotation that could be performed automatically by computer. See Browne (2001) for a review of these and other analytical procedures. A further breakthrough came when Archer and Jennrich (1973) and Jennrich (1973) developed methods for estimating standard errors of analytically rotated factor loadings, see also Jennrich (chap. 15, this volume). This made it possible for researchers to use statistical criteria such as z values to judge whether a factor loading is statistically non-zero.

Previously it was assumed that the factors $\xi_1, \ldots, \xi_k$ in Equation 5.1 are uncorrelated and have variances 1. These assumptions can be relaxed and the factors may be correlated and they need not have variance 1. If ξ has covariance matrix Φ, the covariance matrix of $\mathbf{x}$ is

$$\Sigma = \Lambda \Phi \Lambda' + \Psi \ . \qquad \text{(Equation 5.20)}$$

Let $\mathbf{T}$ be an arbitrary nonsingular matrix of order $k \times k$ and let

$$\xi^* = \mathbf{T}\xi, \, \Lambda^* = \Lambda \mathbf{T}^{-1}, \, \Phi^* = \mathbf{T}\Phi\mathbf{T}' \ .$$

Then

$$\Lambda^* \xi^* \equiv \Lambda \xi, \, \Lambda^* \Phi^* \Lambda^{*'} \equiv \Lambda \Phi \Lambda'.$$

Because $\mathbf{T}$ has k^2 independent elements, this shows that at least k^2 independent conditions must be imposed on Λ and/or Φ to make these identified.

Factor analysis is typically done in two steps. In the first step, one obtains an arbitrary orthogonal solution in which $\Phi = \mathbf{I}$ in Equation 5.20. In the second step, this is rotated orthogonally or obliquely to achieve a simple structure. For the rotated factors to have unit variance, $\mathbf{T}$ must satisfy

$$diag(\mathbf{TT'}) = \mathbf{I} \ , \qquad \text{(Equation 5.21)}$$

for an oblique solution and

$$\mathbf{TT'} = \mathbf{I} \ , \qquad \text{(Equation 5.22)}$$

for an orthogonal solution.

Two-Stage Least-Squares

In addition to the methods of estimation defined previously, the factor analysis model can be estimated by *two-stage least-squares* (TSLS). To explain this, some general information on TSLS is needed.

Suppose we want to estimate the linear relationship between a dependent variable y and a set of explanatory variables $\mathbf{x} = (x_1, x_2, \ldots, x_p)'$:

$$y = \gamma_1 x_1 + \gamma_2 x_2 + \cdots + \gamma_p x_p + u , \qquad \text{(Equation 5.23)}$$

or in matrix form

$$y = \gamma' \mathbf{x} + u , \qquad \text{(Equation 5.24)}$$

where u is a random error term and $\gamma = (\gamma_1, \gamma_2, \ldots, \gamma_p)'$ is a vector of coefficients to be estimated. For simplicity of the argument, we assume that all variables are measured in deviations from their means so that there is no intercept in Equation 5.23 or Equation 5.24.

If u is uncorrelated with $x_1, \ldots, x_p$, ordinary least-squares (OLS) can be used to obtain a consistent estimate of γ, yielding the well-known solution

$$\hat{\gamma} = \mathbf{S}_{xx}^{-1} \mathbf{s}_{xy} , \qquad \text{(Equation 5.25)}$$

where $\hat{\gamma}$ is a $p \times 1$ vector of estimated γ's, $\mathbf{S}_{xx}$ is the $p \times p$ sample covariance matrix of the x variables and $\mathbf{s}_{xy}$ is the $p \times 1$ vector of sample covariances between the x variables and y.

If u is *correlated* with one or more of the x_i, however, the OLS estimate in Equation 5.25 is not consistent, that is, it is biased even in large samples. The bias can be positive or negative, large or small depending on the covariances between u and x. But suppose some *instrumental variables* $\mathbf{z} = (z_1, \ldots, z_q)'$ are available, where $q \geq p$. An instrumental variable is a variable which is uncorrelated with u but correlated with y. Then the following two-stage least-squares (TSLS) estimator:

$$\hat{\gamma} = (\mathbf{S}'_{zx} \mathbf{S}_{zz}^{-1} \mathbf{S}_{zx})^{-1} \mathbf{S}'_{zx} \mathbf{S}_{zz}^{-1} \mathbf{s}_{zy} , \qquad \text{(Equation 5.26)}$$

can be used to estimate γ consistently, where $\mathbf{S}_{zx}$ is the $q \times p$ matrix of sample covariances between the z variables and the x variables, $\mathbf{S}_{zz}$ is the $q \times q$ sample covariance matrix of the z variables, and $\mathbf{s}_{zy}$ is the $q \times 1$ vector of sample covariances between the z variables and y.

The covariance matrix of $\hat{\gamma}$ can be estimated as

$$(n - p)^{-1} \hat{\sigma}_{uu} (\mathbf{S}'_{zx} \mathbf{S}_{zz}^{-1} \mathbf{S}_{zx})^{-1} , \qquad \text{(Equation 5.27)}$$

where

$$\hat{\sigma}_{uu} = s_{yy} - 2\hat{\gamma}' \mathbf{s}_{xy} + \gamma' \mathbf{S}_{xx} \gamma \qquad \text{(Equation 5.28)}$$

is a consistent estimate of the variance of u and $n = N - 1$, where N is the sample size. The standard errors of the estimated γ's are the square roots of the diagonal elements of the matrix in Equation 5.27.

Every x variable that is uncorrelated with u may serve as an instrumental variable z. If all x variables are uncorrelated with u, the x variables themselves serve as instrumental variables. It may be easily verified that if $\mathbf{z} \equiv \mathbf{x}$, then Equation 5.26 reduces to Equation 5.25 and Equation 5.27 reduces to the well-known OLS formula

$$(n - p)^{-1}\hat{\sigma}_{uu}\mathbf{S}_{xx}^{-1} \ .$$

For every x variable that is correlated with u, there must be at least one instrumental variable outside the set of x variables. Usually there is exactly one instrumental variable for each x variable that is correlated with u, but it is possible to use more than one as long as $\mathbf{S}_{zx}$ is of rank p.

We now return to the estimation of the factor analysis model. One way to dispose of the k^2 conditions that may be imposed is to assume that the first k rows of Λ, after suitable ordering of the variables, form an identity matrix. Partitioning $\mathbf{x}$ into two parts $\mathbf{x}_1(k \times 1)$ and $\mathbf{x}_2(q \times 1)$, where $q = p - k$, and δ similarly into $\delta_1(k \times 1)$ and $\delta_2(q \times 1)$, 5.2 can be written

$$\mathbf{x}_1 = \xi + \delta_1 \qquad\qquad \text{(Equation 5.29)}$$

$$\mathbf{x}_2 = \Lambda_2\xi + \delta_2 \ , \qquad\qquad \text{(Equation 5.30)}$$

where $\Lambda_2(q \times k)$ consists of the last $q = p - k$ rows of Λ. Solving Equation 5.29 for ξ and substituting this into Equation 5.30 gives

$$\mathbf{x}_2 = \Lambda_2\mathbf{x}_1 + \mathbf{u} \ , \qquad\qquad \text{(Equation 5.31)}$$

where $\mathbf{u} = \delta_2 - \Lambda_2\delta_1$. Each equation in Equation 5.31 is a linear equation but it is not a regression equation because $\mathbf{u}$ is correlated with $\mathbf{x}_1$, since δ_1 is correlated with $\mathbf{x}_1$.

Let

$$x_i = \lambda_i^{'}\mathbf{x}_1 + u_i \ , \qquad\qquad \text{(Equation 5.32)}$$

be the i-th equation in 5.31, where $\lambda_i^{'}$ is the i-th row of Λ_2, and let $\mathbf{x}_{(i)}(q - 1 \times 1)$ be a vector of the remaining variables in $\mathbf{x}_2$. Then u_i is uncorrelated with $\mathbf{x}_{(i)}$ so that $\mathbf{x}_{(i)}$ can be used as instrumental variables for estimating Equation 5.32. Taking y as x_i, $\mathbf{x}$ as $\mathbf{x}_i$, and $\mathbf{z}$ as $\mathbf{x}_{(i)}$ in Equation 5.26 gives the TSLS estimate of $\lambda_i^{'}$. Provided $q \geq k + 1$, this can be done for each $i = 1, 2, \ldots, q$, thus giving the TSLS estimate of Λ_2.

The method of TSLS goes back to Theil (1953) and Basmann (1957), and the more general method of instrumental variables is due to Sargan (1958). Expository presentations of TSLS is available in most textbooks of econometrics, for example, Theil (1971). TSLS in factor analysis goes back to Madansky (1964) and the instrumental variables method for factor analysis was developed by Hägglund (1982); see also Jöreskog (1983). Further developments of TSLS in factor analysis and structural equation models have been made by Bollen (1996), Bollen & Biesanz (2002), and Bollen & Bauer (2004).

The method of TSLS has the following properties:

- It is noniterative and very fast.
- If the model fits the data well, the TSLS and ML solutions are very close but standard errors are larger for TSLS. However, if the model has a poor fit, the two solutions can differ considerably.
- TSLS does not depend on normality assumptions as strongly as ML.

In its extension to structural equation models, the main advantage of TSLS is that it is sometimes robust to specification error in the model.

Despite the obvious advantages, TSLS has not become popular, neither in factor analysis nor in structural equation modeling (SEM). In SEM it is often used to generate starting values for iterations to ML or other solutions.

CONFIRMATORY FACTOR ANALYSIS

Exploratory factor analysis is used in the following situation. One has a set of tests or other variables, and one would like to know how many factors are needed to account for their intercorrelations and what these factors are measuring. Both the number of factors and the meaning of the factors are unknown. The interpretation and the naming of the factors are usually done after analytic rotation.

In contrast, a *confirmatory factor* analysis begins by defining the latent variables one would like to measure. This is based on substantive theory and/or previous knowledge. One then constructs observable variables to measure these latent variables. This construction must follow certain rules of correspondence, see, for example, Costner (1969). Thus, in a confirmatory factor analysis, the number of factors is known and equal to the number of latent variables. The confirmatory factor analysis is a model that should be estimated and tested.

Factor analysis need not be strictly exploratory or strictly confirmatory. Most studies are to some extent both exploratory and confirmatory because they involve some variables of known and other variables of unknown composition. The former should be chosen with great care in order that as much information as possible about the latter may be extracted. It is highly desirable that a hypothesis that has been suggested by mainly exploratory procedures should subsequently be confirmed, or disproved, by obtaining new data and subjecting these to more rigorous statistical tests. Jöreskog & Lawley (1968) give an example where a model is developed on one sample and replicated on new fresh data; see also Kroonenberg & Lewis (1982). Cudeck & Browne (1983) discuss problems and methods for cross-validation.

Exploratory and confirmatory factor analysis are illustrated with six observed variables x_1 through x_6 and two factors ξ_1 and ξ_2 in Figure 5–1 and Figure 5–2, respectively. In such path diagrams observed variables are enclosed in squares or

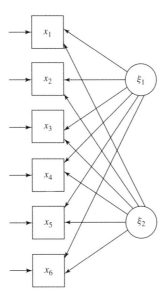

FIGURE 5–1.   Exploratory factor analysis.

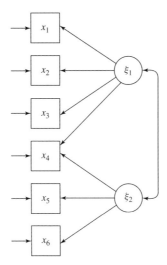

FIGURE 5–2.   Confirmatory factor analysis.

rectangles and latent variables are enclosed in circles or ellipses. In both figures the horizontal arrows on the left represent the error terms δ_1 through δ_6.

In Figure 5–1 each factor affects all variables, which is the same thing as to say that all variables loads on both factors. The factors are uncorrelated. The Λ matrix is a full 6×2 matrix and $\Phi = I$.

In Figure 5–2, it is postulated that x_1, x_2, and x_3 measures ξ_1 and x_5 and x_6 measures ξ_2. The variable x_4 is of unknown composition but it is assumed that it measures either ξ_1 or ξ_2 or both. The two factors are correlated as illustrated by the two-way arrow between ξ_1 and ξ_2. In this case, the Λ matrix has two zeros in the first column and three zeros in the second column. These zeros are specified a priori. The matrix Φ is a correlation matrix. No rotation of the factors is possible because the only matrix T that retains the zero positions in Λ is an identity matrix. The confirmatory factor model is to be estimated subject to the condition that these five elements of Λ are zero.

In a confirmatory factor analysis, the investigator has such knowledge about the factorial nature of the variables that one is able to specify that each measure x_i depends only on a few of the factors ξ_j. If x_i does not depend on ξ_j, $\lambda_{ij} = 0$ in Equation 5.1. In many applications, the latent variable ξ_j represents a theoretical construct and the observed measures x_i are designed to be indicators of this construct. In this case there is only one non-zero λ_{ij} in each Equation 5.1. In general, assuming that Φ is a correlation matrix, one needs to specify at least $k - 1$ zero elements in each column of Λ, but in a confirmatory factor analysis, there are usually many more zeros in each column.

The possibility of a priori specified zero elements in Λ was mentioned in Anderson & Rubin (1956) and in Jöreskog & Lawley (1968), but the term, *confirmatory factor analysis*, was first used in Jöreskog (1969b).

To estimate a confirmatory factor analysis model, one can minimize any of the fit functions ULS, GLS, and ML mentioned previously. The fit function is to be minimized with respect to all free elements of Λ, Φ, and Ψ. In most cases, no analytic solution is available so the minimization must be done numerically. In contrast to exploratory factor analysis, with confirmatory factor analysis, no eigenvalues and eigenvectors are involved and the solution is obtained in one step. No factor rotation is needed. In a way, confirmatory factor analysis shifts the focus from the problems of factor extraction and rotation to the problem of testing a specified model. This is a broad topic that will not be covered in detail in this chapter. For a general discussion of this problem, see Bollen and Long (1993). With the ML method, the most common way of testing the model is to use n times the minimum value of the fit function F_{ML} as a χ^2 with degrees of freedom equal to $\frac{1}{2}p(p+1)$ minus the number of independent parameters in Λ, Φ, and Ψ. For general test criteria see Satorra (1989).

Factorial Invariance

Consider data from several groups or populations of individuals. These may be different nations, states, or regions, culturally or socioeconomically different groups, groups of individuals selected on the basis of some known selection variables, groups receiving different treatments, and control groups, and so forth. In fact, they may be any set of mutually exclusive groups of individuals that are clearly defined. It is assumed that a number of variables have been measured on a number of individuals from each population. This approach is particularly useful in comparing a number of treatment and control groups regardless of whether individuals have been assigned to the groups randomly or not.

Consider the situation where the same tests have been administered in G different groups and the factor analysis model is applied in each group:

$$\mathbf{x}_g = \mathbf{\Lambda}_g \xi_g + \delta_g, \ g = 1, 2, \ldots, G \ , \qquad \text{(Equation 5.33)}$$

where, as before, ξ_g and δ_g are uncorrelated. The covariance matrix of $\mathbf{x}_g$ in group g is

$$\mathbf{\Sigma}_g = \mathbf{\Lambda}_g \mathbf{\Phi}_g \mathbf{\Lambda}'_g + \mathbf{\Psi}^2_g \ . \qquad \text{(Equation 5.34)}$$

The hypothesis of factorial invariance is Equation 5.34 with

$$\mathbf{\Lambda}_1 = \mathbf{\Lambda}_2 = \cdots = \mathbf{\Lambda}_G \ . \qquad \text{(Equation 5.35)}$$

This states that the factor loadings are the same in all groups. Group differences in variances and covariances of the observed variables are due only to differences in variances and covariances of the factors and different error variances. The idea of factorial invariance is that the factor loadings are attributes of the tests and they should therefore be independent of the population sampled, whereas the distribution of the factors themselves could differ across populations. A stronger assumption is to assume that the error variances are also equal across groups:

$$\mathbf{\Psi}_1 = \mathbf{\Psi}_2 = \cdots = \mathbf{\Psi}_G \ . \qquad \text{(Equation 5.36)}$$

Meredith (1964) discussed the problem of factorial invariance from the point of view of multivariate selection. Jöreskog (1971) considered several alternative models for studying differences in covariance matrices across groups. He also showed how the model of factorial invariance can be estimated by the maximum likelihood method. Further problems and issues in factorial invariance are discussed by Millsap and Meredith (chap. 8, this volume).

Sörbom (1974) extended the model of factorial invariance to include intercepts τ in Equation 5.33:

$$\mathbf{x}_g = \tau_g + \mathbf{\Lambda}_g \xi_g + \delta_g, \ g = 1, 2, \ldots, G \ . \qquad \text{(Equation 5.37)}$$

The mean vector μ_g of $\mathbf{x}_g$ is

$$\mu_g = \tau_g + \mathbf{\Lambda} \kappa_g \ , \qquad \text{(Equation 5.38)}$$

where κ_g is the mean vector of ξ_g. The covariance matrix of $\mathbf{x}_g$ is the same as in Equation 5.34.

The model of complete factorial invariance is Equation 5.34, and Equation 5.38 with Equation 5.35 and Equation 5.39.

$$\tau_1 = \tau_2 = \cdots = \tau_G \ , \qquad \text{(Equation 5.39)}$$

Sörbom (1974) showed that one can estimate the mean vector and covariance matrix of ξ in each group on a scale common to all groups. In particular, this makes it possible to estimate group differences in means of the latent variables.

Let $\bar{\mathbf{x}}_g$ and $\mathbf{S}_g$ be the sample mean vector and covariance matrix of $\mathbf{x}_g$ in group g, and let $\mu_g(\theta)$ and $\Sigma_g(\theta)$ be the corresponding population mean vector and covariance matrix, where θ is a vector of all independent parameters in τ, Λ and κ_g, Φ_g, Ψ_g, $g = 1, 2, \ldots, G$. The fit function for the multigroup case is defined as

$$F(\theta) = \sum_{g=1}^{G} \frac{N_g}{N} F_g(\theta) \qquad \text{(Equation 5.40)}$$

where $F_g(\theta) = F[\bar{\mathbf{z}}_g, \mathbf{S}_g, \mu_g(\theta)]$, $\Sigma_g(\theta)$ is any of the fit functions defined for a single group. Here N_g is the sample size in group g and $N = N_1 + N_2 + \cdots + N_G$ is the total sample size. To estimate the model, one usually fixes a one in each column of Λ and the mean vector of ξ to 0 in one group and leaves Φ_g and Ψ_g free in each group, see, for example, Sörbom (1974). If the ML fit function is used, one can use $N - 1$ times the minimum of F as a χ^2 with degrees of freedom $d = Gp(p+1)/2 - t$ for testing the model. Here p is the number of manifest variables and t is the number of independent parameters estimated.

STRUCTURAL EQUATION MODELS

Factor analysis is used to investigate latent variables that are presumed to underlie a set of manifest variables. Understanding the structure and meaning of the latent variables in the context of their manifest variables is the main goal of traditional factor analysis. After a set of factors has been identified, it is natural to go on and use the factors themselves as predictors or outcome variables in further analyses. Broadly speaking, this is the goal of *structural equation modeling*.

We now return to single group analysis. A further extension of the classical factor analysis model is to allow the factors not only to be correlated, as in confirmatory factor analysis, but also to allow some latent variables to depend on other latent variables. Models of this kind are usually called structural equation models and there are many examples of this in the literature. For a recent bibliography, see Wolfle (2003) and for the growth of structural equation modeling in 1994–2001, see Hershberger (2003). Two examples will be considered here: *second-order factor analysis models* and *simplex models*.

Second-Order Factor Analysis

The factors in an oblique factor solution may depend other factors, so called second-order factors. These in turn may depend on still higher order factors. Among the first

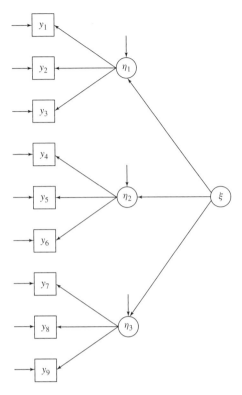

FIGURE 5–3.   Second-order factor analysis model for nine observed variables.

to discuss these ideas are Schmid & Leiman (1957). An example of a second-order factor analysis model is shown in Figure 5–3.

In this model, there are four latent variables η_1, η_2, η_3, and ξ, but they are not freely correlated. Instead, there is a dependence structure among them such that η_1, η_2, and η_3 depend on ξ. In equation form this model is given by two sets of equations;

$$\mathbf{y} = \mathbf{\Lambda}_y \eta + \varepsilon ,\qquad\text{(Equation 5.41)}$$

$$\eta = \mathbf{\Gamma}\xi + \zeta ,\qquad\text{(Equation 5.42)}$$

where $\mathbf{y} = (y_1, y_2, \ldots, y_9)'$, $\eta = (\eta_1, \eta_2, \eta_3)'$ and $\xi = \xi$. The horizontal arrows on the left side represent the measurement errors $\varepsilon = (\varepsilon_1, \varepsilon_2, \ldots, \varepsilon_9)'$ and the vertical arrows in the middle represent the structural errors $\zeta = (\zeta_1, \zeta_2, \zeta_3)$. The latent variables η_1, η_2, and η_3 are first-order factors and the latent variable ξ is a second-order factor. The factor loadings of the first order factors are in the 9×3 matrix $\mathbf{\Lambda}_y$ and the factor loadings of the second-order factor are in the 3×1 matrix $\mathbf{\Gamma}$. In Figure 5–3, $\mathbf{y}$ is supposed to satisfy a confirmatory factor model with three indicators of each of the first-order factors and η is supposed to satisfy a confirmatory factor model with one factor.

Simplex Models

A *simplex model* is a type of covariance structure that often occurs in longitudinal studies when the same variable is measured repeatedly on the same individuals over several occasions. The simplex model is equivalent to the covariance structure generated by a first-order, nonstationary, autoregressive process. Guttman (1954) used the term, *simplex*, also for variables that are not ordered through time but by other criteria. One of his examples concerns tests of verbal ability ordered according to increasing complexity. The typical feature of a simplex correlation structure is that the entries in the correlation matrix decrease as one moves away from the main diagonal. Such a correlation pattern is inconsistent with the factor analysis model with one factor.

Following Anderson (1960), Jöreskog (1970) formulated various simplex models in terms of the well-known Wiener and Markov stochastic processes. A distinction was made between a perfect simplex and a quasi-simplex. A *perfect simplex* is reasonable only if the measurement errors in the observed variables are negligible. A *quasi-simplex*, on the other hand, allows for sizable errors of measurement. Jöreskog (1970) developed procedures for estimation and testing of various simplex models.

The research question and experimental design that leads to a simplex covariance structure is very different than the theoretical rationale of linear factor analysis that leads to its covariance structure in the Explanatory Factor Analysis section. However, the covariance structures for some versions of both models are formally identical, so a simplex model can be viewed as a special kind of factor analysis structure. Consequently, issues of model identification and estimation are the same. One of the useful features of factor analysis is that it provides a general framework for investigating models that initially seem to be unrelated.

Consider p fallible variables $y_1, y_2, \ldots, y_p$. The unit of measurement in the true variables η_i may be chosen to be the same as in the observed variables y_i. The equations defining the model are then

$$y_i = \eta_i + \varepsilon_i, \qquad i = 1, 2, \ldots, p, \tag{Equation 5.43}$$

$$\eta_i = \beta_i \eta_{i-1} + \zeta_i, \qquad i = 2, 3, \ldots, p, \tag{Equation 5.44}$$

where the ε_i are uncorrelated among themselves and uncorrelated with all the η_i and where ζ_i is uncorrelated with η_{i-1} for $i = 2, 3, \ldots, p$. A path diagram of the simplex model with $p = 4$ is given in Figure 5–4.

The parameters of the model are $\omega_1 = \text{Var}(\eta_1)$, $\psi_i = \text{Var}(\zeta_i)(i = 2, 3, \ldots, p)$, $\theta_i = \text{Var}(\varepsilon_i)(i = 1, 2, \ldots, p)$ and $\beta_2, \beta_3, \ldots, \beta_p$. To see the implied covariance structure, it is convenient to reparameterize. Let

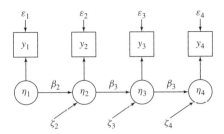

FIGURE 5–4.   A simplex model.

$\omega_i = \mathrm{Var}(\eta_i) = \beta_i^2 \omega_{i-1} + \psi_i \, (i = 2, 3, \ldots, p)$. Then there is a one-to-one correspondence between the parameters $\beta_2, \beta_3, \ldots, \beta_p, \omega_1, \psi_2, \psi_3, \ldots, \psi_p$ and the parameters $\beta_2, \beta_3, \ldots, \beta_p, \omega_1, \omega_2, \ldots, \omega_p$. The covariance matrix of $y_1, y_2, \ldots, y_p$ has the form

$$\Sigma = \begin{pmatrix} \omega_1 + \theta_1 & & & \\ \beta_2 \omega_1 & \omega_2 + \theta_2 & & \\ \beta_2 \beta_3 \omega_1 & \beta_3 \omega_2 & \omega_3 + \theta_3 & \\ \beta_2 \beta_3 \beta_4 \omega_1 & \beta_3 \beta_4 \omega_2 & \beta_4 \omega_3 & \omega_4 + \theta_4 \end{pmatrix}. \qquad \text{(Equation 5.45)}$$

Jöreskog and Sörbom (1988, pp. 182–189; or see Jöreskog & Sörbom, (1999, pp. 230–234) showed that some parameters are not identified and that there are $3p - 3$ independent parameters.

A GENERAL STRUCTURAL EQUATION MODEL

An example of a general structural equation model is the LISREL model shown in the path diagram in Figure 5–5. In such a model, the latent variables are classified into dependent and independent latent variables. The *dependent latent variables* are those that depend on other latent variables. In the path diagram, these have one or more one-way (undirected) arrows pointing toward them. The *independent latent variables* are those that do not depend on other latent variables. In the path diagram, they have no one-way arrows pointing to them. In Figure 5–5, η_1 and η_2 are the dependent latent variables and ξ_1, ξ_2, and ξ_3 are the independent latent variables. The latter are freely correlated, whereas the variances and covariances of η_1 and η_2 depend on their relationships with ξ_1, ξ_2, and ξ_3.

The observed variables are also classified into two categories: y variables and x variables. The y variables are those observed variables that depend on the dependent latent variables, and the x variables are those that depend on the independent latent variables. In Figure 5–5 there is a confirmatory factor model on the left side for the x variables and a confirmatory factor model on the right side for the x variables.

In its most general form, the LISREL model is defined as follows. Consider random vectors $\eta = (\eta_1, \eta_2, \ldots, \eta_m)'$ and $\xi = (\xi_1, \xi_2, \ldots, \xi_n)'$ of latent dependent

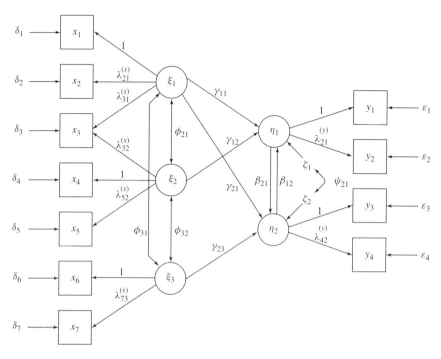

FIGURE 5–5.   The LISREL model.

and independent variables, respectively, and the following system of linear structural relations

$$\eta = \alpha + \mathbf{B}\eta + \Gamma\xi + \zeta \ , \qquad \text{(Equation 5.46)}$$

where α is a vector of intercept terms, $\mathbf{B}$ and Γ are coefficient matrices and $\zeta = (\zeta_1, \zeta_2, \dots, \zeta_m)'$ is a random vector of residuals (errors in equations, random disturbance terms). The elements of $\mathbf{B}$ represent direct effects of η-variables on other η-variables and the elements of Γ represent direct effects of ξ-variables on η-variables. It is assumed that ζ is uncorrelated with ξ and that $\mathbf{I} - \mathbf{B}$ is nonsingular.

Vectors η and ξ are not observed, but instead vectors $\mathbf{y} = (y_1, y_2, \dots, y_p)'$ and $\mathbf{x} = (x_1, x_2, \dots, x_q)'$ are observed, such that

$$\mathbf{y} = \tau_y + \mathbf{\Lambda}_y\eta + \varepsilon \ , \qquad \text{(Equation 5.47)}$$

and

$$\mathbf{x} = \tau_x + \mathbf{\Lambda}_x\xi + \delta \ , \qquad \text{(Equation 5.48)}$$

where ε and δ are vectors of error terms (errors of measurement or measure-specific components) assumed to be uncorrelated with η and ξ, respectively. These equations represent the multivariate regressions of $\mathbf{y}$ on η and of $\mathbf{x}$ on ξ, respectively, with Λ_y and Λ_x as regression matrices and τ_y and τ_x as vectors of intercept terms. It is convenient to refer to $\mathbf{y}$ and $\mathbf{x}$ as the observed variables and η and ξ as the latent variables.

Let κ be the mean vector of ξ. $\mathbf{\Phi}$ and $\mathbf{\Psi}$ the covariance matrices of ξ and ζ, $\mathbf{\Theta}_\varepsilon$ and $\mathbf{\Theta}_\delta$ the covariance matrices of ε and δ, and $\mathbf{\Theta}_{\delta\varepsilon}$ the covariance matrix between δ and ε. Then it follows that the mean vector μ and covariance matrix Σ of $\mathbf{z} = (\mathbf{y}', \mathbf{x}')'$ are

$$\mu = \begin{pmatrix} \tau_y + \Lambda_y(\mathbf{I} - \mathbf{B})^{-1}(\alpha + \mathbf{\Gamma}\kappa) \\ \tau_x + \Lambda_x\kappa \end{pmatrix},$$

$$\Sigma = \begin{pmatrix} \Lambda_y\mathbf{A}(\mathbf{\Gamma}\mathbf{\Phi}\mathbf{\Gamma}' + \mathbf{\Psi})\mathbf{A}'\Lambda_y' + \mathbf{\Theta}_\varepsilon & \Lambda_y\mathbf{A}\mathbf{\Gamma}\mathbf{\Phi}\Lambda_x' + \mathbf{\Theta}_{\delta\varepsilon}' \\ \Lambda_x\mathbf{\Phi}\mathbf{\Gamma}'\mathbf{A}'\Lambda_y' + \mathbf{\Theta}_{\delta\varepsilon} & \Lambda_x\mathbf{\Phi}\Lambda_x' + \mathbf{\Theta}_\delta \end{pmatrix},$$

where $\mathbf{A} = (\mathbf{I} - \mathbf{B})^{-1}$.

The elements of μ and Σ are functions of the elements of κ, α, τ_y, τ_x, Λ_y, Λ_x, $\mathbf{B}$, $\mathbf{\Gamma}$, $\mathbf{\Phi}$, $\mathbf{\Psi}$, $\mathbf{\Theta}_\varepsilon$, $\mathbf{\Theta}_\delta$, and $\mathbf{\Theta}_{\delta\varepsilon}$, which are of three kinds:

- *Fixed parameters* that have been assigned specified values.
- *Constrained parameters* that are unknown but linear or nonlinear functions of one or more other parameters.
- *Free parameters* that are unknown and not constrained.

The LISREL model combines features of both econometrics and psychometrics into a single model. The first LISREL model was a linear structural equation model for latent variables, each with a single observed, possibly fallible, indicator, see Jöreskog (1973b). This model was generalized to models with multiple indicators of latent variables, to simultaneous structural equation models in several groups, and to more general covariance structures, see Jöreskog (1973a, 1974, 1981). Jöreskog & Sörbom (1999) developed the LISREL program.

PATH ANALYSIS, ECONOMETRIC, AND TIME SERIES MODELS

A special case of the LISREL model is when $\Lambda_y = \mathbf{I}$, $\Lambda_y = \mathbf{I}$, $\mathbf{\Theta}_\varepsilon = 0$, and $\mathbf{\Theta}_\delta = 0$. Then $\mathbf{y} \equiv \eta$ and $\mathbf{x} \equiv \xi$ and Equation 5.46 becomes

$$\mathbf{y} = \alpha + \mathbf{B}\mathbf{y} + \mathbf{\Gamma}\mathbf{x} + \zeta .$$ (Equation 5.49)

Models of this kind were used in sociology, mostly with $\mathbf{B}$ as a subdiagonal matrix, under the name of *path analysis*; see, for example, Duncan (1975).

This kind of models, with **y** and **x** as time series variables, were also used in econometrics in the 1950s and 1960s (see, e.g., Klein & Goldberger, 1955) to analyze large systems of interdependent equations. In econometric terminology, **y** are endogenous, **x** are exogenous variables and ζ are random disturbance terms.

Other forms of time series models have been used extensively in econometrics in the last three decades, see, for example, Lütkepohl (1993) and Hatanaka (1996). Du Toit & Browne (2001) considered time-series models in the form of vector autoregressive and moving average (VARMA) models and and gave a closed-form expression for the covariance matrix implied by such models. They also showed that such models can be formulated as LISREL models. Recently, Browne (chap. 13, this volume) extended these models to VARMA models for latent variables. For further background on similar models see Molenaar (1985).

Jöreskog (1978) formulated a general model for multivariate panel data and showed how this model could be formulated as a LISREL model. This model is

$$\mathbf{y}_{it} = \alpha + \mathbf{B}\mathbf{y}_{it} + \mathbf{\Gamma}\mathbf{x}_{it} + \mathbf{C}_t\mathbf{z}_t + \mathbf{u}_{it} , \qquad \text{(Equation 5.50)}$$

It is assumed that there are independent observations $i = 1, 2, \ldots N$ on N individuals over $t = 1, 2, \ldots T$ periods of time (longitudinal data or repeated measurements). Here

- $\mathbf{y}_{it}$ is a vector jointly dependent (endogenous) variables.
- $\mathbf{x}_{it}$ is a vector of explanatory variables, which may be exogenous or lagged dependent variables.
- $\mathbf{z}_i$ is a vector of explanatory variables (background variables) assumed not to vary over time.
- $\mathbf{u}_{it}$ is a vector of unobserved random structural disturbance terms assumed to be uncorrelated with $\mathbf{x}_{it}$ and $\mathbf{z}_i$ both between and within occasions.
- α is a vector of intercepts, $\mathbf{B}$, $\mathbf{\Gamma}$, and $\mathbf{C}_t$ are matrices of structural coefficients.

The disturbance terms $\mathbf{u}_{it}$ are assumed to be composed of two uncorrelated parts, a vector of permanent components μ_i that does not vary over time and a transitory autoregressive component $\mathbf{v}_{it}$ such that

$$\mathbf{u}_{it} = \mu_i + \mathbf{v}_{it} , \qquad \text{(Equation 5.51)}$$

$$\mathbf{v}_{it} = \mathbf{D}\mathbf{v}_{i,t-1} + \mathbf{e}_{it} , \qquad \text{(Equation 5.52)}$$

where $\mathbf{D}$ is a diagonal matrix and $\mathbf{e}_{it}$ is a vector of pure random components uncorrelated both between and within occasions.

Various other models for analysis of longitudinal data have been considered by Jöreskog & Sörbom (1976, 1977), Jöreskog (1979), Steyer & Schmitt (1990), and McArdle (2001; see also McArdle, chap. 7, this volume).

GENERAL COVARIANCE STRUCTURES

The majority of factor analyses and also the majority of SEMs are estimated using ML or ULS. These estimation methods are appropriate for variables that are continuous, and for ML, that are normally distributed. In many research problems, the variables under study are neither normal nor even approximately continuous and the use of ML or ULS is not valid. An important technical development has been in extending the class of estimation methods to procedures that are correct when used with many different kinds of variables. This more general approach to estimation includes ML, GLS, and ULS as special cases. But it also applies to very different statistical distributions.

The statistical inference problem associated with all kinds of structural equation models, including factor analysis models, can be formulated very generally and compactly as follows. For the original formulation, see, for example, Browne (1984) and Satorra (1989).

Let σ and $\mathbf{s}$ be vectors of the nonduplicated elements of $\mathbf{\Sigma}$ and $\mathbf{S}$, respectively, and let

$$\sigma = \sigma(\theta) , \qquad \text{(Equation 5.53)}$$

be a differentiable function of a parameter vector θ. For example, in a LISREL model, θ is a vector of all independent parameters in all parameter matrices $\mathbf{\Lambda}_y, \mathbf{\Lambda}_x, \mathbf{B}, \mathbf{\Gamma}, \mathbf{\Phi}, \mathbf{\Psi}, \mathbf{\Theta}_\varepsilon, \mathbf{\Theta}_\delta,$ and $\mathbf{\Theta}_{\delta\varepsilon}$ but models which are not LISREL models can also be used. For an example see Jöreskog & Sörbom (1999, pp. 347–348). The sample vector $\mathbf{s}$ has a limiting normal distribution when $n \to \infty$:

$$n^{\frac{1}{2}}(\mathbf{s} - \sigma) \xrightarrow{d} N(0, \mathbf{\Omega}) , \qquad \text{(Equation 5.54)}$$

where $\xrightarrow{d}$ denotes convergence in distribution. The elements of the asymptotic covariance matrix $\mathbf{\Omega}$ are given by (Browne, 1984, Equation 2.2)

$$\omega_{ghij} = nCov(s_{gh}, s_{ij}) = \sigma_{ghij} - \sigma_{gh}\sigma_{ij} , \qquad \text{(Equation 5.55)}$$

where $\sigma_{ghij} = E[(z_g - \mu_g)(z_h - \mu_h)(z_i - \mu_i)(z_j - \mu_j)]$ and $\sigma_{gh} = E[(z_g - \mu_g)(z_h - \mu_h)]$.

Consider the minimization of the fit function

$$F(\mathbf{s}, \theta) = [\mathbf{s} - \sigma(\theta)]'\mathbf{V}[\mathbf{s} - \sigma(\theta)] \qquad \text{(Equation 5.56)}$$

where $\mathbf{V}$ is either a fixed positive definite matrix or a random matrix converging in probability to a positive definite matrix $\overline{\mathbf{V}}$. The fit functions ULS, GLS, and ML defined previously correspond to taking

$$\text{ULS}: \mathbf{V} = diag(1, 2, 1, 2, 2, 1, \ldots) \qquad \text{(Equation 5.57)}$$

$$\text{GLS}: \mathbf{V} = \mathbf{D}'(\mathbf{S}^{-1} \otimes \mathbf{S}^{-1})\mathbf{D} \qquad \text{(Equation 5.58)}$$

$$\text{ML}: \mathbf{V} = \mathbf{D}'(\hat{\mathbf{\Sigma}}^{-1} \otimes \hat{\mathbf{\Sigma}}^{-1})\mathbf{D} \qquad \text{(Equation 5.59)}$$

where $\otimes$ denote a Kronecker product and $\mathbf{D}$ is the duplication matrix (see Magnus & Neudecker, 1988), which transforms $\mathbf{s}$ to vec($\mathbf{S}$). Other choices of $\mathbf{V}$ are also possible, see Jöreskog, Sörbom, S. du Toit, and M. du Toit, (2003)

Let θ be the minimizer of $F(\mathbf{s}, \theta)$ and let θ_0 be a unique minimizer of $F(\sigma, \theta)$. We assume here that the model holds so that $F(\sigma, \theta_0) = 0$. See Satorra (1989) for the case where the model does not hold.

Let

$$\mathbf{\Delta} = \left[\frac{\partial \mathbf{\Sigma}}{\partial \theta'}\right]_{\theta_0}. \qquad \text{(Equation 5.60)}$$

Then

$$nACov(\hat{\theta}) = (\mathbf{\Delta}'\overline{\mathbf{V}}\mathbf{\Delta})^{-1}\mathbf{\Delta}'\overline{\mathbf{V}}\mathbf{\Omega}\overline{\mathbf{V}}\mathbf{\Delta}(\mathbf{\Delta}'\overline{\mathbf{V}}\mathbf{\Delta})^{-1}. \qquad \text{(Equation 5.61)}$$

Furthermore, let $\mathbf{W}$ be a consistent estimate of $\mathbf{\Omega}$ and let $\mathbf{\Delta}_c$ be an orthogonal complement to $\mathbf{\Delta}$. Then

$$c = n(\mathbf{s} - \sigma)'\hat{\mathbf{\Delta}}_c(\hat{\mathbf{\Delta}}_c'\mathbf{W}\hat{\mathbf{\Delta}}_c)^{-1}\hat{\mathbf{\Delta}}_c'(\mathbf{s} - \sigma) \qquad \text{(Equation 5.62)}$$

where $\hat{\mathbf{\Delta}}_c$ is $\mathbf{\Delta}_c$ evaluated at $\hat{\theta}$, has an asymptotic χ^2 distribution with degrees of freedom $d = s - t$ where $s = (1/2)p(p + 1)$ and t is the number of independent parameters.

Two special cases are of particular interest:

- If $\mathbf{V}$ is given by Equation 5.58 or Equation 5.59 and the observed variables have a multivariate normal distribution, then $\mathbf{\Omega} = \overline{\mathbf{V}}^{-1}$ and Equation 5.63 reduces to

$$nACov(\theta) = (\mathbf{\Delta}'\overline{\mathbf{V}}\mathbf{\Delta})^{-1}, \qquad \text{(Equation 5.63)}$$

  and c becomes n times the minimum of the fit function.
- Under nonnormality one takes $\mathbf{V} = \mathbf{W}^{-1}$. This gives another fit function called ADF by Browne (1984) and WLS in Jöreskog et al. (2003, Appendix 4). This also reduces Equation 5.62 to Equation 5.63 and c to n times the minimum of the WLS fit function.

For further details and for the extension to mean and covariance structures and to multiple groups, see, for example, Browne (1984) and Satorra (1992, 1993, 2001). These results are also summarized in Jöreskog et al. (2003, Appendix 4).

TETRACHORIC AND POLYCHORIC CORRELATIONS

In the previous sections, it has been assumed that all variables, observed as well as latent variables, are continuous variables. The results have been generalized to observed dichotomous and polytomous categorical variables via the use of tetrachoric and polychoric correlations by various researchers, notably Christoffersson (1975), Muthén (1978, 1984) and Jöreskog (1990, 1994, 2002). Jöreskog (2002) describes how ordinal variables may be used with cross-sectional data, longitudinal data, multiple groups, and with covariates.

A GENERAL PERSPECTIVE

Bartholomew (1985), and Bartholomew & Knott (1999) use the term *latent variable models* in a more general setting. There are two sets of variables, manifest variables $\mathbf{x}$ and latent variables ξ with a joint distribution. If the marginal distribution $h(\xi)$ of ξ and the conditional distribution $g(\mathbf{x}|\xi)$ of x for given ξ exist, then the marginal distribution $f(\mathbf{x})$ of $\mathbf{x}$ must be

$$f(\mathbf{x}) = \int h(\xi)g(\mathbf{x}|\xi)\,d\xi \ . \qquad \text{(Equation 5.64)}$$

This is a tautology in the sense that it always holds if the distributions exist. However, the idea of factor analysis and latent variable models is that the manifest variables should be independent for given latent variables, that is, the latent variables should account for all dependencies among the manifest variables. Thus,

$$g(\mathbf{x}|\xi) = \prod_{i=1}^{p} g(x_i|\xi) \qquad \text{(Equation 5.65)}$$

so that

$$f(\mathbf{x}) = \int h(\xi) \prod_{i=1}^{p} g(x_i|\xi) \qquad \text{(Equation 5.66)}$$

To specify a latent variable model, one must therefore specify $h(\xi)$ and $g(x_i|\xi)$ for all i. The latter distribution may be different for different i.

The manifest variables may be continuous or categorical and the latent variables may be continuous or categorical. Thus there may be four classes of latent variable models as shown in Table 5–1.

- *Class A:* This is the factor analysis model considered in previous sections of this chapter. Assuming normality, one takes $\xi \sim N(0, \mathbf{I})$. The model for normally distributed manifest variables considered previously is obtained by taking $\mathbf{x}|\xi \sim N(\mu + \Lambda\xi, \Psi)$. This implies $\mathbf{x} \sim N(\mu, \Lambda\Lambda' + \Psi)$.

TABLE 5–1
Classification of Latent Variable Models

	Manifest Variables	
Latent Variables	Continuous	Categorical
Continuous	A: Factor analysis models	B: Latent trait models
Categorical	C: Latent profile models	D: Latent class models

- *Class B:* This is called a latent trait model. Moustaki & Knott (2000) considered distributions where $g(x_i|\xi)$ is chosen from the exponential family. A particular case is when the manifest variables are binary or ordinal. Let x_i be an ordinal variable with m_i ordered categories $s = 1, 2, \ldots, m_i$. Then one takes $\xi \sim N(0, \mathbf{I})$ and

$$g_i(x_i = s|\xi) = F\left(\alpha_s^{(i)} - \sum_{j=1}^{k} \beta_{ij}\xi_j\right) - F\left(\alpha_{s-1}^{(i)} - \sum_{j=1}^{k} \beta_{ij}\xi_j\right)$$

(Equation 5.67)

where F is a distribution function and

$$-\infty = \alpha_0^{(i)} < \alpha_1^{(i)} < \alpha_2^{(i)} \cdots < \alpha_{m_i-1}^{(i)} < \alpha_{m_i}^{(i)} = \infty$$

The most common choices of F are (see Jöreskog & Moustaki, 2001).

$$\text{NOR}: \quad F(t) = \Phi(t) = \int_{-\infty}^{t} \frac{1}{\sqrt{2\pi}} e^{-\frac{1}{2}u^2} du \qquad \text{(Equation 5.68)}$$

$$\text{POM}: \quad F(t) = \Psi(t) = \frac{e^t}{1 + e^t} \qquad \text{(Equation 5.69)}$$

In factor analysis terminology, the $\alpha_s^{(i)}$ are intercept terms or threshold parameters and the β_{ij} are factor loadings.

- *Class C:* This is called a latent profile model, see, for example, Bartholomew & Knott (1999).

- *Class D:* This is called a latent class model. This model goes back to Lazarsfeld & Henry (1968) and Goodman (1974). For a more recent update, see Langeheine & Rost (1988), see also Bartholomew (chap. 2, this volume).

For a review of latent trait and latent class models and various approaches to estimate them, see Moustaki (chap. 14, this volume).

REFERENCES

Anderson, T. W. (1960). Some stochastic process models for intelligence test scores. In K. J. Arrow, S. Karlin, & P. Suppes (Eds.), *Mathematical methods in the social sciences* (pp. 205–220). Stanford, CA: Stanford University Press.

Anderson, T. W., & Rubin, H. (1956). Statistical inference in factor analysis. In J. Neyman (Ed.), *Proceedings of the Third Berkeley Symposium* (Vol. 5, pp. 111–150). Berkeley: University of California Press.

Archer, C. O., & Jennrich, R. I. (1973). Standard errors for rotated factor loadings. *Psychometrika, 38,* 581–592.

Bartholomew, D. (1985). Foundations of factor analysis: Some practical implications. *British Journal of Mathematical and Statistical Psychology, 38,* 1–10.

Bartholomew, D. (1995). Spearman, and the origin and development of factor analysis. *British Journal of Mathematical and Statistical Psychology, 48,* 211–220.

Bartholomew, D., & Knott, M. (1999). *Latent variable models and factor analysis.* London: Arnold.

Basmann, R. L. (1957). A generalized classical method of linear estimation of coefficients in a structural equation. *Econometrica, 25,* 77–83.

Bollen, K. A. (1996). An alternative two stage least squares (2SLS) estimator for latent variable equations. *Psychometrika, c1,* 109–121.

Bollen, K. A., & Bauer, D. J. (2004). Automating the selection of model-implied instrumental variables. *Sociological Methods and Research, 32,* 425–452.

Bollen, K. A. & Biesanz, J. C. (2002). A note on a two-stage least-squares estimator for higher-order factor analysis. *Sociological Methods and Research, 30,* 568–579.

Bollen, K. A., & Long, S. A. (1993). *Testing structural equation models.* Newbury Park, CA: Sage Publications.

Boomsma, A., & Hoogland, J. J. (2001). The robustness of LISREL modeling revisited. In R. Cudeck, S. du Toit, & D. Sörbom (Ed.), *Structural equation modeling: Present and future* (pp. 139–168). Lincolnwood, IL: Scientific Software International.

Browne, M. W. (1968). A comparison of factor analytic techniques. *Psychometrika, 33,* 267–334.

Browne, M. W. (1977). Generalized least squares estimators in the analysis of covariance structures. In D. J. Aigner & A. S. Goldberger (Eds.), *Latent variables in socio-economic models* (pp. 205–226). Amsterdam: North-Holland.

Browne, M. W. (1984). Asymptotically distribution-free methods for the analysis of covariance structures. *British Journal of Mathematical and Statistical Psychology, 37,* 62–83.

Browne, M. W. (1985). The information matrix of image factor analysis. *Linear Algebra Applications, 70,* 51–59.

Browne, M. W. (2001). An overview of analytic rotation in exploratory factor analysis. *Multivariate Behavioral Research, 36,* 111–150.

Carroll, J. B. (1953). An analytical solution for approximating simple structure in factor analysis. *Psychometrika, 18,* 23–38.

Cattell, R. B. (1966). The scree test for the number of factors. *Multivariate Behavioral Research, 1,* 245–276.

Christoffersson, A. (1975). Factor analysis of dichotomized variables. *Psychometrika, 40,* 5–32.

Costner, H. L. (1969). Theory, deduction, and rules of correspondence. *American Journal of Sociology, 75,* 245–263.

Cramér, H. (1957). *Mathematical methods of statistics.* Princeton, NJ: Princeton University Press.

Cudeck, R., & Browne, M. W. (1983). Cross-validation of covariance structures. *Multivariate Behavioral Research, 18*, 147–157.

Duncan, O. D. (1975). *Introduction to structural equation models.* New York: Academic Press.

du Toit, S., & Browne, M. W. (2001). The covariance structure of a vector ARMA time series. In R. Cudeck, S. du Toit, & D. Sörbom (Ed.), *Structural equation modeling: Present and future* (pp. 279–314). Lincolnwood, IL: Scientific Software International.

French, J. W. (1951). The description of aptitude and achievement tests in terms of rotated factors. *Psychometric Monographs* 5.

Goodman, L. A. (1974). Exploratory latent structure analysis using both identifiable and unidentifiable models. *Biometrika, 61*, 215–231.

Guilford, J. P. (1956). The structure of intellect. *Psychological Bulletin, 63* 267–293.

Guttman, L. (1944). General theory and methods for matrix factoring. *Psychometrika, 9*, 1–16.

Guttman, L. (1953). Image theory for the structure of quantitative variates. *Psychometrika, 18*, 277–296.

Guttman, L. (1954a). A new approach to factor analysis: The radix. In P. F. Lazarsfeld (Ed.), *Mathematical thinking in the social sciences* (pp. 258–348). New York: Columbia University Press.

Guttman, L. (1954b). Some necessary conditions for common-factor analysis. *Psychometrika, 19*, 149–161.

Guttman, L. (1956). Best possible systematic estimates of communalities. *Psychometrika, 21*, 273–285.

Guttman, L. (1957). A necessary and sufficient formula for matrix factoring. *Psychometrika, 22*, 79–81.

Guttman, L. (1958). To what extent can communalities reduce rank? *Psychometrika, 23*, 297–308.

Hägglund, G. (1982). Factor analysis by instrumental variable methods. *Psychometrika, 47*, 209–222.

Hägglund, G. (2001). Milestones in the history of factor analysis. In R. Cudeck, S. du Toit, & D. Sörbom (Eds.), *Structural equation modeling: Present and future* (pp. 11–38). Lincolnwood, IL: Scientific Software International.

Harman, H. H. (1967). *Modern factor analysis* (3rd ed.) Chicago: University of Chicago Press.

Hatanaka, M. (1996). *Time-series-based econometrics: Unit roots and cointegration.* Oxford, England Oxford University Press.

Hayashi, K., & Bentler, P. M. (2000). On the relations among regular, equal variances, and image factor analysis. *Psychometrika, 65*, 59–72.

Hershberger, S. L. (2003). The growth of structural equation modeling. *Structural Equation Modeling, 10*, 35–46.

Howe, H. G. (1955). *Some contributions to factor analysis* (Rep. 920. ORNL-1919). Oak Ridge, TN: Oak Ridge National Laboratory.

Jennrich, R. I. (1973). Standard errors for obliquely rotated factor loadings. *Psychometrika, 38*, 593–604.

Jennrich, R. I. (1986). A Gauss-Newton algorithm for exploratory factor analysis. *Psychometrika, 51*, 277–284.

Jennrich, R. I. & Robinson, S. M. (1969). A Newton-Raphson algorithm for maximum likelihood factor analysis. *Psychometrika, 34*, 111–123.

Jöreskog, K. G. (1963). *Statistical estimation in factor analysis.* Stockholm: Almqvist & Wiksell.

Jöreskog, K. G. (1967). Some contributions to maximum likelihood factor analysis. *Psychometrika, 32,* 443–482.

Jöreskog, K. G. (1969a). Efficient estimation in image factor analysis. *Psychometrika, 34,* 51–75.

Jöreskog, K. G. (1969b). A general approach to confirmatory maximum likelihood factor analysis. *Psychometrika, 34,* 183–202.

Jöreskog, K. G. (1970). Estimation and testing of simplex models. *British Journal of Mathematical and Statistical Psychology, 23,* 121–145.

Jöreskog, K. G. (1971). Simultaneous factor analysis in several populations. *Psychometrika, 57,* 409–426.

Jöreskog, K. G. (1973a). Analysis of covariance structures. In P. R. Krishnaiah (Ed.), *Multivariate analysis–III* (pp. 263–285). New York: Academic Press.

Jöreskog, K. G. (1973b). A general method for estimating a linear structural equation system. In A. S. Goldberger & O. D. Duncan (Eds.), *Structural equation models in the social sciences* (pp. 85–112). New York: Seminar Press.

Jöreskog, K. G. (1974). Analyzing psychological data by structural analysis of covariance matrices. In D. H. Krantz, R. C. Atkinson, R. D. Luce, & P. Suppes (Eds.), *Contemporary developments in mathematical psychology* (Vol. 2, pp. 1–56). San Francisco: W. H. Freeman.

Jöreskog, K. G. (1977). Factor analysis by least-squares and maximum-likelihood methods. In K. Enslein, A. Ralston, & H. S. Wilf (Eds.), *Statistical methods for digital computers* (pp. 125–153). New York: Wiley.

Jöreskog, K. G. (1978). An econometric model for multivariate panel data. *Annales de l'INSEE, 30–31,* 355–366.

Jöreskog, K. G. (1979). Statistical estimation of structural models in longitudinal developmental investigations. In J. R. Nesselroade & P. B. Baltes (Eds.), *Longitudinal research in the study of behavior and development* (pp. 303–351). New York: Academic Press.

Jöreskog, K. G. (1981). Analysis of covariance structures. *Scandinavian Journal of Statistics, 8,* 65–92.

Jöreskog, K. G. (1983). Factor analysis as an errors-in-variables model. In H. Wainer & S. Messick (Eds.), *Principals of modern psychological measurement: A festschrift in honor of Frederic M. Lord* (pp. 185–196). Hillsdale, NJ: Lawrence Erlbaum Associates.

Jöreskog, K. G. (1990). New developments in LISREL: Analysis of ordinal variables using polychoric correlations and weighted least squares. *Quality and Quantity, 24,* 387–404.

Jöreskog, K. G. (1994). On the estimation of polychoric correlations and their asymptotic covariance matrix. *Psychometrika, 59,* 381–389.

Jöreskog, K. G. (2002). *Structural equation modeling with ordinal variables using LISREL.* Available at http://www.ssicentral.com/techdocs/ordinal.pdf

Jöreskog, K. G., & Goldberger, A. S. (1972). Factor analysis by generalized least squares. *Psychometrika, 37,* 243–250.

Jöreskog, K. G., & Lawley D. N. (1968). New methods in maximum likelihood factor analysis. *British Journal of Mathematical and Statistical Psychology, 21,* 85–96.

Jöreskog, K. G., & Moustaki, I. (2001). Factor analysis of ordinal variables: A comparison of three approaches. *Multivariate Behavioral Research, 36,* 347–387.

Jöreskog, K. G., & Sörbom, D. (1976). Statistical models and methods for test–retest situations. In D. N. M. deGruijter & L. J. T. van der Kamp (Eds.), *Advances in psychological and educational measurement* (pp. 285–325). New York: Wiley.

Jöreskog, K. G., & Sörbom, D. (1977). Statistical models and methods for analysis of longitudinal data. In D. J. Aigner & A. S. Goldberger (Eds.), *Latent variables in socioeconomic models* (pp. 285–325). Amsterdam: North-Holland.

Jöreskog, K. G., & Sörbom, D. (1978). *LISREL 7: A guide to the program and applications.* Chicago: SPSS Publications.

Jöreskog, K. G., & Sörbom, D. (1999). *LISREL 8 User's reference guide* (2nd ed.). Chicago: Scientific Software International.

Jöreskog, K. G., Sörbom, D., du Toit, S., & du Toit, M. (2003). *LISREL 8: New statistical features.* Chicago: Scientific Software International.

Kaiser, H. F. (1958). The varimax criterion for analytical rotation in factor analysis. *Psychometrika, 23,* 187–200.

Kaiser, H. F. (1970). A second generation little jiffy. *Psychometrika, 35,* 401–415.

Klein, L. R., & Goldberger, A. S. (1955). *An econometric model of the united states 1929–1952.* Amsterdam: North-Holland.

Kroonenberg, P. M., & Lewis, C. (1982). Methodological issues in the search for a factor model: Exploration through confirmation. *Journal of Educational Statistics, 7,* 69–89.

Langeheine, R., & Rost, J. (1988). *Latent trait and latent class models.* New York; Plenum.

Lawley, D. N. (1940). The estimation of factor loadings by the method of maximum likelihood. *Proceedings of the Royal Society of Edinburgh, 60,* 64–82.

Lazarsfeld, P. F., & Henry, N. W. (1968). *Latent structure analysis.* New York: Houghton-Mifflin.

Lütkepohl, H. (1993). *Introduction to multiple time series analysis* (2nd ed.). Berlin: Springer-Verlag.

Madansky, A. (1964). Instrumental variables in factor analysis. *Psychometrika, 29,* 105–113.

Magnus, J. R., & Neudecker, H. (1988). *Matrix differential calculus with applications in statistics and econometrics.* New York: Wiley.

McArdle, J. J. (2001). A latent difference score approach to longitudinal dynamic structural analysis. In R. Cudeck, S. du Toit, & D. Sörbom (Eds), *Structural equation modeling: Present and future* (pp. 341–380). Lincolnwood, IL: Scientific Software International.

Meredith, W. (1964). Notes on factorial invariance. *Psychometrika, 29,* 177–185.

Molenaar, P. C. M. (1985). A dynamic factor model for the analysis of multivariate time series. *Psychometrika, 50,* 181–202.

Moustaki, I., & Knott, M. (2000). Generalized latent trait models. *Psychometrika, 65,* 391–411.

Mulaik, S. A. (1972). *The foundation of factor analysis.* New York: McGraw-Hill.

Mulaik, S. A. (1986). Factor analysis and *Psychometrika*: Major developments. *Psychometrika, 51,* 23–33.

Muthén, B. (1978). Contributions to factor analysis of dichotomous variables. *Psychometrika, 43,* 551–560.

Muthén, B. (1984). A general structural equation model with dichotomous, ordered categorical, and continuous latent variable indicators. *Psychometrika, 49,* 115–132.

Romney, D. M., & Bynner, J. M. (1992). *The structure of personal characteristics.* London: Praeger.

Sargan, J. D. (1958). The estimation of economic relationships using instrumental variables. *Econometrica, 26,* 393–415.

Satorra, A. (1989). Alternative test criteria in covariance structure analysis: A unified approach. *Psychometrika, 54,* 131–151.

Satorra, A. (1992). Asymptotic robust inferences in the analysis of mean and covariance structures. In P. V. Marsden (Ed.), *Sociological Methodology 1992* (pp. 249–278). Oxford: Blackwell.

Satorra, A. (1993). Multi-sample analysis of moment structures: Asymptotic validity of inferences based on second-order moments. In K. Haagen, D. J. Bartholomew, & M. Deistler (Eds.), *Statistical modelling and latent variables* (pp. 283–298). New York: Elsevier Science.

Satorra, A. (2001). Goodness of fit testing of structural equation models with multiple group data and non-normality. In R. Cudeck, S. du Toit, & D. Sörbom, (Eds.), *Structural Equation Modeling: Present and Future* (pp. 231–256). Lincolnwood, IL: Scientific Software International.

Satorra, A., & Bentler, P. M. (1988). Scaling corrections for chi-square statistics in covariance structure analysis. *Proceedings of the Business and Economic Statistics Section of the American Statistical Association*, 308–313.

Schmid, J., & Leiman, J. M. (1957). The development of hierarchical factor solutions. *Psychometrika, 22*, 53–61.

Spearman, C. (1904). General intelligence objectively determined and measured. *American Journal of Psychology, 15*, 201–293.

Steyer, R., & Schmitt, M. J. (1990). Latent state-trait models in attitude research. *Quality and Quantity, 24*, 427–447.

Sörbom, D. (1974). A general method for studying differences in factor means and factor structures between groups. *British Journal of Mathematical and Statistical Psychology, 27*, 229–239.

Theil, H. (1953). *Repeated least-squares applied to complete equation systems* [Mimeograph]. The Hague: Central Planning Bureau.

Theil, H. (1971). *Principles of econometrics*. New York: Wiley.

Thurstone, L. L. (1938). Primary mental abilities. *Psychometric Monographs, 1*, 1–121.

Wolfle, L. M. (2003). The introduction of path analysis to the social sciences, and some emergent themes: An annotated bibliography. *Structural Equation Modeling, 10*, 1–34.

CHAPTER 6

On the Origins of Latent Curve Models

Kenneth A. Bollen
University of North Carolina at Chapel Hill

Over the last decade, latent curve models (LCMs) have moved from relative obscurity to being a favored technique for the analysis of longitudinal, social science data. Part of this growing popularity derives from the increasing availability of longitudinal data (e.g., Young, Savola, & Phelps, 1991). The increase in data creates demand for procedures that are adequate to analyze them and LCMs have several desirable characteristics. In addition, the emphasis that LCMs put on individual differences in change corresponds to an increasingly popular view that individuals have different paths of change and that our statistical models need to permit this heterogeneity.

Another reason for the more frequent use of latent curve models is the widespread interest and familiarity with Structural Equation Models (SEMs). The development of several powerful SEM software programs and their accessibility has helped to spread the use and knowledge of SEMs among social scientists. Furthermore, beginning with Meredith and Tisak's (1984, 1990) demonstration that researchers can use standard SEM software to fit latent curve models, numerous researchers have begun to follow their lead and the lead of other researchers who have elaborated on Meredith and Tisak's influential work. The intense interest in multilevel or hierarchical linear models also contributes to the growth of use of LCMs. This occurs because multilevel models have stimulated interest in growth curve models and this in turn has fueled interest in LCMs approached through SEMs.

The sharp increase in the frequency of use of LCMs has created the impression among novice users that these are new and novel techniques. The historical roots of the procedure are not widely appreciated. Furthermore, the LCMs that are best known are straightforward specifications that assume a linear trajectory with the main exception being occasional consideration of a quadratic term to capture nonlinearity.

The primary purpose of this chapter is twofold. First, it acknowledges and encourages an appreciation of several of the pioneers who planted the seeds for LCMs in their work on growth curve models and factor analysis. The review is selective in that it emphasizes several early works that illustrate the manner in which growth curve models and factor analysis contributed to LCMs. It is a testimony to the flexibility of factor analysis that the latent factors play the role of random coefficients and the factor loadings help to define the trajectory curves. A second purpose of the chapter is to see what lessons these early works can teach contemporary users of LCMs. To foreshadow some of my conclusions, I argue that these early works had a more flexible approach to nonlinearity and to defining the number of different curve terms required to describe individual trajectories than do many of today's applications. We would do well to return to these ideas.

In the next section, I present a Generic Model that is capable of incorporating a variety of growth curve, factor analysis, and LCMs. By placing restrictions on this equation, we obtain most of the models that we review and discuss. Following this is the Historic Roots of the Latent Curve Model (LCM) section, with a discussions of papers from the factor analysis and growth curve model traditions that laid the foundation of contemporary LCMs. Issues of Case-by-Case and Factor Analysis Approaches are highlighted in the next section. A section on Meredith and Tisak's Latent Curve Model that grew out of these traditions follows. Then Lessons for Contemporary Latent Curve Models is next. The Conclusion summarizes the papers.

GENERIC MODEL

Repeated measures on a sample of cases are the starting point for growth curves or LCMs. Assume that we have several repeated measures on an outcome of interest. Call the repeated measure, y_{it}, where y is the repeated variable, i indexes the observation in the sample with $i = 1, 2, ..., N$ and t indexes the time of observation with $t = 1, 2, ..., T$. A general equation that is useful throughout the paper is

$$y_{it} = g_1(t)\eta_{i1} + g_2(t)\eta_{i2} + \cdots + g_K(t)\eta_{iK} + \epsilon_{it} \qquad \text{(Equation 6.1)}$$

where $g_k(t)$ is a function of time that describes the kth trajectory, $k = 1, 2, ..., K$, η_{ik} is the random coefficient (weight) or "factor" for the ith individual and the kth trajectory curve, and ϵ_{it} is the random error or disturbance for the ith individual and tth time. The model assumes that $E(\epsilon_{it}) = 0$ (the mean of ϵ_{it} is zero for all cases and all times), $COV(\epsilon_{i,t+s}, \eta_{ik}) = 0$ for all i, s, and k, and $E(\epsilon_{it}\epsilon_{i+j,t+s}) = 0$ for all i, t when j and s are both not zero. The variance of the disturbance is $E(\epsilon_{it}^2) = \theta_{\epsilon_{it}} \equiv VAR(\epsilon_{it})$ for each t. A typical assumption is that all cases have the same variance for each time period (i.e., $E(\epsilon_{it}\epsilon_{jt}) = \theta_{\epsilon_t}$), though there are situations where this assumption is not made. Sometimes researchers assume that the error variances are constant over time and over cases, although this assumption is not routinely needed. Though identifying a model requires some assumptions about the error variances, I only introduce such assumptions as needed. Also, note that the ηs can correlate ("oblique" factors) or not ("orthogonal" factors), depending on the model.

There are several points to make about Equation 6.1. Usually, the t refers to time of measurement, but it also can refer to age, trial, grade, or some other temporal or experience metric to which the repeated measure is linked. The t runs from a minimum of 0 up to a maximum of T. The $g_k(t)$ defines the kth curve that underlies the repeated measures. It is a function of t. Equation 6.1 allows more than one of these curves, though in practice three or fewer of these function terms are common. The ηs are individual weights with separate ones for each of the $g_k(t)$ curves. The larger is the relative magnitude of the η_{ik}, the more the ith case follows the $g_k(t)$ curve. Any individual's trajectory might be dominated by a single $g_k(t)$ curve or several $g_k(t)$ curves that form a composite path of change. In the former case, one η_{ik} is large and the others small. In the latter, at least two η_{ik}s dominate. It also bears emphasis that without further restrictions this model is generally underidentified, even if we assume that all individuals have the same error variance at each time. *Underidentification* means that we cannot find unique values of the model parameters so that it is not possible to determine the "true" and "false" values even with information on the population moments of the repeated measures. In the traditional factor analysis literature, underidentification is often referred to as the "rotation problem." I will have more to say about this issue.

The rich generality of Equation 6.1 contrasts with the typical contemporary (LCM). In practice, it is common to have a linear LCM such as

$$y_{it} = \alpha_i + \lambda_t \beta_i + \epsilon_{it} \qquad \text{(Equation 6.2)}$$

This corresponds to a special case of Equation 6.1 where there are only two curve terms ($K = 2$) to the right of the equal sign. The first "curve" is a constant of one ($g_1(t) = 1$) that creates a random intercept ($\eta_{i1} = \alpha_i$). The second curve term is linear ($g_2(t) = \lambda_t = t - 1$) with a linear random slope ($\eta_{i2} = \beta_i$). The assumptions about the disturbances (ϵ_{it}) match those already described with the addition of assuming that each case in a given time period has the same variance ($E(\epsilon_{it}\epsilon_{it}) = \theta_{\epsilon_t}$) and sometimes assuming that these variances are equal over time ($E(\epsilon_{it}\epsilon_{it}) = \theta_{\epsilon}$). Occasionally, nonlinear relations are included by adding a quadratic term ($\lambda_t^2 \beta_i^2$), and less commonly, by estimating a "freed loading" model where in Equation 6.2, the first two loadings are set to 0 and 1 and the remaining loadings are freely estimated (i.e., $\lambda_1 = 0, \lambda_2 = 1, \; \lambda_3, \lambda_4, ..., \lambda_T$). In this contemporary LCM, there are two latent factors, α_i and β_i, that are the random intercepts and slopes that can differ over cases. The "curve" is captured by the factor loadings, λ_t.

The next section has a selective review of foundation works on growth curve models with factor analysis applications that helps to place our contemporary practice of LCM in historic perspective.

HISTORIC ROOTS OF LATENT CURVE MODELS (LCMs)

In a brief history of trajectory models, Bollen and Curran (2006) summarized early works that contributed to growth curve modeling and LCMs. There we give a broad overview of past work, including 19th-century research that concentrated on group trajectories. Rather than repeating this material, I emphasize several papers that illustrate pivotal turning points in the development of contemporary LCMs, going into greater depth and raising new points that were not covered in our overview. With one noteworthy exception, I restrict the articles to ones published since the 1950s and up until the Meredith and Tisak (1984, 1990) landmark papers on LCMs. My intention is not to be either comprehensive or necessarily representative of the literature on LCMs. Rather I choose papers that illustrate or make major contributions to LCMs.

Pre-1958: Individual Trajectories and Factor Analyses of Growth

Much of the work on growth curve models for longitudinal data prior to 1958 emphasized the analysis of group or mean trajectories in the repeated outcome variable (e.g., Pearl, 1924; Reed, 1921). An important exception is Wishart (1938). Wishart's (1938) study grows out of a reanalysis of data on the impact of protein content of food on the weight of bacon pigs. In the initial study, Wishart looked only at the beginning and end weights of the pigs under three different amounts of protein in their feed. The 1938 reanalysis was motivated by having weight data for 17 times, even though just the first and last were analyzed in the earlier study. Furthermore, Wishart (1938) focused on the growth curves of weight for each pig rather than the average difference in initial and final weights of all pigs in each nutrition group. For each pig, Wishart plotted its weight by week on ordinary and logarithmic paper. Neither indicated a linear relation between time and weight so he fit a second degree parabola for each pig to capture the curvilinear relation. Wishart (1938) then used ANOVA and ANCOVA to analyze the impact of initial weight, sex, and diet on these growth parameters.

The Wishart (1938) paper illustrates several important points. First, it marks a transition from emphasizing group analysis to individual analysis. Much work from this period and earlier placed emphasis on group or average differences. His paper showed the value of examining individual differences. Second, it represents the "case-by-case" analysis of growth curves. That is, the researcher analyzes each individual, one at a time. The growth parameters estimated for one individual have no impact on those of another because the estimation procedure only considers the values of one case over time. This point is closely related to the first, but as I discuss shortly, the case-by-case analysis is not the only way to analyze growth curves or LCMs. Third, Wishart (1938) carefully considered linear and nonlinear curves to best fit the trajectory of weight. He ended up choosing a quadratic model to fit the weight data. Regardless of the functional form chosen, the examination of individual plots and the consideration of nonlinear forms is good practice, but less common in contemporary LCMs analysis. Finally, Wishart developed a conditional growth model in that he used covariates to predict the growth parameters.

Although less well-known in the growth curve literature, Griliches (1957) explored the diffusion of hybrid corn in the United States in an article that grew out of his dissertation. Like Wishart (1938), Griliches (1957) made graphs of growth for individual cases. Figure 6–1 is taken from Griliches (1957) and illustrates these curves for several states. Noting the general S-shaped curves, he then fit a logistic curve to each state. The parameter estimates from these logistic equations summarized the growth curve for each area. Griliches (1957) predicted these parameter estimates by several covariates that characterized the areas and hence had a conditional growth curve model. This early application shares several features with Wishart's (1938) approach: (a) the focus is on individual growth rather than group growth, (b) a case-by-case estimation of the growth curves is done, (c) covariates are used to predict the growth parameters, and (d) a nonlinear functional form is chosen.

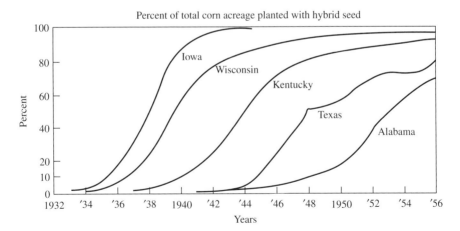

FIGURE 6–1.   Griliches's (1957) graph of percent total acreage planted with hybrid seed. From "Hybrid Corn: An Exploration in the Economics of Technological Change," by Z. Griliches, 1957, *Econometrica, 25*(4), pp. 501–522. Copyright © 1957 by the Econometric Society. Reprinted with permission.

Three years prior to Griliches (1957), Baker (1954) published the first paper that I have found that uses factor analysis techniques to study growth curves.[1] Baker (1954) was not aware of any prior factor analysis work on growth curves as the following quote illustrates: "The application of factor analysis to biological problems of growth seems to be novel so that one of the main purposes of this paper is to suggest such analyses" (p.138). Baker analyzed the correlation matrix of "cheek diameters" of 75 peaches on 20 different dates over several months using factor analysis.[2] Table 6–1 is from Baker (1954) and it contains the loadings on the original and orthogonally rotated factors.

He interpreted the first three factors from the rotated solution as follows:

There is a central time of stability in the relative positions of the peaches extending from May 27, the date of pit hardening ... until August 4. Sizeable loadings on

TABLE 6–1

Baker's (1954) Factor Loadings for Factor Analysis of Growth Curves for Peaches

	Rotated Factors		
1	2	3	4
.330	−.917	.127	.270
.511	−.893	−.140	−.293
.756	−.635	.177	−.112
.848	−.488	.193	.037
.330	−.253	.175	−.059
.960	−.056	.103	−.012
.957	−.041	.026	−.265
.982	.094	.065	−.072
.988	.084	.040	−.098
.986	.123	−.032	−.115
.990	−.002	−.046	−.139
.975	.051	.035	.133
.990	.010	.016	.032
.977	−.028	−.040	.054
.959	−.153	−.110	.321
.959	−.066	−.066	.132
.917	−.094	−.289	.005
.837	.048	−.501	.205
.718	.060	−.665	−.008
.681	.089	−.647	−.004

[1]Robert MacCallum called my attention to a 1936 presidential address of Thurstone that mentions that factor analysis could be applied to over time data (Thurstone, 1937). But the point is not pursued in this chapter.

[2]Citing Cattell (1952), Baker (1954) takes communalities of one for the extraction of the first factor. Factor extraction continued until residuals were suitably small.

this factor occur at all dates. The second factor is most clearly associated with early growth and since the loadings are negative, it is indicated that peaches relatively large at one early measurement tend to be relatively small at a near later measurement. ... Factor 2, F_2', complements Factor 1 in the early stages of growth and fades away as Factor 1 increases. Factor 3 complements Factor 1 in the late stages of growth much the same as Factor 1 does in the early stages. Factor 3 is again negative, which probably indicates that the early ripening fruits complete growth earlier than some that ripen later, which tends to reverse the relative positions of the fruits as they pass through time. (Baker, 1954, p. 141)

In Baker's (1954) approach to growth curves, each column of factor loadings is a different growth curve component. Although, Baker does not formalize his analysis in an equation, the generic Equation 6.1 for LCMs is helpful at this point and is now repeated:

$$y_{it} = g_1(t)\eta_{i1} + g_2(t)\eta_{i2} + \cdots + g_K(t)\eta_{iK} + \epsilon_{it}$$

Baker's analysis would have y_{it} be the diameter of the ith peach at the tth time. His analysis suggest three primary curves, $g_1(t)$ to $g_3(t)$, to describe the growth. The specific function of time is not specified in advance, but is estimated by the factor loadings. For example, the rotated solution in Table 6–1 shows that $g_1(May\ 1) = .330$, $g_1(May\ 6) = .511$ or $g_2(May\ 1) = -.917$ and $g_3(Sept.\ 2) = -0.665$. The preceding quote from Baker (1954) describes the pattern of these curves for each component. The adequacy of any one of these curves in characterizing the growth of a particular peach depends on its latent factor value. Relatively high values on a factor indicate that the corresponding curve is important in describing its growth. Low factor values mean the opposite. Because the factors are latent, the weights are latent and would need to be estimated to determine where a specific case (peach) falls on these curves.

The Baker paper marks a sharp contrast from the Wishart (1938) and Griliches (1957) approach to growth curves. First, rather than a case-by-case estimation as was used by these other authors, Baker (1954) used a "system estimator" and all parameters are estimated simultaneously. Second, Wishart and Griliches used specific functional forms for the growth curves whereas Baker estimated the curves via the factor loadings and a nonspecific functional form. Third, Wishart and Griliches had estimates of the random intercepts, slopes, and other parameters for each individual whereas Baker's factor analysis approach did not predict the latent factor values and hence did not provide weights for the different curves. Fourth, Baker analyzes a correlation matrix, which led to the removal of differences in variances of the repeated measures and kept all means at zero. Generally, differences of means and variances are important components of the growth process that are lost with this standardization. Finally, the exploratory factor analysis model used by Baker is underidentified. This means that there is an arbitrariness to the factor loadings in that many others would be consistent with the data. This rotation problem gives an arbitrariness to the curves that the loadings approximate. Indeed, Cronbach (1967) made this critique of a factor analysis of mental test scores and he discouraged researchers from factor analyzing over time data on individuals.

In this subsection, we described the advancement to case-by-case analyses of growth trajectories as represented in the pioneering work of Wishart (1938) and Griliches (1957). In addition, Baker (1954) is the first author to illustrate the application of factor analysis to growth data. The emphasis on individual cases and the use of factor analysis in growth modeling come together even more clearly in a few years after Baker (1954), as I describe now.

1958: A Turning Point

Two papers published in 1958 marked a turning point in the approach to growth curve models. Rao (1958) and Tucker (1958) provided formal presentations that linked work on factor analysis with work on growth curve models. In this subsection, I review the most relevant aspects of each study.

Rao's (1958) paper made several contributions including developing the connection of the usual case-by-case approach to growth curves and the factor analysis model. For instance, Rao (1958) listed a general equation for an individual growth curve, which using a slight modification of our notation, is

$$y_{it}^* = g_1^*(t)\eta_{i1} + \epsilon_{it}^* \qquad \text{(Equation 6.3)}$$

where the *s signify that Rao (1958) used difference scores so that $y_{it}^* = (y_{it} - y_{i,t-1})$, $g_1^*(t) = g_1(t) - g_1(t-1)$, and $\epsilon_{it}^* = (\epsilon_{it} - \epsilon_{i,t-1})$. In other words, the dependent variables in Rao's work were change scores. Rao then noted the similarity of this model to the factor analysis model of

$$y_{it}^* = g_1^*(t)\eta_{i1} + g_2^*(t)\eta_{i2} + \cdots + g_K^*(t)\eta_{iK} + \epsilon_{it}^* \qquad \text{(Equation 6.4)}$$

where the * variables are defined analogously. In the factor analysis model, the $g_k^*(t)$ are not explicitly specified functions, but are the estimated factor loadings that define the trajectory curve of the change scores (y_{it}^*). The η_{ik}s are the latent factors or weights of the ith case for the corresponding curve component.[3] Rao also discussed the relation of these models to principal component analysis, the estimation of factors, and tests of significance for differences between groups. His work provided a formal basis to show that growth curve models could be placed in a factor analysis or principal component framework. Rao's use of change scores departed slightly from growth curve or factor analysis models of the original repeated measure, but it does not change the essential points about the ties between factor analysis and growth curve models. Furthermore, his use of change

---

[3]Rao (1958) notes that one difference of this model from a factor analysis model occurs if the factor analysis model includes a constant for each time.

scores in growth curve models was a precursor to the renewed interest in them in contemporary research (e.g., Boker, 2001; McArdle, 2001).

In the same year, Tucker (1958) published a paper that moved the field in a similar direction. He considered a functional relation $[\phi(.,.)]$ for individual i between y_i and x such that

$$y_i = \phi(\theta_i, x) \qquad \text{(Equation 6.5)}$$

where θ_i contains one or more parameters for individual i. In the context of LCMs, x is most often t, a metric of time, and we can write this function at a particular value of t as

$$y_{it} = \phi(\theta_i, t) \qquad \text{(Equation 6.6)}$$

Tucker (1958) suggested that researchers approximate or reproduce such functions with products of two different functions

$$y_{it} = \sum_{k=1}^{K} f_k(t) h_k(\theta_i) \qquad \text{(Equation 6.7)}$$

The number of terms, K, required will depend on the original function, $\phi(\theta_i, t)$, and the degree of accuracy sought. Defining $g_k(t) \equiv f_k(t)$ and $\eta_{ik} \equiv h_k(\theta_i)$ leads to

$$y_{it} = \sum_{k=1}^{K} g_k(t) \eta_{ik} \qquad \text{(Equation 6.8)}$$

which matches Equation 6.1 with the exception that there is no disturbance, ϵ_{it}, and its accompanying assumptions.[4] Thus, Tucker (1958) showed that a factor analysis expression can represent a function of two variables in general (see Equation 6.5) and a growth curve model in specific.

Tucker's (1958) conclusions were very similar to Rao's (1958). They showed the generality of factor analysis in capturing possibly complex growth curve models without specifying the exact nature of the function of time or function of the parameters in θ_i. It provided an empirical approach by which researchers could find the trajectory curves and estimate the importance of each curve for each case through predicting the values of the latent factors. But as I have already noted and as Tucker (1958) noted long ago, there is a rotation issue or identification problem that makes unique solutions elusive.

Tucker (1966) was a powerful demonstration of how researchers could use these results in exploring the number of factors required and in reproducing the trajectory of individuals. To explain this further, I reproduce some of his results here. Tucker's empirical example was of learning curves for a probability learning

---

[4]The disturbance would be recovered if an additional $g_k(t)\eta_{ik}$ term was included and $g_k(t)$ was set to 1 and η_{ik} was treated as ϵ_{it}. Furthermore, ϵ_{it} would need to satisfy the previously described assumptions of the disturbance term.

task. The subjects were enlisted army men and each subject was exposed to 420 presentations of one of four letters. Prior to the presentation, the subject guessed what letter would appear and then would observe the actual letter. The probabilities of the letters appearing differed such that S had a .7 probability and the letters of L, N, and D each had a .10 probability. "The 420 presentations were grouped arbitrarily into 21 'trials' of 20 presentations each, and a score for each trial for each man was the number of times he guessed the predominant letter" (Tucker, 1966, p. 484). Tucker settled on a three-factor orthogonal solution for these data and predicted the factor scores. Table 6–2 reproduces Tucker's estimated factor loadings. In this model, the factor loading estimates give the shape of the growth curves over the 21 trials.

Tucker describes these curves as follows:

These curves are generally near zero or positive and their slopes are either nearly zero or positive. ... Factors B and C start near zero while Factor A is well above zero at all times. Factor C follows the base line for about six trials before starting to rise. All three curves seem to arrive at an asymptote by about trial 13 or 14. We might characterize A as early learning, B as middle learning, and C as late

TABLE 6–2
Tucker (1966, Table 16–12) Factor Loadings for
Learning Data 21 Trials

| | Group 70–10–10–10 Factor | |
1	2	3
6.17	−.23	.22
11.28	.51	.14
11.73	1.54	1.15
10.77	3.00	−.10
11.89	4.93	.21
12.86	4.72	.20
13.38	5.58	.83
14.87	5.94	.88
13.57	4.70	1.23
14.17	5.08	2.33
13.73	5.14	3.16
13.59	5.18	3.48
14.72	6.06	3.86
14.80	6.05	4.22
14.59	5.64	4.06
14.74	6.27	4.17
14.44	5.18	4.66
14.43	5.76	4.30
15.24	5.57	4.01
14.40	5.74	3.81
15.13	6.32	4.28

learning. The curve of Factor *A* appears to have the shape of a negative exponential curve used extensively in learning theory while the curve of factor *C* appears to be more of the sigmoid shape, which is also used in learning theory. Factor *B* lies somewhere between these two in shape. (Tucker, 1966, p. 495)

Table 6–3 contains the factor score predictions for the three factors.

The impact of each curve on a specific individual depends on the relative weight or the factor score predictions given in Table 6–3. Tucker (1966) showed how the combination of factor score predictions and the three curves, predicted the original data. Figure 6–2 reproduces his diagram for six persons. The dots are the observed values and the solid lines are the predicted ones.

The predicted curves result from multiplying the factor score predictions (the weights) times the factor loadings (the curves), so, for instance, Person 7 in the upper left diagram has his factor score estimates shown as 1.13, −.09, and .06. These values are multiplied by the factor loadings corresponding to a given trial and added together to form the predicted value. It is impressive to see the closeness

TABLE 6–3
Tucker's (1966, Table 16–13) Predicted Factor Scores for
Learning Data With 3 Factors

	Rotated Factors		
Individual	1	2	3
1	1.16	−.70	.12
2	.75	1.46	−.48
3	.88	.04	.96
4	.52	1.48	.82
5	.84	−.04	.47
6	1.52	−.86	−.20
7	1.13	−.09	.06
8	1.25	−.86	.12
9	.61	.58	.51
10	1.40	−.57	−.30
11	1.71	−1.04	−.03
12	.81	.37	.75
13	.39	1.96	.32
14	.84	1.20	−.86
15	.56	.98	.92
16	.69	.47	.52
17	1.42	−.56	−1.24
18	.79	.78	−.59
19	.74	.99	−.91
20	.38	1.96	−.21
21	.58	1.72	−.76
22	.11	.18	3.93
23	1.34	−.63	.30
24	1.47	−.50	.36

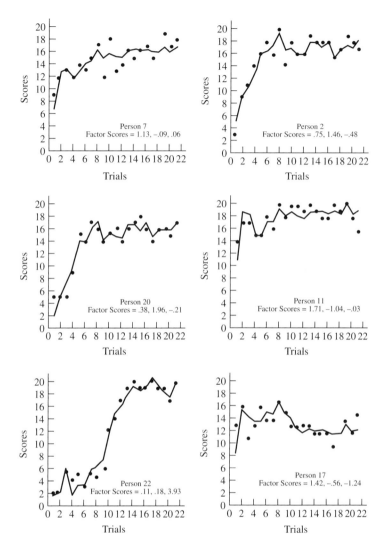

FIGURE 6–2.   Tucker's (1966) individual learning curves predicted by model. From "Learning theory and multivariate experiment: Illustration by determination of generalized learning curves" by L. R. Tucker, 1966. In R. B. Cattell (Ed.), *Handbook of multivariate experimental psychology: Theoretical, empirical, and classroom perspectives* (Diagram 15-5, p. 499). Chicago: Rand McNally. Copyright © 1966 by Rand McNally. Reprinted with permission.

of the model predicted values to the observed, particularly given the nonlinear patterns in the observed data. Thus, Rao (1958) and Tucker (1958, 1966) provided a powerful justification for using factor analysis to study individual growth curves, even when growth is highly nonlinear.

ISSUES OF CASE-BY-CASE AND FACTOR ANALYSIS APPROACHES

The previous sections described the growth curve and factor analysis traditions to modeling. Now I highlight several issues that characterize the precursors to contemporary LCMs. One issue is the nature of the error or disturbance term in growth curve models. Some treatments have no error term. For instance, Tucker (1958) presented the repeated measure as an exact function of parameters and named variables.[5] Other treatments that included an error term, say, ϵ_{it}, described it as *measurement error* in the repeated measure. Rogosa, Brandt, and Zimowski (1982) illustrated this case where the true score was a deterministic function of time and any error in the trajectory was due to measurement error. Meredith and Tisak (1984) described the error as due to measurement with the possibility that it also included "errors of approximation." I interpret this as errors due to the real trajectory having a more complex form than the estimated trajectory. Errors might also be due to omitted variables or an inherent stochastic component that affect the repeated measures. In virtually all social science applications, the most plausible assumption is that the disturbance includes at least some error due to each source: (a) measurement error in the repeated measure, (b) errors of approximation in the functional form, (c) errors due to omitted variables, and (d) errors due to an inherent stochastic component. In general, it will not be possible to separately estimate each of these components of error. However, if a latent variable is the repeated variable and there are multiple indicators of the latent variable, then it will be possible to separate the measurement error variance from the variance due to the combined effect of the other error components (e.g., McArdle, 1988; Bollen & Curran, 2006).

Another issue is the contrast between the case-by-case and the factor analytic approaches to growth curve models. The case-by-case approach chooses an explicit functional form to capture the relation between a repeated measure and a metric of time. It then fits this functional form to each case individually and collects together the parameter estimates of individuals for further analysis. In contrast, the factor analysis approach to growth curve models is a systemwide approach to estimation. In the earliest approach, temporal differences in the means and variances were surpressed by analyzing correlation matrices (e.g., Baker, 1954). But analysts turned to factor analysis of the covariance matrix, means, or the moment matrix (e.g., Tucker, 1966). These factor analyses led to the estimation of one or more curves of growth as reflected in the factor loadings. Only if the latent factor values were predicted would the weights for each case for each curve be available.

An issue for the case-by-case method to growth curves is determining the appropriate functional form to fit each case. Transformations of the repeated measures or of the time metric might help; or trying several different functional forms

---

[5]For example, see Equation (2) on p. 19, or Equation (4) on p. 20, of Tucker (1958).

might help. A problem is created by the need to try these alternatives for each case in the sample and for the possibility that different cases might have different optimal functional forms.

The factor analysis approach to growth curve modeling is very flexible in determining the curves because the factor loadings in Exploratory Factor Analysis (EFA) are freely estimated. However, the factor loading matrix is generally underidentified, so that different rotations will lead to different loadings. A simple structure rotation in LCM seems less desirable than in other factor analysis contexts. One reason is that our interest might be more focused on rotations that lead to smooth curves rather than high or low factor loadings. Indeed, little attention has been given to factor rotation in the context of EFA applied to LCMs. Another issue of the factor analysis approach is that you need to predict the latent factor values so that you have the weights for each case on each factor. These weights give the relative impact of the different curves on the individual trajectory. In the case-by-case approach, these weights were the estimated coefficients for the individual runs for the model.

In sum, several issues characterize the historic case-by-case and EFA approaches to growth curve models. One is that both approaches assume that the major source of error in repeated measures was measurement error, whereas it is likely that there are other sources of error. Another issue is the contrast between the case-by-case and the factor analysis approach where the case-by-case has the problem of determining the functional form of the trajectory but given the functional form, straightforwardly obtains estimates of the random coefficients. In contrast, the factor analysis method permits estimation of complex and flexible functional forms, but does not routinely provide predictions of the values of the random coefficients. Furthermore, the EFA factor loadings that define the functional forms are not uniquely identified. In the next section, I describe how this latter problem was overcomed.

MEREDITH AND TISAK'S LATENT CURVE MODEL

In the years following Rao's (1958) and Tucker's (1958, 1966) papers, the factor analysis model underwent many developments. Among the important advances most relevant to LCMs were the development of confirmatory factor analysis (CFA), work on the identification of CFA models, and SEM software capable of estimating CFAs (e.g., Bentler, 1985; Jöreskog, 1969; Jöreskog & Sörbom, 1981). Meredith and Tisak (1984, 1990) took Tucker's (1958, 1966) and Rao's (1958) exploratory factor analysis approach to growth curves and incorporated it into the CFA and SEM framework and software. Meredith and Tisak's (1984, 1990) work marks the transition to the contemporary factor analysis approach to growth curves. Like the earlier factor analysis approaches to growth curve modeling, they used the factor loadings to determine the shape of the growth curves and the predicted values of the factors as the random coefficients or weights that determined the influence of the corresponding curve on the case. But unlike previous research, they used a CFA model, not EFA.

This difference was important for several reasons. It forced the issue of identification that is essential to CFA models. Meredith and Tisak discussed identification conditions that corrected the underidentification (or rotation problem) raised in the previous literature on using factor analysis for growth curves. For example, Meredith and Tisak's (1990) "freed loading" model is an interesting hybrid of the EFA method, where all loadings were freely estimated but underidentified, and exchanged this for a CFA approach with a slope factor that has two loadings set to zero and one, respectively, and the rest freely estimated. These latter constraints are sufficient to identify the model, yet provide flexibility in fitting a curve by using the freely estimated factor loadings.[6] The simulated data example from Meredith and Tisak (1990) illustrated the freed loading model and its use in determining the functional form of a growth curve. Plots of the fixed and estimated factor loadings with time helped them to find the nonlinear functional form that generated the data.

Meredith and Tisak's (1984, 1990) transition from the traditional EFA into CFA also enabled the use of likelihood ratio tests to compare the fit of different LCMs for the same data. For instance, the fit of a linear LCM with the factor loadings set to $0, 1, 2, \ldots$ could be compared to the same model where just two loadings are fixed and the others are freely estimated. They also gave a LCM for a cohort sequential design where a long span of ages of individuals is studied longitudinally within a relatively short period of time. An empirical example illustrated its use (Meredith & Tisak, 1990).

Another contribution of Meredith and Tisak's (1984, 1990) that should not be underestimated was their clear demonstration of how conventional SEM software was capable of implementing the LCMs. Their use of LISREL type notation and their references to SEM programming enabled most researchers with the appropriate data and access to SEM software capable of estimating LCMs. Thus the Meredith and Tisak (1984, 1990) papers helped to form the basis for the contemporary SEM approach to LCMs.

LESSONS FOR CONTEMPORARY LATENT CURVE MODELS

Although the placement of growth curve models into the CFA model has created many opportunities for new analysis and testing, the current practice of LCMs has lost some valuable aspects of the case-by-case and traditional factor analysis approaches. One aspect largely lost in contemporary LCMs, but present in the case-by-case growth curve approach, is the emphasis on the individual case. The

---

[6]Bollen and Curran (2006) give more details on the identification conditions of the freed loading model in LCMs and give other conditions that must be met for identification.

traditional individual growth curve modelers estimated their model for each case and had parameter estimates for all in the sample. Many contemporary researchers using LCMs direct attention to the covariance matrix and means of the repeated measures and away from the individual. This is unfortunate in that examination of individual cases reveal the fit of the model at the individual level. Outliers from such an examination can provide insight into possible changes to the model or the need for transformation of the variables. The loss of the individual is not a necessary consequence of LCMs. Indeed, predicting the value of the factor scores together with the factor loadings would enable plots of individual trajectories compared to observed trajectories. Tucker (1966) illustrated this approach in the context of EFA, but there is no reason that this could not be done with the CFA model for LCMs (see Bollen & Curran, 2006). This is not without complications, such as selecting the optimal method for factor score prediction. But directing attention to individual cases would have more rewards than drawbacks.

Closely related to the neglect of the individual in current LCM practice is the greater neglect of nonlinear trajectories in contemporary LCM practice than was true in earlier research. Wishart (1938), for instance, considered linear, logarithmic transforms of time, and a quadratic model in his case-by-case analysis of the weights of pigs. Griliches (1957) employed a logistic curve for repeated measures of hybrid corn. More generally, the case-by-case approach to growth curves applications exhibited greater sensitivity to the issue of nonlinear functional forms than is true of contemporary LCMs. Linear trajectories in LCMs seem the norm with an occasional treatment of quadratic functional forms. Least one might think that this linear functional form bias is due to the factor analysis approach to LCM, consider the work of Tucker (1966) with EFA. Tucker fitted highly nonlinear forms and made use of the estimated factor loadings that could shift with the patterns found in the data. Meredith and Tisak (1984, 1990) illustrated a modified freed loading model, which is flexible in modeling nonlinear patterns of change in the trajectories. Plots of these freed loadings against time suggest the nature of the nonlinearity that might lead to modifications. Others are examining methods to incorporate more flexible nonlinear functional forms in LCMs (e.g., Bollen & Curran, 2006; Browne, 1993). There also is the possibility of selecting different metrics of time rather than the wave of measurement (e.g., age, grade) or to use transformations (e.g., square root, logarithmic) of the metric of time. If we return to comparing individual predicted and observed trajectories as I discussed in the last paragraph, then such plots could be helpful in exploring nonlinearity. Thus, researchers can pursue nonlinearity in LCMs as was done in the past.

The traditional EFA approach to growth curve models also was valuable in its extraction of multiple rather than single factors to reproduce the growth trajectories observed in the data. Baker (1954) and Tucker (1958), for example, extracted more than a single factor for the growth curves. Each set of factor loadings described a curve and the factor scores gave the influence of that curve on the individual pattern of change. This gave them a great deal of flexibility to match trajectories. The main drawback of the EFA approach was the underidentification (rotation) problem when more than one factor is extracted. LCMs generally are restricted to two or three factors including the first that serves to measure individual differences in initial values. To extend multiple factors to the LCMs requires that identification problem be solved for multiple factors, particularly with the use of freed loadings. Thus, the traditional factor analysis and individual growth curve modeling approaches offer lessons on how we can improve contemporary methods.

CONCLUSIONS

A primary focus of this chapter was to examine the origins of the contemporary LCM in the case-by-case growth curve and factor analysis traditions. A useful way to conclude is to review the basic ingredients that make up LCMs and to summarize what ingredients were contributed by what works. Though any list is somewhat arbitrary, I identify seven characteristics necessary to the development of LCMs: (a) an approach that permits individual trajectories, (b) the ability to include prespecified linear or nonlinear trajectories, (c) formulation of the model as a factor analysis, (d) the treatment of random trajectory coefficients as latent variables, (e) the ability to estimate shapes of curves or trajectories, (f) identifying the model parameters, and (g) full incorporation of LCMs into SEMs so as to take advantage of the associated software and tools.

The preceding historical review indicates that the idea of individual trajectories is one that was contributed by the traditional growth curve model approach. Early literature in this area focused on group trajectories, but later research gave more attention to individual differences in growth curves. Wishart (1938) and Griliches (1957), whom I reviewed, are good examples of studies of individual growth curves. These same two studies are good illustrations from the growth curve literature that use linear and nonlinear trajectories. The functional forms that they included were specified in advance, although the specific parameter values were estimated separately for each case.

The demonstration that growth curve models could be formulated in a traditional factor analysis model marks a major transition to the LCMs. Baker (1954) gave an early empirical demonstration of this with traditional factor analysis. Rao (1958) and Tucker (1958) provided a more formal grounding on the connection between growth curve models and factor analysis. These same three references contributed two other key ingredients. They showed that the random coefficients of the trajectories could be treated as latent factors and they illustrated that rather than prespecified functional forms, the factor loadings provided flexible estimates of the curves.

A problem with the traditional factor analysis approach to growth curve models was that the arbitrariness of the rotation and the accompanying factor loadings created an arbitrariness of the curves. This identification issue was addressed in Meredith and Tisak's (1984, 1990) creation of the LCMs. In addition, their work clearly demonstrated that the LCM could be incorporated into SEMs so that researchers could easily estimate and test these models, and also could take full advantage of the other features (e.g., multiple group analysis) available in SEM software.

The review of the literature suggests both the continuity of the LCMs with earlier work, but also its points of departure. Furthermore, the review suggested that the previous growth curve and factor analysis literatures are more than of just historical interest. Rather, these past works still hold lessons for future research. Specifically, one example is that contemporary practice using LCMs has leaned too heavily on analyzing covariance matrices and means and it has neglected the individual. Past growth curve models heavily focused on individual trajectories. Even some of the early factor analysis approaches gave attention to individual trajectories and their match to the predicted changes (e.g., Tucker, 1966). A return to the individual in LCMs through the prediction of factor scores and predicted trajectories would be beneficial.

Another lesson we should take from past work is the flexibility of estimating curves via factor loadings. The early factor analysis literature such as Baker (1954) and Tucker (1958) estimated factor loadings that gave great flexibility in the fitting of curves. Plots of these factor loadings against the metric of time might suggest specific functional forms or transformations of the repeated measure or the time metric. A closely related feature of the early factor analysis literature was the use of multiple factors to describe trajectories. Tucker (1966) gives an early demonstration of the power of this approach in matching individual growth patterns. Using multiple factors and freed loadings does raise issues of identification, but given the flexibility that this could bring suggests that it would be worthwhile to pursue identified multifactor models. In brief, contemporary LCMs could still benefit from incorporating features from the traditional growth curve and factor analysis approaches to change.

REFERENCES

Baker, G. A. (1954). Factor analysis of relative growth. *Growth*, *18*, 137–143.

Bentler, P. M. (1985). *Theory and implementation of EQS: A structural equations program, manual for program version 2*. Los Angeles: BMDP Statistical Software, Inc.

Boker, S. M. (2001). Differential structural equation modeling of intraindividual variability. In L. M. Collins & A. G. Sayer (Eds.), *New methods for the analysis of change* (pp. 5–27). Washington, DC: American Psychological Association.

Bollen, K. A., & Curran, P. J. (2006). *Latent curve models: A structural equation perspective*. New York: Wiley.

Browne, M. W. (1993). Structured latent curve models. In C. M. Cuadras & C. R. Rao (Eds.), *Multivariate analysis: Future directions 2* (pp. 171–197). New York: Elsevier Science.

Cronbach, L. J. (1967). Year-to-year correlations of mental tests: A review of the Hofstaetter analysis. *Child Development*, *38*, 283–289.

Griliches, Z. (1957). Specification bias in estimates of production functions. *Journal of Farm Economics, 39*, 8–20.

Jöreskog, K. G. (1969). A general approach to confirmatory maximum likelihood factor analysis. *Psychometrika, 34* (2), 183–202.

Jöreskog, K. G., & Sörbom, D. (1981). *LISREL V: Analysis of linear structural relationships by maximum likelihood*. Chicago: National Educational Resources.

McArdle, J. J. (1988). Dynamic but structural equation modeling of repeated measures data. In J. R. Nesselroade & R. B. Cattell (Eds.), The handbook of multivariate experimental psychology (2nd ed., pp. 561–614). New York: Plenum.

McArdle, J. J. (2001). A latent difference score approach to longitudinal dynamic structural analyses. In R. Cudeck, S. du Toit, & D. Sörbom (Eds.), *Structural equation modeling: Present and future* (pp. 342–380). Lincolnwood, IL: Scientific Software International.

Meredith, W., & Tisak, J. (1984). *On "Tuckerizing" curves*. Paper presented at the annual meeting of the Psychometric Society, Santa Barbara, CA.

Meredith, W., & Tisak, J. (1990). Latent curve analysis. *Psychometrika, 55* (1), 107–122.

Pearl, R. (1924). *Studies in human biology*. Baltimore: Williams & Wilkens Co.

Rao, C. R. (1958). Some statistical methods for comparison of growth curves. *Biometrika, 51*, 83–90.

Reed, L. J. (1921). On the correlation between any two functions and its application to the general case of spurious correlation. *Journal of the Washington Academy of Sciences, 11*, 449–455.

Rogosa, D., Brandt, D., & Zimowski, M. (1982). A growth curve approach to the measurement of change. *Psychological Bulletin, 92*, 726–748.

Thurstone, L. L. (1937). Psychology as a quantitative rational science. *Science, 85*, 227–232.

Tucker, L. R. (1958). Determination of parameters of a functional relation by factor analysis. *Psychometrika, 23*, 19–23.

Tucker, L. R. (1966). Learning theory and multivariate experiment: Illustration by determination of generalized learning curves. In R. B. Cattell (Ed.), Handbook of multivariate psychology (pp. 476–501). Chicago: Rand McNally.

Wishart, J. (1938). Growth-rate determinations in nutrition studies with the bacon pig, and their analysis. *Biometrika, 30* (1/2), 16–28.

Young, C. H., Savola, K. L., & Phelps, E. (Eds.). (1991). *Inventory of longitudinal studies in the social sciences*. Newbury Park, CA: Sage.

CHAPTER 7

Five Steps in the Structural Factor Analysis of Longitudinal Data

John J. McArdle
University of Southern California

It is well known that the factor analysis model was created and developed by Charles Spearman (1904) in his classical studies of the concept of *general intelligence*. In this conception, a large number of observed behaviors are a direct result of a smaller number of unobserved or latent sources termed *common factors*. Over the next 25 years, Spearman posed more technical problems and invented several key mathematical and statistical solutions still used to solve psychometric and substantive problems (Spearman, 1927; see also Deary, Bell, Bell, Campbell, & Fazal, 2004). He formalized the basic algebraic model for multiple observed variables based on a single common latent variable. He considered different ways that the parameters in this model could be uniquely calculated. He considered ways to evaluate the statistical goodness-of-fit of this model to empirical data. In this classic work, Spearman raised the general factor model to the high level of a scientifically respectable theory by creating a strong and rejectable method for an improved understanding of individual differences in cognitive abilities.

The first theme of this chapter is a focus on Spearman's strategies to examine the mathematical and statistical evidence used to evaluate common factor theories. Forms of *exploratory* or *traditional factor analysis* have now been applied in a wide variety of empirical studies to isolate and identify latent factors representing parsimonious and reliable sources of differences between individuals and groups (e.g., Cattell, 1971; Mulaik, 1972, 1987). During the past three decades, there has been an increasing use on what can be termed *confirmatory* or *structural factor analysis* (see McArdle, 1996; McDonald, 1985; Nesselroade & Baltes, 1984). In contrast to traditional methods, the newer structural factor methods allow precise and meaningful restrictions on parameters in any common factor model, including statistical tests of hypotheses about factor loadings and factor scores. As a result, these structural factor techniques are useful in dealing with formal hypotheses about longitudinal data, including hypotheses of *factorial invariance*.

As a second theme of this chapter, we examine structural factor models designed for use with a collection of information on the same individuals over some period of time—*longitudinal data* with *repeated measurements* (Nesselroade & Baltes, 1979). In a general sense, this bridging of longitudinal data with factor analysis is an attempt to provide clarity about the nature of changes in the underlying factors in both: (a) the *qualitative* meaning of the factors over time, and (b) the *quantitative* differences in the level of the factors over time. That is, although the same variables are measured at repeated occasions, this does not ensure that the same constructs are being measured at each occasion. It is common to assume that a lack of construct equivalence can occur when (a) there is an experimental intervention between occasions, or (b) if the persons measured have developed in different ways, or (c) if both have occurred.

The third theme of this chapter is to offer a framework for dealing within the factor analysis of multiple-wave longitudinal data on the same group of persons and variables. This chapter offers five basic building blocks, or steps along the way, as a methodological strategy to deal with any longitudinal factor analysis. We assume that multivariate data (M) have only been collected on a relatively few time points (e.g., $T = 2$ to 10) on a relatively large sample (e.g., $N > 50*T$). This collection is often referred to as "panel data" or "cohort-sequential" data, and "times-series" analysis (e.g., where $T > N$) will not directly be considered. In Step 1, we define the common factor model for single-occasion data and highlight key issues about goodness-of-fit and factor rotation. In Step 2, we use the common factor model to deal with the analysis of two-occasion data, and we focus on alternative models of factor invariance and change over time. In Step 3, we consider new techniques for dealing with longitudinal mean changes, incomplete data, and factor rotation. In Step 4, we expand these common factor model concepts for use with data from more than two occasions based on traditional modeling concepts. In Step 5, we extend these models and examine alternative forms of the dynamic relationship of factor scores over time. We conclude with a discussion of related factor analysis models for repeated measures data, and future issues of current concern. To preserve space, key references are only presented at the beginning of each section.

STEP 1: BASIC ISSUES IN THE STRUCTURAL FACTOR ANALYSIS OF SINGLE-OCCASION DATA

It is usually a reasonable idea to start a multivariate longitudinal analysis by dealing with the problems apparent using only a single-occasion of data. These data can come from a specific occasion of testing (e.g., the first, the last), from one occasion of testing (e.g., year 2005 data), or from a common age of testing (e.g., as adults), but at first we ignore the available longitudinal information. Useful references for this first step include Thurstone (1947), Jöreskog (1969), Lawley and Maxwell (1971), Cattell (1971, 1987), Mulaik (1972), McDonald (1985), Browne and Cudeck (1993), and McArdle (1996).

The "Structure" of the Common Factor Model

To clarify the key issues, we now use a formal notation for the common factor model. Let us first assume we have collected information on $n = 1$ to N people on $m = 1$ to M measures. We represent measures for each person in the $(M \times 1)$ vector Y where, for simplicity, the subscript n is often assumed but not written. In the case of single occasion data we can subtract the observed means to obtain deviation scores ($Y^* = Y - m_y$). The linear factor model for $m = 1$ to M variables with $k = 1$ to K common factors is written as

$$Y^* = \Lambda f + u \quad \text{and} \quad E\{ff'\} = \Phi, \; E\{uu'\} = \Psi^2, \qquad \text{(Equation 7.1)}$$

where the $(K \times 1)$ vector f represents the common factor scores, the $(M \times K)$ matrix Λ represents the factor loadings relating the common factors to observed measures, and the $(M \times 1)$ vector u represents the *unique* factor scores for each measure. We presume a $(K \times K)$ symmetric matrix of common factor covariances Φ, with an $(M \times M)$ diagonal matrix of unique factor variances in the main diagonal of Ψ^2. (All Greek letters here refer to estimated parameters—that is, factor scores are not estimated, so we use f not η.) Most importantly, the unique factors are presumed to be uncorrelated with each other ($E\{u_i u'_j\} = 0$), and uncorrelated with the common factors ($E\{fu'\} = 0$) These standard assumptions are used to allow an indirect test of the fit of the common factor hypothesis and also imply the factor loadings Λ to be conditional linear regression coefficients.

These assumptions lead us directly to the classical set of expectations for the $(M \times M)$ symmetric matrix Σ of covariances for all measured variables. We can write the *structural expectations* for the common factor model as

$$E\{Y*Y*'\} = E\{[\Lambda f + u][\Lambda f + u]', \quad \text{or} \quad \Sigma = \Lambda \Phi \Lambda' + \Psi^2, \quad \text{(Equation 7.2)}$$

The final elements of these equations are termed the *structural covariance hypotheses* of a K common factor model.

In the first substantive case studied by Spearman (1904), the number of common factors was presumed to be $K = 1$. This structural model is depicted in the path diagram of Figure 7–1a to help visualize the implications of all the structural equations. In this diagram, squares are used to represent the observed or *manifest variables* (e.g., Y and X) and circles to represent the unobserved or *latent variables*

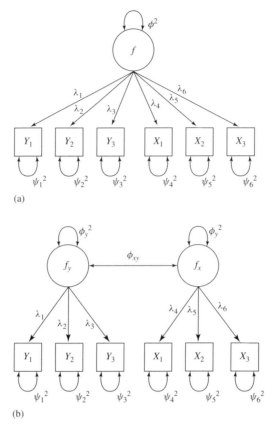

(a)

(b)

FIGURE 7–1.   Path diagrams of for the structural factor analysis of single-occasion data. (a) A structural path diagram of a one common-factor model. (b) A structural path diagram of a two common-factor model.

(e.g., f). The factor loadings (λ) are drawn as one-headed arrows (from f to Y) and represent the regression slope of the factor score on the observed score. The two-headed arrows are used to represent variance or covariance terms.

Model Fitting and Evaluating Goodness-of-Fit

One of the most important aspects of this structural approach is that this technique can be used to reject the common factor hypothesis. This explicit definition of the structural factor model suggests: (a) for some population of individuals P, (b) if the K-common factor model of Equation 7.1 holds, then (c) the covariances among the M variables Y in that population should exhibit a Σ consistent with equation 7.2. In applied research, of course, we can only hope to have a representative sub-sample of persons from the population, so we deal with this problem as a statistical issue of goodness-of-fit.

Using these classical factor analysis definitions, we can define a broad scalar index of differences between observations and expectations in the shorthand notation of

$$L^2 \simeq \sum_{i=1}^{S} (\mathbf{C} - \mathbf{\Sigma})^2 \mathbf{\Omega}^{-1} \qquad \text{(Equation 7.3)}$$

where $\mathbf{C}$ is the $(M \times M)$ symmetric matrix of observed covariance statistics (with $S = M(M + 1))/2$ elements), and $\mathbf{\Omega}$ is an $(M \times M)$ symmetric weight matrix used to obtain specific estimates:that is, $\mathbf{\Omega} = \mathbf{C}$ or $\mathbf{\Omega} = \mathbf{\Sigma}$. If we calculate the parameters based on the principle of *maximum likelihood estimation* (MLE where $\mathbf{\Omega} = \mathbf{\Sigma}$) we obtain a *likelihood ratio statistic* (L^2) of "misfit." Under standard assumptions (e.g., normality of the residuals) it has been shown that the L^2 follows a χ^2 distribution with df equal to the number of statistics minus the number of parameters estimated. We use L^2 type tests to ask, "Should we reject the hypothesis of local independence given K-common factors?" Often we rephrase this question as, "Are the observed data *consistent* with the hypothetical model?" or "Is the model plausible?" or "Does the model fit?"

As in every statistical model (e.g., regression), there is a tradeoff between accuracy (e.g., closer fit) and parsimony (e.g., numbers of parameters estimated). Fit indices based on penalties are now popular, including Aikaike's Information Criterion (AIC) and Schwarz's Bayesian Information Criterion (BIC). One useful criterion of fit is the *Root Mean Square Error of Approximation*, written as

$$\varepsilon_a = \{[L^2/(N-1)]/df - [1/(N-1)]\}^{1/2}. \qquad \text{(Equation 7.4)}$$

This equation shows the ε_a is a rescaling of the likelihood into an index of the *misfit per person and per degree-of-freedom*. Among other benefits, this index of fit can be compared across many different kinds of experiments, even those with very large sample sizes. Browne & Cudeck (1993) emphasized the sampling distribution of ε_a, and proposed $\varepsilon_a < .05$ as a "close fit" of the structural factor model. While a strict adherence to statistical cutoff rules are not fully justified across different kinds of experiments and data, the case for using close fit criteria (rather than perfect fit) is compelling and useful in most cases.

Factor Rotation and Simple Structure

One of the classic problems in common factor analysis is the possibility of the need for multiple factors. In Figure 7–1b we use the same factor model notation (Equation 7.1 to Equation 7.4) to define one specific alternative form of a $K = 2$ common factor model. Here the first common factor (f_y) is indicated by three variables $(Y_1, Y_2,$ and $Y_3)$, the second factor (f_x) is indicated by three other variables $(X_4, X_5,$ and $X_6)$. The two common factors both have variance (ϕ_y^2, ϕ_x^2) and a non-zero covariance (ϕ_{yx}).

In a *confirmatory approach* to factor analysis, a variety of alternative models and the salient loadings are stated in advance of the model fitting. This is illustrated in Figure 7–1b where a restricted two-factor model is considered. First, the variables Y_1, Y_2, and Y_3 are allowed to load only on factor f_1, so the description of this factor is based on the common description of these variables. Second, the variables Y_4, Y_5, and Y_6 are allowed to load only on factor f_2, so the description of this second factor is based on the common description of these other variables. Even if the factors are orthogonal (i.e., uncorrelated) in the population, due to the practical necessity of sampling of individuals from a population, it is always reasonable for common factors in a model to be correlated. If these restrictions do not fit (i.e., $\varepsilon_a > .05$) then we examine alternatives with more loadings, different loadings, or more common factors.

In contrast, *an exploratory approach* to factor analysis approach starts with a less restrictive multiple factor model and considers a more global test of the fit of any K-factor model. For any K-factor solution (Λ) we define a $(K \times K)$ transformation matrix $\mathbf{T}$,

$$\Lambda^* = \Lambda \mathbf{T}^{-1}, \; \Phi^* = \mathbf{T}\Phi\mathbf{T}', \; \text{so} \; \Sigma = \Lambda^* \, \Phi^* \, \Lambda' + \Psi^2, \quad \text{(Equation 7.5)}$$

and we achieve the same fit with a new set of rotated factor loadings (Λ^*) and a new set of rotated factor covariances (Φ^*). It is now well known that the minimum requirement to uniquely identify a K-factor factor model is to place K^2 (the number of elements of $\mathbf{T}$) fixed constraints in Λ and Φ. If we impose exactly K^2 constraints, we achieve an *exactly identified* rotation with the optimal fit for a K-factor solution. Typically, K constraints are placed on the main diagonal of $\Phi = \mathbf{I}$ and $K(K - 1)$ are placed on the columns of Λ (see Jöreskog, 1969). In an important insight into the development of traditional factor analysis, Thurstone (1947) proposed *simple structure* as a solution to the optimal choice of these constraints. The Simple structure concept was initially based on moving tests from one battery to another, but can now be written as a set of structural restrictions (see Browne, 2001).

In contemporary uses of structural factor analysis, we can impose more than K^2 constraints and obtain an *overidentified* or *unrotatable* solution, but this restricted model Σ might not fit the observed $\mathbf{C}$ very well. Often these hypotheses are based on simple factor patterns, especially those where each measured variable loads on one and only one factor (i.e., Fig. 7–1b). In contemporary uses of structural factor analysis the choice of these constraints is used to test the critical hypotheses, and the cost due to these restrictions is judged in the same way as described (i.e., using χ^2, *df*, and ε_a). A simple structure pattern is not a necessary requirement for a good structural factor analysis, but the set of alternative models considered for the single occasion data is important because this information will be carried over in all further longitudinal steps.

STEP 2: LONGITUDINAL CHANGES AND THE FACTOR ANALYSIS OF TWO-OCCASION DATA

The repeated observation of multiple variables leads to a broader and more focal set of questions about changes over time (or experimental condition). To start these kinds of analyses, we first select a set of data that only represent two occasions of measurement. Two occasions of data provide a first opportunity to characterize some of the key longitudinal questions about change. These data can come from the first and second occasion, or the first and last occasions, or the two most substantively meaningful occasions. References for this second include Meredith (1964), step Corballis and Traub, (1970), Nesselroade (1970), Hakstain (1973), Nesselroade and Cable (1974), McDonald (1984), Burr and Nesselroade (1990), Horn and McArdle (1992), McArdle and Nesselroade (1994), and Meredith and Horn (2001).

A Longitudinal Factor Analysis Model

In two-occasion longitudinal data where the same variables ($Y[1]$ and $Y[2]$) are repeatedly measured at a second occasion (over time, or over age, etc.) we typically remove the means and start with deviation scores ($Y[t]^* = Y[t] - m_y[t]$) and write

$$Y[1]^* = \Lambda[1]f[1] + u[1] \text{ and } Y[2]^* = \Lambda[2]f[2] + u[2] \qquad \text{(Equation 7.6)}$$

where each matrix now has a bracketed 1 or 2 designating the occasion of measurement. Given the same assumptions, we assume a set of expectations for the joint covariance matrix of both occasions in terms of ($2M \times 2M$) matrix with three subpartitions

$$\Sigma[1, 1] = \Lambda[1]\Phi[1, 1]\Lambda[1]' + \Psi[1, 1]^2,$$

$$\Sigma[2, 2] = \Lambda[2]\Phi[2, 2]\Lambda[2]' + \Psi[2, 2]^2, \text{ and} \qquad \text{(Equation 7.7)}$$

$$\Sigma[1, 2] = \Lambda[1]\Phi[1, 2]\Lambda[2]' + \Psi[1, 2].$$

The first two submatrices ($\Sigma[1,1]$ and $\Sigma[2,2]$) show the structural factor model within each occasion and the third submatrix ($\Sigma[1,2]$) shows the structure of the model between the two occasions. The structure of this last submatrix permits over-time covariance within the common factors ($\Phi[1,2]$) and within the unique factors on the diagonal of $\Psi[1,2]$ but not between common and unique factors over time. Figure 7–2a is a path diagram of this two-occasion deviation score model (McArdle & Nesselroade, 1994).

This organization of the factor model permits a few key questions to be examined using specific model restrictions. The first question we can evaluate is whether or not the same number of factors are present at both occasions—"Is the number $K[1] = K[2]$?" Based on this evaluation, we can also ask questions about the invariance of the factor loadings $\Lambda[t]$ over time—"Does $\Lambda[1] = \Lambda[2]$?" Another set of questions can be asked about the invariance of the factor score $f[t]$ over time—"For all persons N, is $f[1]_n = f[2]_n$?" This last question is examined through the correlations over time—"Does $\rho[1, 2] = 1$?" As many researchers have noted, these questions about the stability of the factor pattern and the stability of the factor scores raise both methodological and substantive issues. Most usefully, this use of multiple indicators allows us to clearly separate the stability due to (a) the internal

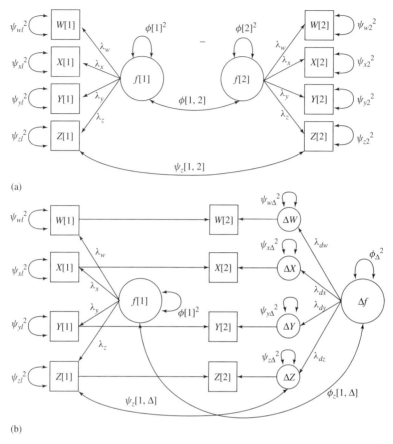

(a)

(b)

FIGURE 7–2.   Path diagrams of longitudinal structural factor analysis of two-occasion data. (a) A longitudinal model of "factor invariance over time" (after Jöreskog, 1977). (b) A "factor of difference scores" model (from McArdle & Nesselroade, 1994).

consistency reliability of the factors and (b) the test–retest correlation of the factor scores. Each set of model restrictions of factor invariance deals with a different question about *construct equivalence over time*. We can examine the evidence for these questions using the structural goodness-of-fit techniques.

Principles of Factorial Invariance in Longitudinal Data

In a seminal series of papers, Meredith (1964) extended selection theorems to the common factor case (see Meredith & Horn, 2001; Millsap & Meredith, chap. 8, this volume). The initial papers proved the following postulates: If (1) a common factor model Equation 7.2 holds in a population, and (2) samples of persons are selected into subgroups from that population in any way, randomly or nonrandomly, then (3) the factor loadings Λ will remain invariant within each subgroup, (4) but the common and unique factor variances and covariances Φ and Ψ^2 need not remain invariant across these subgroups. These principles of factorial invariance for multiple groups also apply to multiple occasions.

We often start with the primary hypothesis that there are the same numbers of common factors within each occasion (i.e., $K[1] = K[2]$?). Assuming the same numbers of factors are present, we turn to the factor loadings $\Lambda[t]$. These $\Lambda[t]$ are latent variable regression coefficients used to define the meaning and the name we assign to the common factor based on the pattern of relationships with the observed variables. That is, questions about whether or not we have measured the same factor over time are based solely on answering, "Does $\Lambda[1] = \Lambda[2]$?" In structural factor analysis we focus on different hypotheses about the equality of these loadings over time:

1. *Metric Invariance* is the exact equality of *every* loading—$\Lambda[1] = \Lambda[2]$.
2. *Partial Invariance* is the exact equality of *some* loadings—$m\{\Lambda[1]\} = m\{\Lambda[2]\}$.
3. *Configural Invariance* is equality of *zero loadings*—$z\{\Lambda[1]\} = z\{\Lambda[2]\}$.
4. *Noninvariant* is the *lack of equality* of the size or pattern—$\Lambda[1] \neq \Lambda[2]$.

These tests are a fundamental starting point in any traditional longitudinal factor analysis. To the degree we achieve a good fit with metric loading invariance, we can further examine changes in the common factor scores as if they have the properties of repeated measures. These questions about the equality of slopes can be confounded with scale differences so, if any form of rescaling is desired, it must be done using the same mean and standard deviation for all occasions (i.e., $z[t]_n = \{Y[t]_n - m_y[1]\}/s_y[1]$).

In general, the structural factor logic defined here suggests that whether or not we have the same factor over time is not based on the factor score parameters. Of course, the common factor scores $f[t]$ are not directly observed (or uniquely identified), but their variances ($\phi[t]^2$) and covariances ($\phi[t,t+j]$) define the relative position of each individual on the factor scores. But in all forms of invariance already listed, no additional restrictions are imposed on the covariances of the common factors, and this differs from prior research on this problem that focused on the stability of the factor scores. Orthogonality restrictions are important in any structural models, but these restrictions are avoided here when they seem inconsistent with the logic of Meredith's theorems.

Two occasions also allows the examination of additional forms of invariance of the unique variances over time (i.e., $\Psi[1, 1]^2 = \Psi[2, 2]^2$). If some or all of the unique variances are deemed equal, we have a simplification of the factorial descriptions—all covariation over time can be captured among the common factor scores. But it also seems reasonable to relax restrictions on the covariance over time among the parallel unique factors in the diagonal of $\Psi[1,2]$, and one of these is depicted as the dashed line in Figure 7–2a. These parameters represent *parallel specific factors over time* (and not the popular oxymoron "correlated errors"), and can simplify the interpretation of the other model parameters, so these parameters should be allowed in any longitudinal factor analyses.

Alternatives Based on Longitudinal Difference Scores

The model of Figure 7–2a is the most typical structural factor model examined with longitudinal data, but it is not the only useful organization of these data. One of the purposes of collecting longitudinal data is to examine changes over time, so it is useful to reconsider the model with change as a primary goal. In this context we can rewrite a factor model with a simple set of *difference scores* as

$$\Delta Y = Y[2] - Y[1] \text{ or } Y[2] = Y[1] + \Delta Y$$
$$\Delta f = f[2] - f[1] \text{ or } f[2] = f[1] + \Delta f \qquad \text{(Equation 7.8)}$$
$$\Delta u = u[2] - u[1] \text{ or } u[2] = u[1] + \Delta u$$

where the Δ operator is used to represent vectors of first differences among manifest or latent scores. Assuming the factor model of Equation 7.6 holds, we can write

$$
\begin{aligned}
Y[2] - Y[1] &= \{\Lambda[2]f[2] + u[2]\} - \{\Lambda[1]f[1] + u[1]\} \\
&= \{\Lambda[2](f[1] + \Delta f) + (u[1] + \Delta u)\} - \{\Lambda[1]f[1] + u[1]\} \\
\Delta Y &= (\Lambda[2] - \Lambda[1])f[1] + \Lambda[2]\Delta f + \Delta u.
\end{aligned}
$$
$$\text{(Equation 7.9)}$$

This final model suggests the changes in the observed scores can be assessed in three parts—(a) the differences in the loadings over time ($\Lambda[2] - \Lambda[1]$) multiplied by the initial common factor score ($f[1]$); (b) the loadings at time 2 multiplied by the differences in the factor scores (Δf); and (c) the differences in the unique factors (Δu). It is most interesting that this difference score form does not alter the interpretation or statistical testing of factor invariance over time. If the factor loadings are invariant over time ($\Lambda[2] = \Lambda[1]$), then the first term in the model drops out and the result is $\Delta Y = \Lambda \, \Delta f + \Delta u$. This result is practically useful If the loadings are invariant over time, the factor pattern *between* occasions equals the factor pattern within occasions. This is not a necessary result so the differences in the between and *within* factor loadings may be meaningful.

This basic result for difference scores is consistent with previous multivariate work on this topic, especially by Nesselroade (e.g., 1970; Nesselroade & Cable, 1974). In this work, a clear distinction was made between factors representing "traits" ($f[1]$) and factors representing "states" (Δf). However, several authors raised issues about the problems of measurement error in the observed difference scores (e.g., Cronbach & Furby, 1970). To illuminate solutions to these problems, McArdle and Nesselroade (1994) wrote the difference scores as part of the model rather than as a part of the data. That is, instead of creating the ΔY by direct calculation in the data (i.e., $Y[2] - Y[1]$), the differences ΔY were implied as latent variables by using *fixed unit weights* (i.e., $Y[2]_n = 1 \times Y[1]_n + 1 \times \Delta Y_n$), and these scores are allowed to be correlated with the starting points.

A path diagram illustrating this structural model is presented in Figure 7–2b. In this figure, the simple restriction of pairs of fixed unit values (one pair per variable) across time allows us to model differences at the level of the observations (ΔY) and at the level of the common factors (Δf). McArdle and Nesselroade (1994) showed how this set of structural equations can be fitted simultaneously and all implications about model testing and goodness-of-fit can be accomplished without the need to calculate difference scores. As it turns out, all results for the factor of difference scores (Fig. 7–2b) model are identical to the results of the previous models—that is, the invariance of the loadings of the starting points and the loadings of latent difference scores are the same. Perhaps most importantly, if metric invariance does not fit both the starting point factors and difference factors, then the factorial interpretation of the changes can be interpreted from these difference loadings.

STEP 3: ADDITIONAL OPPORTUNITIES IN THE FACTOR ANALYSIS OF TWO-OCCASION DATA

The two-occasion data problem allows us to deal with some additionally critical issues. First, the means of the variables should always be considered in any multivariate model even if they are only used to describe the sampling of subjects. Second, we must address the practical and persistent problem of incomplete data due to loss of persons over time. Third, we can reconsider the basic resolution of factorial structure using the longitudinal data, especially as this choice impacts the tests of factorial invariance. References for the third step include Jöreskog (1969), Jöreskog and Sörbom (1979), Horn and McArdle (1981), McArdle (1994), and McArdle and Cattell (1994).

Adding Latent Means in Two-Occasion Longitudinal Data

To deal with means in factor models, we start by writing a common factor model for raw scores with single-occasion data as Equation 7.2 with the addition of

$$E\{f\} = \theta, \, E\{u\} = v, \text{ so } E\{Y\} = \Lambda\theta + v \qquad \text{(Equation 7.10)}$$

where the ($K \times 1$) vector θ represents the means of the common factor scores, while the ($M \times 1$) vector v represents the intercepts of the unique factor scores for each measure. Restrictions on the means of the common factors only if the unique means are fixed (e.g., $v = 0$) so there is the potential for misfit of the observed means ($m_y - \Lambda\theta$).

The inclusion of means in the longitudinal model allows group differences over time to be taken into account. In many studies, this is viewed as a different question typically asked by the classical MANOVA techniques where we calculate an optimal component of mean differences over time, which may or many not be related to the within-occasion covariances. If we have two-occasion data and the factor loadings Λ are invariant over time, we can write the expected means in Equation 7.6 as

$$E\{Y[1]\} = \Lambda\theta[1] + v[1] \text{ and } E\{Y[2]\} = \Lambda\theta[2] + v[2]. \qquad \text{(Equation 7.11)}$$

If we can further assume all intercepts are equal $(v[2] - v[1])$, then the difference in the observed means over time must be accounted for by the latent means $(\theta[d] = \theta[2] - \theta[1])$. This simplification represents another important multivariate hypothesis—"Are all the mean changes over time in Y[t] accounted for by changes in the common factors f[t]?"

One benefit of including mean restrictions at this step is that this classical question of mean differences in multivariate analysis is directly related to the question of factorial invariance. In such models, we are interested in the mean changes over time, and this focus naturally leads to another variation on the latent difference Equation 7.9. We can write a latent difference score at the factor score level by forcing unit weights (i.e., $f[2]_n = 1 \times f[1]_n + 1 \times \Delta f_n$). the key restrictions are that all factor loadings (Λ) and mean intercepts (v) are forced to be equal over time for each variable, so all differences must be accounted for by the parameters of the factor of the difference Δf—that is, the mean (θ_Δ), variance (ϕ_{Δ^2}), and covariance $(\phi[1]_\Delta)$. In this model, the mean changes allow direct evaluation of the mean of the latent difference factor $(\theta_\Delta = \Delta\theta = \theta[2] - \theta[1])$. The additional covariance parameters define the factor scores at time 1 and the changes in the factor scores from time 1 to time 2.

One form of a latent variable model of mean differences is depicted in the path diagram of Figure 7–3a. To represent means or intercepts in the path diagram, we can include a one-headed arrow from a unit constant (drawn as a triangle; e.g., McArdle, 1994) to the variables. In this figure, we assume the intercepts at time 1 are all zero, but we estimated means at time 1 $(\theta[1] = 0)$ and on the difference factor (θ_Δ). This factor model must be fitted using both means and covariances formed from the raw scores.

Including Incomplete Data Over Occasions

As some attrition is expected in every longitudinal study, it seems important to consider alternative ways to deal with subject losses in the context of these models. As it turns out, the mathematical and statistical issues of means and incomplete data in common factor models are directly related to one another and can be investigated as a natural next step for two-occasion data. A typical indicator of attrition bias due to dropouts is expressed as the mean differences at time 1 between the groups of persons who (a) participate at both occasions versus (b) those who dropout

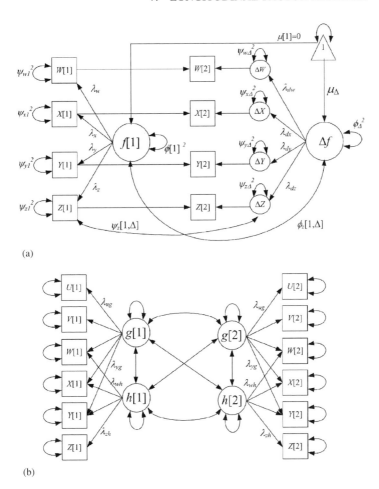

(a)

(b)

FIGURE 7-3.   Path diagrams of alternative structural factor analysis of two-occasion data.
(a) Adding latent means to the latent difference score model (McArdle & Nesselroade, 1994). (b)
Two-factor invariance by confactor rotation with repeated measures.

at the second occasion. For this simple reason, if we allow for models with mean
structures, this leads us to be able to deal with incomplete longitudinal data as well.

   In structural factor models with incomplete data, we estimate the parameters of
the factor model with an overall fitting function written in terms of a sum of misfits
for $g = 1$ to G groups where the multiple groups are now defined by persons with
similar patterns of incomplete data (see McArdle, 1994). All available information
for any subject on any variable is used to build up *maximum likelihood estimates*
(MLE) by a numerical routine that optimizes the model parameters with respect to
any available data.

One underlying assumption of all MLE-based techniques is that the incomplete data are *missing at random* (MAR; Little & Rubin, 1987), and this is a convenient starting point. Under MAR, we imply that the available data points allow us to distinguish any differences in the cases with complete and incomplete data points. Most new structural equation computer programs can be used to estimate the model parameters using raw data under these incomplete data assumptions—for example, Mplus, Mx, AMOS, LISREL, and so forth. In general, this approach makes use of all available data on any measured variable.

The addition of any model for the means combined with a raw score maximum likelihood fitting function also allows the inclusion of all longitudinal and cross-sectional data. This approach provides the best estimate of the parameters of the latent differences as if everyone had continued to participate. The inclusion of all the cases, both complete and incomplete, allows us to examine the impact of attrition, and possibly correct for these biases. We recognize that nonrandom selection to measurement remains a potential confound, especially if it is related to other key variables, such as age-based mortality or cohort differences. But the basic principles and indices of goodness-of-fit provide key test statistics in this two-occasion longitudinal model of latent differences. There are many more complex issues related to these topics, but it is essential to deal with incomplete data using two-occasion data before going onto further analyses.

Longitudinal Alternatives to Simple Structure Rotation

In the absence of metric factorial invariance, we do not assert the same factors are measured with the same variables. Although we might be interested in evidence for a *qualitative* change, it is difficult to go much further because we do not have analytic tools to "compare apples to oranges." Unfortunately, in many applied cases, the tests in the battery are not chosen by a clear simple structure theory, but are packaged together to span a broad range of attributes. In these cases, we might find that some specific variables may be the reason for lack of invariance and rely on a model with "partial invariance."

Different numbers of common factors can emerge at each occasion. But we can always consider any common factor solution to include factors with zero variance (i.e., as nodes or phantom variables). This structural expression is usually not meaningful in single-occasion data, but in two-occasion data, it now plays a role in the evaluation of equal number of factors at each time. That is, we can essentially restate the number of factors problem in terms of "How many factors are needed for the equality of the factor loadings?" or "How many common factors are needed to *accept metric invariance*?" This type of evaluation strategy sets up an important trade-off between the utility of invariant factors versus the cost of dealing with different factors at different occasions.

In some important work on this topic, Cattell (1944) proposed an alternative to Thurstone's simple structure in terms of factorial invariance over multiple groups. In subsequent work on this problem, Meredith (1964) showed covariances were required for Cattell's form of "parallel proportional profiles" with multiple groups (G). Following this lead, McArdle & Cattell (1994) provided conditions for structural factor identification of "confactor rotation" with multiple groups. In multiple-group problems, it is possible to identify all rows and columns of the invariant factor loadings (Λ) model by only requiring restrictions on multiple-group covariances matrices. The extension of this confactor logic to longitudinal factor problems implies there may be a unique but complex set of loadings that are invariant over all occasions T. We can write the multiple group as corresponding multiple occasion constraints as

$$\Phi^{(1)} = \mathbf{I}, \; \Phi^{(2)} = diag(\phi^2), \; \text{with } \Phi^{(g>2)} \text{ and } \Lambda = \text{unrestricted,}$$

which turns into

$$\Phi[1, 1] = \mathbf{I}, \; \Phi[2, 2] = diag(\phi^2), \; \text{with } \Phi[t > 2, t > 2] \text{ and } \Lambda = \text{unrestricted.}$$

$$\text{(Equation 7.12)}$$

This set of restrictions uses covariance constraints within the occasions ($\Sigma[t, t]$) as if each occasion were a separate group but allows all other over-time covariance matrices ($\Phi[t > 2, t > 2]$) to be unrestricted. This result is practically useful because it suggests that the multiple-occasion factor constraints can be placed so that an invariant factor pattern can be identified without any restrictions. These invariant factor loadings may then be rotated using any procedure, but the factor pattern Λ used for all occasions will remain invariant over even after any rotation, and thus can lead to parsimony (i.e., when $T > K$).

The basis for this premise of complex but invariant factors is illustrated in the diagrams of Figure 7–3b. In the left-hand side of this, we presume the existence of a population model with 6 observed variables (V, U, W, X, Y, and Z) and 2 common factors (g and h). As depicted here, the first 2 variables (V and U) load only on the first factor (g), and the last variable (Z) loads only on the second factor (h). This is a complex pattern that might not be clear in a single-occasion simple structure rotation. Our analysis would be simpler if we selected (or measured) only the first second variables and the last second variables, but if we measured the middle four variables, all of which have complex loadings on both factors, we would obtain a complex structural result. Although the latter situation is not desirable, and it is often avoided by good test design (i.e., pure markers), it is a reasonable possibility when we must examine an existing test battery (e.g., the WAIS). The key opportunity that two-occasion data offers is the possibility that this set of loadings is parsimonious—complex but invariant with no cross-occasion loadings.

STEP 4: TRADITIONAL FACTOR MODELS FOR MULTIPLE-OCCASION LONGITUDINAL DATA

The availability of multiple-occasion longitudinal data creates many new opportunities and problems for structural factor analysis. There are many alternative ways to extend the previous ideas to this more general case. In this step, we consider the most traditional and most widely used alternatives. Key references for this step include Jöreskog (1969), Horn (1972), Goldstein and McDonald (1988), McArdle and Woodcock (1997), du Toit and Browne (2001), and Kroonenberg and Oort (2003).

A Longitudinal Factor Model for Multiple Occasions

We assume variables $Y[t]$ are repeatedly measured for $t = 1$ to T occasions, and write

$$Y[t] = \Lambda[t] f[t] + u[t] \qquad \text{(Equation 7.13)}$$

where each matrix now has a subscript t designating the occasion of measurement. Given the same presumptions as before, and we can write a set of expectations for the joint covariance matrix of both occasions in terms of $(TM \times TM)$ matrix with subpartitions

$$\Sigma[t, t] = \Lambda[t]\Phi[t, t]\Lambda[t]' + \Psi[t, t]^2, \text{ for } t = 1 \text{ to } T, \text{ and}$$

$$\Sigma[t, t+j] = \Lambda[t]\Phi[t, t+j]\Lambda[t+j]' + \Psi[t, t+j]$$

$$\text{for } t = 1 \text{ to } T \text{ and } j = 1 \text{ to } T (j \neq t). \text{ (Equation 7.14)}$$

The first sub-matrices ($\Sigma[t, t]$) are symmetric and appear on the main diagonal blocks and show the structural factor model within each occasion. The second submatrices ($\Sigma[t, t+j]$) appear in the off-diagonal blocks and show the structure of the model between the occasions. As in Equation 7.7, the structure of the last submatrix permits over-time covariance within the common factors ($\Phi[t, t+j]$) and within the unique factors ($\Psi[t, t+j]$) but not between common and unique factors over time.

The addition of many occasions ($T > 2$) has multiplied the data available as well as the complexity of the models of invariance we may consider. Nevertheless, the primary questions we can evaluate are the same as those considered for the two occasion data: Are the same number of factors present within all occasions? Are the factor loadings $\Lambda[t]$ invariant over time? Are the factor scores $f[t]$ invariant over time? Are the unique variances $\Psi^2[t]$ invariant over time? Are there parallel over-time specific covariances? Can we account for all group differences using latent means $\theta[t]$?" We can examine any of these alternatives in multi-occasion longitudinal data using the same goodness-of-fit techniques.

Variance Components for Longitudinal Factor Models

The multioccasion longitudinal data has led to a variety of other alternatives. One of the first structural factor models for longitudinal data was presented by Jöreskog (1969) in terms of the structuring of the covariance into different factorial components. We can rewrite the longitudinal factor model as

$$Y[t] = \Lambda_s f[t] + \Lambda_s[t]s + u[t] \qquad \text{(Equation 7.15)}$$

where the observed scores at any occasion are decomposed into (1) a factor ($f[t]$), which is common over all measures and times, (2) a factor (fs), which is specific to each measured variable, and (3) a factor ($u[t]$), which is unique to ever variable at each time. This decomposition of the specific covariances of one variable into a specific factor is not possible without multiple manifestations of the same specific factor, but Jöreskog (1969) recognized that this was possible with multioccasion data of the same measurement. Provisions can also be made for the invariance of the common factors and lack of invariance for the specific factors, allowing a structured form of the prior model of *partial invariance*.

One potential problem with using this model is that the identification constraints needed to separate the common factors and the specific factors are based on an orthogonality restriction typically used in multimode models of Kenny & Zautra (1995), McArdle and Woodcock (1997), and Kroonenberg and Oort (2003). All of these models offer a decomposition of factorial influence based on the orthogonality of the common and specific components, and between the specific factors as well. These alternatives models have interesting interpretations, but they do not provide the same result as some the other models described here (i.e., latent differences model).

A Multilevel Longitudinal Factor Model

The collection of multioccasion longitudinal data creates opportunities for several other alternatives. One practical solution for the problem of factor loading invariance in multioccasion data comes in the form of a *multilevel factor analysis* model (after Goldstein & McDonald, 1988; McArdle & Hamagami, 1996). We can rewrite the longitudinal factor model for a set of individual average scores over time as

$$\begin{aligned} Y[+] &= \Lambda[+]f[+] + u[+] \text{ or} \\ \sum_{t=1}^{T}\{Y[t]\}/T &= \sum_{t=1}^{T}\{\Lambda[t]f[t] + u[t]\}/T, \end{aligned} \qquad \text{(Equation 7.16)}$$

a common factor model for the *between* occasions cross-products $\Sigma[+]$. Similarly, we can use this rewrite the model in terms of T sets of individual deviation scores over time as

$$\begin{aligned} Y[-] &= \Lambda[t-]f[t-] + u[t-] \text{ or} \\ Y[t] - Y[+] &= \Lambda[t]f[t] + u[t]\} - \{\Lambda[+]f[+] + u[+]\} \text{ for } t = 1 \text{ to } T. \end{aligned}$$

(Equation 7.17)

Using this approach, we remove the individual averages over time from the observed scores to obtain deviations for a $(T \times T)$ *within* occasion covariance matrix $\Sigma[-]$ based on $N \times (T - 1)$ pieces of information. The person-centering technique used in Equation 7.17 and Equation 7.18 resembles other classical approaches: (a) a standard between-within factor analysis of family data (Nagoshi, Phillips, & Johnson 1987), (b) the multiple situation FANOVA approach used by Gollob (1968), and (c) the occasion-discriminant approach created by Horn (1972).

Using contemporary structural modeling software (e.g., Mplus, Mx, NLMIXED, etc.) we can carry out a precise form of these operations by fitting both directly. We can next consider Equation 7.16 and Equation 7.17 together by writing the score model as

$$Y[t] = Y[+] + Y[t-] = \Lambda[+]f[+] + u[+]\} + \{\Lambda[t-]f[t-] + u[t-]\}t = 1 \text{ to } T.$$

(Equation 7.18)

In this form of a multilevel model, we consider both a first-order latent variable model ($\Lambda[-]$) for a person in terms of the deviations around the averages over time, and a second-order model ($\Lambda[+]$) of the variation between people over time. By restating the original model in this way, we can now use a structural principle discussed earlier; if the loadings are invariant over time, the factor pattern between occasions $\Lambda[+]$ should equal all the factor pattern within occasions $\Lambda[-]$. Given this setup, in order to test the broad hypothesis of multioccasion loading invariance over time, we simply have to test whether or not the same pair of variable loadings between occasions equals the variable loadings within occasions no matter how many time points are available. Using this multilevel approach, we can also effectively consider cases where each person has different amounts of longitudinal data (i.e., incomplete data due to attrition, etc.).

The process of factorial modeling of longitudinal data is now easily extended to include many occasions. First we fit a one-factor model to up to T occasions of data per person with (a) an $(M \times 1)$ vector of loadings (Λ) equal over all times, (b) M unique variances (Ψ^2) equal over all times, (c) a restricted factor variance at time 1 ($\Phi[1]^2 = 1$), and (d) no restriction on the later factor variances ($\Phi[t > 1]^2$) or covariances ($\Phi[t > 1, t + j]$). Next, we use the same models but we relax the assumption of strict metric invariance over the loadings between occasions and within occasions and examine the change in fit. The relaxation of invariant loadings in the same configuration may yield important information about specific occasions of measurement, and virtually any model can fit or fail. Although the constraints on the between and within occasion matrix yields much smaller restrictions (i.e., dfs) than in other models, the basic result and conclusions are often identical, so the key question remains the same: "Do these data display a reasonable form of invariance over time?" If this test fails, we must conclude that we do not have repeated constructs, and other forms of the factor models might be more useful.

There are a few caveats about the use of this general approach to multiple occasion data based on multilevel factor analysis. First, in the typical multilevel estimation we require the between and within components to be uncorrelated, and this may not be a reasonable assumption for some constructs. Second, and in contrast to other longitudinal latent variables models, information about the time-based order of occasions is not used here. Thus, any representation of the sequence of events over time is not used and is uninformative. Third, the within group estimation of the factor model also does not depend on a strict time order, so within-person and within-measure specific covariance is now aggregated as a part of the overall within-time variance (i.e., no specific over-time covariances). Fourth, in this multilevel format, the MAR assumptions are used, but they are more difficult to evaluate than in other models (e.g., see Fig. 7–3a). Thus, this multilevel model is especially useful at a first stage of multioccasion analysis to test the key questions of factorial invariance. Once metric invariance is established, we can move on to other models in a later stage of analysis (e.g., using latent difference models).

Adding Latent Score Regressions to Longitudinal Factor Models

Once the basic pattern of the common factors are established, it is now quite typical to examine further restrictions on the factor scores. The traditional models used here can be seen to come from the time-series literature (e.g., du Toit & Browne, 2001; Geweke & Singleton, 1981; Molenaar, 1985). One popular model for longitudinal panel data is an autoregressive Markov simplex model applied to the factor scores written as

$$f[t] = \beta f[t-1] + d[t] \qquad \text{(Equation 7.19)}$$

where the common factor scores at a current time ($f[t]$) are essentially predicted by scores on the same factor at an earlier time ($f[t-1]$) plus a disturbance term ($d[t]$). Figure 7–4a presents a picture of this popular model using separate loadings (λ_y and λ_x) for sets of $Y[t]$ and $X[t]$ variables. Due to the inclusion of common factors, this is termed a *Quasi-Markov Simplex* (after Jöreskog, 1970). If we presume the factor loadings are identical over time, then the key hypothesis here is that all over-time information can be accounted for by using the same single factor at each occasion. Of course, the general structure of this model can be extended further to include other predictors as needed, including multiple back-shifts $f[t-2]$, $f[t-3]$, and so fourth (see du Toit & Browne, 2001).

The restrictions of the auto-regressive factor model Equation 7.19 do not necessarily provide a good fit to longitudinal data (e.g., McArdle & Woodcock, 1997). There are many alternatives to consider at this point, but most are based on less restricted regressions (i.e., $\beta[1]$, $\beta[2]$, etc.), or models with multiple factors. For

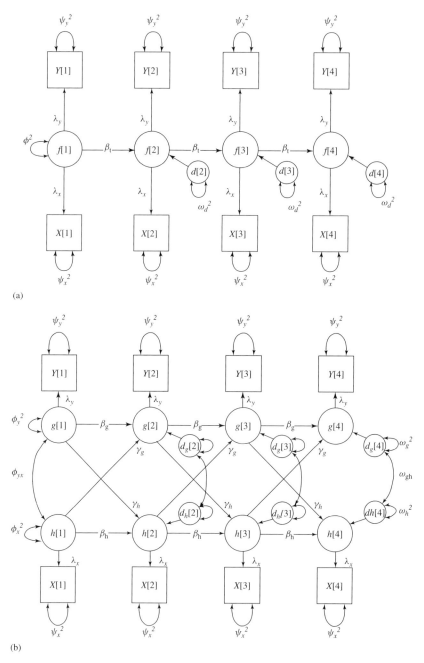

(a)

(b)

FIGURE 7–4.   Path diagrams of traditional models for the structural factor analysis of multioccasion data. (a) A quasi-markov-simplex for common factors (after Jöreskog, 1970). (b) An alternative cross-lagged regression with latent variables.

example, suppose we have a set of Y variables with common factors g and a set of X variables with common factors h, (e.g., Fig. 7–1b), and we write

$$g[t] = \beta_g g[t-1] + \gamma_g g[t-1] + d_y[t] \text{ and}$$
$$h[t] = \beta_h h[t-1] + \gamma_h g[t-1] + d_x[t],$$

(Equation 7.20)

so each common factor is predicted by itself with time-lag parameters (β) and by the other factor with crossed parameter (γ). This is the formal basis of a *cross-lagged latent variable longitudinal model*, and Figure 7–4b presents this kind of model (after Jöreskog, 1970, 1977). It is appropriate to use either model Equation 7.19 or Equation 7.20 when the phenomena under study appear to represent a stationary (nonevolving) process (see Duncan, 1975). In these cases, the direct comparison of fit of longitudinal models Equation 7.19 and Equation 7.20 is a rigorous way to evaluate the number of factors question not available in single-occasion data.

STEP 5: DYNAMIC EXTENSIONS IN THE FACTOR ANALYSIS OF MULTIPLE-OCCASION DATA

If we presume metric factorial invariance holds for most of the key indicators of the factors, the factor scores can also be presumed to have the key property repeated constructs. Given a sequential ordering of the observations, it can also be meaningful to examine systematic changes in the factor scores using more advanced models for repeated observations. These models have been collectively termed *dynamic factor models*, and we consider a few alternatives in this last section. Key references here include Tucker (1966), McArdle (1988), Meredith and Tisak (1990), Browne and du Toit (1991), and McArdle (2001).

Adding Longitudinal Curves to Factor Models

An approach to multivariate dynamic modeling is based on a *latent curve model*, presented as a factor model by Tucker (1958), detailed as a structural model by Meredith and Tisak (1990) and drawn in path diagrams by McArdle (1988, 1991). Although the parameters of a latent curve model are usually estimated from the observed means and covariances, it is possible to estimate a latent curve of the latent scores ($f[t]$). Under metric invariance restrictions, we rewrite the ($K \times 1$) factor scores at each occasion as

$$f[t] = g_0 + A[t]g_1 + d[t]$$

(Equation 7.21)

where the basis weights $A[t]$ are fixed or estimated so the latent scores can be interpreted as constant intercepts g_0, systematic slopes g_1, and random disturbance terms $d[t]$. If we presume a metric invariant factor pattern Λ (with K^2 constraints), we can place fixed constraints on $A[t]$ to represent, say, a linear model (i.e., $A[t] = t$) representing growth of the factor scores. However, if we do not have an a priori hypothesis about the basic shape, we can place minimal constraints (e.g., $\alpha[1] = 0$ and $\alpha[T] = 1$) and describe an optimal shape of the curve of factor scores over time. If we further constrain the intercepts on the observed variables to be equal over time, and we can fix the latent intercept ($\theta_0 = 0$ or 1) and examine the group mean of the slope of the common factor scores (θ_1). Figure 7–5a is a path diagram of this basic model, and includes the means and the deviations of the level and slope scores.

The previous model development also leads to other common factor-based alternatives. For example, we can write a latent curve model for each variable as

$$
\begin{aligned}
Y[t] &= g_{y0} + A[t]g_{y1} + d_y[t] \text{ with} \\
g_{y0} &= \Lambda_0 f_0 + u_0 \text{ and } g_{y1} = \Lambda_1 f_1 + u_1
\end{aligned}
\qquad \text{(Equation 7.22)}
$$

where we introduce the M different sets of basis weights $A[t]$, $(M \times 1)$ latent vectors of intercepts g_{y0}, slopes g_{y1} and residuals $d_y[t]$. In the same model, but at a second level, we introduce a separate factor model for the intercepts (Λ_0) and a factor model for the latent slopes (Λ_1). Due to the often arbitrary position of the intercept (at $t = 0$), we allow the higher order factors of the intercepts (f_0) and the higher order factors of the slopes (f_1) to covary (ϕ_{01}), and the residuals $d_y[t]$ may be correlated across variables within occasions.

This was termed the *factor of curve scores* model by McArdle (1988) and it has not been used very much since. One key feature of this alternative multivariate longitudinal model is that it does not seem to require any form of factor loading invariance; the changes in the measured variables are recast into curve components that are then considered as variables in a higher order factor analysis. However, on a formal basis, the invariance problem is merely shifted up, as it were, to an interpretation of the factors of the intercepts (Λ_0) and factors of the slopes (Λ_1). This alternative now permits us to ask if the loadings of the M intercepts and the slopes are invariant (i.e., "Is $\Lambda_0 = \Lambda_1$?"), and we do not permit arbitrary centering to have any impact on this test statistic. As stated earlier in the two-occasion case, the invariance of the initial levels and slopes has the same interpretation and goodness-of-fit index as the test of invariance of $\Lambda[t]$ over all occasions. But if invariance does not hold at this second level, a substantive interpretation about the difference in the loadings for intercepts and slopes may provide a direct and meaningful summary about the lack of invariance over all occasions. When invariance is not found at this second level, this model has a structural similarity with the canonical components of change model suggested by Harris (1963).

Adding Dynamic Systems Models to Factor Models

In recent research, we recast the previous growth models using latent difference scores (McArdle, 2001). These models encompass the latent growth models just described, but they are formed in a different way and have properties that permit easy extensions to multivariate forms. More formally, we first assume we have

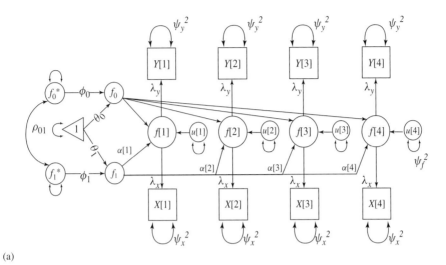

(a)

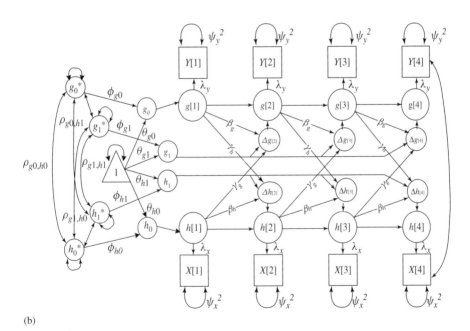

(b)

FIGURE 7–5.   Path diagrams of dynamic extensions for the structural factor analysis of multioccasion data. (a) A latent curve model of the common factors (from McArdle, 1988). (b) A bivariate latent difference score model (from McArdle, 2001).

observed scores $Y[t]$ and $Y[t-1]$ measured over a defined interval of time (Δt), but we assume the latent variables are defined over an equal interval of time ($\Delta t = 1$). This definition of an equal interval latent time scale is nontrivial because it allows us to eliminate Δt from the rest of the equations. This allows us to use latent scores $y[t]$ and $y[t-1]$, residual scores $e[t]$, representing measurement error, and latent difference scores $\Delta y[t]$. Even though this difference $\Delta y[t]$ is a theoretical score, and not simply a fixed linear combination, we can write a structural model for any latent change trajectory by simply writing

$$Y[t]_n = g_{0,n} + \left(\sum_{i=1}^{t} \Delta y[i]_n \right) + u[t]_n. \qquad \text{(Equation 7.23)}$$

This simple algebraic device allows us to generally define the trajectory equation based on a summation ($\Sigma_{i=1,t}$) or accumulation of the latent changes ($\Delta y[t]$) up to time t, and these structural expectations are automatically generated using any standard SEM software (e.g., LISREL, Mplus, Mx, etc.). That is, we do not directly define the basis ($A[t]$) coefficients of a trajectory equation but we directly define changes as an accumulation of the first differences among latent variables.

This latent difference score approach makes it possible to consider many kinds of change models. This is most useful when we start to examine time-dependent interrelationships among multiple-growth processes. In general, we write an expansion of our previous latent difference scores logic as the *bivariate dynamic change score* model

$$\begin{aligned}
\Delta g[t] &= \alpha_g g_{1,n} + \beta_g g[t-1] + \gamma_{gh} h[t-1] + z_g[t], \text{ and} \\
\Delta h[t] &= \alpha_h h_{1,n} + \beta_h h[t-1] + \gamma_{hg} g[t-1] + z_h[t].
\end{aligned} \qquad \text{(Equation 7.24)}$$

In this model, the g_1 and h_1 are the latent slope score that is constant over time, and the changes are based on additive parameters (α_g and α_h), a multiplicative parameters (β_g and β_h), and *coupling* parameters (γ_{gh} and γ_{hg}). The coupling parameter (γ_{gh}) represents the time-dependent effect of latent $h[t]$ on $g[t]$, and the other coupling parameter (γ_{hg}) represents the time-dependent effect of latent $g[t]$ on $h[t]$.

This bivariate dynamic model is described in the path diagram of Figure 7–5b. The key features of this model include the use of fixed unit values (unlabeled arrows) to define $\Delta g[t]$ and $\Delta h[t]$, and equality constraints within a variable (for the α, β, and γ parameters) to simplify estimation and identification. These latent difference score models can lead to more complex nonlinear trajectory equations (e.g., nonhomogeneous equations). These trajectories can be described by writing the implied basis coefficients ($A_j[t]$) as the linear accumulation of first differences for each variable ($\Sigma \Delta g[j], j = 0$ to t). Additional unique covariances within occasions ($u_g[t]$ $u_h[t]$) are possible, but these will be identifiable only when there are multiple ($M > 2$) measured variables within each occasion. These dynamic models permit new features of the factor analytic assessment of the previous models (e.g., McArdle & Hamagami, 2003, 2004; Ferrer & McArdle, 2004).

Longitudinal Rotation to Simple Dynamics

Multiple-occasion data can be used to help resolve the factorial complexity of a population model (e.g., Fig. 7–3b), especially when it is considered in the context of a dynamic model (e.g., Fig. 7–5b). Given a K-factor hypothesis at several occasions, we may identify all factor loadings (Λ) by creating restrictions (e.g., Equation 7.12). But we may also expand upon the possibilities for other restrictions by considering

$$\Phi[1, 2] \;=\; \mathbf{0}, \; \Phi[1, 1] = \mathbf{P}\text{(correlations)}, \; \Phi[2, 2] = diag(\phi^2), \text{ or}$$

$$\Phi[t, t+j] \;=\; diag(\phi^2), \text{or } \Phi[t, t+j] = \mathbf{AB'}.$$

$$\text{(Equation 7.25)}$$

The first set of constraints identifies the invariant K-factor pattern by using information in the cross-time matrices, $\Sigma[t, t+j]$. Although this does free up the restrictions at the first occasion (from $\mathbf{I}$ to $\mathbf{P}$), it requires the factors to be uncorrelated over time ($\Phi[1, 2] = \mathbf{0}$), and this is unlikely with real data. The second set of longitudinal constraints can be formed from restrictions with variables having no cross-correlation over time, $\Phi[t, t+j] = diag(\phi^2)$, or be based on specific dynamic structures with zero elements. In the third set we identify all factor loadings by using latent variable regression restrictions where $\Phi[t, t+j] = \mathbf{AB'}$, so the partial covariances among residual factors are zero. This final set of restriction can be use to identify factor model where we posit "Factor 1 factor is the leader of factor 2." In all cases, we can identify these factors with no restrictions on the factor loadings.

Using model restrictions over time to identify factor loadings was a main theme of work on "Rotation to Smooth Functions" by Arbuckle and Friendly (1977). The focus on invariant factor loadings and, hence, the invariant factors, was initially described as "Rotation to Simple Dynamics" (McArdle & Nesselroade, 1994, 2003). A contemporary approach to selection of these kinds of restrictions can be evaluated by computational procedures for identification, and further explorations of dynamic forms of confactor rotation in longitudinal multiple-occasion data are needed.

DISCUSSION

Summary of the Five-Step Strategy

A five-step strategy was presented here to organize and deal with the complexity of longitudinal factor modeling. Step 1 started the examination of the common-factor alternatives at the first occasion of measurement. These analyses can be carried out while the remainder of the longitudinal data collection is being carried out. In Step 2, we considered two-occasion models, which highlight the information about individual differences in change. The standard-factor models and latent-difference models should be considered. In Step 3, we suggested that it is useful to deal with means, incomplete data, and factor rotation in two-occasion data before going further with models of more than two occasions. In Step 4, we dealt with multiple-occasion data and overviewed some traditional alternatives from a contemporary point of view. In Step 5, we considered longitudinal alternatives with a dynamic focus.

These five steps form a sequence with increasing levels of practical and theoretical inquiry. For these reasons, a longitudinal researcher should consider the issues within each step before moving on to the next step. Of course, it is easy to envision situations where it would be best to apply the steps is a different sequence, or even to focus on just one step for the research. For example, when dealing with multiple-occasion data, it may be most practical to use a pair-wise approach, that is, Step 2 and Step 3 for occasions 2 and 3, and then Step 2 for occasions 3 and 4, and so on. Obviously, models of the complexity of Step 3 and Step 4 and certainly Step 5 may only be useful in the more advanced stages of research. Further steps beyond these are possible, and should deal with dynamic models from a time-series perspective (e.g., Nesselroade, McArdle, Aggen, & Meyers, 2001), models based on differential equations (e.g., Oud & Jansen, 2000), consider selection effects due to survival (e.g., McArdle, Small, Backman, & Fratiglioni, 2005), and deal with experimental group dynamics (e.g., McArdle, 2006). The five-step sequence is primarily intended to organize the otherwise daunting task of analyses of multiple-variable and multiple-occasion data.

Extensions to Nonlongitudinal Repeated Measures

There are many other situations where the basic factor analysis models described here can be used. One important case is where some of the measurements are not the exactly the same from one time to the next, and this is quite common in long-term longitudinal studies. One solution to this problem is to fit a metric invariant factor model based on all the variables ever measured at any time with latent variables as placeholders for the incomplete data (as in Horn & McArdle, 1980). The incomplete measurement approach clearly presumes that the same factors are measured in the same way over time even though the measured variables have changed. The limitation of this model is that it strongly presumes but does not test metric invariance. A potentially more practical solution is to recast this problem as an item response problem and calibrate common measures of each variable at each time (e.g., see McArdle & Nesselroade, 2003).

The longitudinal factor models described here may also be combined with several other forms of repeated-measures analysis. This kind of problem comes in the analysis of dyads or other nested sets of individuals (i.e., spouses, partners, siblings). Our questions about factor invariance now extended to include questions about invariance of factor structure across these dyads, both within time and across time. Other extensions of the longitudinal factor model can also be made to situations where the persons are not ordered but have a specific nested structure. One of the more interesting cases here is the dynamic assessment of longitudinal changes in MZ and DZ twin pairs (McArdle & Hamagami, 2003). The importance of the factor model in these behavioral genetic studies should not be overlooked; the factor model provides a measurement base for the further interpretation of common genetic and nongenetic variation, and this is crucial for the rotation and interpretation of the resulting factors (McArdle & Goldsmith, 1990).

Factor Analysis at the Crossroads

Over 100 years ago, Spearman made a clear methodological suggestion—a model dealing with latent variables was possible to put to a rigorous empirical test by measuring multiple realizations of it in the form of indicators. The second contribution made by Spearman 100 years ago was the substantive theory of a single underlying and unifying driving force behind all intellectual activity—the factor he labeled g. In the first example presented in Spearman (1904), he calculated the first factor-analysis model using a matrix of correlations from data collected on the school grades (and one mental test) of children ($N = 101$; for details, see chap. 11 by Horn & McArdle in this volume). The original g-factor theory of multiple cognitive tests was considered to fit nicely, but the specific selection of subjects and variables he used essentially guaranteed a good fit to this highly restricted model. It was not too surprising that in subsequent research, the single factor model often failed to fully fit the data.

One attempt to solve this problem was given by Spearman's student, Cyril Burt (1909) as an "orthogonal group factors" solution (a reapplication of the single-factor extraction method to the residual matrix). Somewhat later, L. L. Thurstone (1931, 1947) and R. Tryon (1932) presented intriguing arguments about the need for multiple factors from both methodological and substantive perspectives. Thurstone's view was in one part based on a lack of fit at the first-order, and he suggested the possibility of g-theory at the second-order level. In a similar approach, Schmid and Leiman (1957) showed how the multiplication of the first- and second-order factor loadings could be used to create an orthogonal decomposition of the second-order factor on the observed variables (i.e., Burt's group-factor solution). Another of Spearman's students, R. B. Cattell's (1971, 1987) analyses suggested we drop g and adopt a multiple general-factor theory (g_f and g_c).

In the view of many contemporary scientists, Spearman's g theory has been soundly accepted by the factor analysis methods he created and many researchers and educators strongly support some form of a g theory (e.g., Jensen, 1998; Lubinski, 2004). However, in the view of many other contemporary scientists, Spearman's g theory has been soundly rejected by the very factor analysis methods he created. Carroll (1993) followed Thurstone (1947) and suggested we pursue the g model at higher order levels. Horn (1989) expressed concern about different experiments with different variables yielding a different g factor in each case. In more recent work, some researchers have found g theory lacking developmental or dynamic validity (see Ferrer & McArdle, 2004; McArdle & Hamagami, 2003; McArdle & Woodcock, 1997). This curious schism among contemporary scientists has placed factor analysis at an important crossroad.

When dealing with what might otherwise appear to be largely philosophical concepts based on latent variables, we need to pay more attention to Spearman's testable and rejectable factor model. Unfortunately, because decisions about rejection and goodness-of-fit are always relative to the data and substantive problem at hand, the appeal to absolute rules for goodness-of-fit indices rests on shaky ground. In practical applications, substantive and theoretical knowledge is always needed in the interpretation of a factor-analysis, and the goals of the factor analysis problems are not always the same, so different factor analysis interpretations of the same data are both natural and reasonable.

If we are to continue to make progress in the next century of factor analysis, we must carefully consider the powerful lessons of this *g*-theory debate. Some attacks on the factor-analysis methods are really about the misuses of factor analysis by factor analysts (e.g., Gould, 1981). Other critiques address alternative aspects of theory, data, and models (e.g., Horn, 1989). From a longitudinal perspective, the single-factor models (e.g., Fig. 7–4a and Fig. 7–5a) do not account for the apparent dynamic influences nearly as well as the more complex multifactor versions (e.g., Fig. 7–4b and Fig. 7–5b). So, in my view, there is irony in applauding the merits of Spearman's factor analysis approach—Spearman's factor-analysis methods should now be considered an outstanding scientific achievement largely because his more well-known *g* theory should not! If scientists are to fulfill Spearman's initial goal of creating an "objectively determined" set of scientifically useful and dynamically informative factors, then we need to pay closer attention to the basic evidence and further clues that actually emerge from our longitudinal factor analyses.

ACKNOWLEDGMENTS

This research was supported by a grant from the *National Institute on Aging* (AG07137). This chapter is dedicated to John L. Horn who taught me, among other things, the basic concepts of factor analysis. I also thank my close colleague John R. Nesselroade who encouraged me to study the advanced concepts of longitudinal factor analysis. Reprints of this chapter can be obtained from the author at the Department of Psychology, National Growth and Change Study (NGCS) laboratory, SGM 824, University of Southern California, Los Angeles, CA 90089.

REFERENCES

Arbuckle, J. L., & Friendly, M. (1977). On rotation to smooth functions. *Psychometrika, 42,* 127–140.

Browne, M. W. (2001). An overview of analytic rotation in exploratory factor analysis. *Multivariate Behavioral Research, 36*, 111–150.

Browne, M., & Cudeck, R. (1993). Alternative ways of assessing model fit. In K. Bollen & S. Long (Eds.), *Testing structural equation models* (pp. 136–162). Beverly Hills, CA: Sage.

Browne, M., & du Toit, S. H. C. (1991). Models for learning data. In L. Collins & J. L. Horn (Eds.), *Best methods for the analysis of change* (pp. 47–68). Washington, DC: APA Press.

Burr, J. A., & Nesselroade, J. R. (1990). Change measurement. In A. von Eye (Ed.), *New statistical methods in developmental research* (pp. 3–34). New York: Academic Press.

Burt, C. (1909). Experimental tests of general intelligence. *British Journal of Psychology, 3*, 94–177.

Carroll, J. B. (1993). *Human cognitive abilities: A survey of factor-analytic studies.* New York: Cambridge University Press.

Cattell, R. B. (1944). "Parallel proportional profiles" and other principles for determining the choice of factors by rotation. *Psychometrika 4*, 267–283.

Cattell, R. B. (1971). *Abilities: Their structure, growth and action.* Boston: Houghton-Mifflin.

Cattell, R. B. (1987). *The scientific use of factor analysis in the behavioral and life sciences.* New York: Plenum Press.

Corballis, M. C., & Traub, R. E. (1970). Longitudinal factor analysis, *Psychometrika, 35*, 79–98.

Cronbach, L. J., & Furby, L. (1970). How we should measure change—or should we? *Psychological Bulletin, 74*, 68–80.

Deary, I. J., Bell, P. J., Bell, A. J., Campbell M. L., & Fazal, N. D. (2004). Sensory discrimination and intelligence: Testing Spearman's other hypothesis. *American Journal of Psychology, 117*(1), 1–18.

Duncan, O. D. (1975). Some linear models for two-wave, two-variable panel analysis. with one-way causation and measurement error. In H. M. Blalock (Ed.), *Quantitative sociology* (pp. 285–306). New York: Academic Press.

du Toit, S. H. C., & Browne, M. W. (2001). The covariance structure of a vector time series. In R. Cudeck, S. H. C. du Toit, & D. Sörbom (Eds.), *Structural equation modeling: present and future* (pp. 279–314). Chicago: Scientific Software International, Inc.

Ferrer, E., & McArdle, J. J. (2004). An experimental analysis of dynamic hypotheses about cognitive abilities and achievement from childhood to early adulthood. *Developmental Psychology, 40*(6), 935–952.

Geweke, J., & Singleton, K. (1981). Maximum likelihood 'confirmatory analysis' of economic time series. *International Economic Review, 22*, 37–54.

Goldstein, H., & McDonald, R. P. (1988). A general model for the analysis of multilevel data. *Psychometrika, 53*(4), 455–467.

Gollob, H. F. (1968). A statistical model which combines features of factor analytic and analysis of variance techniques. *Psychometrika, 33*(1), 73–115.

Gould, S. J. (1981). *The mismeasure of man.* New York: Penguin.

Hakstain, A. R. (1973). Procedures for the factor analytic treatment of measures obtained on different occasions. *British Journal of Mathematical and Statistical Psychology, 26*, 219–239.

Harris, C. W. (Ed.). (1963). *Problems in measuring change.* Madison, WI: University of Wisconsin Press.

Horn, J. L. (1972). State, trait, and change dimensions of intelligence. *The British Journal of Mathematical and Statistical Psychology, 42*(2), 159–185.

Horn, J. L. (1989). Models for intelligence. In R. Linn (Ed.), *Intelligence: Measurement, theory and public policy* (pp. 29–73). Urbana, IL: University of Illinois Press.

Horn, J. L., & McArdle, J. J. (1980). Perspectives on mathematical and statistical model building (MASMOB) in research on aging. In L. Poon (Ed.), *Aging in the 1980's: Psychological Issues* (pp. 503–541). Washington, DC: American Psychological Association.

Horn, J. L., & McArdle, J. J. (1992). A practical guide to measurement invariance in research on aging. *Experimental Aging Research, 18*(3), 117–144.

Jensen, A. R. (1998). *The g factor: The science of mental ability.* London: Praeger.

Jöreskog, K. G. (1969). *Factoring the multi-test multi-occasion correlation matrix* [Research Bulletin no. 69–62]. Princeton, NJ: Educational Testing Service.

Jöreskog, K. G. (1970). Estimation and testing of simplex models. *British Journal of Mathematical and Statistical Psychology, 23,* 121–145.

Jöreskog, K. G. (1977). Analysis of longitudinal data. In D. V. Aigner & A. S. Goldberger (Eds.), Latent variables in socioeconomic models (pp. 91–110). Amsterdam: North Holland.

Jöreskog, K. G., & Sörbom, D. (1979). Advances in factor analysis and structural equation models. Cambridge, MA: Abt Books.

Kenny, D. A., & Zautra, A. (1995). The trait-state-error model for multiwave data. *Journal of Consulting and Clinical Psychology, 63,* 52–59.

Kroonenberg P. M., & Oort F. J. (2003). Three-mode analysis of multimode covariance matrices *British Journal of Mathematical and Statistical Psychology, 56*(2), 305–335.

Lawley, D. N., & Maxwell, A. E. (1971), *Factor analysis as a statistical method.* New York: Macmillan.

Little, R. T. A., & Rubin, D. B. (1987). *Statistical analysis with missing data.* New York: Wiley.

Lubinski, D. (2004). Introduction to the special section on cognitive abilities: 100 years after spearman's (1904) *"General intelligence, objectively determined and measured." Journal of Personality & Social Psychology, 86*(1), 96–111.

McArdle, J. J. (1988). Dynamic but structural equation modeling of repeated measures data. In J. R. Nesselroade & R. B. Cattell (Eds.), *The handbook of multivariate experimental psychology,* (Vol. 2, pp. 561–614). New York: Plenum.

McArdle, J. J. (1991). Structural models of developmental theory in psychology. In P. Van Geert & L. P. Mos (Eds.), *Annals of theoretical psychology,* (Vol. 7, pp. 139–160). New York: Plenum.

McArdle, J. J. (1994). Structural factor analysis experiments with incomplete data. *Multivariate Behavioral Research, 29*(4), 409–454.

McArdle, J. J. (1996). Current directions in structural factor analysis. *Current Directions in Psychological Science, 5*(1), 11–18.

McArdle, J. J. (2001). A latent difference score approach to longitudinal dynamic structural analyses. In R. Cudeck, S. du Toit, & D. Sörbom (Eds.), *Structural equation modeling: Present and future* (pp. 342–380). Lincolnwood, IL: Scientific Software International.

McArdle, J. J. (2006). Dynamic structural equation modeling in longitudinal experimental studies. In K. van Montfort, H. Oud, & A. Satorra (Eds.), *Longitudinal models in the behavioural and related sciences* (pp. 159–188). Mahwah, NJ: Lawrence Erlbaum Associates.

McArdle, J. J., & Cattell, R. B. (1994). Structural equation models of factorial invariance in parallel proportional profiles and oblique confactor problems. *Multivariate Behavioral Research, 29*(1), 63–113.

McArdle, J. J., & Goldsmith, H. H. (1990). Some alternative structural equation models for multivariate biometric analyses. *Behavior Genetics, 20*(5), 569–608.

McArdle, J. J., & Hamagami, F. (1992). Modeling incomplete longitudinal and cross-sectional data using latent growth structural models. *Experimental Aging Research, 18*(3), 145–166.

McArdle, J. J., & Hamagami, F. (1996). Multilevel models from a multiple group structural equation perspective. In G. Marcoulides & R. Schumacker (Eds.), *Advanced structural equation modeling techniques* (pp. 89–124). Mahwah, NJ: Lawrence Erlbaum Associates.

McArdle, J. J., & Hamagami, F. (2003). Structural equation models for evaluating dynamic concepts within longitudinal twin analyses. *Behavior Genetics, 33*(3), 137–159.

McArdle, J. J., & Hamagami, F. (2004). Longitudinal tests of dynamic hypotheses intellectual abilities measured over sixty years. In S. M. Reaker (Ed.), *Quantitative methods in contemporary psychology*. Mahwah, NJ: Lawrence Erlbaum Associates.

McArdle, J. J., & Nesselroade, J. R. (1994). Structuring data to study development and change. In S. H. Cohen & H. W. Reese (Eds.), *Life-span developmental psychology: Methodological innovations* (pp. 223–267). Mahwah, NJ: Lawrence Erlbaum Associates.

McArdle, J. J., & Nesselroade, J. R. (2003). Growth curve analyses in contemporary psychological research. In J. Schinka & W. Velicer (Eds.), *Comprehensive handbook of psychology, volume two: Research methods in psychology* (pp. 447–480). New York: Pergamon.

McArdle, J. J., Small, B. J., Backman, L., & Fratiglioni, L. (2005). Longitudinal models of growth and survival applied to the early detection of Alzheimer's disease. *Journal of Geriatric Psychiatry and Neurology, 18*(4), 234–241.

McArdle, J. J., & Woodcock, J. R. (1997). Expanding test-rest designs to include developmental time-lag components. *Psychological Methods, 2*(4), 403–435.

McDonald, R. P. (1984). The invariant factors model for multimode data. In H. G. Law, C. W. Snyder, Jr., J. A. Hattie, & R. P. McDonald (Eds.), *Research methods for multimode data analysis* (pp. 285–307). New York: Praeger.

McDonald, R. P. (1985), *Factor analysis and related methods*. Hillsdale, NJ: Lawrence Erlbaum Associates.

Meredith, W. (1964). Notes on factorial invariance. *Psychometrika, 29*, 177–185.

Meredith, W., & Horn, J. L. (2001). The role of factorial invariance in modeling growth and change. In A. G. Sayer & L. M. Collins (Eds.), *New methods for the analysis of change* (pp. 203–240). Washington, DC: American Psychological Association.

Meredith, W., & Tisak, J. (1990). Latent curve analysis. *Psychometrika, 55*, 107–122.

Molenaar, P. C. M. (1985). A dynamic factor model for the analysis of multivariate time series. *Psychometrika, 50*, 181–202.

Mulaik, S. A. (1972). *The foundations of factor analysis,* New York: McGraw-Hill.

Mulaik, S. A. (1987). A brief history of the philosophical foundations of exploratory factor analysis. *Multivariate Behavioral Research, 22*, 267–305.

Nagoshi, C. T., Phillips, K., & Johnson, R. C. (1987). Between- versus within-family factor analyses of cognitive abilities. *Intelligence, 11*, 305–316.

Nesselroade, J. R. (1970). A note on 'longitudinal factor analysis.' *Psychometrika, 20*, 173–192.

Nesselroade, J. R., & Baltes, P. B. (Eds.). (1979). *Longitudinal research in the study of behavior and development*. New York: Academic Press.

Nesselroade, J. R., & Baltes, P. B. (1984). From traditional factor analysis to structural–causal modeling in developmental research. In V. Sarris & A. Parducci (Eds.), *Perspectives in psychological experimentation* (pp. 267–287). Hillsdale, NJ: Lawrence Erlbaum Associates.

Nesselroade, J. R., & Cable, D. G. (1974). Sometimes it's okay to factor difference scores: The separation of state and trait anxiety. *Multivariate Behavioral Research, 9*, 273–282.

Nesselroade, J. R., McArdle, J. J., Aggen, S. H., & Meyers, J. (2001). Dynamic factor analysis models for multivariate time series analysis. In D. M. Moskowitz & S. L. Hershberger (Eds.), *Modeling individual variability with repeated measures data: Advances and techniques* (pp. 235–265). Mahwah, NJ: Lawrence Erlbaum Associates.

Oud, J. H. L., & Jansen, R. A. R. G. (2000). Continuous time state space modeling of panel data by means of SEM, *Psychometrika, 65*, 199–215.

Schmid, J., & Leiman, J. M. (1957). The development of hierarchical factor solutions. *Psychometrika, 22*, 53–61.

Spearman, C. E. (1904). 'General intelligence,' objectively determined and measured. *American Journal of Psychology, 15*, 201–293.

Spearman, C. E. (1927). *The abilities of man: Their nature and measurement.* New York: Macmillan.

Thurstone, L. L. (1931). Multiple factor analysis. *Psychological Review, 38*, 406–427.

Thurstone, L. L. (1947). *Multiple factor analysis.* Chicago: University of Chicago Press.

Tryon, R. C. (1932). Multiple factors vs. two factors as determiners of abilities. *Psychological Review, 39*, 324–351.

Tucker, L. R. (1958). Determination of parameters of a functional relation by factor analysis. *Psychometrika, 23*, 19–23.

Tucker, L. R. (1966). Learning theory and multivariate experiment: Illustration by determination of generalized learning curves. In R. B. Cattell (Ed.), *Handbook of multivariate experimental psychology* (pp. 476–501). Chicago: Rand McNally.

CHAPTER 8

Factorial Invariance: Historical
Perspectives and New Problems

Roger E. Millsap
Arizona State University

William Meredith
University of California–Berkeley

It is no exaggeration to say that at present, interest in the study of factorial invariance and related topics is higher than at any time in the last 100 years. One explanation for this interest lies in the wide availability of relevant software, but other influences are at work as well. The importance of invariance for the interpretation of group differences on psychological measures is becoming more widely recognized. For example, cross-cultural researchers are now actively engaged in examining invariance in factor structure on measures adapted for use across cultures (see Steenkamp & Baumgartner, 1998, for one review). Vandenberg and Lance (2000) provide a general review of the current use of methods for studying invariance across many social science disciplines. Furthermore, recent developments in longitudinal data analysis such as latent growth modeling require some assumptions about the stationarity of factor structure, compelling further interest in invariance investigations.

Given the current interest in factorial invariance, it is curious that no one appears to have thoroughly described the history of this topic. This chapter begins to fill this gap by giving some historical perspective on methods for the study of factorial invariance. It will become clear that great progress has been made on the technical problems associated with statistical methods for investigating invariance. The statistical tools resulting from this progress carry their own problems of use and interpretation however. We describe two of these problems, along with their possible solutions.

We begin with a brief statement of the problem of *factorial invariance*. Our focus will be on invariance across independent populations of individuals, rather than invariance or stationarity of factor structure over time. Many of the same ideas apply to either domain. Following the problem statement, we give a historical account of research on the invariance problem. We divide this history into three phases. The historical account leads into our description of two current problems facing users of factorial invariance methods. Neither problem is fully solved at present, but we describe some attempts to do so. We hope this account will inspire more researchers to examine these problems.

THE FACTORIAL INVARIANCE PROBLEM

Suppose that K distinct populations of individuals exist and are to be compared on their factor structures for a $p \times 1$ vector of observed random variables $\mathbf{X}$. We will subscript $\mathbf{X_k}$ to denote measures taken in the kth population. The populations are usually defined by demographic variables such as gender, ethnicity, age, or language status, but other applications exist, as in comparisons across groups created through randomization in an experiment. Within the kth population, it is assumed that

$$\mathbf{X_k} = \tau_k + \Lambda_k \mathbf{W_k} + \mathbf{u_k}, \qquad \text{(Equation 8.1)}$$

where τ_k is a $p \times 1$ vector of measurement intercept parameters, Λ_k is a $p \times r$ matrix of factor loading parameters, $\mathbf{W_k}$ is an $r \times 1$ vector of common factor scores, and $\mathbf{u_k}$ is a $p \times 1$ vector of unique factor scores. Note that the number of factors r is taken to be the same across populations. This number could vary across populations, but for now we will assume that the same number of factors exist in each population. Traditionally, we also assume that

$$\text{Cov}(\mathbf{W_k}, \mathbf{u_k}) = \mathbf{0}, \quad \text{Cov}(\mathbf{W_k}) = \Phi_k, \quad \text{Cov}(\mathbf{u_k}) = \Theta_k, \qquad \text{(Equation 8.2)}$$

where Φ_k is a $r \times r$ factor covariance matrix and Θ_k is a $p \times p$ diagonal unique factor covariance matrix. The unique factors are mutually uncorrelated and are uncorrelated with the common factors. For some results relating to the implications of selection for invariance, stronger assumptions about the relationship between $\mathbf{W_k}$ and $\mathbf{u_k}$ are needed (e.g., independence of $\mathbf{W_k}$ and $\mathbf{u_k}$). We also define

$$\text{E}(\mathbf{W_k}) = \kappa_k, \quad \text{E}(\mathbf{u_k}) = \mathbf{0}, \qquad \text{(Equation 8.3)}$$

with κ_k an $r \times 1$ vector of factor means. Together, all of these assumptions lead to expressions for the covariance and mean structure for $\mathbf{X_k}$ as

$$\text{Cov}(\mathbf{X_k}) = \Sigma_k = \Lambda_k \Phi_k \Lambda_k' + \Theta_k, \qquad \text{(Equation 8.4)}$$

$$\text{E}(\mathbf{X_k}) = \mu_k = \tau_k + \Lambda_k \kappa_k. \qquad \text{(Equation 8.5)}$$

Before proceeding, it is useful to consider that the unique factors are traditionally defined as consisting of two portions: a specific factor s_k that is reliable but unique to the measure, and measurement error e_k, which is unsystematic:

$$\mathbf{u_k} = \mathbf{s_k} + \mathbf{e_k}. \qquad \text{(Equation 8.6)}$$

The measurement error portion is usually viewed as having null means $E(\mathbf{e_k}) = \mathbf{0}$, and zero covariances $Cov(\mathbf{e_k}) = \mathbf{\Theta}_{ek}$, with $\mathbf{\Theta}_{ek}$ being diagonal. This measurement error follows the assumptions regarding error of measurement in classical test theory (Lord & Novick, 1968). The specific factor s_k may not follow these assumptions. Specific factors may have nonzero means $E(\mathbf{s_k}) = \boldsymbol{\mu}_{sk} \neq \mathbf{0}$ and may fail to be mutually uncorrelated in all populations: $Cov(\mathbf{s_k}) = \mathbf{\Theta}_{sk}$, with $\mathbf{\Theta}_{sk}$ a symmetric matrix. In this event, the unique factor scores $\mathbf{u_k}$ will also have nonzero expectations, with correlations among the unique factors. In practice, nonzero means for the specific factors will be absorbed in the measurement intercepts:

$$E(\mathbf{X_k}) = \boldsymbol{\tau}_k + \boldsymbol{\Lambda}_k \boldsymbol{\kappa}_k + \boldsymbol{\mu}_{sk} = \boldsymbol{\tau}_k^* + \boldsymbol{\Lambda}_k \boldsymbol{\kappa}_k, \qquad \text{(Equation 8.7)}$$

where $\boldsymbol{\tau}_k^* = \boldsymbol{\tau}_k + \boldsymbol{\mu}_{sk}$. This absorption will ordinarily go unnoticed. Nonzero covariances among the unique factors will be noticed however, and will contribute to lack of fit in the model. Tests of invariance for intercepts will be affected by group differences in specific factor means. Covariances among the specific factors may affect tests of invariance in unique factor variances, along with model fit. If the specific factors are mutually uncorrelated, group differences in their variances will affect tests of invariance for the unique factor variances. For a general discussion of the consequences that may follow from weaker assumptions about the unique factors $\mathbf{u_k}$ in models of invariance, see Bloxom (1972) and Meredith (1993).

Given an initial factor model in each group, the study of invariance proceeds sequentially through a series of steps, with each step introducing additional constraints on the initial factor model. These sequential stages each have names that denote particular levels of invariance. *Configural invariance* (Thurstone, 1947) denotes an invariance condition on the factor pattern matrix such that the same number of common factors are represented in each group, and the locations of the zero elements in the factor pattern matrices are identical across groups. Non-zero elements in the pattern matrices are unconstrained. Configural invariance implies that the same indicators define a given factor in all groups. Rejection of configural invariance may suggest the need for different numbers of factors across groups, or for different factor configurations. If configural invariance is tenable, the next step is to constrain the factor pattern matrices to invariance ($\boldsymbol{\Lambda}_k = \boldsymbol{\Lambda}$ for all k), a condition known as *weak factorial invariance* (Widaman & Reise, 1997) or *metric invariance* (Horn & McArdle, 1992; Thurstone, 1947). Weak factorial invariance implies that any systematic group differences in the covariances among the measured variables are due to the common factors, rather than other sources of association. If weak factorial invariance is retained, the measurement intercepts are constrained to invariance next ($\Lambda_k = \Lambda$, $\tau_k = \tau$ for all k), yielding *strong facto-rial invariance* (Meredith, 1993) or *scalar invariance* (Steenkamp & Baumgartner, 1998). Strong factorial invariance implies that any systematic group differences in either the means or the covariances among the measured variables are due to the common factors. The final step imposes invariance on the unique factor vari-ances ($\Lambda_k = \Lambda$, $\tau_k = \tau$, $\Theta_k = \Theta$ for all k), leading to *strict factorial invariance* (Meredith, 1993). Strict factorial invariance implies that any systematic group dif-ferences in the means, variances, or covariances for the measured variables are due to the common factors, rather than group differences in factor structure. For example, systematic group differences in the means on the measured variables are due to differences in the factor means. Strict factorial invariance is useful if present because it clarifies the interpretation of any group comparisons on observed means or covariance structures.

An analogous series of models is typically examined in longitudinal data, where the focus lies in the stationarity of the factor structure across repeated occasions of measurement. An additional consideration in longitudinal data is the autocorrelation structure among the specific portions of the unique factors. These autocorrelations are often needed to adequately represent covariation across time. Traditional lon-gitudinal factor models are nomothetic in orientation, seeking to provide a single model that applies to all individual trajectories. A different orientation is repre-sented in P-technique factor analysis (Cattell, Cattell, & Rhymer, 1947), and in more recent developments in dynamic factor models as described by Browne and Zhang (chap. 13) in this volume. These models are specified separately for each individual, permitting variations in factor structure across individuals as needed. Viewed within traditional invariance theory, these individual differences in factor structure seem to violate the notion of invariance as an essential requirement for valid measurement. On the other hand, it can be argued that stationarity of factor structure is a more important consideration than homogeneity of such structures across individuals, especially if change is the focus of study. Nesselroade (chap. 12, this volume) argues forcefully for a more general theory of invariance in longitu-dinal data that can encompass individual differences in structure while permitting valid scientific generalizations. Developments of this sort may well occupy the second century of factor analysis.

HISTORICAL PERSPECTIVES

A complete history of research on factorial invariance has yet to be written, but it is clear that issues of invariance arose early in the history of factor analysis. Charles Spearman appears to have had little to say on the topic of invariance. For Spearman, group differences in scores on intelligence tests largely reflect differences in the distribution of "g." The idea that such tests might have factor structures that differ across groups does not seem to have concerned Spearman. As is described however, subsequent factor analytic theorists were more concerned about potential group differences in factor structure. In fact, the apparent inevitability of such differences led some investigators to question the usefulness of factor analysis for scientific purposes (Thomson, 1939).

In this section, we divide the history of research on factorial invariance into three periods. The first and earliest period was concerned with the impact of selection on the factor structure in selected groups. The second period turned from questions about the origins of group differences to rotational strategies for detecting invariance or violations of invariance. In the third period, rotational strategies were replaced with confirmatory factor analysis as the method of choice for evaluating invariance in factor structure. This third period has continued up to the present day.

Selection Theory and Factorial Invariance

Formally, it is always possible to view multiple subpopulations as having their origin in some larger "super population" through a selection process. The mechanism involved in that process may or may not be clear. For example, genetic subpopulations can be created through different processes, including mutation, mating patterns, or geographical isolation. In invariance studies, the populations we study are usually defined by demographic characteristics such as age or gender. Interest in how the factor structure might vary across subpopulations led to consideration of selection processes that created these subpopulations. Fortunately, statisticians had already developed some theory regarding how selection on elements of a vector-valued random variable would affect the covariance matrix for that random variable. Aitken (1934), building on earlier work by Pearson (1902), gave theorems regarding how direct selection on elements of a multivariate random variable would affect both the covariance structure of these elements and the covariance structure of the other elements that covary with the elements on which selection has operated directly. This work is not concerned with factor analysis, but because the factor model provides a representation of the covariance structure, the work has relevance for factor analysis.

Thomson and Ledermann (1939) developed the implications of Aitken's results for the effects of selection on the factor structure in the created subpopulations. These implications can be stated simply as follows. Assume first that selection operates directly on more than one variable from the set of variables under study (i.e., *multivariate selection*). The first implication of Aitken's results is that if r common factors underlie a set of variables prior to selection, there will be $r + q$ common factors underlying the variables after selection, with $q \geq 0$. Second, if $q > 0$, the additional q common factors involve only the subset of the original variables on which selection operated directly. The remaining variables are only involved in r factors. Third, the factor loadings of the variables on the r factors are different following selection from the loadings prior to selection. Finally, Thomson and Ledermann (1939) noted that if selection only operates on a single variable (i.e., *univariate selection*), then $q = 0$ and r common factors underlie the variables both before and after selection, although the factor loadings will change following selection.

The fact that selection might operate to create new common factors, and will certainly alter the factor loadings, led Thomson (1939) to a pessimistic evaluation of the prospects for factorial invariance. Thomson (1939) argued that because selection is always operating to some extent, we cannot expect to replicate the same factor structure or even the same number of factors across different subpopulations. Thomson (1939) concluded "All these considerations make it very doubtful indeed whether any factors, and any loadings of factors, have absolute meaning. They appear to be entirely dependent upon the population in which they are measured . . ." (p. 194). According to this view, it becomes difficult if not impossible to claim any generality for the factors discovered in a particular subpopulation.

One feature of Thomson and Ledermann's (1939) developments was crucial to their results: Selection is assumed to operate directly on a subset of the measured variables. Thurstone (1947) posed a different locus for selection by assuming that selection operates on either the common factors directly, or on unobserved variables that are correlated with the common factors. This alteration requires no new mathematical theory because Aitken's (1934) results can be applied to a supervector of random variables that includes both the original measured variables and the common factors. Thurstone (1947) showed that these results have several implications for the factor structure after selection. First, if the factor loadings have simple structure prior to selection, this simple structure is preserved after selection for the original r common factors. *Simple structure* here refers primarily to the presence of zero loadings in each row of the pattern matrix. Second, the correlations among the r common factors are usually altered by selection. Third, multivariate selection can induce additional common factors beyond the original r factors. These "incidental" factors will depend heavily on the specific selection, and will generally vary as selection is varied. For Thurstone, it is the simple-structure loading pattern that is the defining characteristic of the factor solution. If simple structure is preserved under selection, selection is not a barrier to generalization across the resulting subpopulations. Thurstone was less concerned about invariance in the values of the nonzero loadings over selection than with the placement of the zero loadings. In the end, Thurstone (1947) was optimistic about the prospects for factorial invariance under selection: "The analysis of these various cases of selection is very encouraging, in that a simple structure has been shown to be invariant under widely different selective conditions" (p. 471).

The widely different outlooks of Thomson and Thurstone with regard to the likelihood of invariance in factor structure is an outcome of their contrasting views of how selection operates. For Thomson, selection operates directly on the observed variates under study. This viewpoint would apply in cases in which groups are explicitly selected on a subset of the measured variables, as in situations involving direct selection on test scores in personnel selection or educational testing

(Muthén, 1989). For demographic subpopulations (e.g., males vs. females) however, the observed variate that defines the groups is not in the set being analyzed, and the "selection" that distinguishes the groups occurs via mechanisms that are unobserved. Thomson's viewpoint is not directly applicable in such cases. Thurstone's view is more consistent with cases involving natural populations if it can be assumed that the variates on which selection operates are (a) not among the set being analyzed, and (b) are related to the common factors in a way that permits application of Aitken's theorems.

The Aitken/Pearson selection theorems originally were posed in the context of a multivariate normal distribution for the measured variables under study. Thomson and Ledermann (1939) mentioned that the theorems were probably applicable over a wider range of conditions than multivariate normality, but they did not pursue this question. Lawley (1943) finally showed that multivariate normality was not required for the theorems to hold. The required conditions concerned the regression functions in the regression of the variables under study on the selection variables (i.e., the variables on which selection operates). These regression functions are required to be linear and homoscedastic. The shapes of the distributions are not important if these two conditions are met. This generalization of the required conditions will be used by later investigators to argue for the reasonableness of invariance.

Rotational Strategies: How to Find Invariance

Although the theoretical selection arguments were useful as explanations for why invariance might or might not hold, in the first half of the 20th century, it was very difficult to verify that invariance holds in real data. Prior to modern computers, even a single factor analysis required extensive and time-consuming hand calculations. In studies comparing factor solutions across multiple groups, multiple factor analyses must be conducted. Given that the initial factor solutions in these analyses lie in an arbitrary orientation, it is unlikely that the factor pattern matrices in these solutions are very similar even if invariance holds. A further consideration lies in the decision about whether to require orthogonality in all groups simultaneously. The importance of orthogonality as an influence on the apparent invariance of the factor pattern matrix was not initially appreciated. All of these considerations led to the question: Are there one or more rotational transformations, that when applied in each group, will reveal the invariance in the pattern matrices?

Work proceeded on this question from a variety of directions. Cattell (1944) developed the principle of *parallel proportional profiles* as a rotational goal in factor comparisons across two populations. The principle suggests that in two populations, it should always be possible to rotate the factor pattern matrices so that they are columnwise proportional across groups. This proportionality would preserve any simple structure that exists in the pattern matrices. Furthermore, the resulting solutions can be taken as orthogonal within both populations. One requirement however is that the observed measures must not be standardized separately within each group. This requirement precludes the analysis of correlation matrices, and leads to the analysis of covariance matrices instead. Cattell (1944) may have been the first to recognize that the matrix being analyzed has important consequences for the search for invariance. Unfortunately, the principle of parallel proportional profiles does not generalize to more than two populations. In more than two populations, it is generally not possible to require both proportional pattern matrices and orthogonal factor solutions.

Apart from Cattell (1944), the major early contribution to the rotational strategy for invariance was Ahmavaraa (1954). Ahmavaraa provided proof of Thurstone's claim about the preservation of simple structure under multivariate selection. Most importantly, Ahmavaraa presented expressions for the factor pattern matrix after selection. The factor pattern in these expressions excludes any measured variables that were the basis for direct selection. It was acknowledged that the factors after selection are generally correlated, rather than orthogonal. Ahmavaraa also reaffirmed the importance of analyzing the covariance matrix when invariance is to be studied. Given that the covariance matrix is analyzed and that the measured variables on which selection is based are excluded from consideration, the pattern matrices for the remaining measures will be columnwise proportional across groups. This result resembles Cattell's earlier work on parallel proportional profiles.

Meredith (1964a, 1964b) considered both Ahmavaraa's (1954) results and Cattell's (1944) work on parallel proportional profiles in extending the rotational approach to a more stringent form of invariance. First, Meredith applied Lawley's theorem by assuming that selection operates on a vector of selection variables that are external to the common factors, but are associated with those common factors. The regressions of the common factors on these selection variables are assumed to be linear and homoscedastic. Assuming that neither the common factors nor the measured variables are standardized within each subpopulation, the factor pattern matrix is invariant across subpopulations under multivariate selection. The resulting factors are generally oblique within the subpopulations, with correlations that vary across subpopulations. Ahamvaraa's (1954) results achieved only proportionality in the factor patterns due to the insistence that the factors have unit variance in all subpopulations. If this requirement is dropped and the covariance matrices are analyzed across groups, invariance in the factor pattern matrix can be achieved.

Meredith (1964a, 1964b) presented two methods for finding the best-fitting invariant factor pattern matrix. This pattern matrix is not unique because any nonsingular transformation of the matrix will also satisfy the requirements, assuming that the same transformation is used in all groups. One can rotate the invariant pattern matrix to approximate simple structure, for example. The requirement of invariance for the factor pattern matrix results in some loss of fit in the factor model relative to the data. No statistical tests or sampling theory were developed for the invariant solution, but several indices based on least squares were suggested.

A key insight leading to Meredith's results was the shift in the locus of selection to a set of hypothetical selection variables, instead of defining selection by either the measured variables being analyzed or by the common factors. The linearity and homoscedasticity assumptions are then applied to the relations between the selection variables and the common factors. Importantly, the selection variables need not be measured or even known. It is enough to assume that selection variables exist and that they satisfy the linearity and homoscedasticity assumptions in relation to the factor scores. For invariance studies with naturally occurring groupings (e.g., male vs. female), the selection variables are assumed to lead to the groupings under study. The mechanisms by which these groups are created are usually not obvious.

A related but different stream of research on rotational strategies was the development of procrustes rotation methods (Browne, 1967; Green, 1952; Horst, 1941; Mosier, 1939; Jöreskog, 1966; Meredith, 1977; Schönemann, 1966). The idea here is to rotate the pattern matrix to approximate a prespecified target pattern matrix. The target matrix represents a hypothesized structure based on theory. The procrustes method has applications outside of the realm of invariance studies, but the idea of rotating pattern matrices from independent groups to approximate common target is an important application. The adequacy of the resulting approximation could be measured using indices of closeness, such as *Tucker's congruence coefficient* (Tucker, 1951). An important development within this area concerned the use of "partially-specified" target patterns in which not all elements of the target matrix need be prespecified (Browne, 1972a, 1972b; Meredith, 1977). For example, it is possible to specify the locations only of the zero elements in the target matrix, permitting the nonzero elements to assume any values. This hyperplane-fitting strategy represents the use of simple structure as the guiding rotational principle, leading to configural invariance.

Two weaknesses in all of the rotational strategies eventually became obvious. First, the rotational methods did not resolve the issue of fit assessment for the resulting factor solutions. Descriptive indices of congruence among the rotated factor patterns are not measures of fit to the data. Congruence indices only assess the similarities in the factor structure across groups. One could apply existing fit indices such as the maximum likelihood chi-square test statistic to the overall factor solution in each group separately, but no method existed for incorporating the invariance restrictions explicitly into the fit indices. The rotational procedures simply applied rotations to an existing factor solution whose fit was deemed acceptable, and did not alter the fit. The idea of building invariance explicitly into the estimation method was not yet realized in any practical procedure.

A second problem with rotational procedures is that they only permitted the study of invariance in a single feature of the factor model—the factor loadings. The factor loadings are clearly important and should be the first feature of the model to be examined, but they are not the only feature of interest. The unique variances are also of interest. The influence of the factor model on the mean structure of the measured variables is of even greater interest, given that groups are often compared on their means. Rotational procedures did not address these issues, but the next stage in methodological development did eventually do so.

Confirmatory Factor Analysis

Jöreskog (1971) appears to have been the first application of *confirmatory factor analysis* (CFA) to the problem of invariance. CFA had already been proposed as a method for incorporating theory-driven constraints into the common factor model, to be followed by fit assessment. Jöreskog (1971) extended this method to simultaneous models in multiple groups, with invariance constraints being permitted on any model parameter. The investigator would first fit a model without any invariance constraints to evaluate the plausibility of the initial model. Assuming the fit of this model was acceptable, the next model would incorporate the invariance constraints that were of early interest, such as constraints on loadings. The change in fit from the initial model to the constrained model would then be noted as a way of assessing the appropriateness of the added invariance constraints. This sequence of model fits could continue until all invariance constraints of interest were examined. The use of CFA in tests of invariance permitted the hypothesis of exact invariance to be tested, rather than relying on rotational procedures to achieve approximate invariance.

A further step was made with the introduction of mean structures in the factor model for multiple groups (Sörbom, 1974). The distinction in this model between the means of the common factors and the measurement intercepts allowed investigators to test invariance in either set of parameters. Invariance in the measurement intercepts is needed to justify group comparisons on the means of the measured variables. When both the intercepts and the factor loadings are invariant, systematic group differences in the means on the measured variables are attributable to group differences in common factor means. The common factor means themselves can also be directly tested for invariance using CFA.

Growing in parallel with these developments was the extension of CFA methods to the case of discrete, ordinal measured variables. Factor models for dichotomous measures had been of interest for many years due to the widespread use of dichotomously scored items in testing. The pitfalls in applying ordinary factor analysis to such items were known (Carroll, 1945; Ferguson, 1941), and alternative factor models were considered. None of this work had been extended to the multiple group case for invariance analyses. Muthén and Christoffersson (1981) extended CFA to include factor models for dichotomous items in multiple groups, with tests of invariance constraints. The further extension to polytomous items would come later (Muthén, 1984). Given that most items in psychological scales are ordinal or dichotomous, these extensions could be immediately applied to invariance studies on such items. The relations between these factor models and the models for test items in item response theory were noted early (Lord & Novick, 1968).

Estimation and fit assessment in CFA typically relies heavily on assumptions of multinormality, although other options are available. Simulation studies have shown that violations of these normality assumptions can disrupt tests of fit and standard errors, leading to an interest in finding fit procedures that are robust under nonnormality. This interest has extended to the multiple group case also. Satorra (1993, 2000) and Bentler, Lee, and Weng (1987) have developed robust fit statistics that are designed for multiple group applications with both mean and covariance structures.

Meredith (1993) positioned the factorial invariance problem within the more general context of measurement invariance, and showed the implications of various forms of measurement invariance for factorial invariance. He emphasized the importance of assumptions regarding specific factors as they affect invariance after selection. Useful selection results were developed without recourse to Lawley's (1943) selection theorems. He described the consequences of selection for mean structures, noting that studies of factorial invariance must consider mean structures in addition to covariance structures. Multiple-group CFA including mean structures is the natural approach in this case.

CFA is now the primary method for studying factorial invariance. Using CFA, we can examine invariance hypotheses on any factor model parameter, for both the mean and covariance structures. These investigations can be conducted for both continuous and discrete measured variables. Robust fit procedures help protect against violations of normality assumptions. From a technical viewpoint, tremendous progress has been made in the last 100 years on methods for studying factorial invariance. Some problems remain unresolved in spite of this progress, however. As will become clear, some problems concern issues of interpretation or meaning, rather than additional technical challenges. Other problems do concern gaps in technical knowledge. In what follows, we examine two of these problems and some possible solutions. We begin with an interpretive problem.

THE MEANINGFULNESS PROBLEM

Strict factorial invariance represents an ideal that is often unattainable in real invariance applications. More commonly, investigators must settle for some level of invariance that falls short of strict invariance. Partial factorial invariance, in which some but not all parameters in the set $\{\tau_k, \Lambda_k, \Theta_k\}$ are found to be invariant, is a frequent finding in real applications. Assuming that one can determine which model parameters are invariant, the next question is: What should be done in response to the partial invariance? Several courses of action might be considered in response to finding group differences in loadings, for example. First, one might simply do nothing, arguing that the differences are too small to warrant any action. Unfortunately, no clear guidelines exist for deciding when a loading difference is "small." Alternatively, one could choose to do nothing because the number of items showing group differences in loadings is small. The problem here is that simple counts of the number of items showing differences do not consider the magnitudes of these differences. Also, we again have no rational procedure for deciding when the number of items is small. Another course of action might be to drop any items that show group differences in loadings, relying on the remaining items. If this course of action is taken by different investigators who use the same scale, many different versions of the scale will be generated as different subsets of the items are removed by different investigators. A third course of action might be to simply not use the scale if any items are found to have loadings that differ across groups, arguing that such differences may indicate that the construct underlying the scale is not comparably measured. Given that violations of strict factorial invariance are quite common, this course of action would lead to the suspension of measurement in many domains. Each of these options faces difficulties, but the important point is that there is almost no literature that addresses how investigators should think about the problem. A large literature exists on how to decide whether a measure violates factorial invariance. Once that decision is made, however, the next step is unclear. How should we decide whether a violation of invariance is meaningful? If the violation is meaningful, what action should be taken?

One approach to answering these questions is to consider the purpose for which the measure under study is being used. What do we hope to accomplish through the use of the measure? The meaningfulness of the violation of invariance can be judged in relation to this purpose. To what extent does the violation of invariance interfere with the purpose for the measure? We can define a "meaningful" violation of invariance as one that interferes with the purpose of the measure.

A common purpose for a psychological test is to identify individuals who are at one end of the dimension being measured by the test. In clinical applications, we might refer individuals to treatment who score highly on a measure of psychopathology, for example. Would the violation of invariance interfere with this identification by rendering the identification less accurate in one or more groups? In an educational setting, we might use the measure to select individuals to be admitted to a graduate program. Would the violation of invariance lead to less accurate selection in one or more groups? This selection approach could be applied even in situations where no explicit selection will take place. We still might gauge the value of a test by whether it would permit, in theory, accurate identification of individuals at one end of the latent continuum. If the violations of invariance would substantially reduce this accuracy, we should be concerned about those violations.

Millsap and Kwok (2004) proposed one method for assessing the impact of violations of invariance on selection accuracy. The method assumes that a single-factor model fits the measured variables, and that the question of which model parameters are invariant has been settled. Estimates for all model parameters must be available. The method also assumes that any selection is to be based on a simple sum of the scores on the measured variables. The single factor model underlying these variables assumes that every individual's status on the factor is measured by a single, unobserved factor score. Consistent with the multivariate normal model typically assumed in CFA, the joint bivariate distribution of the measured composite and the factor score is assumed to be bivariate normal, with moments that are functions of the factor model parameters. For example, let $\mathbf{X}$ be the $p \times 1$ vector of measured variables, and let $Z = \mathbf{1}'\mathbf{X}$ be the measured composite. If in the factor model we have

$$\mu_x = \mathrm{E}(\mathbf{X}) = \boldsymbol{\tau} + \boldsymbol{\lambda}\kappa, \qquad \text{(Equation 8.8)}$$

we must also have

$$\mu_z = \mathrm{E}(Z) = \tau^* + \lambda^*\kappa, \qquad \text{(Equation 8.9)}$$

with $\tau^* = \mathbf{1}'\boldsymbol{\tau}$ and $\lambda^* = \mathbf{1}'\boldsymbol{\lambda}$. For the variance of Z, we have

$$\boldsymbol{\Sigma}_x = \mathrm{Cov}(\mathbf{X}) = \boldsymbol{\lambda}\boldsymbol{\lambda}'\phi + \boldsymbol{\Theta}, \qquad \text{(Equation 8.10)}$$

so that

$$\sigma_z^2 = \mathrm{Var}(Z) = \lambda^{*2}\phi + \theta^*, \qquad \text{(Equation 8.11)}$$

with $\theta^* = \mathbf{1}'\boldsymbol{\Theta}\mathbf{1}$. Finally, the correlation between Z and the factor score ξ can be shown to be

$$\rho_{z\xi} = \frac{\lambda^*\sqrt{\phi}}{\sqrt{\lambda^{*2}\phi + \theta^*}}. \qquad \text{(Equation 8.12)}$$

If parameter estimates for all model parameters are available, we can estimate all of the moments for the joint bivariate distribution of (Z, ξ) using the factor model parameter estimates. We have then identified the bivariate normal distribution for (Z, ξ).

The next step requires the specification of a cutpoint on the distribution of the composite Z beyond which we would select individuals. If we wish to select the top 20%, we can find the value of Z that corresponds to this percentile. We can also find the corresponding cutpoint on the factor scale that marks the top 20% of the factor score distribution. The two cutpoints jointly divide the bivariate distribution for (Z, ξ) into four quadrants. The "true positive" quadrant includes scores that are in the top 20% on both Z and ξ. The quadrant in which composite scores are below the composite cutpoint, but above the factor score cutpoint, are the "false negatives." These people would not be selected based on their composite scores, yet would have been selected if their factor scores were known. The next quadrant consists of people who score below the cutpoints on both the composite and the factor score distributions: the "true negatives." Finally, the remaining quadrant includes people who score above the cutpoint on the composite but below the cutpoint on the factor score distribution. These "false positives" would be selected given their composite scores, but their factor scores indicate that they should not have been selected.

The relative proportions of the population to be found in each of the four quadrants is a function of the shape of the bivariate distribution for (Z, ξ), together with the cutpoints. The factor model parameters help determine the shape of the bivariate distribution. Group differences in these parameters will create differences in the bivariate distributions, and these distribution differences in turn affect measures of accuracy in selection.

Several measures of accuracy in selection can be directly formulated based on the proportions in the four quadrants. The sensitivity of the composite as a measure of the factor score can be defined as

$$\text{Sens} = \frac{A}{A + D},$$ (Equation 8.13)

where A is the proportion of true positives, and D is the proportion of false negatives. Sensitivity denotes the probability of scoring above the cutpoint on the composite, given that one is above the cutpoint on the factor score. The specificity of the composite is defined as

$$\text{Spec} = \frac{C}{C + B},$$ (Equation 8.14)

where C is the proportion of true negatives and B is the proportion of false positives. Specificity is the the probability that an individual scores below the cutpoint on the composite, given that the individual's factor score is below the factor score cutpoint. Finally, we can define the positive predictive value of the composite as

$$\text{PPV} = \frac{A}{A + B}.$$ (Equation 8.15)

The **PPV** gives the probability that an individual's factor score is above the factor cutpoint, given that the composite score is above the composite score cutpoint. Taken together, these three accuracy indices provide a complete picture of the accuracy of decisions using the composite, relative to the factor score.

To illustrate how the accuracy indices might be used to gain insight into the implications of partial invariance, we consider an example taken from Millsap and Kwok (2004). This example consists of a single-factor model for $p = 4$ measured variables in each of two populations, denoted as reference and focal populations (see Holland & Thayer, 1988, for the origin of this terminology). In the reference group, the factor model parameters are

$$\lambda_r = \begin{bmatrix} .7 \\ .6 \\ .5 \\ .4 \end{bmatrix}, \quad \tau_r = \begin{bmatrix} .1 \\ .2 \\ .3 \\ .4 \end{bmatrix}, \quad diag[\Theta] = \begin{bmatrix} .3525 \\ .3525 \\ .3525 \\ .3525 \end{bmatrix},$$

with $\phi_r = 1$ and $\kappa_r = .5$. In the focal group, the unique factor variances are identical to those in the reference group. The remaining parameters in the focal group were

$$\lambda_f = \begin{bmatrix} .4 \\ .5 \\ .5 \\ .4 \end{bmatrix}, \quad \tau_f = \begin{bmatrix} .0 \\ .1 \\ .2 \\ .3 \end{bmatrix},$$

with $\phi_f = 1$ and $\kappa_r = .0$. Under this parameterization, the correlation between (Z, ξ) is .88 in the reference group and .83 in the control group.

TABLE 8–1

Partial Invariance Case

	SENS	PPV	SPEC
Focal	.390	.655	.987
Reference	.751	.643	.931

Table 8–1 gives figures for selection accuracy under partial invariance as revealed in the parameter values given earlier: partial invariance holds for loadings, with no invariance for intercepts. Table 8–2 gives the same figures on selection accuracy when all loadings and intercepts are invariant at values found in the reference group. Comparison of the selection accuracy under the two conditions shows that the largest difference is that sensitivity shrinks in the focal group under partial invariance. The shrinkage is considerable in percentage terms. The next step is to decide whether the shrinkage in meaningful in practical terms. This decision would need to consider the context of the research, and whether shrinkage in sensitivity in the focal group would have negative consequences. The decision may be difficult, but it is greatly facilitated by the selection perspective in comparison to pondering group differences in factor model parameters whose practical interpretation is often unclear.

THE SPECIFICATION SEARCH PROBLEM

The foregoing discussion assumed that the degree of invariance that holds across the groups being compared had been determined, with estimates of all parameters being available. In reality, this determination is not always easily made. Invariance testing is usually conducted in stages, beginning with configural invariance in which no invariance constraints are introduced except with regard to the number of factors and the locations of any zero elements in the loading matrix. If the configural model is found to fit, the next model will constrain all loadings to invariance, resulting in metric invariance (Horn & McArdle, 1992; Thurstone, 1947). If this model does not fit, the inference is made that at least some factor loadings are not invariant. Which loadings are invariant? The answer to this question may not be immediately obvious from the results of the metric invariance model, and so further analyses are often needed. These analyses combine educated guesses based on previous

TABLE 8–2

Full Invariance Case

	SENS	PPV	SPEC
Focal	.642	.592	.973
Reference	.678	.700	.952

experience with the scale or relevant theory, and exploratory fit evaluations of models that incorporate partial loading invariance.

Two problems are encountered in attempts to locate the proper configuration of invariance constraints through model respecification. First, it is unclear whether such searches are likely to be successful under realistic conditions. The literature on specification searches in SEM (MacCallum, 1986; MacCallum, Roznowski, & Necowitz, 1992) suggests that searches guided primarily by the data will often be misleading, especially in modest samples and with many models to be evaluated. In invariance applications, the models to be examined are confined to a narrow subset of the total set of alternative models that might be considered. For example, once metric invariance is rejected, interest focuses on model alternatives that relax invariance constraints on some subset of loadings. Other alternative models (e.g., adding new factors) are not considered. The moderate number of alternative models may enhance the chances of a successful specification search. The available literature on the accuracy of these searches in invariance studies is quite small (Meade & Lautenschlager, 2004; Oort, 1998).

The second problem to be faced in any specification search concerns the handling of constraints needed for identification during the search. As noted by Cheung and Rensvold (1998, 1999), the presence of invariance constraints used to identify the model can complicate the specification search if doubt exists about the actual invariance of the parameters that are constrained for identification. A factor loading that is fixed to 1.0 in all groups can create spurious violations of invariance in the loadings of other indicators if the loading really violates invariance. The same problem exists in choosing identification constraints for the mean structure (e.g., fixing measurement intercepts to zero); poor choices here may lead to spurious violations of intercept invariance. Unfortunately, the potential for these distortions is nearly always present because only rarely will we be certain about the a priori invariance of particular parameters.

Cheung and Rensvold (1998, 1999) studied the second problem, and have proposed a systematic empirical approach for its solution (Rensvold & Cheung, 2001). Consider the case of invariance in factor loadings. In this approach, invariance constraints on pairs of loadings are tested by comparing a model with both loadings constrained to invariance with a weaker model that constrains only one of the loadings. In both models, all other nonzero loadings are unconstrained. The two models are evaluated using a chi-square difference test, with Bonferroni adjustments for the entire series of tests. If p loadings are to be evaluated, the entire series will include $p(p-1)/2$ tests. Once the entire series is completed, the results should suggest which loadings may be taken as invariant. Rensvold and Cheung (2001) describe this process and illustrate it using real data. One benefit of this method is that it not only addresses the identification problem, it also provides a solution to the general specification search problem. The solution is an exhaustive one however, with the number of tests growing rapidly as the number of variables p increases. We do not yet have a detailed study of the performance of the method in data where the solution is known.

The aforementioned approach begins from a model in which only invariance constraints needed for identification are included, and then adds further constraints. We can label this as a *forward addition* approach in which constraints are added sequentially. In contrast, we could begin with a model that includes invariance constraints on all parameters in the set under study (e.g., metric invariance for loadings). Constraints are then eliminated in order to improve the fit of the model, creating a *backward elimination* approach to the specification problem. The forward approach must face the identification problem by choosing which parameters to constrain for identification initially. Rensvold and Cheung (2001) deal with this problem by cycling through many identification choices and comparing results. The backward approach constrains all parameters in the studied set to invariance initially, but avoids any commitment to a particular choice. Constraints are removed sequentially with no necessary impact on identification as long as at least one parameter remains constrained. The backward approach thus avoids any confrontation with the identification problem until late in the process of respecification.

To illustrate the backward approach, consider an invariance study that compares two populations on a single-factor model for $p = 6$ measured variables. Suppose that metric invariance has been tested and rejected, but that a single-factor model with no invariance constraints apart from identification constraints provides a good fit. The metric invariance model in this case can be identified by (a) fixing the factor variance to one in one of the two groups, and (b) fixing one intercept to zero in both groups. The backward approach begins by freeing one invariance constraint on the loadings, yielding partial metric invariance. The logical candidate for elimination would be the constraint with the largest Lagrange multiplier statistic, in the absence of any theory to guide selection. Invariance constraints on the remaining five loadings remain in place. The fit of the model is reevaluated, and a second constraint is removed, again guided by the Lagrange multiplier statistic or by theory. This process is repeated until either an adequate fit is achieved or only one loading constraint remains. One constraint must be retained for identification. This backward elimination approach is feasible, but how likely is it that the method will distinguish invariant loadings from those that violate invariance?

Yoon (2004) conducted simulations to evaluate the accuracy of the backward method. Data were simulated to fit a single-factor model in each of two groups. Mean structures were not included in the model because the focus of the study was the detection of partial invariance in loadings. Several potential influences on detection accuracy were manipulated (a) sample size ($N = 200, 500$), (b) the number of measured variables ($p = 6, 12$), (c) the proportion of loadings that differ between the groups (one third vs. two thirds), and (d) the size of the loading difference (low = .1, medium = .2, high = .3). Data were simulated under multivariate normality for all common and unique factor scores. Within each combination of the four manipulated influences, 100 replications were performed. The results now reported refer to percentages of outcomes across these 100 replications. All analyses were performed using LISREL 8.52 (Jöreskog & Sörbom, 1996).

The backward elimination process was implemented as follows. For a given replication, the metric invariance model with a single factor was first fit to the data. Assuming that this model revealed statistically significant misfit as indicated by chi-square, the next step was to release the single loading invariance constraint corresponding to the largest modification index (Lagrange multiplier), followed by another global fit evaluation. If this new model showed no significant misfit as indicated by the global chi-square fit statistic, the process ended. If misfit was found, another constraint was removed again based on the modification indices. The entire process was repeated until no further statistically significant improvements in fit were possible through removal of loading constraints. Once the process was completed for a given replication, two quantities were recorded. The first was a count of the number of loadings that actually varied across groups and that were detected as varying across groups by the specification search. This count can be denoted the "true positive" (TP) count. This count could assume values from zero up to the number of loadings that actually varied. The second quantity was the count of the loadings that did not vary across groups but were falsely detected as varying by the specification search. This count can be denoted the "false positive" (FP) count. This number could range from zero up to the number of truly invariant loadings.

Here we will only consider one set of scenarios from the many conditions studied: $N = 500$, $p = 6$, with one third of the loadings varying across groups (i.e., two of the six loadings varied). This condition represents an optimal case in that the sample is substantial, the number of variables is modest, and only a few loadings varied. Table 8–3 shows the results. The columns represent the three levels of the group difference in the loading size. The first row gives the percentage of replications for which the true positive count was two (all loadings that violate invariance were found). The second row gives the percentage of replications for which the numbers of false positives was greater than zero. It is clear that the size of the loading difference plays a major role. One is virtually certain to detect all loadings that vary across groups if the group differences are large, but when the differences are small, little power is found. Conversely, when the loading differences are small, there is a greater chance of erroneously concluding that a truly invariant loading shows lack of invariance. This chance is reduced when the loading differences are large.

An implication of the aforementioned results is that the performance of the backward elimination approach will depend on data conditions and the extent of

TABLE 8–3
Specification Search Accuracy

	Low	Medium	High
TP = 2	11	66	98
FP > 0	25	24	16

the group differences. For example, the communalities of the variables used in the scenarios ranged from .22 to .48. These values are reasonable for item-level data, but perhaps too small for scale-level data. Preliminary simulations prior to those reported showed that as communalities increased, the backward procedure virtually always detects the loadings that differed between groups, with no false detections. At lower communality values, performance of the backward procedure was much more variable.

These simulation results may or may not mirror experience with specification searches in real data. The search in the simulation was guided strictly by the chi-square test, with the search proceeding until the global chi-square was no longer statistically significant. In practice, most researchers rely on approximate fit indices and would suspend the search if these approximate fit indices reached adequate levels. This practice will reduce power. Another consideration is that the single-factor model was known to fit the data in the simulations, but in real data the initial baseline model (e.g., configural invariance) may not fit well by the chi-square criterion. The use of a model whose fit is marginal as the starting point for the analyses might alter the specification search.

A different approach to the partial invariance problem with respect to measurement intercepts is based on a method outlined in Meredith and Horn (2001). The intent of this method is to reveal group differences in intercepts while avoiding the standard practice of fixing one or more intercepts to zero in all groups to achieve identification. The first step in this approach is to evaluate metric invariance, without requiring simple structure in the factor loadings if the model has multiple factors. Meredith and Horn (2001) argue that simple structure should be imposed following the establishment of metric invariance, rather than before. The analysis proceeds to the second step only if metric invariance is confirmed, given that group differences in slopes are generally accompanied by differences in intercepts. In the second step, invariance in intercepts is evaluated. Assuming that invariance is rejected, estimates of the factor means κ_k are obtained by fixing Λ and Θ_k to their values as estimated in the first step. Intercepts are held invariant in this estimation. The estimated factor means are then centered to sum to zero across groups. In the third step, the parameters Λ and Θ_k are fixed as in the second step, and the factor means κ_k are fixed to the mentioned values. The intercepts τ_k are then estimated, with no invariance constraints. Group differences in the intercepts are revealed in this final step.

In the just-cited approach, the factor means in Step 2 are forced to account for as much of the group difference in the means on the measured variables as possible. The intercepts then account for any differences that remain in Step 3, providing a perfect fit to the mean structure. One can subsequently compare the intercept estimates across groups by inspection. A statistical test for differences in intercepts based on these estimates is unavailable at present. The method does provide intercept estimates that are not tied to a particular choice of identification. More practical experience with this method is needed.

CONCLUSION

One hundred years of progress on the problem of factorial invariance has brought forth some precise statistical tools. These tools have in turn created new problems of use and interpretation. In some applications, the precision of the available tools has outpaced the theoretical understanding of the psychological scale under study. Current statistical tools for investigating invariance require a fairly detailed understanding of the factor structure that likely underlies the studied scale. Without this understanding, attempts to evaluate the fit of various invariance constraints are likely to be confounded with other sources of misfit, leading to ambiguity. In other words, researchers who study invariance must also be good psychologists. This is a lesson that Charles Spearman would have understood, and heartily endorsed.

REFERENCES

Ahmavaara, Y. (1954). The mathematical theory of factorial invariance under selection. *Psychometrika, 19*, 27–38.

Aitken, A. C. (1934). Note on selection from a multivariate normal population. *Proceedings of the Edinburgh Mathematical Society, 4*, 106–110.

Bentler, P. M., Lee S. Y., & Weng, J. (1987). Multiple population covariance structure analysis under arbitrary distribution theory. *Communication in Statistics-Theory, 16*, 1951–1964.

Bloxom, B. (1972). Alternative approaches to factorial invariance. *Psychometrika, 37*, 425–440.

Browne, M. W. (1967). On oblique procrustes rotation. *Psychometrika, 32*, 125–132.

Browne, M. W. (1972a). Oblique rotation to a partially specified target. *Psychometrika, 25*, 207–212.

Browne, M. W. (1972b). Orthogonal rotation to a partially specified target. *Psychometrika, 25*, 115–120.

Carroll, J. B. (1945). The effect of difficulty and chance success on correlations between items or between tests. *Psychometrika, 10*, 1–19.

Cattell, R. B. (1944). "Parallel proportional profiles" and other principles for determining the choice of factors by rotation. *Psychometrika, 9*, 267–283.

Cattell, R. B., Cattell, A. K. S, & Rhymer, R. M. (1947). P-technique demonstrated in determining psychophysical source traits in a normal individual. *Psychometrika, 12*, 267–288.

Cheung, G. W., & Rensvold, R. B. (1998). Cross-cultural comparisons using non-invariant measurement items. *Applied Behavioral Science Review, 6*, 93–110.

Cheung, G. W., & Rensvold, R. B. (1999). Testing factorial invariance across groups: A reconceptualization and proposed new method. *Journal of Management, 25*, 1–27.

Ferguson, G. A. (1941). The factorial interpretation of test difficulty. *Psychometrika, 6*, 323–329.

Green, B. F. (1952). The orthogonal approximation of an oblique structure in factor analysis. *Psychometrika, 17*, 429–440.

Holland, P. W., & Thayer, D. T. (1988). Differential item performance and the Mantel-Haenszel procedure. In H. Wainer & H. Braun (Eds.), *Test validity* (pp. 129–145). Hillsdale, NJ: Lawrence Erlbaum Associates.

Horn, J. L., & McArdle, J. J. (1992). A practical guide to measurement invariance in research on aging. *Experimental Aging Research, 18*, 117–144.

Horst, A. P. (1941). A non-graphical method for transforming an arbitrary factor matrix into a simple structure factor matrix. *Psychometrika, 6*, 79–99.

Jöreskog, K. G. (1966). Testing a simple structure hypothesis in factor analysis. *Psychometrika, 31*, 165–178.

Jöreskog, K. G. (1971). Simultaneous factor analysis in several populations. *Psychometrika, 36*, 409–426.

Jöreskog, K. G., & Sörbom, D. (1996). *LISREL 8: User's reference guide.* Chicago: Scientific Software Inc.

Lawley, D. N. (1943). A note on Karl Pearson's selection formulae. *Proceedings of the Royal Society of Edinburgh, 2*, 28–30.

Lord, F. M., & Novick, M. R. (1968). *Statistical theories of mental test scores.* Reading, MA: Addison-Wesley.

MacCallum, R. C. (1986). Specification searches in covariance structure modeling. *Psychological Bulletin, 100*, 107–120.

MacCallum, R. C., Roznowski, M., & Necowitz, L. B. (1992). Model modifications in covariance structure analysis: The problem of capitalization on chance. *Psychological Bulletin, 111*, 490–504.

Meade, A. W., & Lautenschlager, G. J. (2004). A Monte-Carlo study of confirmatory factor analytic tests of measurement equivalence/invariance. *Structural Equation Modeling, 11*, 60–72.

Meredith, W. (1964a). Notes on factorial invariance. *Psychometrika, 29*, 177–185.

Meredith, W. (1964b). Rotation to achieve factorial invariance. *Psychometrika, 29*, 187–206.

Meredith, W. (1977). On weighted procrustes and hyperplane fitting in factor analytic rotation. *Psychometrika, 42*, 491–522.

Meredith, W. (1993). Measurement invariance, factor analysis, and factorial invariance. *Psychometrika, 58*, 525–543.

Meredith, W., & Horn, J. (2001). The role of factorial invariance in modeling growth and change. In L. M. Collins & A. G. Sayer (Eds.), *New methods for the analysis of change* (pp. 203–240). Washington DC: American Psychological Association.

Millsap, R. E., & Kwok, O. M. (2004). Evaluating the impact of partial factorial invariance on selection in two populations. *Psychological Methods, 9*, 93–115.

Mosier, C. I. (1939). Determining a simple structure when loadings for certain tests are known. *Psychometrika, 4*, 149–162.

Muthén, B. O. (1984). A general structural equation model with dichotomous, ordered categorical and continuous latent variable indicators. *Psychometrika, 49*, 115–132.

Muthén, B. O. (1989). Factor structure in groups selected on observed scores. *British Journal of Mathematical and Statistical Psychology, 42*, 81–90.

Muthén, B. O., & Christoffersson, A. (1981). Simultaneous factor analysis of dichotomous variables in several groups. *Psychometrika, 46*, 407–419.

Oort, F. J. (1998). Simulation study of item bias detection with restricted factor analysis. *Structural Equation Modeling, 5*, 107–124.

Pearson, K. (1902). On the influence of natural selection on the variability and correlation of organs. *Philosophical Transactions of the Royal Society, A, 200*, 1–66.

Rensvold, R. B., & Cheung, G. W. (2001). Testing for metric invariance using structural equation models: Solving the standardization problem. *Research in Management, 1*, 25–50.

Satorra, A. (1993). Asymptotic robust inferences in multiple-group analysis of augmented-moment structures. In C. M. Cuadras & C. R. Rao (Eds.), *Multivariate analysis: Future directions 2* (pp. 211–229). Amsterdam: Elsevier.

Satorra, A. (2000). Scaled and adjusted restricted tests in multi-sample analysis of moment structures. In D. D. H. Heijmans, D. S. G. Pollock, & A. Satorra (Eds.), *Innovation in multivariate statistical analysis: A festschrift for Heinz Neudecker* (pp. 233–247). Dordrecht: Kluwer.

Schönemann, P. H. (1966). The generalized solution of the orthogonal procrustes problem. *Psychometrika, 31*, 1–16.

Sörbom, D. (1974). A general method for studying differences in factor means and factor structure between groups. *British Journal of Mathematical and Statistical Psychology, 27*, 229–239.

Steenkamp, J. E. M., & Baumgartner, H. (1998). Assessing measurement invariance in cross-national consumer research. *Journal of Consumer Research, 25*, 78–90.

Thomson, G. H. (1939). *The factorial analysis of human ability.* Boston: Houghton-Mifflin.

Thomson, G. H. & Lederman, W. (1939). The influence of multivariate selection on the factorial analysis of ability. *British Journal of Psychology, 29*, 288–305.

Thurstone, L. L. (1947). *Multiple factor analysis.* Chicago: University of Chicago Press.

Tucker, L. R. (1951). *A method for synthesis of factor analysis studies* [PRS Rep. No. 984]. Educational Testing Service, Research Contract No. DA-49-083-OSA-116, Department of the Army.

Vandenberg, R. J., & Lance, C. E. (2000). A review and synthesis of the measurement invariance literature: Suggestions, practices, and recommendations for organizational research. *Organizational Research Methods, 3*, 4–70.

Widaman, K. F. & Reise, S. P. (1997). Exploring the measurement invariance of psychological instruments: Applications in the substance use domain. In K. J. Bryant, M. Windle, & S. G. West (Eds.), *The science of prevention: Methodological advances from alcohol and substance abuse research* (pp. 281–324). Washington DC: American Psychological Association.

Yoon, M. (2004). *Detecting violations of factorial invariance using data-based specification searches: A Monte Carlo study.* Unpublished masters thesis, Arizona State University.

CHAPTER 9

Factor Analysis Models as Approximations

Robert C. MacCallum
University of North Carolina at Chapel Hill

Michael W. Browne
Ohio State University

Li Cai
University of North Carolina at Chapel Hill

A fundamental principle inherent in any application of factor analysis is that a factor analysis model is not an exact representation of real-world phenomena. Such a model, at least in any parsimonious form, is always wrong to some degree, even in the population. There is a variety of ways in which such models may be incorrect. For example, most factor analysis models specify a linear influence of latent variables on measured variables, when in fact that relationship may be nonlinear in the real world. Factor analysis models also attempt to account for relationships among measured variables using a small number of common factors and are not capable of fully representing the undoubtedly large number of minor common factors that influence measured variables and account in part for their intercorrelations. There are many other sources of error in such models. At best, a factor analysis model is an approximation of real-world phenomena.

Of course this is the nature of scientific models in general and has been discussed frequently in a variety of literatures. In our own field, Cudeck and Henly (1991) emphasized "... no model is completely faithful to the behavior under study. Models usually are formalizations of processes that are extremely complex. It is a mistake to ignore either their limitations or their artificiality. The best one can hope for is that some aspect of a model may be useful for description, prediction, or synthesis" (p. 512). This view is now widely understood and accepted in our use of models for representing psychological processes and the structure in data gathered in psychological research, with factor analysis models being one special case.

In the current chapter we consider two aspects of this principle. First, we examine the evolution of this idea in the history of factor analysis, focusing on how the view of the relationship between a factor analysis model and the real world has changed over the past 100 years. Second, we examine one important practical implication of this fundamental characteristic of such models: its relevance to the performance of different methods of parameter estimation. We demonstrate important differences among common estimation methods and account for these differences in terms of the nature of the correspondence between our models and the data we gather.

HISTORICAL PERSPECTIVE ON FACTOR ANALYSIS MODELS AS APPROXIMATIONS

Although the principle of the approximate nature of our models seems self-evident now, it was not part of the mindset among Charles Spearman and other psychological researchers a century ago. In part, this was because the models in question were not yet being formally expressed. Mathematical equations and statistical theory came much later. But even without equations for a model, the notion of formal implications of a theory for observed data was clearly present in early writings on factor analysis. In many ways, the model was implicit rather than explicit, as it became later, and the notion of a relationship between the implied model and the real world is often not difficult to discern in these early writings. So we begin with Spearman (1904) and attempt to examine the evolution of the perspectives regarding the relationship between the model and the real world. In this brief review, we must state two disclaimers. First, our review of the literature is not exhaustive but is rather selective. We focus primarily on major contributors to the factor analytic literature and on classic papers. Second, our review is necessarily interpretive in places. Authors are not always explicit about the issues of interest here, but the reader can often make inferences rather directly. Of course, reasonable alternative interpretations may well exist for some of the sources and statements that we cite here.

Comments on Spearman (1904)

Spearman (1904) focused of course on a theory of the structure of intelligence. His objective was to provide support for his theory that performance on any given mental test is determined in part by an individual's level of general ability, g, and the rest by whatever specific ability is required by that test. He sought to show that *g* alone was sufficient to account for correlations among various measures of mental ability, and he conducted analyses of observed correlation coefficients in pursuit of that objective. Although his 1904 paper does not include an equation for a factor analysis model, his theory can be clearly interpreted to imply that a single general common factor accounts for the intercorrelations of the measured variables.

Spearman's extensive review of earlier studies revealed inconsistent patterns of correlations among mental tests and no consistent support for his theory. He attributed failure of those studies to weakness of methods, noting problems associated with design, sampling, measures, and analyses. He clearly believed that if studies were done properly, then results would support his theory, and he undertook such a series of studies with great care, exhibiting his rigorous training in experimental methods under his mentor, Wilhelm Wundt. In these studies, Spearman employed a variety of measures of intellectual performance along with measures of sensory discrimination and he focused on correlations among such measures both within and between these domains. A cornerstone of the case for his theory was the effort to show that the true correlations between the separate domains were essentially perfect, indicating that sensory discrimination and measures of other sorts of intellectual performance were simply different manifestations of *g*. To this end, he applied new and creative corrections to observed sample correlations, including correction for attenuation and partialing out of effects of other variables. In the end, he showed that corrected correlations were consistently around 1.00, a finding that he took to reflect strong support for his theory. In addition, he noted importantly that tables (matrices) of correlations among various tests, when rows and columns were properly arranged, tended to exhibit a hierarchical order, meaning that the magnitude of correlations decreased as one moved down each column away from the diagonal. Spearman argued that this pattern was further evidence for his theory and that the ordering of the tests in such a table reflected their saturation with *g*.

Spearman (1904) offered some strongly stated conclusions based on these results:

> On the whole then, we reach the profoundly important conclusion that there really exists a something that we may provisionally term "General Sensory Discrimination" and similarly a "General Intelligence," and further that the functional correspondence between these two is not appreciably less than absolute. . . . When branches of intellectual activity are at all dissimilar, then their correlations with one another appear wholly due to their being all variously saturated with some common fundamental Function (or group of Functions). (pp. 272–273)

We perceive a clear theme in Spearman's 1904 paper in that he believed there was an absolute truth with regard to the structure of intelligence, and that that truth was represented by his two-factor theory. Importantly, he believed that truth to be accessible via sufficiently careful design, methods, and analyses, and that the evidence he had thereby obtained verified the truth of his two-factor theory.

Translated into more modern language, he believed that the model implied by his theory accounted exactly for the relevant real-world phenomena.

A Long Period of Debate

During the next 20 to 30 years, Spearman invested much effort in the refinement of criteria for verification of his theory and in attempting to develop further compelling evidence of the truth of that theory. Hart and Spearman (1912) discussed several criteria for testing the theory based on the pattern of intercorrelations among the measured variables. Based on the anticipated hierarchical structure of the sample correlation matrix, **R**, under Spearman's theory, Hart and Spearman focused on the computation and use of *intercolumnar correlations*, which are correlations among coefficients in different columns of **R**. After correction for attenuation and for other sources of bias, Hart and Spearman used as a criterion the mean of the intercolumnar correlations obtained from correlating pairs of columns in **R**. If it were to hold exactly, Spearman's theory would imply that such correlations should be 1.0. Hart and Spearman also defined and discussed the subsequently famous tetrad differences as another criterion for evaluating Spearman's theory, pointing out that the truth of the theory would require that all tetrad differences be zero.

The Hart and Spearman (1912) paper provides an interesting early example of the evaluation of competing theories. They described several different factor analytic theories about the structure of intelligence (Spearman's two-factor theory, the theory of group factors, and the theory that intelligence is composed of a complex array of elementary functions) and then determined the implications of each theory for the pattern of elements in **R**, arguing that each theory predicted a different pattern. Hart and Spearman obtained data from 14 previous empirical studies and then applied the intercolumnar correlation criterion to each data set. However, prior to computing this value, they eliminated from each data set variables that were highly similar, in addition to applying various corrections for bias. Their results yielded mean intercolumnar correlations of approximately 1.0 in each of the 14 studies, leading them to the conclusion that Spearman's theory had now been "proved true" (p. 60). Again such a statement clearly implies that they believed there to be an exact and invariant truth about the structure of intelligence, that that truth was accessible by use of sufficiently careful techniques, and that the resulting evidence verified that Spearman's theory was purely correct.

The Hart and Spearman (1912) findings seemed compelling. In a later review of the early factor analytic literature Dodd (1928) wrote, "it seemed to be the most striking quantitative fact in the history of psychology" (p. 214). Dodd, however, quickly pointed out that there were significant concerns and questions pertaining to this finding that had become the focus of much subsequent work. A major antagonist of Spearman's efforts to prove his theory true was Godfrey Thomson. In a series of papers beginning in 1916, Thomson pushed two major arguments. First, he showed that alternative theories could produce essentially the same pattern of elements in

R as implied by Spearman's theory; second, he argued that Spearman's methods of analysis were highly suspect and biased in favor of confirming his theory.

Thomson (1920a, 1920b) presented an alternative theory of the structure of intelligence based on the notion that there exists a very large number of simple, elemental abilities and that any mental test requires some sample of these abilities. Correlations among tests are then attributable to the overlap in the sample of abilities that they require. Thomson showed that this sampling theory of mental abilities would also imply intercolumnar correlations of 1.0 and zero tetrad differences, just as did Spearman's theory. He also simulated these phenomena via experiments with dice (Thomson, 1919). Thus, Thomson was arguing that satisfaction of the criteria laid out by Hart and Spearman (1912) and used often to evaluate the validity of Spearman's theory were not in fact sufficient criteria for such evaluation. Thomson also attacked much of the evidence for Spearman's theory on the grounds that investigators routinely removed selected tests prior to final statistical evaluation of the theory, and evaluated the theory based only on correlations among the remaining tests. Numerous studies supportive of Spearman's theory deleted tests that caused violations of the usual criteria (e.g., Brown & Stephenson, 1933; Hart & Spearman, 1912) and then showed that the criteria were satisfied when applied to the remaining tests. Commenting on this approach, Thomson (1920b) stated, ". . . the Hart and Spearman criterion for the degree of perfection is erroneous and creates the extreme perfection it purports to detect" (p. 326). Of note is the fact that Thomson (1920a) also discussed the futility of requiring that these criteria be perfectly satisfied. Thomson's primary criticisms of Spearman's theory and the criteria and research supporting it are summarized by Brown and Thomson (1921).

For years, Spearman firmly stood his ground against Thomson's assault, arguing that Thomson's dice simulations were misleading and that g was introduced in his simulations and in his sampling theory in a hidden fashion. Spearman continued to believe his theory was correct and stated in response to Thomson (Spearman, 1920) ". . . as regards the fundamental theory, I venture to maintain that this has now been demonstrated with finality" (p. 172).

Much of the theoretical and applied work during this early era seemed to revolve around a debate about the truth or falsity of Spearman's two-factor theory. It was clear that the theory implied a particular pattern of correlations among measured variables. The Spearman school operated from the position that if empirical data could be shown to exhibit those characteristics exactly, then the theory was proven. The Thomson school, on the other hand, held the view that methods used for assessing common criteria in empirical data were badly flawed and biased, and furthermore that alternative theories were not sufficiently differentiated by those criteria. Even granting the hazy distinction between the substantive theory and a corresponding formal model that was inherent in much of the early work, from a modern perspective it seems unfortunate that so much energy was invested in evaluating the truth or falsity of Spearman's original theory. As stated earlier, the view that such theories or models are simplifications and approximations of the real world was not yet part of the mindset.

During the 1920s and 1930s, the focus gradually shifted away from establishing the truth or falsity of Spearman's theory. Spearman himself gave ground as evidence accumulated that his theory often did not adequately account for observed data. In his 1927 book, and elsewhere, he gradually came to acknowledge the need for group factors, but as few as possible and only after g was extracted. In this context, he acknowledged the failure of his theory to perfectly account for data when measures represented abilities that overlap and he went so far as to note that it was useful to consider as a general criterion the degree of truth in competing theories. This view could be interpreted as a significant shift in his perspective on the correspondence between models and real-world phenomena. In this same vein, Thomson (1939) wrote explicitly about seeking factor analytic solutions that provided the best approximation to observed data and he differentiated methods such as components analysis and factor analysis in terms of the type and degree of approximation that they sought. Notions of approximation were clearly taking hold both conceptually and analytically.

Increased Understanding of the Nature of Models

In the late 1920s and early 1930s, L. L. Thurstone turned his attention to the theory and methodology of factor analysis and brought with him a clear perspective on models as approximations of reality. This perspective can be found in many of his writings, and is especially clear in the following quotations from his monograph on the Primary Mental Abilities (Thurstone, 1938). Consider the following quotations regarding the assumptions inherent in the common factor model: "Our assumptions oversimplify the phenomena we are trying to comprehend" (p. 89). "While working with this simplifying assumption, we can expect to find the principal landmarks or dimensions of mind" (p. 89). Regarding the common factor model as an approximation, he wrote "... performance can be expressed, in first approximation, as a linear function of the primaries," (p. 2) and "Perhaps the equation 9.1 should be very much more complex" (p. 3), referring to an equation for the basic common factor model and its inadequacy to represent the complexities of the real world. As Thurstone moved the factor analysis literature toward more explicit and complete expression of models (e.g., using matrix algebra), he also was consistently explicit that these models were simplifications and approximations of the phenomena for which they were intended to account. In his development of substantive theory on the structure of intelligence, he argued that Spearman's two-factor model was usually inadequate and that more factors were necessary, although the full set of factors retained might well include g. The decision about the number of factors to retain became an important aspect of carrying out factor analysis, with full recognition that the object was not to retain enough factors to exactly account for observed data, but rather to achieve a close but parsimonious approximation. Rather than

employ rigid criteria such as tetrad differences, Thurstone focused on residual correlations and the goal of making the residuals small enough that one could believe
that all major factors had been extracted, even though there may be a wide array
of random and nonrandom influences contributing to remaining lack of fit of the
model. Thurstone's views and methods clearly caused the general perspective in
the field of factor analysis to move away from notions of proof and truth, and
toward notions of models as approximations.

The next major step in this direction can be attributed to the full representation of the common factor model as a statistical model by Lawley and Maxwell
(1963). This development incorporated (a) distribution theory, (b) the notion of
population parameters with unknown values, (c) estimation of parameters by minimization of discrepancy functions, and (d) statistical inference including model
testing. Application of these methods became feasible in the 1960s and 1970s
through the work of Jöreskog (1967) and others and is now routine. Most importantly, in the present context of considering the evolution of the notion of factor
analysis models as approximations, these developments provided a clear basis for
understanding many various ways in which the model could be incorrect, including
violation of distributional assumptions, violation of linearity, the influence of minor
common factors not represented in the model, and violation of the assumption that
factor loadings are invariant across individuals. Clearly, such explicit representation of the model and underlying assumptions made it more evident that this model
cannot be exactly correct in the real world. Without this formal representation and
accompanying perspective, early researchers struggled with notions of truth and
proof, and with defining and assessing quantitative criteria to evaluate their theories.
In commenting on the great changes that occurred between 1904 and the development of a full statistical formulation of factor analysis models many decades
later, Bartholomew (1995) suggested that factor analysis "was born before its
time" (p. 216).

Fortunately the formal mechanisms for model specification and estimation are
now well developed and allow us to conduct factor analyses easily while also
understanding that we are employing a model that is a simplification and approximation of that which it is meant to represent and explain. This view is now part of
the general perspective on such models and is reflected in numerous classic papers
on the subject. For example, Jöreskog (1969) in his famous paper on confirmatory
factor analysis comments on how the likelihood ratio test of exact fit is problem-
atic because exact fit will never hold in practice. In a classic Monte Carlo study
of the performance of various methods of factor analysis, Tucker, Koopman, and
Linn (1969) constructed artificial correlation matrices incorporating effects of large
numbers of minor factors. Tucker and Lewis (1973) developed a widely used fit
index for maximum likelihood factor analysis whose rationale was based explicitly
on the differentiation between sampling error and error in the model itself. Work
by Steiger, Shapiro, and Browne (1985) established the distribution of the likelihood ratio test statistic under the condition that the model did not hold exactly in

the population, and subsequent work on model fit has made explicit use of this statistical theory (e.g., Browne & Cudeck, 1993).

Some fairly recent papers have focused directly on the approximate nature of factor analysis and related models. MacCallum and Tucker (1991) teased apart sources of error in the common factor model, differentiating among error due to sampling and error due to the approximate nature of the model both in the population and the sample. Cudeck and Henly (1991) borrowed a framework from Linhart and Zucchini (1986) and adapted it to represent different sources of error in covariance structure models, and they used that framework as a basis for differentiating various aspects of model fit and model comparison. In general, then, this perspective of factor analysis models as approximations has become a central feature of the mainstream methodological literature in the field.

Of course, this perspective holds across scientific disciplines and has been stated firmly and often by some of the most prominent statisticians of our time. John Tukey (1961) put it this way: "In a single sentence, the moral is: Admit that complexity increases, first from the model you fit to the data, thence to the model you use to think and plan about the experiment and its analysis, and thence to the true situation" (p. 210). George Box, in his 1979 Presidential Address to the American Statistical Association, stated "Models, of course, are never true, but fortunately it is only necessary that they be useful. For this it is usually needful only that they not be grossly wrong" (p. 2).

Thus, we accept the fact that our factor analysis models are always wrong to some degree and in various ways, but that they still may be useful if they are not grossly wrong. And we can also see that this perspective has evolved over the past 100 years, from early arguments about truth and proof to current recognition that, at best, we can hope for a model that has some utility and that provides a good approximation to what we have observed.

IMPLICATIONS FOR PARAMETER ESTIMATION

A number of papers (Cudeck & Henly, 1991; MacCallum, 2003; MacCallum & Tucker, 1991) have focused explicitly on implications of the fact that our models are merely approximations. This phenomenon has been shown to bear directly on issues such as sample size, statistical power, model fit, and model comparison. In the current chapter, we focus on implications regarding parameter estimation. We draw on and extend previous work by MacCallum, Tucker, and Briggs (2001) and Briggs and MacCallum (2003) to show that the presence and nature of error in a model has direct and strong implications for the performance of different estimation methods.

The central issue is the nature of error in our data. Observed data can be viewed as containing error of various types. Overall error can be understood as arising from two distinct sources, which we refer to as *sampling error* and *model error*. Sampling error arises from the lack of correspondence between the sample and the population from which it was drawn. Thus, even if a model were to be exactly true in a population, the presence of sampling error would result in that model not holding perfectly in a sample from that population. Sampling error arises routinely of course even in perfect random sampling, but its degree and nature may be affected in any variety of ways due to nonrandomness in sampling. Model error refers to the lack of fit of a model in the full population and may also arise from a variety of sources. As mentioned earlier, in the context of factor analysis, we can easily understand model error arising from sources such as nonlinearity in the relationships of factors to measured variables, the influences of large numbers of minor common factors, and many other effects not represented in a parsimonious factor analysis model.

A variety of estimation methods is available in factor analysis, and these methods differ with respect to assumptions they make about the nature of error. For instance, maximum likelihood (ML) estimation is based on the assumption that the model is exactly correct in the population and that all error is normal theory random sampling error. In other words, it is assumed under ML estimation that there is no model error. Other estimation methods make different assumptions, as is discussed later in this chapter. When using a particular method of estimation, a reasonable concern is the issue of the degree of correspondence between the assumptions about the nature of error and the actual nature of error in the data, and whether that correspondence has any practical implications or consequences regarding the results of our analyses. This is the central question to be considered here.

Example of Differences in Estimation Methods

To illustrate potential consequences associated with the issue just raised, we begin with an artificial example first presented by MacCallum and Tucker (1991). The example is extended in a number of ways as we proceed. Using a modified version of simulation methods developed by Tucker et al., (1969), a population correlation matrix was generated that included effects of model error. Specifically, correlations among 12 measured variables were constructed as arising from effects of three major common factors and 50 minor factors simulated to represent a type of model error. It is important to note that no sampling error was introduced. Thus, the simulated correlation matrix can be viewed as a population correlation matrix, **P**, with all lack of fit attributable to model error. The data generating parameters are shown in Table 9–1. The three major domain factors are clearly of unequal strength, decreasing from a very strong first factor to a moderately strong second factor to a relatively weak third factor. Under the simulation method, variance in each measured variable not accounted for by these three major factors was attributed partly to a unique factor for each measured variable with the remainder attributable to effects of the 50 minor factors. Note that the variance due to minor factors was identical for each measured variable. Following methods described in

TABLE 9–1
Data Generating Parameters for Simulated Population Correlation Matrix

	Major Domain Factors			Uniqueness	Minor Variance
Variable	1	2	3		
1	.95	0	0	.000	.098
2	.95	0	0	.000	.098
3	.95	0	0	.000	.098
4	.95	0	0	.000	.098
5	.95	0	0	.000	.098
6	0	.70	0	.413	.098
7	0	.70	0	.413	.098
8	0	.70	0	.413	.098
9	0	.70	0	.413	.098
10	0	0	.50	.653	.098
11	0	0	.50	.653	.098
12	0	0	.50	.653	.098

TABLE 9–2
Simulated Population Correlation Matrix

	1	2	3	4	5	6	7	8	9	10	11	12
1	1.00											
2	.94	1.00										
3	.87	.88	1.00									
4	.89	.90	.95	1.00								
5	.96	.94	.89	.86	1.00							
6	−.01	−.01	.06	.08	−.04	1.00						
7	−.06	−.06	.06	.03	−.06	.53	1.00					
8	.00	−.06	−.04	.02	−.06	.49	.52	1.00				
9	−.01	.05	−.02	−.06	.04	.45	.45	.42	1.00			
10	.06	.07	−.02	.02	.05	.02	.06	.04	.02	1.00		
11	.04	.05	−.05	−.06	.07	−.05	−.05	−.04	.05	.29	1.00	
12	.01	−.06	−.02	−.07	.04	−.06	.00	.02	.00	−.21	.27	1.00

detail by MacCallum and Tucker (1991) the parameters in Table 9–1 were used to generate the population correlation matrix, **P**, shown in Table 9–2. A glance at **P** reveals two interesting features. First, the three blocks of large correlations along the diagonal clearly reflect the influences of the three major domain factors. Second, the effects of the minor factors are also clearly evident. Given that there is no sampling error, without the minor factors all elements outside of the three diagonal blocks would be exactly zero, and elements within each diagonal block would be identical ($.95^2$ in the first block, $.70^2$ in the second block, and $.50^2$ in the third block). Deviations of elements in **P** from these values are attributable to influences of minor factors.

TABLE 9–3

OLS and ML Results From Factor Analyzing the Population Correlation Matrix

	OLS Solution				ML Solution			
	Factor 1	Factor 2	Factor 3	Uniqueness	Factor 1	Factor 2	Factor 3	Uniqueness
1	**.96**	−.01	.06	.07	**.96**	−.02	.10	.06
2	**.96**	−.02	.04	.07	**.96**	−.01	.06	.08
3	**.94**	.05	−.10	.11	**.95**	.05	−.13	.08
4	**.94**	.06	−.12	.09	**.96**	.06	−.28	.00
5	**.96**	−.06	.10	.06	**.97**	−.03	.25	.00
6	.01	**.72**	.00	.48	.01	**.72**	−.12	.47
7	−.03	**.75**	−.01	.44	−.02	**.74**	−.06	.44
8	−.04	**.69**	.03	.53	−.03	**.67**	−.03	.54
9	−.01	**.61**	.14	.61	−.01	**.64**	.30	.50
10	.04	−.04	**.45**	.79	.04	−.03	**.06**	.99
11	.01	−.07	**.63**	.60	.01	.04	**.23**	.94
12	−.02	−.04	**.42**	.82	−.01	−.02	**.19**	.96

The matrix in Table 9–2 was subjected to unrestricted factor analysis using two different estimation methods: ML and ordinary least squares (OLS). Three factors were retained in each solution and the factors were rotated using oblique target rotation with the major domain factors as the target. The ML and OLS solutions are shown in Table 9–3. Loadings that correspond to the nonzero loadings in the major domain are shown in bold. (Factor intercorrelations are not shown, but for both ML and OLS, the rotated factors were nearly orthogonal; the largest interfactor correlation in either solution was approximately .10.) A major difference between loadings obtained in the two solutions is immediately apparent. Both estimation methods recover the first two major domain factors quite accurately, but ML does not recover the weak third factor whereas OLS does. (In further discussion of this illustration, MacCallum et al., 2001, showed that the failure of ML was not due to retaining an insufficient number of factors and also could not be attributed to the presence of two Heywood cases in the ML solution.)

The current focus is to consider whether the differential performance of ML and OLS in this illustration might be attributable to the degree of correspondence between the nature of error in the data and the assumptions made about such error by each of these estimation methods. Recall that in the example there is no sampling error, with all error being model error arising from influences of minor factors. Under ML estimation, all error is assumed to be random sampling error under normal distribution theory. The model is assumed to be correct in the population. (Note that if this assumption holds, then ML estimates are more efficient than those provided by any other method, and ML would be the estimation method of choice. Here we consider the behavior of ML and other methods when this assumption is violated and model error is present.) Under the ML assumptions, larger correlations among measured variables would be less influenced by error, whereas smaller correlations would tend to be more affected by error. Compare these assumptions to those made under OLS estimation. Under OLS, no distributional assumptions are made and no assumption is made about sampling error versus model error. From this basis, the magnitude of error is assumed to be unrelated to the size of the correlation coefficients. Given this difference between ML and OLS with regard to assumptions about error in the correlation coefficients that are being analyzed, it is of interest to consider whether this difference might be the source of the differential performance of the methods seen in Table 9–3. More specifically, the illustration presented involves construction of simulated data wherein the magnitude of error in the correlation coefficients is unrelated to the size of the correlations (see Table 9–2). Clearly this error structure is more consistent with assumptions under OLS than under ML. The possibility that this difference may explain results in the illustration presented earlier and that it may in fact be one instance of a more general difference in performance of ML and OLS has been examined in some detail by MacCallum et al. (2001) and by Briggs and MacCallum (2003). In those papers, the issue was studied using other major domain structures (i.e., structures different from that presented in Table 9–1), different numbers of strong and weak factors, and different amounts and types of error in the data. The general finding was a distinct advantage of OLS over ML in recovery of weaker common factors. We now pursue this issue further in an effort to provide a deeper understanding and also extend the issue to involve yet another estimation method.

Estimation Methods and the Relationship Between Residuals and Data

In this section, we extend analysis of one condition considered in the study by Briggs and MacCallum (2003). (Details not presented here can be found in that paper.) The condition involves simulation of data for 16 measured variables influenced by four major domain factors, with the first three major factors being quite strong and the fourth being relatively weak. (Specifically, four variables had loadings of .95 on the first factor, four had loadings of .85 on the second factor, four had loadings of .80 on the third factor, and four had loadings of .45 on the relatively weak fourth factor.) Model error was introduced into the data by simulating effects of 50 minor factors, as in the previous example. Holding the minor variance contributions to each measured variable fixed in the population, analogous to our earlier example, we generated 500 population correlation matrices, with those matrices varying with respect to the random nature of the minor factor influences on the correlations among the measured variables. In addition, sampling error was introduced into these simulated data. For each of the 500 **P** matrices, we generated 200 sample correlation matrices using $N = 100$ and sampling under the assumption of multivariate normality. Thus, the entire procedure yielded 100,000 sample correlation matrices, with each matrix influenced by randomness both with respect to model error and sampling error. Each of these 100,000 matrices was then factor analyzed using both ML and OLS, retaining four factors and rotating the solution using oblique target rotation with the major domain loadings as the target.

Of special interest in evaluating these results was the degree of recovery of the weak fourth factor. Recovery of the fourth factor was measured using the congruence coefficient between the fourth estimated factor and the fourth major domain factor already defined. (The congruence coefficient is the cosine of the angle between these two factors when represented in the same space; values in the low to mid .90s are considered to reflect relatively close congruence.) Figure 9–1 shows a plot of these congruence coefficients for OLS vs. ML solutions from the 100,000 replications. The striking triangular form of the plot shows that across 100,000 replications, it rarely occurred that ML recovered the weak factor better than did OLS, and it never occurred that ML recovered that factor accurately while OLS did not. The mean congruence coefficients were .90 for OLS and .78 for ML, a very substantial difference. In addition, recovery by OLS was much more stable, with coefficients exhibiting a standard deviation of .08 under OLS and .21 under ML.

This large scale example, including both model error and sampling error, shows that the advantage of OLS over ML observed in the limited first illustration presented earlier in fact is not a narrow one. It is a difference that can have important implications in empirical research, and it also is a difference that demands explanation and understanding.

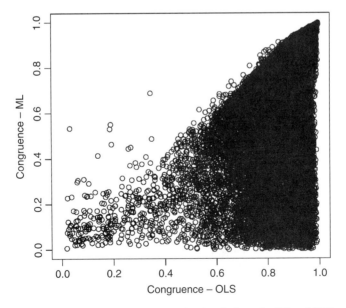

FIGURE 9–1.   Recovery of weak major domain factor by ML and OLS.

We believe that such understanding can be advanced through a careful consideration of the discrepancy functions being minimized under ML and OLS. The discrepancy function under ML estimation is generally written as

$$F_{ML} = \ln|\Sigma| - \ln|S| + tr(S\Sigma^{-1}) - p \qquad \text{(Equation 9.1)}$$

where Σ is the population covariance matrix, S is the sample covariance matrix, and p is the number of measured variables. It has been shown that this function can be closely approximated by a different function expressed as a sum of squares of weighted residuals:

$$F_{ML} \cong \sum_j \sum_k \left[(s_{jk} - \hat{\sigma}_{jk})^2 / u_j^2 u_k^2 \right] \qquad \text{(Equation 9.2)}$$

where s_{jk} and $\hat{\sigma}_{jk}$ are elements of the sample covariance matrix and the implied covariance matrix, respectively, and u_j^2 and u_k^2 are sample unique variances of variables j and k (e.g., Browne, 1969). The important feature of this expression is that squared residuals are inversely weighted according to the product of the unique variances of the associated variables, meaning squared residuals associated with a larger product of unique variances receive less weight in contributing to this approximation of F_{ML}. It is informative to compare this discrepancy function to the corresponding OLS function:

$$F_{OLS} = \sum_j \sum_k (s_{jk} - \hat{\sigma}_{jk})^2 \qquad \text{(Equation 9.3)}$$

Obviously the OLS discrepancy function is defined in terms of unweighted squared residuals, meaning that all squared residuals contribute equally to F_{OLS}.

The different weighting of residuals under F_{ML} and F_{OLS} suggests that residuals associated with pairs of variables that exhibit a higher product of unique variances may in fact be larger under ML than OLS estimation, because they receive less weight under ML than under OLS. We examined results from the simulation study described earlier to investigate this phenomenon. From the 100,000 data sets generated in that study, we selected 400, consisting of 20 sample correlation matrices drawn from populations represented by each of 20 different population matrices. Aggregating across these 400 data sets, we examined the relationship between squared residual correlations and products of unique variances for corresponding pairs of variables. The resulting plots are shown in Figure 9–2 and Figure 9–3, for ML and OLS respectively. These plots indicate a clear tendency for ML to produce higher squared residuals than OLS for those pairs of variables characterized by higher unique variance products. Pairs of variables, where both exhibit relatively large unique variances, would naturally exhibit smaller intercorrelations. That is, if $u_j^2 u_k^2$ is relatively high for variables j and k, then the correlation between variables j and k would tend to be small. Thus, it should also be of interest to examine the association between squared residual correlations and the magnitude of the correlations themselves. These plots are shown in Figure 9–4 and

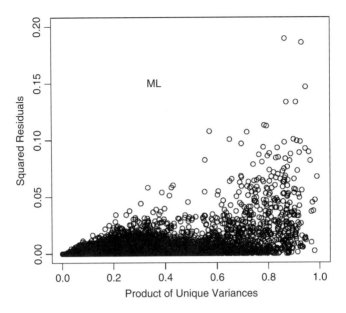

FIGURE 9–2.   Relationship of squared residuals and unique variance products under ML.

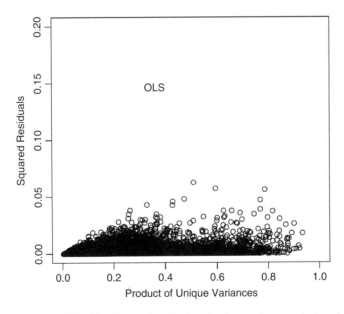

FIGURE 9–3.   Relationship of squared residuals and unique variance products under OLS.

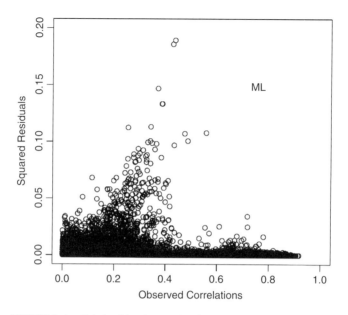

FIGURE 9–4.   Relationship of squared residuals and correlations under ML.

Figure 9–5, for ML and OLS respectively. The plots indicate a tendency for ML squared residuals associated with smaller correlations in the matrix being fitted to be larger than corresponding squared residuals obtained from OLS.

We suggest that this observation helps to explain the phenomenon observed earlier, wherein OLS showed a clear superiority in recovering weaker common factors. The rationale for this explanation is as follows. The ML and OLS estimation methods make different assumptions about the nature of error. These different assumptions are manifested formally as differential weighting of squared residual correlations. Specifically, ML estimation, because it assumes all error to be normal theory sampling error, will allow for more error in smaller correlations and will attach lower weight to the associated squared residuals, as reflected in Equation 9.2. OLS estimation, with no distributional assumptions and no explicit differentiation of model error and sampling error, weights all squared residuals equally as in Equation 9.3. Considering the issue of recovery of weaker common factors, the critical point is that such factors will manifest themselves through the presence of smaller correlations among measured variables, whereas stronger factors produce larger correlations among measured variables. Given that ML tolerates larger squared residuals in smaller correlations while seeking to make squared residuals associated with larger correlations as small as possible, there will be a natural tendency for it to perform more poorly than OLS in recovering common factors that produce smaller correlations.

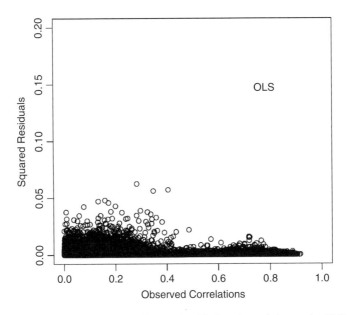

FIGURE 9–5.   Relationship of squared residuals and correlations under OLS.

If this explanation is valid, it should hold up in considering other estimation methods. To investigate this issue, we considered the *Alpha factor analysis* method (Kaiser & Caffrey, 1965) from the same perspective. The Alpha approach makes different assumptions about the nature of error than does ML or OLS. Under Alpha factor analysis it is assumed that there is no sampling error with respect to individuals. Rather, sampling error is assumed to arise from the sampling of measured variables from the universe of variables of interest. That is, it is assumed that there exists a universe (or a population) of all measured variables of potential interest in a given study. The universe represents the content domain of interest. From this universe a set of variables is chosen for empirical measurement, but this set of observed variables cannot fully represent the universe or domain of interest, just as a sample of individuals will exhibit properties different from the population from which it was drawn. More specifically, in the universe of variables, there will exist a set of common factors, but these common factors would not be recovered exactly from the set of observed variables. Error arising from not having access to the full universe of variables is called *psychometric error*, and in Alpha factor analysis, all error is assumed to be psychometric error. Given these assumptions, the objective of Alpha factor analysis is then defined as determining common factors from the sample of measured variables that will have maximum correlation with the corresponding factors in the universe of variables. This is achieved by extracting factors that exhibit maximum coefficient alpha. In terms of a discrepancy function to be minimized, the discrepancy function for Alpha factor analysis can be approximated very closely as the following sum of weighted squared residuals (Browne, 1969):

$$F_{ALPHA} \cong \sum_{j} \sum_{k} \left[(s_{jk} - \hat{\sigma}_{jk})^2 / (1 - u_j^2)(1 - u_k^2) \right] \qquad \text{(Equation 9.4)}$$

A comparison of Equation 9.4 and Equation 9.2 reveals a most interesting difference in the weighting applied to squared residuals under Alpha versus ML estimation. Whereas ML weights the squared residuals inversely according to the products of the unique variances, Alpha weights them inversely according to the products of the *complements* of those same unique variances. Equivalently, Alpha weights residuals inversely to the magnitude of the product of communalities for the given pair of variables. For a pair of measured variables with high unique variances (low communalities), the corresponding squared residual would receive low weight under ML but high weight under Alpha. Relating this point to the notion that such a pair of variables would tend to exhibit a low intercorrelation, it can in turn be understood that, whereas ML tends to apply lower weight to squared residuals associated with lower correlations, Alpha will tend to apply higher weight to those same squared residuals. And finally relating this observation to the issue of recovery of weaker common factors, we can anticipate that Alpha should recover weaker factors better than ML because it should emphasize fitting of lower correlations more than does ML. It might even be the case that Alpha would be superior to OLS at this same task.

The same 100,000 simulated sample correlation matrices that were analyzed earlier by ML and OLS were also analyzed using the Alpha method of factoring, and recovery of the weak fourth factor was assessed. Figure 9–6 and Figure 9–7 show scatterplots indicating the congruence coefficient for Alpha versus ML (Figure 9–6) and Alpha versus OLS (Figure 9–7). Figure 9–6 shows evidence of superiority of Alpha over ML, with better recovery of the weak factor by Alpha than by ML in the vast majority of replications. On the other hand, Figure 9–7 shows ambiguous results for the comparison of Alpha to OLS, with no consistent advantage to either method. Earlier the mean congruence coefficients for ML and OLS were reported as .90 and .78, respectively; the mean for Alpha was .91. The standard deviations for ML and OLS were reported earlier as .21 and .08; the standard deviation under Alpha was .08. Thus, Alpha tends to show the same sort of advantage over ML as did OLS. We suggest that this advantage occurs because of the difference already described with regard to weighting of squared residuals, which in turn emanates from the assumptions made about the nature of error. In Figure 9–7, there is a hint of an advantage of Alpha over OLS. There are more instances where Alpha recovers the weak factor accurately and OLS misses it badly, as indicated by points in the lower right portion of the Figure, than vice versa. Although the advantage appears minor in our results, it is consistent with expectations as mentioned earlier.

Examination of residuals sheds further light on the differences between these estimation methods. For the same 400 matrices for which results were shown earlier in Figures 9–2 through 9–5 for ML and OLS, corresponding results are

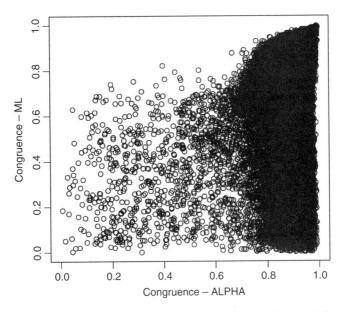

FIGURE 9–6. Recovery of weak major domain factor by ML and Alpha.

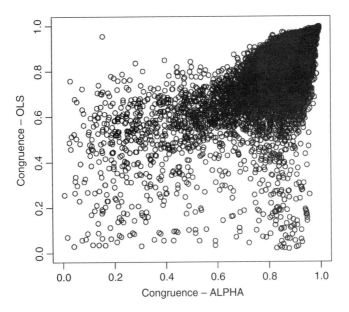

FIGURE 9–7. Recovery of weak major domain factor by OLS and Alpha.

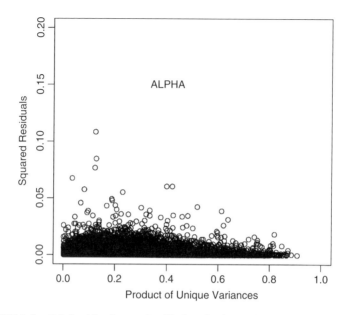

FIGURE 9–8.   Relationship of squared residuals and unique variance products under Alpha.

shown in Figure 9–8 and Figure 9–9 for Alpha. The plot in Figure 9–8 should be compared to those in Figure 9–2 and Figure 9.3 to see the difference in the relationship between squared residuals and unique variance products under each method. This comparison shows a difference among ML, OLS, and Alpha with regard to characteristics of pairs of variables that exhibit the smaller squared residuals. Figure 9–2 shows that under ML, larger residuals tend to be associated with variables with larger products of unique variances. Such a pattern is not present for OLS (Figure 9–3) or Alpha (Figure 9–8). Finally, Figure 9–9 shows the association between squared residuals and magnitude of observed correlations under Alpha factoring. A progression from ML (Figure 9–4) to OLS (Figure 9–5) to Alpha is evident with squared residuals associated with smaller correlations gradually becoming smaller.

Summary of Implications for Parameter Estimation

The general principle that factor analysis models are approximations implies that not all error in observed data is sampling error, but that some is model error. Different estimation methods are based on different assumptions about the nature of error, as described already in some detail. Those assumptions will differ with regard to how closely they correspond to the nature of error in real data, and we have demonstrated that that correspondence has real consequences for parameter estimation. We provided clear evidence for differential performance in estimation

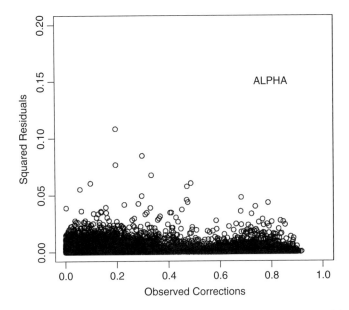

FIGURE 9–9.   Relationship of squared residuals and correlations under Alpha.

methods with regard to recovery of weaker common factors. It may well be that performance of these methods will differ significantly under other circumstances as well, such as when sampling error is quite high (small N) even though model error is quite small. Further study of such questions may well provide evidence of further important differences among methods. Most importantly, these observable consequences of differential assumptions about the nature of error apparently have implications for how we might best do factor analysis in practice. For example, results just presented suggest that if the investigator has reason to believe that some common factors of substantive interest may be relatively weak, then the investigator would probably have a better chance of recovering those factors using OLS or Alpha estimation methods rather than ML.

CONCLUSIONS

Like all other scientific models, factor analysis models must be viewed as simplifications or approximations of real-world phenomena. In the early years of the development of factor analytic methods and their application to empirical data, this concept was not well understood and it appears that some early controversy about theories of mental ability may have been due in part to that circumstance. However, now that the principle is well understood, it must be kept in mind when we do factor analysis and interpret our findings. It has observable and important consequences and implications for how we do factor analysis.

REFERENCES

Bartholomew, D. J. (1995). Spearman and the origin and development of factor analysis. *British Journal of Mathematical and Statistical Psychology, 48*, 211–220.

Box, G. E. P. (1979). Some problems of statistics and everyday life. *Journal of the American Statistical Association, 74*, 1–4.

Briggs, N. E., & MacCallum, R. C. (2003). Recovery of weak common factors by maximum likelihood and ordinary least squares estimation. *Multivariate Behavioral Research, 38*, 25–56.

Brown, W., & Stephenson, W. (1933). A test of the theory of two factors. *British Journal of Psychology, 23*, 352–370.

Brown, W., & Thomson, G. (1921). *The essentials of mental measurement.* London: Cambridge University Press.

Browne, M. W. (1969). Fitting the factor analysis model. *Psychometrika, 34*, 375–394.

Browne, M. W., & Cudeck, R. (1993). Alternative ways of assessing model fit. In K. A. Bollen & J. S. Long (Eds.), *Testing structural equation models* (pp. 136–162). Newbury Park, CA: Sage.

Cudeck, R., & Henly, S. J. (1991). Model selection in covariance structures analysis and the "problem" of sample size: A clarification. *Psychological Bulletin, 109*, 512–519.

Dodd, S. C. (1928). The theory of factors. *Psychological Review, 35*, 211–234.

Hart, B., & Spearman, C. (1912). General ability, its existence and nature. *British Journal of Psychology, 5*, 51–84.

Jöreskog, K. G. (1967). Some contributions to maximum likelihood factor analysis. *Psychometrika, 32*, 443–482.

Jöreskog, K. G. (1969). A general approach to confirmatory maximum likelihood factor analysis. *Psychometrika, 34*, 183–202.

Kaiser, H. F., & Caffrey, J. (1965). Alpha factor analysis. *Psychometrika, 30*, 1–14.

Lawley, D. N., & Maxwell, A. E. (1963). *Factor analysis as a statistical method.* London: Butterworths.

Linhart, H., & Zucchini, W. (1986). *Model selection.* New York: Wiley.

MacCallum, R. C. (2003). Working with imperfect models. *Multivariate Behavioral Research, 38*, 113–139.

MacCallum, R. C., & Tucker, L. R (1991). Representing sources of error in the common factor model: Implications for theory and practice. *Psychological Bulletin, 109*, 502–511.

MacCallum, R. C., Tucker, L. R, & Briggs, N. E. (2001). An alternative perspective on parameter estimation in factor analysis and related methods. In R. Cudeck, S. du Toit, & D. Sörbom (Eds.), *Structural equation modeling: Present and future.* (pp. 39–57). Lincolnwood, IL: SSI.

Spearman, C. (1904). "General intelligence," objectively determined and measured. *American Journal of Psychology, 5*, 201–293.

Spearman, C. (1920). Manifold sub-theories of "the two factors." *Psychological Review, 27*, 159–172.

Spearman, C. (1927). *The abilities of man, their nature and measurement.* New York: Macmillan.

Steiger, J. H., Shapiro, A., & Browne, M. W. (1985). On the multivariate asymptotic distribution of sequential chi-square statistics. *Psychometrika, 50*, 253–264.

Thomson, G. (1919). The proof or disproof of the existence of general ability. *British Journal of Psychology, 9*, 321–326.

Thomson, G. (1920a). General versus group factors in mental activities. *Psychological Review, 27*, 173–190.

Thomson, G. (1920b). The general factor fallacy in psychology. *British Journal of Psychology, 10*, 319–326.

Thomson, G. (1939). The factorial analysis of ability. *British Journal of Psychology, 30*, 71–77.

Thurstone, L. L. (1938). *Primary mental abilities*. Chicago: University of Chicago Press, Psychometric Monographs, 1, 1–121.

Tucker, L. R, Koopman, R. F., & Linn, R. L. (1969). Evaluation of factor analytic research procedures by means of simulated correlation matrices. *Psychometrika, 34*, 421–459.

Tucker, L. R, & Lewis, C. L. (1973). A reliability coefficient for maximum likelihood factor analysis. *Psychometrika, 38*, 1–10.

Tukey, J. W. (1961). Discussion, emphasizing the connection between analysis of variance and spectrum analysis. *Technometrics, 3*, 191–219.

CHAPTER 10

Common Factors Versus Components: Principals and Principles, Errors and Misconceptions

Keith F. Widaman
University of California at Davis

During the past century, common factor analysis (CFA) has enabled researchers to investigate the structure of behavioral domains in ways unsurpassed by other methods. Historically, factor analysis was first applied in the ability domain. The current received view of the structure of this domain, based on thousands of contributions published over the past 100 years, is that the ability domain is characterized by at least 25 to 30 primary mental ability dimensions at the lowest, first-stratum level and by about 9 broad, second-stratum factors (Carroll, 1993; Horn & Noll, 1997). Similar agreement has arisen in the personality domain based on research over the past 40 years or so with the identification of the Big 5 structure, which has become the standard taxonomy for broad personality dimensions (e.g., Digman, 1997; Goldberg, 1990; John & Srivastava, 1999). In neither the ability nor personality domains has final consensus yet been reached, as arguments continue on multiple issues, including whether any additional dimensions should be included in the taxonomies and whether higher order structures are warranted. However, attesting to its continuing importance, factor analysis is central to the framing of opposing positions on these current issues and is also the analytic method of choice for providing answers to the theoretical questions posed.

The transcendent position of factor analysis as a method for uncovering the dimensional structure of a domain has led to increasing complexity in methods of analysis. A dizzying array of options confront the analyst at each step in an analysis, with numerous methods for estimating communalities, extracting factors, selecting the number of factors, and rotating factors. One of the most basic choices—and the topic for the current contribution—is that between CFA and principal component analysis (PCA). Fundamentally, the choice between these methods is one regarding whether communalities are explicitly represented during the extraction of factors. This seemingly minor issue has many consequences, some well-known, others unintended or unacknowledged.

The structure of this chapter follows the lead provided by its title. First, I provide a historical backdrop by discussing some of the principal figures and events during the past century that are related to the distinction between common factors and principal components. Next, I identify basic principles regarding statistical analyses that can be used to organize thinking about matters, stressing the principled implications of these basic tenets for evaluating the alternative procedures of CFA and PCA. Then, I give a short and nontechnical introduction to the matrix formulations of CFA and PCA, the two primary methods for identifying the principal dimensions of a domain. The final part of the chapter covers errors and misconceptions. One intended meaning of the term, *errors*, is allied with the residual variables in CFA and PCA, which represent variance in manifest variables that is unrelated to the major dimensions retained in the solution; central here is the covariance structure for residual variables in CFA and PCA. A second denotation of errors is the misconceptions that accompany the use of CFA and PCA.

The overarching goals of this presentation are to compare and contrast CFA and PCA with regard to their applicability to data and utility as scientific tools for establishing fundamental, replicable findings. In so doing, I outline key assumptions, some of which are rarely discussed in depth, that lead to differences in the representations achieved by CFA and PCA.

PRINCIPALS AND PRINCIPLES

Principal Persons and Events

Spearman (1904) provided the first conceptualization of the nature of a common factor as the element in common to two or more indicators. As is well known, Spearman stressed the presence of two classes of factor. The first class of factor has a single member, identified as *g* (for general intelligence); *g* was identified as a, or more correctly *the*, common factor, influencing all tests of mental ability and therefore representing the single, common element shared by all tests of mental ability. The second class of factor has a potentially infinite number of members, as this class contains what are now termed *unique factors*, with one unique factor for each individual test.

Within a decade of the initial publication by Spearman (1904), the two-factor theory was in dispute. Burt (1909) offered an initial challenge to the unitary nature of the ability domain, presenting data and arguments that more than a single factor was required to represent ability data. Next, Thomson (1916) recognized the elusiveness of the connection between theory and data, specifically in relation to Spearman's two-factor theory. That is, Thomson demonstrated that the hierarchical pattern of correlations among variables predicted by Spearman's theory and subsequently observed in several studies could be consistent with underlying mechanisms for which no single mental function was common to all tests. Instead, Thomson argued that the mind could consist of a virtually infinite number of potential "bonds," that bonds might be statistically independent, that different mental tests may require different and overlapping sets of bonds to arrive at correct solutions to problems, and that this conception would lead to the same pattern in correlations among tests as predicted by the two-factor theory proposed by Spearman (1904).

A decade and a half later, Thurstone (1931) made his initial foray into factor analysis. Here, Thurstone developed what he termed a "center of gravity" method for estimating factor loadings, an approach that later became the *centroid method*. Important for the distinction between common factors and principal components, the diagonal entries in the correlation matrix were explicitly disregarded, as Thurstone formulated a method that used only the off-diagonal correlations among variables in calculations, as these were the principal data to be explained.

Only 2 years later, Hotelling (1933) proposed a method of estimating the principal components of a battery of manifest variables. Hotelling's method yielded a least-squares representation of the manifest variables, a representation in which the components were uncorrelated (or orthogonal) and conditionally variance maximized. That is, regardless of the correlations among the manifest variables, scores on the principal components were uncorrelated across components, and the components were estimated so that each successive component explained the greatest amount of variance in the manifest variables that was independent of variance explained by preceding components. Two key aspects of the developments by Hotelling (1933) are relevant to the present chapter: (a) Hotelling left unities on the diagonal of the correlation matrix analyzed, and (b) he interpreted the unrotated solution. Thus, it is clear that both models and methods are involved. That is, Hotelling was dealing, explicitly or not, with a different analytic model by retaining unities on the diagonal of the correlation matrix and retaining their influence on the resulting solution, even as he was proposing a new extraction method—the method of principal axes—for estimating the loadings of manifest variables on dimensions.

Two years hence, Thurstone (1935) published *The Vectors of Mind*, his first extended treatment of the common factor model. Most germane to our current interest, Thurstone identified three major problems with the methods developed by Hotelling (1933): (a) leaving unities on the diagonal of the correlation matrix and thereby assuming that all of the variance of each manifest variable should be explained by the derived dimensions; (b) retaining and interpreting the full set of components (i.e., the number of principal components equaled the number of manifest variables); and (c) failing to rotate dimensions into a more interpretable orientation. In my opinion, Thurstone appeared far more concerned about the latter two issues than the first.

Shortly after the publication of *The Vectors of Mind*, two articles were published in *Psychometrika* that are directly relevant to the CFA–PCA comparison. In the first, McCloy, Metheny, and Knott (1938) presented a matrix of hypothetical loadings of 10 manifest variables on 3 factors, computed correlations among manifest variables implied by the loadings, and then applied the CFA procedures developed by Thurstone (1935) and the PCA procedures by Hotelling (1933) to this population correlation matrix. McCloy et al. (1938) extracted and rotated three common factors and separately extracted and rotated three principal components. Foreshadowing results presented over a half-century later by Snook and Gorsuch (1989), McCloy et al. concluded that the loadings based on PCA tended to be larger than loadings from CFA and that CFA loadings were closer to the population loadings that generated the correlational structure. The McCloy et al. paper was followed the next year by a paper by Wilson and Worcester (1939), who argued that PCA was poorly suited to the goal of identifying known relations among measurements, although their argument seems to cast aspersions on CFA as well.

Following closely after the preceding papers, Thomson (1939) provided an illuminating discussion of the differing goals of CFA and PCA. Because this contribution is discussed later in more detail, I do not discuss it further here, aside from observing that Thomson (1939) deserves re-reading even today for its clarity and conciseness.

About a decade and a half later, Guttman published several papers on the role of communalities in factor analysis. In one of these papers, Guttman (1954) derived three lower bounds for the number of common factors. These bounds are (a) the weakest lower bound, or the number of dimensions with eigenvalues $\geq$ unity when unity is used as the communality estimate; (b) the middle lower bound, or the number of dimensions with eigenvalues ≥ 0 when the square of the highest correlation in the row is used as the communality estimate; and (c) the strongest lower bound, or the number of dimensions with eigenvalues ≥ 0 when the squared multiple correlation of each variable with all remaining manifest variables is used as the communality estimate.

Kaiser (1960, 1971) built on the ideas of Guttman to develop a simple approach to factor analysis, an approach that Chester Harris later dubbed the "Little Jiffy": PCA extraction, retention of all components with eigenvalues $\geq$ unity (à la Guttman), and varimax rotation of the retained components (à la Kaiser, 1958). The ability of the Little Jiffy to identify meaningful solutions for several classic data sets led to the institution of the Little Jiffy options as the defaults in virtually all computer programs for exploratory factor analysis, even to the present day.

With the issue of basic analytic options "solved" through the Kaiser–Guttman approach, the focus of CFA–PCA contrasts shifted. The 1970s saw a substantial flurry of publications on the factor score indeterminacy problem, an issue that had lain largely dormant for about 40 years. Any detailed consideration of this issue is far beyond the scope of the present chapter. An abbreviated rendition of the fray is as follows: Schönemann and his colleagues (e.g., Schönemann, 1971; Schönemann & Steiger, 1978; Schönemann & Wang, 1972) revived concerns by Wilson (1928) about the indeterminacy of common factor scores and extended these ideas in inventive ways. Note that the early writings on factor indeterminacy were by the same E. B. Wilson who later (Wilson & Worcester, 1939) argued that PCA was unable to arrive at a defensible representation of data. The central contrast between models is that CFA has indeterminate factor scores, whereas PCA has determinate component scores. Several authors, including McDonald (1974) and Mulaik (1976; Mulaik & McDonald, 1978) answered with defenses of common factor scores. The history of the contentious debate was well summarized by Steiger (1979), which is worth consulting for a balanced consideration of the issues involved. The matter of factor score indeterminacy was not resolved by this work in the 1970s; indeed, the issue remains unresolved. An updated view on the topic was given in a special issue of *Multivariate Behavioral Research* published in the mid-1990s (see Maraun, 1996, and associated responses and replies).

Shifting the focus of comparisons once again, Snook and Gorsuch (1989) reported a Monte Carlo study comparing CFA and PCA with regard to accuracy in reproducing population factor loadings. They found that CFA led to fairly accurate reproduction of population loadings and that PCA loadings tended to be positively biased. This positive bias was lessened as a function of (a) increasing communality of manifest variables, and (b) the number of manifest variables in the analysis. Snook and Gorsuch (1989) argued that nonnegligible differences between CFA and PCA estimates will be present unless 40 or more manifest variables are included in an analysis.

The next year, Velicer and Jackson (1990) summarized contrasts between CFA and PCA in terms of seven issues, such as the contentions that CFA and PCA typically lead to essentially identical representations of data, differences between results obtained by the two techniques arise only if too many, unnecessary dimensions are retained, and calculations associated with PCA are less computer intensive than those for CFA. On each of their seven issues, Velicer and Jackson argued that properties of PCA were either equal to or superior to those of CFA.

Shortly thereafter, Widaman (1993) disputed certain conclusions by Velicer and Jackson (1990). As discussed in this chapter, Widaman showed how inaccurate communality estimates can lead to biased over- or underrepresentation of population loadings by either CFA or PCA and also showed how overrepresentation of loadings leads to underrepresentation of correlations between optimally rotated dimensions. Because systematic overestimates of communality (i.e., unities) are used in PCA, component loadings are typically larger and correlations among rotated components are correspondingly smaller than population values for these parameters. Widaman also derived analytic expressions that showed that the overrepresentation of population loadings by PCA was a function of the number of manifest variables loading on a factor or component, not the total number of variables included in the analysis, as Snook and Gorsuch (1989) had argued.

Two recent contributions also deserve mention, one quite technical and the other less so. The first of these contributions concerns standard errors of factor loadings, a topic of considerable current concern. Ogasawara (2003) provided a highly technical account of standard errors for factor and component loadings in the spherical case, where the spherical case is one in which the endpoints of all indicator vectors fall on a sphere and therefore all loadings on all dimensions in a solution are equal and all error variances (or unique factor variances) are equal. Ogasawara confirmed findings by Widaman (1993), specifically overrepresentation of loadings by PCA relative to CFA and attendant underrepresentation of correlations between rotated dimensions by PCA. Ogasawara also reported smaller standard errors for PCA loadings than for CFA loadings. However, demonstrations presented in this chapter may undermine the validity of this finding, through questioning the veracity of the notion of a population PCA loading for a given variable.

In the second contribution, Goldberg and Velicer (in press) wrote for the relative novice, providing a summary of many options a researcher must consider when designing a study, assembling a battery of measures, and then performing an exploratory factor or component analysis. Although their chapter contains much to admire, Goldberg and Velicer explicitly dismissed the claim that CFA and PCA lead to different representations of data. Later, I spend more time discussing their position, but note here that researchers may be led seriously astray if they attend too closely to Goldberg and Velicer on the issue of CFA versus PCA.

Principles—Mislaid or Forgotten

As noted already, principles can help us organize our thoughts or concerns about any area of investigation. This structuring or organizing function is welcome for any attempt to compare and contrast CFA and PCA, methods that have been the topic of much controversy. In this section, I offer a set of principles that can be used to draw distinctions between the two methods. Some might dispute my contention that these principles have been either mislaid or forgotten; however, most would acknowledge that these principles are rarely considered or emphasized when CFA and PCA are applied, but certainly deserve to be.

Principle 1: Common factor analysis and principal component analysis have different goals, so different outcomes should not be surprising.

As Thomson (1939) elegantly argued, the goals of common factor analysis and principal component analysis differ. The goal of CFA is to explain off-diagonal correlations among manifest variables, by positing the presence of one or more latent variables that represent the correlations among manifest variables. To this end, methods of estimating or extracting factors have been developed that either disregard diagonal elements of the matrix of correlations among observed variables or alter the diagonal elements to contain estimates of the common variance of each variable. With the influence of diagonal elements of the correlation matrix either disregarded or deemphasized, the goal is accurate representation of the off-diagonal correlations among variables, as these correlations reflect the influence of shared, or common, latent variables.

In contrast, the goal of PCA is to explain as much of the variance in the matrix of raw scores as possible in the lowest possible rank (or with the minimum number of dimensions). Thus, all of the standardized variance (i.e., unity) of each manifest variable is retained in an analysis so that the method of PCA can explain a maximal amount of the total variance of the set of manifest variables. Under PCA, explaining off-diagonal covariation among variables is a side issue, achieved more-or-less well as the goal of explaining total variance is pursued.

If Thomson (1939) so clearly delineated the differing goals of CFA and PCA, one would think that researchers should expect differences in results when using the two techniques. But, consideration of publications during the past 15 years shows that this is not the case. Among several comparisons between CFA and PCA, Velicer and Jackson (1990) argued that CFA and PCA provide similar representations of data. Steiger (1994) supported Velicer and Jackson's position, citing Velicer's work as showing that "usually there is no substantial difference between solutions produced by the two methods" (p. 214). More recently, Ogasawara (2003) compared the sampling variability of CFA and PCA loadings, arguing that PCA loadings tend to have slightly smaller standard errors than corresponding CFA loadings, even as he acknowledged some differences between mean loadings derived from CFA and PCA. Finally, Goldberg and Velicer (in press) essentially ruled out the ability to consider differences between the two techniques. They claimed that, if CFA and PCA lead to substantially different results, neither procedure should be used because the data lack sufficient structure for any analyses. So, according to Goldberg and Velicer, if no substantial differences arise, it matters little if one uses CFA or PCA; but, if substantial differences in results arise, one should use neither technique. Clearly, at least some technical experts and leading applied users downplay the presence of any notable differences in results produced by CFA and PCA.

Principle 2: Common factor analysis is a theory regarding manifest variables as well as a theory regarding latent variables; in contrast, principal component analysis emphasizes the component scores that are combinations of manifest variables.

In the initial paper on factor analysis, Spearman (1904) showed how correlations among manifest variables depend on the saturation of each variable with g, or general intelligence. Later, Spearman (e.g., Spearman & Holzinger, 1924) developed a statistical criterion based on tetrad equations to verify whether a single factor adequately represented correlations among variables, leaving residual correlations approximating those arising from sampling variability alone. He also propounded the doctrine of the indifference of the indicator, which holds that the same g factor is identified regardless of the set of manifest variables included in a battery. If a single *g* factor underlies the ability domain, then the particular tests used in an analysis are unimportant; each test has its saturation with *g*, and different selections of tests will allow one to estimate both the *g* saturation of each test and individual differences in *g* regardless of the nature of the test battery.

Later, citing the manner in which CFA represents manifest variables, Thurstone (1935) argued that a valid method of factor analysis must yield invariant weights for a given test, regardless of the battery of tests into which that test is placed. Because the issue of invariance is the core of Principle 3 (to come), the emphasis by Thurstone on invariance will not be discussed here in any detail. Suffice it to say that Thurstone considered the data model—representing relations between latent and manifest variables—to be the core of the CFA approach.

In contrast, much work on PCA has emphasized qualities of the scores for individuals on the summary dimensions, whether these be factor or component scores. Proponents of PCA argue that representations achieved by CFA and PCA—for example, the loadings of manifest variables on factors or components—are rarely so different that interpretation of results would be affected, so CFA and PCA arrive at essentially identical representations of data (cf. Velicer & Jackson, 1990). But, PCA has component scores that are unique and that can be calculated as simple weighted sums of manifest variables. In contrast, CFA leads to factor scores that can only be estimated or, following Steiger (1994), can be calculated but are not unique, with different methods of calculating factor scores giving different numerical values for these scores.

Thus, one way to understand the controversy between proponents of CFA and PCA is to see that, to a great extent, they have been talking past one another. Supporters of CFA stress differences between the two techniques in the values of certain parameters (factor loadings, correlations among dimensions), often downplaying the importance of the issue of factor score indeterminacy; in contrast, supporters of PCA concentrate on differences in the status and qualities of the scores for individuals on the summary dimensions, the factors or components, ignoring the frequently large differences in parameters defined by the two techniques.

Principle 3: Invariance of the psychological and/or mathematical description of each manifest variable is a fundamental issue.

Principle 3 is sufficiently important that an extended quote from Thurstone (1935) is in order:

> The test coefficients [i.e., factor loadings] therefore constitute a psychological description of the test. *It is a fundamental criterion for a valid method of isolating primary abilities that the weights of the primary abilities for a test must remain invariant when it is moved from one test battery to another test battery.* If this criterion is not fulfilled, the psychological description of a test will evidently be as variable as the arbitrarily chosen battery into which the test may be placed. (p. 55)

To fulfill this principle, one must assume that all common factors that contribute to a given test are represented or identifiable in each battery in which the test is included.

The issue of factorial invariance has been of great importance for over 50 years. The majority of this work has considered invariance within the CFA framework, although some work has invoked forms of component analysis. Whether the CFA or PCA frameworks were involved, most work on factorial invariance has concentrated on factorial invariance under sampling of observations from a population. But, consistent with Principle 2, researchers must remain aware that CFA embodies a theory about manifest variables as well as about latent variables. Thus, factorial invariance should also be studied when a manifest variable is moved from one battery to another or when one or more manifest variables are added to an existing battery of manifest variables. If a statistical procedure exhibits lack of factorial invariance in either of these two scenarios, then that procedure would run afoul of Principle 3, and its validity as a method of isolating primary factors should be questioned.

Principle 4: The researcher must be aware and beware of all assumptions underlying a method of analysis, the mathematical consequences of these assumptions, and their relations to the hypotheses pursued, data collected, and outcomes of statistical modeling in order to perform a meaningful analysis.

This principle is *truism*, an abiding assumption accompanying any type of statistical analysis. Still, despite its universality, one should not forget its applicability. When comparing CFA and PCA, I now argue that certain assumptions in the use of these techniques usually remain implicit. Every time a practicing scientist opts for a statistical or mathematical method, he or she endorses and accepts, even if implicitly, all assumptions associated with the method. Once assumptions are made explicit, the practicing scientist may be less likely to adopt a given mathematical/statistical technique if its assumptions or their implications are difficult to justify.

THE COMMON FACTOR AND PRINCIPAL COMPONENT FORMULATIONS

In this section, I outline the representations of data obtained using CFA and PCA. Given limited space, I deal little with derivations or matters of estimation. Instead, I concentrate on what I view as central distinctions between these two mathematical methods—the similarities and differences between methods in the ways in which they represent manifest variables.

The Common Factor Analysis Model

The CFA model is first and foremost a model for representing manifest variables as linear functions of underlying latent variables. The linear model that relates latent variables to manifest variables—the CFA data model—is the fundamental equation of CFA. Because exploratory CFA and PCA are typically applied to correlation matrices, I concentrate on the way in which these techniques represent correlation structures. The CFA data model can be written as:

$$z_{ij} = l_{j1}\eta_{1i} + l_{j2}\eta_{2i} + \cdots + l_{jr}\eta_{ri} + l_{ju}\eta_{jui} \qquad \text{(Equation 10.1)}$$

where all manifest variables are in standardized form ($M = 0$, $SD = 1$), z_{ij} is the score of person i on manifest variable j ($i = 1, \ldots, N$; $j = 1, \ldots, p$), l_{jk} is the loading of manifest variable j on latent variable k ($k = 1, \ldots, r$), η_{ki} is the score of person i on latent variable k, l_{ju} is the loading of manifest variable j on its unique factor, and η_{jui} is the score of person i on the unique factor for manifest variable j. The data model in Equation 10.1 can also be written in matrix form as:

$$\mathbf{z} = \mathbf{P}\eta_{\mathrm{c}} + \mathbf{U}\eta_{\mathrm{u}} \qquad \text{(Equation 10.2)}$$

where $\mathbf{z}$ is a ($p \times 1$) vector of scores for an individual, $\mathbf{P}$ is a ($p \times r$) matrix of loadings of the p manifest variables on the r common factors, η_{c} is an ($r \times 1$) vector of common factor scores for the individual, $\mathbf{U}$ is a ($p \times p$) diagonal matrix of unique factor loadings for the manifest variables, and η_{u} is a ($p \times 1$) vector of unique factor scores for the individual.

Based on Equation 10.2, parameters in the $\mathbf{P}$ and $\mathbf{U}$ matrices can be identified if certain assumptions are made. These assumptions include: expected value of $\eta_{\mathrm{c}} =$ expected value of $\eta_{\mathrm{u}} = 0$, linear relations between latent and manifest variables, unique factors in η_{u} are mutually uncorrelated, and the common factors η_{c} and unique factors η_{u} are uncorrelated. Postmultiplying each side of Equation 10.2 by its transpose and taking expectations leads to:

$$\mathbf{R} = \mathbf{FF}' + \mathbf{U}^2 = \mathbf{P}\mathbf{\Phi}\mathbf{P}' + \mathbf{U}^2 \qquad \text{(Equation 10.3)}$$

where $\mathbf{R}$ is the ($p \times p$) matrix of correlations among manifest variables, $\mathbf{F}$ is a ($p \times r$) unrotated common factor matrix, $\mathbf{P}$ is a ($p \times r$) matrix of rotated common factor loadings, $\mathbf{\Phi}$ is an ($r \times r$) matrix of correlations among the common factors, and $\mathbf{U}^2$ is the ($p \times p$) diagonal matrix of unique factor variances. If factors are rotated orthogonally, $\mathbf{\Phi}$ is an identity matrix; if factors are rotated obliquely, the diagonal of $\mathbf{\Phi}$ contains unities, but off-diagonal values can depart from zero.

Equation 10.3 is often termed the fundamental equation of factor analysis, but more properly should be identified as the CFA correlation structure model. Equation 10.1 truly deserves to be called the fundamental equation of CFA, as it postulates that manifest variables are linear functions of the latent variables or common factors. Still, parameters in the $\mathbf{P}, \mathbf{\Phi}$, and $\mathbf{U}^2$ matrices in Equation 10.3, and estimates of these parameters based on sample data, are usually the focus of interpretation when CFA is applied. Thus, Equation 10.3 is an important representation of the CFA model.

Approaches to Principal Component Analysis

At least two approaches to the conception of principal components can be articulated, approaches that can be identified by the labels of *data reduction* and *explanation*. A PCA usually begins with the raw data matrix **Z**, an ($N \times p$) matrix of the standardized scores of N individuals (or observations) on p manifest variables. Following the data reduction approach, the researcher's goal is to represent as much of the variability in the raw data matrix **Z** as possible in an efficient, reduced-rank representation. To meet this goal, the first principal component explains the maximal amount of variance in **Z**; the second principal component explains the most variance in **Z** remaining after the influence of the first component is partialed (or removed); the third principal component explains the most variance in **Z** remaining after the influences of the first two components are partialed (or removed); and so on. The result is a mathematical representation in which the p principal components are (a) orthogonal (or statistically uncorrelated), and (b) conditionally variance maximized (ordered with regard to variance explained). To achieve a reduced-rank representation, researchers often retain only the r largest principal components, discarding the ($p - r$) remaining components because they explain little variance. Also, under the strict data reduction approach, the principal components usually are not rotated, as this would destroy the conditional variance maximization property.

In contrast to the data reduction rationale, many researchers use PCA to serve the function of explanation. These researchers wish to arrive at an interpretable rotated solution that approximates that achieved via Equation 10.3 and CFA, but use PCA to arrive at the solution.

Regardless of the approach taken, a PCA proceeds in a fashion that is similar to that of CFA. Specifically, the PCA data representation can be written as:

$$z_{ij} = a_{j1}s_{1i} + a_{j2}s_{2i} + \cdots + a_{jp}s_{pi} \qquad \text{(Equation 10.4)}$$

where a_{jk} is the loading of manifest variable j on component $k (k = 1, \ldots, p)$, s_{ki} is the score of person i on component k, and other terms are as defined above. Equation 10.4 can also be written as:

$$\mathbf{z} = \mathbf{As} \qquad \text{(Equation 10.5)}$$

where **z** is a ($p \times 1$) vector of scores for an individual, **A** is a ($p \times p$) matrix of loadings of the p manifest variables on the p components, and **s** is a ($p \times 1$) vector of component scores for the individual. To obtain an equation that parallels Equation 10.2, rewrite Equation 10.5 as:

$$\mathbf{z} = \mathbf{F_c s_r} + \mathbf{G s_d} \qquad \text{(Equation 10.6)}$$

where $\mathbf{F_c}$ is a ($p \times r$) matrix containing the loadings of manifest variables on the r principal components to be retained for analysis (the first r columns of **A**), $\mathbf{s_r}$ is an ($r \times 1$) vector of scores for a random person on the first r principal components, **G**

---

is a $(p \times p - r)$ matrix of loadings of manifest variables on the discarded principal components $r + 1$ through p, and s_d is a $(p - r \times 1)$ vector of scores on the discarded components. From Equation 10.6, parameters in the F_c and G matrices can be identified if certain assumptions are made, assumptions including: expected value of s_r = expected value of $s_d = 0$, and all component scores in s_r and s_d are mutually uncorrelated. Taking the expectation of the product of each side of Equation 10.2 by its transpose leads to:

$$R = F_c F_c' + GG' = F_c F_c' + V^2 \qquad \text{(Equation 10.7a)}$$

$$R = P_c \Phi_c P_c' + GG' = P_c \Phi_c P_c' + V^2 \qquad \text{(Equation 10.7b)}$$

where F_c is a $(p \times r)$ matrix of loadings of the manifest variables on the r unrotated components retained for further analysis, G is a $(p \times \{p - r\})$ unrotated loading matrix for the $(p - r)$ components that are discarded, P_c is a $(p \times r)$ matrix of rotated component loadings, Φ_c is an $(r \times r)$ matrix of correlations among rotated components, $V^2 (= GG')$ is the $(p \times p)$ matrix of covariances among residuals of manifest variables after extraction of r components, the c subscript distinguishes several matrices from their CFA counterparts in Equation 10.3, and other symbols are as already defined. As in CFA, if components are rotated orthogonally, Φ_c is an identity matrix; but, if components are rotated obliquely, the off-diagonal values of Φ_c can depart from zero.

Equations such as 10.7a and 10.7b are usually not written in this fashion, tending to delete the representations of residual variances and covariances in $V^2 (= GG')$, leaving simply $R = F_c F_c'$ or, if rotations are allowed, $R = P_c \Phi_c P_c'$. Equation 10.7a is consistent with the data reduction rationale for PCA, as it retains the principal components in their unrotated, conditionally variance maximized orientation. In contrast, equation 10.7b provides for rotation of components, presumably into a more easily interpreted orientation (i.e., to simple structure), which negates the properties enjoyed by equation 10.7a, but gains interpretability of the resulting structure.

COMPARISONS BETWEEN CFA AND PCA: ESTABLISHING REGULARITY CONDITIONS

Comparisons between CFA and PCA can be made at various levels. The preceding section and Equation 10.1 through Equation 10.7b constitute one set of comparisons. But, differing numerical results obtained by CFA and PCA are additional ways to compare the two techniques. The aim of the present section is to discuss various aspects of CFA and PCA solutions and to develop what I call *regularity conditions* for these outcomes. By regularity conditions, I mean patterns in results that are expected, based on the model fit to data and patterns in the data to which models are fit. In this section, I concentrate on regularity conditions for five aspects of the outcomes of CFA and PCA analyses: (a) correlations among manifest variables and resulting represented structures, (b) eigenvalues, (c) loadings of manifest variables on factors or components, (d) correlations among optimally rotated dimensions, and (e) the structure of unique factors or residual variables.

Correlations Among Manifest Variables and Represented Structures

The basic tenet of CFA is that latent variables explain or account for the correlations among manifest variables (cf. Thomson, 1939). Most experts on multivariate models (e.g., Browne & Cudeck, 1993) argue that our statistical models are over-simplifications of reality, so cannot be correct. I concur strongly with this view, assuming that none of our statistical models can fully and accurately represent reality. But, for the rest of this chapter, I consider an ideal (i.e., unreal) world in which the CFA model fits perfectly in the population. I use this ruse to simplify comparisons I wish to draw between CFA and PCA. Model misfit in the population always occurs when applying models to real data, and sampling variability always affects results absent the presence of population data; both model misfit and sampling variability only obscure comparisons between CFA and PCA. Here, I consider only structures that are not spoiled by model misfit or sampling variability; investigating the influences of these two distorting agents is left to the future.

CFA Population, CFA Parameters.   If the CFA model with simple structure in r factors (with r substantially less than p; i.e., $r \leq [p/3]$) fits perfectly in the population, then a bidirectional relation of implication holds between the population correlation matrix and the factor solution. I denote this relation as $\mathbf{R} \leftrightarrow [\mathbf{P\Phi P'}]$. The $\leftrightarrow$ operator represents the contention that, provided the simple-structure CFA model holds, (a) a given population correlation matrix $\mathbf{R}$ implies one and only one set of parameters in the CFA solution $[\mathbf{P\Phi P'}]$ (or, more correctly, an infinite number of sets of parameters that can be rotated to coincide exactly with $[\mathbf{P\Phi P'}]$); *and* (b) a particular set of parameters in a CFA model $[\mathbf{P\Phi P'}]$ implies one and only one population correlation matrix $\mathbf{R}$. Thus, a one-to-one correspondence holds between a matrix of population correlations among manifest variables and a set of parameters of the CFA model if the CFA model holds in the population. One may commence with either the population correlation matrix or the set of population parameters in the CFA model. If one begins with the latter, the parameters in $[\mathbf{P\Phi P'}]$ can be used to calculate $\mathbf{R}$, and then $\mathbf{R}$ can be analyzed to recover the solution in $[\mathbf{P\Phi P'}]$. Or, if one begins directly with $\mathbf{R}$, CFA can recover the parameters in $[\mathbf{P\Phi P'}]$ that are consistent with $\mathbf{R}$. In large part, this is a tautology: If I assume that the CFA model holds in the population, then it should come as no surprise that (a) given $\mathbf{R}$, CFA can be used to find $[\mathbf{P\Phi P'}]$, and (b) given $[\mathbf{P\Phi P'}]$, I can calculate $\mathbf{R}$ from which I can again recover $[\mathbf{P\Phi P'}]$. But, I offer this tautology for CFA because of the contrast it affords with PCA.

One further, important criterion is offered: If one or more manifest variables are added to a battery of measures and any additional variables rely only on factors already well represented in the initial battery of p manifest variables (i.e., the additional variables rely on no new common factors), then all parameters associated with the original set of p manifest variables—including correlations among the p manifest variables, their loadings on the r common factors, and correlations among rotated factors—remain unchanged by the inclusion of the additional variables.

CFA Population, PCA Parameters.   Retaining the assumption that the CFA model with simple structure in r factors fits perfectly in the population, only a unidirectional relation of implication holds between a population correlation matrix and a PCA solution. This unidirectional relation can be denoted as $\mathbf{R} \to [\mathbf{P}_c\mathbf{\Phi}_c\mathbf{P}_c']$. The relation means that a particular population correlation matrix $\mathbf{R}$ implies the presence of a particular set of parameters in the PCA solution $[\mathbf{P}_c\mathbf{\Phi}_c\mathbf{P}_c']$. So, barring bizarre occurrences such as a malfunctioning computer program, every application of PCA to a particular correlation matrix $\mathbf{R}$ will return the same set of parameters in $[\mathbf{P}_c\mathbf{\Phi}_c\mathbf{P}_c']$. But, a given set of parameters in the PCA solution $[\mathbf{P}_c\mathbf{\Phi}_c\mathbf{P}_c']$ can be consistent with more than one population matrix of correlations among manifest variables. That is, a one-to-many—or [one set of PCA parameters]-to-[many correlation matrices]—relation holds for PCA, one implication of work by ten Berge and Kiers (1999).

A second property similar to that for CFA parameters—whether inclusion of additional manifest variables influences any PCA parameter values for the p manifest variables in the initial battery—is of importance here. As shown now, adding one or more manifest variables alters PCA parameter values associated with the p manifest variables in the initial battery, supporting the claim that parameters derived using PCA do not generalize beyond the battery that is analyzed.

PCA Population.   For symmetry, the notion of a population matrix $\mathbf{R}$ that is consistent with parameters in a PCA solution $[\mathbf{P}_c\mathbf{\Phi}_c\mathbf{P}_c']$ should be considered. A method of constructing $\mathbf{R}$ matrices with this structure has only recently been proposed (ten Berge & Kiers, 1999). Clearly, if an $\mathbf{R}$ matrix is constructed to represent a given PCA solution, PCA should recover this solution accurately, and CFA should do a poorer job of recovering the population PCA parameters. I conjecture that an acceptable CFA solution cannot be found for certain $\mathbf{R}$ matrices for which PCA can easily recover the population parameters that generated the correlations. Due to limited space, this intriguing area of inquiry must be left for the future, but deserves further study.

Eigenvalues

An *eigenvalue* is the variance explained by a common factor or principal component. One simple way to obtain eigenvalues is to obtain sums of squared loadings down each column of the unrotated CFA factor matrix $\mathbf{F}$ or the unrotated PCA matrix $\mathbf{F_c}$. This method of computing eigenvalues circumvents methods of estimating these quantities, but the simplified procedure presented is adequate to the current goal—to establish regularity conditions for eigenvalues.

If communalities reduce the rank of the correlation matrix $\mathbf{R}$, one should observe r nonzero eigenvalues and $(p - r)$ zero eigenvalues when using CFA to analyze $\mathbf{R} - \mathbf{U}^2$. As noted, model misfit in the population and sampling variability will obscure a simple pattern of this sort. But, in our rarified world in which the CFA model fits perfectly, the prescribed pattern will hold.

In contrast, if the correlation matrix $\mathbf{R}$ is positive definite, all r eigenvalues from a PCA solution will be positive, nonzero values. The first r eigenvalues correspond to the components to be retained for further analysis, and the remaining $(p - r)$ eigenvalues are for components to be discarded. On an a priori basis, it is difficult to determine what pattern of numerical values should hold for eigenvalues associated with components to be discarded, so inspecting results from several ideal cases may help establish regularity conditions.

Factor or Component Loadings

One key set of parameters evaluated when using CFA or PCA is the set of loadings in the factor loading matrix $\mathbf{P}$ or component loading matrix $\mathbf{P_c}$. For convenience, I deal here only with loading matrices rotated to simple structure. In the restricted spherical case, in which each manifest variable loads on only one of the r factors (i.e., no manifest variables load on two or more factors) and all factor loadings in the solution are equal, Equation 10.8 (from Widaman, 1993) shows the relation between the "true," population factor loading, l_{jk}, and the loading represented by a technique, $\hat{l}_{jk}$, as a function of the difference between true and estimated communalities of the variable, Δh_j^2, and the number of manifest variables, m, loading on the factor, as:

$$\hat{l}_{jk} = \sqrt{l_{jk}^2 + \left(\frac{\Delta h_j^2}{m}\right)}. \qquad \text{(Equation 10.8)}$$

Equation 10.8 shows that accurate estimation of communality leads to accurate representation of the population loading, because $\Delta h_j^2 = 0$. For example, consider a population in which all manifest variables loading on a factor have loadings of .60; the communality of each variable would be .36. If PCA were used to analyze data, the difference between true and estimated communality would be .64. If three manifest variables load on the dimension, the resulting component loadings would be .76; if six manifest variables load on the dimension, the component loadings would be .68.

Equation 10.8 was used to derive values shown in Table 10–1. The first column of Table 10–1 lists the magnitudes of off-diagonal correlations in a matrix,

TABLE 10–1

Relation Between Off-Diagonal Correlations and CFA and PCA Loadings: Spherical Case

Off-diagonal Correlations	CFA Loading	PCA Loading					
		$m = 3$	$m = 6$	$m = 9$	$m = 12$	$m = 15$	$m = 20$
1.00	1.00	1.00	1.00	1.00	1.00	1.00	1.00
.64	.80	.87	.84	.82	.82	.81	.81
.36	.60	.76	.68	.66	.64	.63	.63
.16	.40	.66	.55	.50	.48	.46	.45
.04	.20	.60	.40	.38	.35	.32	.30
.00	.00	.58	.41	.33	.29	.26	.22

Note. The tabled results assume all off-diagonal correlations are equal; therefore, a single factor or component can be evaluated. m = number of manifest variables in the matrix.

assuming that all these values are equal. The second column lists the common factor loadings consistent with the listed correlations. The number of variables analyzed has no effect on CFA loadings; whether 3, or 6, or 36 variables are included in an analysis, a matrix for which all off-diagonal correlations are .36 will lead to loadings of exactly .60 for each manifest variable on the factor. Such is not the case for PCA. The number of manifest variables m loading on a component influences the resulting component loading, with higher numbers of variables loading on a component leading to consistently lower component loadings that converge on the CFA loading as m increases. Note also that a CFA of an identity matrix (with all off-diagonal values = 0) will result in loadings of zero. But, because the first principal component must have an eigenvalue of unity or greater (or it would not be the first principal component), the first principal component of an identity matrix has loadings of $[1/m]^{1/2}$. Thus, if an analysis of empirical data found a component with three variables loading on the component and each loading was .60, this would be an unimpressive result, as loadings of .58 would be obtained even if the variables were statistically uncorrelated with one another.

Correlations Among Rotated Dimensions

Correlations among optimally rotated common factors, Φ, or principal components, Φ_c, are also of critical concern. Gorsuch (1983) argued that obliquely rotated factors should correlate about as highly as manifest indicators for one factor correlate with manifest indicators for the second factor. But, these raw correlations understate the strength of correlation between oblique factors. The proper index is derived by estimating the average cosine between vectors for indicators for one factor with the vectors for indicators for a second factor. No equations are offered here to estimate these values (see Ogasawara, 2003; Widaman, 1993), but one must attend to correlations among optimally rotated dimensions to compare CFA and PCA fully.

The Structure of Unique Factors or Residual Variances

A final set of parameters that must be considered in the contrast between CFA and PCA is the structure of the residual variables, where residual variables represent variability in manifest variables after extracting r common factors or principal components. In CFA, these residual variables are termed *unique factors*. The unique factor covariance matrix was identified as $\mathbf{U}^2$ in Equation 10.3; by assumption, unique factors are mutually uncorrelated, so $\mathbf{U}^2$ is a diagonal matrix.

In PCA, the residuals of the p manifest variables are represented by the discarded components in $\mathbf{GG}'$ (see Equation 10.7a and Equation 10.7b), which can also be evaluated as the matrix $\mathbf{V}^2(= \mathbf{GG}')$. Matrix $\mathbf{V}^2$ is a covariance matrix, with variances of residuals on the diagonal and covariances among residuals off the diagonal. As outlined, all principal components are orthogonal when extracted, and the space defined by the retained components in $\mathbf{F}_c$ is orthogonal to the space defined by the discarded components in $\mathbf{G}$. However, the residual covariance matrix $\mathbf{V}^2$ contains nonzero off-diagonal elements and is, therefore, not a diagonal matrix. If the original matrix of correlations among manifest variables $\mathbf{R}$ is of full rank p, and at least one principal component is retained ($r \geq 1$), $\mathbf{V}^2$ is a matrix that must have deficient rank, having a maximal rank of $(p - 1)$. Even though it is rarely examined, $\mathbf{V}^2$ is an integral part of the PCA model, as the variances and covariances of manifest variable residuals are, mathematically, the complement of the solution provided by the retained components $\mathbf{F}_c\mathbf{F}'_c$. Consistent with Principle 4 already discussed, anyone using PCA must be aware of, understand, and accept the patterns of relations contained in $\mathbf{V}^2$; if the patterns of values in $\mathbf{V}^2$ are difficult to justify, PCA may be an indefensible form of analysis.

REGULARITY CONDITIONS IN THE POPULATION: ERRORS AND MISCONCEPTIONS

In this section, I demonstrate the CFA and PCA parameters in several structured population cases. In each case, the CFA model was used to develop a correlation matrix, and the matrix was then analyzed using CFA and PCA. Although this approach may bias results in favor of the CFA model, the key outcomes are contrasts between CFA and PCA parameters.

One-Dimensional, Spherical Case

A correlation matrix consistent with a one-dimensional, spherical CFA model (all factor loadings = .60) is shown above the diagonal in the top half of Table 10–2. When all off-diagonal correlations are equal, the pattern of observed correlations among manifest variables is simple to discern, and a researcher would not be surprised to uncover the influence of only a single dimension when using CFA.

TABLE 10–2

Population Correlations Among Six Manifest Variables

Variable						
Variable	V1	V2	V3	V4	V5	V6
	One-dimensional data					
V1	—	.36	.36	.36	.36	.36
V2	.48	—	.36	.36	.36	.36
V3	.32	.24	—	.36	.36	.36
V4	.64	.48	.32	—	.36	.36
V5	.48	.36	.24	.48	—	.36
V6	.32	.24	.16	.32	.24	—
	Two-dimensional data					
V1	—	.36	.36	.18	.18	.18
V2	.48	—	.36	.18	.18	.18
V3	.32	.24	—	.18	.18	.18
V4	.32	.24	.16	—	.36	.36
V5	.24	.18	.12	.48	—	.36
V6	.16	.12	.08	.32	.24	—

Note. In the top section of the table, correlations above the diagonal are for one factor, spherical case, medium-communality (all loadings = .6), and correlations below the diagonal are for one factor, nonspherical case (average loading = .6). In the bottom section of the table, correlations above the diagonal are for two correlated factors, spherical case, medium communality (all loadings = .6), and those below the diagonal are for two correlated factors, nonspherical case (average loading = .6).

Whether one principal component would also be consistent with the data is a less obvious outcome, but should become apparent as we proceed.

Results from four analyses, two CFAs and two PCAs, are shown in Table 10–3. On the left side of Table 10–3, results from two CFAs are shown. In the analysis reported in the top half of the table, only the first three variables (V1–V3) were included in the analysis; in the bottom half of the table, results of analyzing all six manifest variables are shown. Several things should be noted about the two CFAs. First, only a single eigenvalue was nonzero in each analysis, consistent with the construction of the data to reflect a single factor. Second, the nonzero eigenvalue in the second analysis was exactly twice as large as the corresponding eigenvalue in the first analysis, because the first eigenvalue was (3×0.6^2) and the second was (6×0.6^2). Third, adding the second set of variables (V4–V6) in the second analysis left all parameters associated with the first three manifest variables (V1–V3) completely unchanged. That is, if one compares factor loadings and unique factor variances for V1–V3 in the top half of the table, these parameters are identical to the corresponding values for these same variables in the bottom half of the table.

The preceding results for the CFAs contrast with those for the PCAs, shown in the right half of Table 10–3. In the top half of Table 10–3, the first three manifest variables (V1–V3) were included in the analysis; the remaining three manifest

TABLE 10–3

Results of CFA and PCA of 3 and 6 Manifest variables: One-Dimensional, Spherical Case

									PCA					
	CFA								Residual covariance matrix, V^2					
Eigen-values	Var.	P	U^2	h_f^2	Eigen-values	Var.	P_c	V1	V2	V3	V4	V5	V6	h_c^2
Analysis of 3 manifest variables														
1.08	V1	.60	.64	.36	1.72	V1	.76	*.43*	−.50	−.50				.57
.00	V2	.60	.64	.36	.64	V2	.76	−.21	*.43*	−.50				.57
.00	V3	.60	.64	.36	.64	V3	.76	−.21	−.21	*.43*				.57
Analysis of 6 manifest variables														
2.16	V1	.60	.64	.36	2.80	V1	.68	*.53*	−.20	−.20	−.20	−.20	−.20	.47
.00	V2	.60	.64	.36	.64	V2	.68	−.11	*.53*	−.20	−.20	−.20	−.20	.47
.00	V3	.60	.64	.36	.64	V3	.68	−.11	−.11	*.53*	−.20	−.20	−.20	.47
.00	V4	.60	.64	.36	.64	V4	.68	−.11	−.11	−.11	*.53*	−.20	−.20	.47
.00	V5	.60	.64	.36	.64	V5	.68	−.11	−.11	−.11	−.11	*.53*	−.20	.47
.00	V6	.60	.64	.36	.64	V6	.68	−.11	−.11	−.11	−.11	−.11	*.53*	.47

Note. Var. = variable name (names from V1–V6), P = common factor loadings, U^2 = diagonal values from U^2 matrix, h_f^2 = communality based on CFA, P_c = principal component loadings, h_c^2 variance in manifest variable explained by retained components. The residual covariance matrix, V^2, is symmetric; I report residual variances (italicized) on diagonal, residual covariances below diagonal, and residual correlations above diagonal (after extracting one principal component from correlations among manifest variables).

variables (V4–V6) were added to the initial battery for the analysis shown in the bottom half of the table. In the top half of the table, the loadings on the first principal component were all equal (.76). Moreover, the residual covariance matrix was compound symmetric (i.e., all diagonal values were equal, all off-diagonal values were equal), with variances of .43 and covariances of −.21, consistent with correlations among residuals of −.50. Contrasting with CFAs, PCA results revealed the following: First, all eigenvalues were nonzero; interestingly, all eigenvalues after the first were equal to one another and equal across solutions. Second, the eigenvalue for the single, major dimension in the second analysis was *not* exactly twice as large as the corresponding eigenvalue in the first analysis, because loadings on the first component in the second analysis were not equal to loadings on the first component in the first analysis, or $[2 \times (3 \times 0.76^2)] \neq (6 \times 0.68^2)$. Third, all parameters associated with the first three variables (V1–V3) changed markedly across the two analyses. Specifically, loadings were reduced from .76 to .68, residual variables on the diagonal of V^2 increased from .43 to .53, and covariances among residuals (off-diagonals in V^2) decreased from −.21 to −.11, corresponding to correlations among residuals that decreased from −.50 to −.20. The V^2 matrix still retained its compound symmetry, but the structure of this matrix was altered importantly across the two analyses.

TABLE 10–4

Results of CFA and PCA of three and six Manifest Variables: One-Dimensional, Nonspherical Case

		CFA					PCA							
								Residual covariance matrix, V^2						
Eigen-values	Var.	P	U^2	$h_f{}^2$	Eigen-values	Var.	P_c	V1	V2	V3	V4	V5	V6	$h_c{}^2$
					Analysis of 3 manifest variables									
1.16	V1	.80	.36	.64	1.70	V1	.83	*.32*	−.47	−.58				.68
.00	V2	.60	.64	.36	.79	V2	.78	−.16	*.39*	−.55				.61
.00	V3	.40	.84	.16	.51	V3	.64	−.21	−.26	*.59*				.41
					Analysis of 6 manifest variables									
2.32	V1	.80	.36	.64	2.85	V1	.82	*.32*	−.23	−.21	−.12	−.23	−.21	.68
.00	V2	.60	.64	.36	.84	V2	.70	−.09	*.52*	−.19	−.23	−.24	−.19	.48
.00	V3	.40	.84	.16	.79	V3	.51	−.10	−.12	*.74*	−.21	−.19	−.14	.26
.00	V4	.80	.36	.64	.64	V4	.82	−.04	−.09	−.10	*.32*	−.23	−.21	.68
.00	V5	.60	.64	.36	.52	V5	.70	−.09	−.12	−.12	−.09	*.52*	−.19	.48
.00	V6	.40	.84	.16	.36	V6	.51	−.10	−.12	−.10	−.10	−.12	*.74*	.26

Note. Var. = manifest variable names (V1–V6), P = common factor loadings, U^2 = diagonal values from U^2 matrix, $h_f{}^2$ = communality based on CFA, P_c = principal component loadings, $h_c{}^2$ variance in manifest variable explained by retained components. The residual covariance matrix, V^2, is symmetric; I report residual variances (italicized) on the diagonal, residual covariances below diagonal, and residual correlations above diagonal (after extracting one principal component from correlations among manifest variables).

One-Dimensional, Nonspherical Case

A correlation matrix derived from a one-dimensional, nonspherical CFA model (mean factor loading = .60) is shown below the diagonal in the top half of Table 10–2. Even experts in factor analysis might have difficulty determining that this correlation matrix reflected a single common factor, so CFA and PCA should help to discern patterns in this matrix.

Results from four analyses are shown in Table 10–4. As with Table 10–3, results of CFAs are shown in the left half of Table 10–4, and results of PCAs are reported on the right half; results of analyzing only the first three variables (V1–V3) are shown in the top half of the table, and results of analyzing all six variables (V1–V6) are shown in the bottom half of the table.

Considering first the CFAs shown in the left half of Table 10–4, once again we see a single nonzero eigenvalue in each analysis, and the single nonzero eigenvalue in the second analysis was exactly twice the eigenvalue in the first analysis, because the factor loadings for the second set of three variables (V4–V6) were identical on a one-to-one basis with the factor loadings for the first set of three variables (V1–V3). Note as well that the factor analytic descriptions—the factor loadings and unique factor variances—of the first three variables (V1–V3) were identical in both analyses. That is, introducing three new manifest variables (V4–V6) in the battery left the factorial description of variables V1 through V3 completely unchanged.

Turning to the PCAs shown in the right half of Table 10–4, we see that all eigenvalues were once again nonzero, but eigenvalues following the first were no longer equal. Thus, when we move to the nonspherical case, the pattern expected in eigenvalues for nonretained components is unclear. Note also that the loadings were not consistent with loadings shown in Table 10–1 for the spherical case. Specifically, in the analysis in the top half of Table 10–4, certain loadings (for V1 and V3) were larger than corresponding CFA loadings, but were lower than expected based on Table 10–1, whereas the remaining loading was higher than expected (compare the loading for V2 with values in Table 10–1). Thus, moving to the nonspherical case, which is likely to hold in empirical populations, clear trends based on the spherical case did not generalize. The covariance matrix for the residuals, $\mathbf{V}^2$, was no longer compound symmetric, having varying diagonal values (varying from .32 to .59), varying off-diagonal covariances (varying from $-.16$ to $-.26$), and varying off-diagonal correlations. Also, the highest of the off-diagonal correlations, $-.58$, was between the variables that had the highest and lowest loadings on the component (V1 and V3). Finally, observe what happened when three new variables (V4–V6) were added to the battery, results shown in the bottom half of Table 10–4. Of primary importance here are the distinctly altered parameters for variables V1 through V3 when compared to comparable values in the top half of Table 10–4. Specifically, component loadings fell differentially (little for V1, more substantially for V2 and V3), residual variances and covariances were altered in haphazard fashion, and the highest of the three covariances among the residuals for V1 through V3 was now between V1 and V2.

Multidimensional, Spherical Case

A correlation matrix consistent with a two-dimensional, spherical CFA model (all factor loadings = .60; factor correlation = .50) is shown above the diagonal in the bottom half of Table 10–2. This correlation matrix has such a clear structure that a two-dimensional solution would be expected by visual inspection alone.

Results from two analyses are shown in Table 10–5. On the left side of Table 10–5, results from a CFA of the matrix are shown. Here, the first two eigenvalues are nonzero, consistent with the construction of a two-factor population, and remaining eigenvalues are zero. All factor loadings are identical (.60), and the correlation between factors is recovered at its population value of .50.

Results of a PCA of the matrix are shown on the right side of Table 10–5. There we see two large eigenvalues and four smaller eigenvalues, and all of the small eigenvalues are equal, similar to the one-dimensional spherical case already investigated. The rotated component loadings were, interestingly, precisely as predicted from Equation 10.8, so Equation 10.8 can be used to estimate component loadings

WIDAMAN

TABLE 10–5
Results of CFA and PCA of Six Manifest Variables: Two-Dimensional, Spherical Case

		CFA							PCA							
										Residual covariance matrix, V^2						
Eigen-values	Var.	F1	F2	U^2	h_f^2	Eigen-values	Var.	C1	C2	V1	V2	V3	V4	V5	V6	h_c^2
						Rotated factor patterns and residual variances										
1.62	V1	.60	.00	.64	.36	2.26	V1	.76	.00	.43	−.50	−.50	.00	.00	.00	.57
.54	V2	.60	.00	.64	.36	1.18	V2	.76	.00	−.21	.43	−.50	.00	.00	.00	.57
.00	V3	.60	.00	.64	.36	.64	V3	.76	.00	−.21	−.21	.43	.00	.00	.00	.57
.00	V4	.00	.60	.64	.36	.64	V4	.00	.76	.00	.00	.00	.43	−.50	−.50	.57
.00	V5	.00	.60	.64	.36	.64	V5	.00	.76	.00	.00	.00	−.21	.43	−.50	.57
.00	V6	.00	.60	.64	.36	.64	V6	.00	.76	.00	.00	.00	−.21	−.21	.43	.57
						Correlations between obliquely rotated dimensions										
	F1	1.00					C1	1.00								
	F2	.50	1.00				C2	.31	1.00							

Note. Var. = manifest variable name (V1–V6), F1 and F2 are names for the two common factor, U^2 = diagonal values from U^2 matrix, h_f^2 = communality based on CFA, C1 and C2 are names for the two principal components, h_c^2 = variance in manifest variable explained by retained components. The residual covariance matrix, V^2, is symmetric; I report residual variances (italicized) on the diagonal, residual covariances below diagonal, and residual correlations above diagonal (after extracting two principal components from correlations among manifest variables).

in multidimensional solutions as long as the spherical case holds. The hyperplanar loadings were all precisely zero, so the solution in Table 10–5 was an optimal oblique rotation of the two components. But, the correlation between components, .31, was substantially smaller than the .50 correlation between oblique common factors. The matrix of covariances among residuals also had an interesting, yet unexpected appearance. Specifically, residual covariances for variables V1 through V3 were identical to those observed in the upper section of Table 10–3 when only variables V1 though V3 were included in the PCA; the residual covariances for variables V4 through V6 were also identical to this pattern. But, surprisingly, the residual covariances of variables V1 through V3 with variables V4 through V6 were exactly zero, so the correlations among these residuals were zero. Thus, at least in the spherical case, the PCA model represented perfectly the observed correlations among indicators for different factors, but failed to represent perfectly the correlations among indicators for a given factor.

Multi-Dimensional, Nonspherical Case

Finally, in the multidimensional, nonspherical case, more than one dimension is present in data, and manifest variables have varied loadings on factors. This is the most interesting case, as it likely represents what researchers will confront in any analysis of empirical data. A correlation matrix consistent with a two-dimensional, nonspherical CFA model (mean factor loading = .60; factor correlation = .50) is shown below the diagonal in the bottom half of Table 10–2. The pattern in this matrix is difficult to discern; hopefully, CFA and PCA will shed light on the structure.

Results of a CFA of this correlation matrix are shown in the left half of Table 10–6. Three variables loaded on each of the factors, with one variable loading .80, another .60, and the third .40. These loadings fall in a 4:3:2 ratio relation to one another. The factors correlated .50, consistent with population parameters that generated the correlations among manifest variables.

When PCA is used to analyze the data, the results obtained are shown in the right half of Table 10–6. Large loadings on each component were .77, .77, and .71, which are very close to being equal, rather than having the proper 4:3:2 ratio relation. Note particularly the altered appearance of the covariances among residuals. This matrix is not compound symmetric nor does it have the zero correlations between residuals for V1–V3 and those for V4–V6 observed in Table 10–5. Indeed, this residual covariance matrix has both positive and negative values, as the correlations between residuals vary between −.59 and +.16. Note as well that the highest correlation is now between the two variables with the lowest population

TABLE 10–6

Results of CFA and PCA of Six Manifest Variables: Two-Dimensional, Nonspherical Case

| | | CFA | | | | | | PCA | | | | | | | | |
| | | | | | | | | | | Residual covariance matrix, V^2 | | | | | | |
Eigen-values	Var.	F1	F2	U^2	h_f^2	Eigen-values	Var.	C1	C2	V1	V2	V3	V4	V5	V6	h_c^2
						Rotated factor patterns and residual variances										
1.74	V1	.80	.00	.36	.64	2.27	V1	.77	.11	*.34*	−.38	−.49	−.13	−.11	.01	.66
.58	V2	.60	.00	.64	.36	1.16	V2	.77	.00	−.14	*.41*	−.59	−.11	−.04	.07	.59
.00	V3	.40	.00	.84	.16	.79	V3	.71	−.12	−.21	−.28	*.54*	.01	.07	.16	.46
.00	V4	.00	.80	.36	.64	.77	V4	.11	.77	−.04	−.04	.00	*.34*	−.38	−.49	.66
.00	V5	.00	.60	.64	.36	.52	V5	.00	.77	−.04	−.02	.03	−.14	*.41*	−.59	.59
.00	V6	.00	.40	.84	.16	.49	V6	−.12	.71	.00	.03	.08	−.21	−.28	*.54*	.46
						Correlations between obliquely rotated dimensions										
	F1	1.00					C1	1.00								
	F2	.50	1.00				C2	.32	1.00							

Note. Var. = manifest variable name (V1–V6), F1 and F2 are names for the two common factor, U^2 = diagonal values from U^2 matrix, h_f^2 = communality based on CFA, C1 and C2 are names for the two principal components, h_c^2 variance in manifest variable explained by retained components. The residual covariance matrix, V^2, is symmetric; I report residual variances (italicized) on the diagonal, residual covariances below diagonal, and residual correlations above diagonal (after extracting two principal components from correlations among manifest variables).

loadings on each component (V2 and V3). One can only describe the pattern of covariances and correlations among residual variables as haphazard.

DISCUSSION

The aim of this chapter was to compare CFA and PCA, an issue that has spawned perhaps the most strident arguments of any in the factor analytic literature. First, I outlined some historical threads related to this issue. Considering these led to the statement of four principles that aid in comparing CFA and PCA. I attempted to derive regularity conditions in the parameters defined by the CFA and PCA models and then evaluated the degree to which these conditions were satisfied in systematically varied populations. The upshot of this work is that (a) clear regularities held for parameters defined by CFA for both the spherical and nonspherical cases; (b) if data satisfied the spherical case, certain regularities were discernible in parameters defined by PCA, but these varied uncomfortably with alterations in the test battery; and (c) departures from the spherical case led to a breakdown of all regularities for PCA. Because empirical data almost surely depart from the spherical case and batteries of manifest variables vary across studies, the breakdown of regularities under PCA casts doubt on its utility for representing psychological data.

As adumbrated in Principle 1, CFA and PCA have differing goals, so different outcomes should not be surprising. Contrary to views offered by some observers, differences encountered in CFA and PCA parameters (e.g., in the magnitude of correlations between rotated dimensions) are often sufficiently large that interpretations should be altered in important ways. Aligned with Principle 2, the core of CFA is a linear model relating latent variables to manifest variables, and CFA reproduced parameters in this model consistently and well. In contrast, the core of PCA is the development of a linear weighting system to capture variability in manifest variables, but the parameters of this weighting system varied unsystematically with changes in the test battery.

Invariance of parameters, the heart of Principle 3, offers yet another distinction between CFA and PCA. When constructing data, variable V2 had a consistent population description—a factor loading of .6 on the first (or only) common factor and unique variance of .64. Across all six CFAs reported in Table 10–3 through Table 10–6, the population description of V2 was reproduced precisely. In contrast, the description of V2 across the six PCAs varied considerably; component loadings varied between .68 and .78, residual variances varied between .39 and .58, and correlations with other residuals varied between −.55 and +.07—and these are (so-called) population parameters! Contrary to recent work, including Ogasawara (2003), speaking of *the* population component loading of a manifest variable is a category mistake, in the sense of Ryle (1969). No population component loading exists for a manifest variable; instead, the component loading for a variable based on a population correlation matrix varies widely as a function of the matrix in which the variable appears. Moreover, because no population component loading for a manifest variable exists, the notion of standard errors for component loadings is also a category mistake.

Finally, covariances among unique factors or residuals were very different for CFA and PCA. Unique factors are unlikely to be uncorrelated in a sample even if they are uncorrelated in the population (cf. MacCallum & Tucker, 1991); still, imposing this structure is standard practice in CFA. In PCA, these parameters are rarely, if ever, examined. Results in Table 10–3 through Table 10–6 showed haphazard changes in residual covariances across analyses; if users of PCA cannot justify or account for these results, PCA runs afoul of Principle 4, whereas CFA does not.

The final word on comparisons between CFA and PCA has not yet been written. But, surely we can reach agreement on several conclusions: the ideas first broached by Spearman (1904) have maintained scientific currency ever since their appearance and promise to do so for at least another century, scientific psychology and the toilers in this field are the beneficiaries, and the choice between CFA and PCA will continue to provide interesting, if contentious, insights into our methods for understanding psychological data.

ACKNOWLEDGMENTS

This research was partially supported by grants from the National Institute of Child Health and Human Development, the National Institute on Drug Abuse, and the National Institute of Mental Health (HD047573, HD051746, and MH051361). I would like to thank Katie Gibbs, Betsy Feldman, Gary Stockdale, and the editors of this volume for valuable comments made on an earlier version of this chapter.

REFERENCES

Browne, M. W., & Cudeck, R. (1993). Alternative ways of assessing model fit. In K. A. Bollen & J. S. Long (Eds.), *Testing structural equation models* (pp. 136–162). Newbury Park, CA: Sage.

Burt, C. (1909). Experimental tests of general intelligence. *British Journal of Psychology, 3*, 94–177.

Carroll, J. B. (1993). *Human cognitive abilities: A survey of factor-analytic studies.* Cambridge, England: Cambridge University Press.

Digman, J. M. (1997). Higher-order factors of the Big Five. *Journal of Personality and Social Psychology, 73*, 1246–1256.

Goldberg, L. R. (1990). An alternative "description of personality:" The Big-Five factor structure. *Journal of Personality and Social Psychology, 59*, 1216–1229.

Goldberg, L. R., & Velicer, W. F. (in press). Principles of exploratory factor analysis. In S. Strack (Ed.), *Differentiating normal and abnormal personality* (2nd ed.). New York: Springer.

Gorsuch, R. L. (1983). *Factor analysis* (2nd ed.). Hillsdale, NJ: Lawrence Erlbaum Associates.

Guttman, L. (1954). Some necessary conditions for common-factor analysis. *Psychometrika, 19*, 149–161.

Horn, J. L., & Noll, J. (1997). Human cognitive abilities: Gf-Gc theory. In D. P. Flanagan & J. L. Genshaft (Eds.), *Contemporary intellectual assessment: Theories, tests, and issues* (pp. 53–91). New York: Guilford.

Hotelling, H. (1933). Analysis of a complex of statistical variables into principal components. *Journal of Educational Psychology, 24,* 417–441, 498–520.

John, O. P., & Srivastava, S. (1999). The Big Five trait taxonomy: History, measurement, and theoretical perspectives. In L. A. Pervin & O. P. John (Eds.), *Handbook of personality: Theory and research* (2nd ed., pp. 102–138). New York: Guilford.

Kaiser, H. F. (1958). The varimax criterion for analytic rotation in factor analysis. *Psychometrika, 23,* 187–200.

Kaiser, H. F. (1960). The application of electronic computers to factor analysis. *Educational and Psychological Measurement, 20,* 141–151.

Kaiser, H. F. (1971). A second generation little jiffy. *Psychometrika, 35,* 401–415.

MacCallum, R. C., & Tucker, L. R. (1991). Representing sources of error in the common factor model: Implications for theory and practice. *Psychological Bulletin, 109,* 502–511.

Maraun, M. D. (1996). Metaphor taken as math: Indeterminacy in the factor analysis model. *Multivariate Behavioral Research, 31,* 517–538.

McCloy, C. H., Metheny, A., & Knott, V. (1938). A comparison of the Thurstone method of multiple factors with the Hotelling method of principal components. *Psychometrika, 3,* 61–67.

McDonald, R. P. (1974). The measurement of factor indeterminacy. *Psychometrika, 39,* 203–222.

Mulaik, S. A. (1976). Comments on "the measurement of factor indeterminacy." *Psychometrika, 41,* 249–262.

Mulaik, S. A., & McDonald, R. P. (1978). The effect of additional variables on factor indeterminacy in models with a single common factor. *Psychometrika, 43,* 177–192.

Ogasawara, H. (2003). Oblique factors and components with independent clusters. *Psychometrika, 68,* 299–321.

Ryle, G. (1969). *The concept of mind.* New York: Barnes & Noble.

Schönemann, P. H. (1971). The minimum average correlation between equivalent sets of uncorrelated factors. *Psychometrika, 36,* 21–30.

Schönemann, P. H., & Steiger, J. H. (1978). On the validity of indeterminate factor scores. *Bulletin of the Psychonomic Society, 12,* 287–290.

Schönemann, P. H., & Wang, M. M. (1972). Some new results on factor indeterminacy. *Psychometrika, 37,* 61–91.

Snook, S. C., & Gorsuch, R. L. (1989). Component analysis versus common factor analysis: A Monte Carlo study. *Psychological Bulletin, 106,* 148–154.

Spearman, C. (1904). "General intelligence," objectively determined and measured. *American Journal of Psychology, 15,* 201–293.

Spearman, C., & Holzinger, K. J. (1924). The sampling error in the theory of two factors. *British Journal of Psychology, 15,* 17–19.

Steiger, J. H. (1979). Factor indeterminacy in the 1930's and the 1970's: Some interesting parallels. *Psychometrika, 44,* 157–167.

Steiger, J. H. (1994). Factor analysis in the 1980's and 1990's: Some old debates and some new developments. In I. Borg & P. P. Mohler (Eds.), *Trends and perspectives in empirical social science* (pp. 201–224). Berlin: DeGruyter.

ten Berge, J., & Kiers, H. (1999). Retrieving the correlation matrix from a truncated PCA solution: The inverse principal component problem. *Psychometrika, 64,* 317–324.

Thomson, G. H. (1916). A hierarchy without a general factor. *British Journal of Psychology, 8,* 271–281.

Thomson, G. H. (1939). The factorial analysis of ability. I. The present position and the problems confronting us. *British Journal of Psychology, 30,* 71–77.

Thurstone, L. L. (1931). Multiple factor analysis. *Psychological Review, 38,* 406–427.

Thurstone, L. L. (1935). *The vectors of mind.* Chicago: University of Chicago Press.

Thurstone, L. L. (1947). *Multiple factor analysis.* Chicago: University of Chicago Press.

Velicer, W. F., & Jackson, D. N. (1990). Component analysis versus common factor analysis: Some issues in selecting an appropriate procedure. *Multivariate Behavioral Research, 25,* 1–28.

Widaman, K. F. (1993). Common factor analysis versus principal component analysis: Differential bias in representing model parameters? *Multivariate Behavioral Research, 28,* 263–311.

Wilson, E. B. (1928). Review of 'The abilities of man, their nature and measurement' by C. Spearman. *Science, 67,* 244–248.

Wilson, E. B., & Worcester, J. (1939). Note on factor analysis. *Psychometrika, 4,* 133–148.

CHAPTER 11

Understanding Human Intelligence
Since Spearman

John L. Horn and John J. McArdle
University of Southern California

One hundred years have passed since Charles Spearman (1904a, 1904b) published papers in which–it has been said–nearly all the basic formulas that are particularly useful in test theory are found (Gulliksen, 1950), and *g*, "a general mental ability that enters into every kind of activity requiring mental effort, was discovered" (Jensen, 1998, p. 18). Such thoughts led to a question that led to organizing a conference, which led to writings and the idea of putting the writings together in a book. The question was, "What have we learned about test theory and human intelligence since Spearman wrote those articles that seemed to say it all?" In this chapter, we talk about the part of the question that pertains to human intelligence.

To deal with this part of the question, we lay out knowledge acquired from Spearman's work. In doing this, we find that what often is assumed to be known is not known. We find, also, that we learned a lot that did not come directly from Spearman's work even as it did come from following leads that Spearman laid down. We consider those leads first, and then look at the major substantive contributions of Spearman's work.

SPEARMAN'S THEORY OF GENERAL INTELLIGENCE

A scientific theory must be falsifiable; that is what distinguishes scientific theory from other theory. In his initial 1904a paper, Spearman put forth a scientific theory of general intelligence. Others of his time had theories about intelligence, but they had no test that could falsify their theory. Binet and Simon (1905) were prominent among these others. They said intelligence is a collection of cognitive abilities. That collection-of-abilities theory became the accepted theory, the standard used throughout the world in psychology and education.

Still today, it is the theory of the large majority of people who talk and write about human cognitive abilities. Jenson (1998), for example, one of the best known members of that majority, argues that intelligence is the first principal factor in any large collection of diverse mental ability tests. The first principal factor is simply a weighted sum of the test scores. The theory thus argues that intelligence is a sum of the scores obtained with a diverse collection of mental ability tests—and this is basically what Binet and Simon (1905) said.

Such theories are not really scientific theories because there is no test that can possibly falsify them; one collection-of-abilities theory of intelligence is no better, or worse, than another. Collection-of-abilities theories spawn commercial enterprise; indeed, many marketed intelligence tests have derived from such theories, but they do not spawn a science.

Spearman's theory was different. It described what the results of doable experiments would be if the theory was correct—and, just as important, what the results would be if the theory was not correct. It required that one identify intelligence, whatever it was, and distinguish it from what was not intelligence. Spearman's theory thus directed the fledgling field of psychology toward research that could build a science to describe what people referred to when they used the term, *human intelligence*.

The Essence of the Theory

It may seem on first consideration that Spearman's theory is no better than collection-of-abilities theories, for it argues that intelligence is a common factor manifested in every kind of mental effort. Thus one might think that this would be the first principal factor in any large collection of diverse mental ability tests—just what Jensen argued. But it isn't. Spearman's theory requires that that factor be the only common factor, not just the first principal factor.

The theory requires an experiment in which people are measured with separate devices[1] for each kind of activity requiring mental effort. It argues that the measures

---

[1]In this context to keep "test" in the sense of testing a theory separate from "test" in the sense of a psychological test to measure an ability, we use the term, *measurement device* or simply *device* to refer to a psychological test.

obtained with such devices involve two things—general intelligence and a specific factor. Persons scoring well on a device may do so by virtue of having and using general intelligence, but also by virtue of having and using ability, or other abilities, or by luck. Such other ability or abilities or luck is referred to with the singular term, *specific factor*. In an experiment required to test Spearman's theory, it is necessary that there be no duplication of any specific factor in the devices selected to measure different kinds of mental effort. If this condition is met, and the theory of general intelligence is correct, then every one of the off-diagonal 2-by-2 determinants of the matrix of intercorrelations among the measurement devices will be zero (to within chance variation). On the other hand, if the theory is not correct, or an experiment is not adequately designed (to meet the conditions of the theory), then the 2-by-2 determinants will not be zero. The 2-by-2 determinants came to be called *tetrad differences*. The tetrad differences will all be zero if each of the sampled measurement devices measure one (and only one) factor in common. The tetrad differences will not be zero—even if the theory is correct—if any specific factor is reliably measured in more than one measurement device of an experiment.

Again, it might seem on first consideration that Spearman's theory is not scientific because it requires that intelligence be general; that is, operate in every activity requiring mental effort. This necessitates representative sampling of all such activities, which is impossible, so experiments to test the theory are not doable; therefore, the theory is not testable, and thus is not scientific. But this reasoning misconstrues what is required of a scientific theory. A scientific theory need not be testable in a limiting statement of the theory. Most scientific theories are not testable in this sense.

For example, the kinetic theory of molecules states that all molecular motion stops at absolute zero ($-273°$ Centigrade). Such a condition can never be sampled; Brownian motion can never be stopped entirely. This does make the theory unscientific. It merely indicates the impossibility of testing the absolute limiting condition of the theory. The theory specifies potential experiments that could falsify it. That is what makes it a scientific theory. Similarly, the ideal of obtaining a representative sample of all indicators of intelligence need not be realizable in order for Spearman's theory to be testable.[2]

For any scientific theory, there are hypotheses that are not testable. This does not render a theory unscientific; it renders it not fully tested, never proven for sure, which is a hallmark of scientific theories. This is in stark contrast to nonscientific theories, which claim to be fully and absolutely proven. The requirement for a theory to be scientific is that it be falsifiable in doable experiments, and Spearman's theory meets that requirement.

---

[2]More specifically to the point, Meredith (1964), citing Lawley (1943–1944) as the originator of the theorem, has shown that a common factor of a population can be identified when neither the sample of indicator variables nor the sample of subjects is representative of their respective populations.

The Origins of the Theory

Spearman had studied for the doctoral degree with Wilhelm Wundt, usually regarded as one of the founders of experimental psychology—that is, research based on experimental versus control-group designs. But Spearman also read the works of Francis Galton (1869, 1952, 1883), often regarded as the founder of differential psychology; that is, research based on covariation designs (studies of individual differences). Spearman's theory of general intelligence, and his specifications for testing it, derived primarily from the Galton school of psychology.

Galton had theorized that individual differences in intellectual achievements—particularly the differences between the achievements of eminent people and ordinary people—reflect hereditary differences in the power of the mind. He thought this power would be indicated by keenness of sensory discrimination (acuity in seeing, hearing, tasting, smelling, sensing, touch). He reasoned that thinking is required in the intellectual achievements that indicate power of the mind, and because all thinking must depend on the five senses (a premise that Locke had advanced), individual differences in sensory discrimination should indicate individual differences in power of the mind. He sought evidence to support this idea.

He had established an Anthropometric Laboratory in London's South Kensington Science Museum. Visitors to the museum were allowed to pay 3 pence to have their sensory discriminations measured (and provide other information). Thousands of people paid the 3 pence and thus provided Galton with data (see Johnson, McClearn, Yuen, Nagoshi, Ahern, & Cole, 1985). He had developed a way of calculating the correlation between variables. He reasoned that if keenness of sensory discrimination indicated intellectual achievement, then the intercorrelations among the discrimination measures for the different senses and the correlations of these measures with intellectual achievements should be large. This is not what he found; the correlations he calculated were very small—near zero.

By the time Spearman undertook his 1904 studies, he had created methods for estimating reliability of measurement and had proved that correlations can be low primarily because the reliabilities of the measures are low. He had invented a method for correcting correlations for attenuation due to unreliability. Had such corrections been used with the correlations Galton obtained, the estimated correlations would have been larger, so the results would have presented a more favorable case than Galton presented for the hypothesis that measures of sensory discrimination are interrelated and related to intellectual achievements. Spearman's 1904a article is largely a presentation of this more favorable case.[3]

---

[3]The other 1904 article (Spearman, 1904b) is a presentation of test theory, not a study of intelligence. Here we refer to some results from that article, for example, the idea of correcting correlations for attenuation due to unreliability, but we do not review it here.

First Studies by Spearman

The Spearman (1904a) article is a 93-page report of four studies of measures of sensory discrimination and measures of "the intelligences." In these studies, he did more than merely correct correlations for attenuation due to unreliability. To obtain what he regarded as proper data for analyses, (a) he eliminated subjects from initial samples to control for experience differences, (b) he rescaled variables to remove possible practice effects, (c) he adjusted for age and gender differences, (d) he partialled out a variety of what he called irrelevant influences, (e) he "arbitrarily assumed observational errors" to estimate reliabilities. Then, after all this, he corrected the correlations for attenuation due to measurement unreliability.

With the data adjusted in these ways, Spearman directed analyses at showing that there is a "correspondence"—by which he meant a single common factor—among the different forms of sensory discrimination, a comparable correspondence among different measures of intelligence, and a correspondence among both "the discriminations and the intelligences." Surveying the outcomes of these analyses, Spearman (1904a) concluded "... these results ... and other analogous observed facts indicate that all branches of intellectual activity have in common one fundamental function (or group of functions), whereas the remaining or specific elements of the activity seem in every case to be wholly different from that in all others" (p. 284).

The calculations for the critical test of Spearman's hypothesis in these earliest studies were not literally those we described previously; Spearman did not calculate all the tetrad differences and compare their distribution around zero with the standard error of the distribution. Those calculations, in the days before computers, would have taken a great amount of time. Spearman worked out calculations that approximated results that would obtain if all the tetrad differences were zero, and that could be done in a reasonable amount of time. We can illustrate such calculations with Spearman's analyses to show *hierarchical order*. Such an order occurs if the tetrad differences are zero. The correlations Spearman (1904a) presented to show this hierarchy are shown in Table 11–1.

If the tetrad differences are zero, the partial correlation between any two variables will be zero when the general factor[4] is partialed out; then the correlation between the two variables will be equal to the product of the correlation of each variable with the general factor. Spearman recognized that it follows directly from this condition that the correlations in the same rows of any two columns of the matrix of intercorrelations will be proportional. Such proportionality indicates, he said, "a very remarkable uniformity," what he called "The hierarchy of the intelligences": If all the correlations are due to one common factor and they can be arranged in a table in order of magnitude—from the top left corner to the bottom

---

[4]There was no mention of *g* in this early article. Reference to *g* appears in Spearman (1914), Theory of Two Factors, and is very prominent in Spearman (1927).

TABLE 11–1

Intercorrelations on Which Spearman Based His Analysis of the Hierarchy of the
Intelligences, as Reported in Spearman (1904a)

	Classics	French	English	Math	Discrim.*	Music
Classics	1.00					
French	.83	1.00				
English	.78	.67	1.00			
Math	.70	.67	.64	1.00		
Discrim.*	.66	.65	.54	.45	1.00	
Music	.63	.57	.51	.51	.40	1.00

*Pitch discrimination.

right corner of the table, as seen in Table 11–1—then it will be seen that the correlations decrease in the same proportion in both vertical and horizontal directions throughout the table. This is what Spearman called a "perfectly constant Hierarchy.[5]"

The subjects in the study on which Table 11–1 is based were 22 boys[6] "... in a preparatory school of the highest class, which principally trained boys for Harrow." There were six kinds of measurements. Four were said to be measures of "the intelligences." These were rank-orders of the sums of percentage-grades the boys received within courses in Classics (Latin and Greek), French, English, and Mathematics. There were two kinds of measures of sensory discrimination, one a measure of pitch discrimination, the other—said to be a measure of discrimination in music–was the rank-order of the sum of percentage-grades the boys received in their music course.

Spearman described the hierarchy in Table 11–1 in this way:

> ... if we consider the correspondences between the four branches of school study, a very remarkable uniformity may be observed. English and French, for instance, agree with one another in having a higher correlation with Classics than with Mathematics. Quite similarly, French and Mathematics agree in both having a higher correlation with Classics than with English. And the same will be found to be the case when any other pair is compared with the remainder. The whole thus forms a perfectly constant Hierarchy in the following order: Classics, French, English, Mathematics. This unbroken regularity becomes especially astonishing

---

[5]In Table 11–1, compare the elements in the same rows of any two columns—say, columns 1 and 2. Perfect fit of the model requires $r_{31}/r_{32} = r_{41}/r_{42} = r_{51}/r_{52} = r_{61}/r_{62}$. In Table 11–1, the proportions are .78/.67 = 1.16; .70/.67 = 1.04; .66/.65 = 1.02; .63/.57 = 1.11. Throughout the table, the average of the 90 independent proportions for off-diagonal elements is 1.07.

[6]To control for practice effects in music and pitch discrimination, only the boys who were taking music lessons were selected from the entire class of 33 boys; the 11 boys who were not taking music lessons were excluded from the sample.

when we regard the minuteness of the variations involved, for the four branches have average correlations of 0.77, 0.72, 0.70, and 0.67 respectively.

When... we turn to the Discrimination of Pitch, we find its correlations to be of slightly less magnitude (raw) but in precisely the same relative rank, being: 0.66 with Classics, 0.65 with French, 0.54 with English, and 0.45 with Mathematics....

Just the same principle governs even Musical Talent... For it is not only correlated with all the other functions, but once again in precisely the same order: with Classics 0.63, with French 0.57, with English 0.51, with Mathematics 0.51, and with Discrimination 0.40.

Altogether, we have a uniformity that is very nearly perfect and far surpasses the conceivable limits of chance coincidence ... when we consider that the probable error varies between about 0.01 for the ordinary studies to about 0.03 for music ... (Spearman, 1904a, pp. 274–275)

Spearman estimated the correlation of each variable with the common factor by dividing the sum of the correlations in each column by the square root of the sum of all the correlations. He then ordered (from high to low) the variables in accordance with the squares of these correlations to show "the full absolute saturation of each variable with General Intelligence" (Spearman, 1904a, p. 276).

These, then, are the kinds of analyses, results, and statements of proof that are referred to when Spearman's (1904a) paper is cited to support a claim that he did the first factor analysis and discovered general intelligence. They are not the crisp calculations we outlined when we argued that Spearman was the first to put forth a testable theory of intelligence, but in his arguments for "correspondences," displays of "very remarkable uniformity" and marshalling of results, Spearman is, indeed, putting forth a form of common factor analysis[7] and presenting evidence in support of the principal hypothesis of his theory of general intelligence.

---

[7]The claim that Spearman invented factor analysis needs to be understood in the context of mathematical inventions that preceded him (much of which history is discussed elsewhere in this book). Spearman did not invent or prove the principles of determinants and matrices that are the crux of his test. These principles were developed by others well before Spearman's time. Grattan-Guinness and Ledermann (1994) provide a good history indicating how and when these ideas came into use. They report that as early as the 17th century, in the writings of Leibniz in Europe and Seki in Japan, both in the 1680s, it was known that in solving linear equations, determinants comprised of the coefficient multipliers of the unknowns indicate the number of consistent equations needed to solve for—determine—a solution for the unknowns. As early as 1812, in the work of Cauchy, the concepts of matrix, characteristic equation, and characteristic values (eigenvalues) were in use. In the writings of Frobenius, Sylvester, and Caley in the 1870s and 1880s there were proofs that a matrix satisfies its own characteristic equation, that the number of linearly independent (basis) variables among a set of variables is the rank of the product-moment matrix (Gram product) of these variables, that rank is equal to the number of nonzero eigenvalues, and is one less than the largest non-zero minor of that Gram-product matrix. In the 1890s, Pearson developed the product moment correlation and Yule described partial and semipartial correlation.

So these ideas on which factor analysis is based were known and in available publications in the days when Spearman read mathematics and studied for his degrees in engineering and psychology. They

In a later paper, Spearman (1914) would present a more mathematically rigorous argument for the proportionality of columns and hierarchical order. He would then argue, first, that if the column proportionality holds good throughout the correlation matrix, the correlation of a column of that matrix with any other column will be 1.0,[8] and, second, that the "... theory now ... possesses one of the most valuable characteristics in highest degree: the capability of being readily submitted to crucial quantitative verification" (Spearman, 1914, p. 108). He would use this criterion of near-perfect correlations among the columns of the correlation matrix in later studies, in which he made the claim that one common factor described the data (Spearman, 1923). It his 1927 book, Spearman applied the tetrad difference test in the manner we described in the first part of this chapter.

Today, the kind of calculations Spearman so arduously worked through to imperfectly estimate the tetrad difference condition would be compressed into fitting, and estimating the goodness of fit of, a one-common factor model. Once the raw scores were in the computer, this would take only a small fraction of a second using a computer with any contemporary modeling program (e.g., Mx; Neale, Boker, Xie, & Maes, 1999). Results of such analysis for the correlations of Table 11–1 are shown in Figure 11–1. Here we see that an estimate of the probability that the model fits the one common factor model is .99 and the root mean square error of approximation (RMSEA; Browne & Cudeck, 1993; Steiger, 1990), which estimates departure from fit, rounds to zero. These two statistics indicate that one, and only one, common factor very well accounts for the intercorrelations among the measures of sensory discrimination and the classroom grades.

CRITICISMS AND RESPONSES

Today the adjustments Spearman applied to the data—for example, estimating reliability from "arbitrarily assumed observational errors," adjusting correlations for

---

indicate that if measurements can be regarded as real numbers (at the interval level of measurement) in parametric equations for which there are unknowns, then mathematical analyses can be applied to solve for the unknowns. Spearman's invention of factor analysis involved applying these principles to the idea that, indeed, measurements of persons might be assumed to be real numbers in equations and therefore the mathematical principles of determinants and matrices can be applied to solve for the unknowns. His idea—the basic idea of common factor analysis—was that there may be both common and unique basis variables and that only the off-diagonal elements (the covariances) of the Gram product indicate the common basis variables. This is different from the way the principles of determinants and matrices had been applied in eigenvalue–eigenvector decomposition analysis, and in the method of scaling the eigenvectors that is called *principal components analysis* (Pearson, 1901). In stating and applying the principles of determinants and matrices in this novel way, Spearman invented the one common factor form of factor analysis.

[8]Spearman (1914) gives the product moment correlation formula for this. Kendall's (1962) tau had not yet been invented. Although Spearman (1904b) had developed the product moment correlation for ranks, he did not argue for use of that formula here.

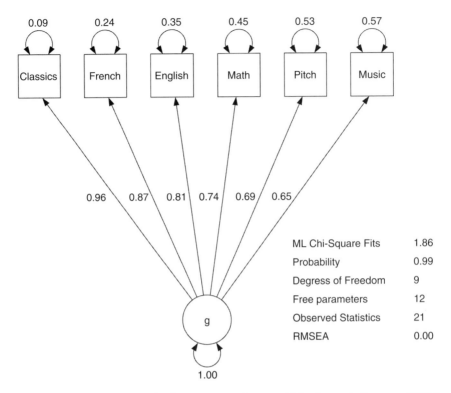

FIGURE 11–1.   Fit of a one and only one common factor model for the matrix Spearman (1904a) presented to show a perfectly constant hierarchy for the intercorrelations among four measures of "the intelligences" and two measures of "the sensory discrimination" of 22 boys in a preparatory school of the highest class.

attenuation due to unreliability—would render his study unacceptable for publication in a scientific journal. But such procedures were not a principal concern in those early days in psychology. The concerns were with the ideas and the logic of the methods for garnering support for ideas.

Early Problems

Burt (1909, 1911) appears to have been the first (in publication) to question the ideas and logic of Spearman's (1904a) study. His principal point was that the Spearman's results did not indicate that intelligence was general because important activities requiring mental effort were not considered in Spearman's analyses. Burt brought together and analyzed broader samples of cognitive abilities extracted a general factor, in accordance with Spearman's stipulations, and found that one common factor would not account for the correlations; he had to calculate a second (numerical) factor and third (verbal) factor to do this.

In his answer to these criticisms, Spearman (1914, 1923; Hart & Spearman, 1912) presented results that showed that the one-common factor hypothesis was retainable for correlation matrices on different particular sets of abilities. Burt (1924) replied with analyses of even broader samples of "indicators of intelligence" that showed that one common factor was not sufficient and that group factors of memory span, scholastic aptitude and manual skills, as well as the verbal and numerical factors were needed to account for the correlational data. In the years immediately following, other studies by other investigators (Carter, 1928; Cox, 1928; Kelley, 1928; Paterson & Elliot, 1930) were presented to show that when samples of what were well-regarded as indicators of intelligence were analyzed, more than one common factor was indicated. *Cognitive speed* and *visualization* were added to the list of replicable group factors.

A general factor was always extracted in these early studies. Some reasoned that perhaps that general factor was the factor of Spearman's theory. But a flaw in that reasoning was spotted; the general factors of different studies were different. The factor had a different composition in each study. It came to be realized that a general factor could always be calculated, but this factor was simply a summary of the correlations among the collection of variables sampled in a particular study. There was no test of whether the general factor in one study represented the same phenomenon as the general factors in other studies. Simply calculating the general factor of each particular battery did test Spearman's hypothesis that one—the same one—common factor was required in all mental activities.

Spearman's Major Response

In his much-cited book, *The Abilities of Man: Their Nature and Measurement*, Spearman (1927) marshaled a comprehensive response to criticisms of his theory. He brought together the empirical findings of his previous studies, but he also called in evidence and theory from different branches of psychology and a variety of other sources. He aimed: "... to set forth the conditions under which every ability is divisible into two factors, one universal and the other specific" (Spearman, 1927, p. 87). He also described the nature, origins, development, and correlates of the universal factor. *Comprehensiveness* was a principal feature of this statement of his theory. Spearman tried to bring together all that was known in psychology to help us understand human intelligence. This 1927 statement, more than Spearman (1904a) or any of his other early works, most influenced subsequent research on human cognitive capabilities (i.e., human intelligence).

The theory Spearman produced owes much to Galton's thinking. But Spearman, much more than Galton, appealed to evidence of the field of psychology, generally, to give credence to his principal arguments. For example, what Galton had described as *power of the mind*, Spearman described as *mental energy*; but where Galton had left power of the mind largely as only a metaphor, Spearman used two chapters and major sections of other chapters to bring together evidence and arguments to show that the mental energy concept was well based on findings and explanations of general psychology—findings that supported concepts of *mental competition, fatigue, retentivity, conative control*, and *primordial potencies*. His claim was that these various lines of evidence indicate, first, that there is a form of mental energy that "... is wanted to explain the general factor," and, second, that there is a system of "... mental engines that might go far toward explaining the specific factors" (Spearman, 1927, p. 135).

The mental energy of the general factor was said to be manifested in cognitive behavior, but Spearman suggested that underlying this mental energy is a neural energy that flows from throughout the brain and affects all abilities. He suggested that different neural systems serve the specific-factor engines.

This thinking is similar to that of a prominent neurologist of the time— Lashley (1929)—although Spearman (1927) makes no reference to Lashley, and Lashley (1929) makes no reference to Spearman. Lashley argued that although specific, somewhat different cognitive deficits are produced by injuries to different parts of the brain, the brain functions as a whole, so that an injury anywhere in the brain produces general cognitive decline. He spoke of a mass action of the neural system that, to some extent, determines all intellectual capabilities.

Spearman's theory also specified that individual differences in the general factor were, to some extent, innate. Again his thinking is similar to Galton's, but much more based on appeal to evidence. To arrive at the main points of this argument, Spearman reviewed findings from some 28 studies of mean ability differences for groupings of people classified in accordance with nationality, occupation, race, familial relationship, social class, gender, and educational training. He concluded, "... education has a dominant influence on specific abilities, but normally it has little if any influence in respect to the general factor" (Spearman, 1927, p. 32). On this point, he acknowledged, "... the question is, no doubt, in great need of further more exact investigation" (p. 32).

Emergence of the Theory of g

Spearman's early theory was about intelligence—general intelligence. But increasingly in his writings over the years preceding his 1927 book, he had expressed concerns about using the word, "intelligence." It referred to too many things. Then, in 1927, he characterized it as "cankered with equivocality ... Chaos itself can go no farther! Disagreement ... has reached its apogee ... In truth, 'Intelligence' has become a mere vocal sound, a word with so many meanings that finally it has none" (Spearman, 1927, p. 14). He had used the letter "g" to stand for general intelligence in some of his earlier writings. Now he used the letter g, always italicized, to replace "general intelligence," and sought to define g in a way that would eradicate equivocality.

This g, he said,

> ... is primarily not any concrete thing but only a value or magnitude. Further, that which this magnitude measures has not been defined by declaring what it

is like, but only by pointing out where it can be found. It consists in just that constituent—whatever it may be—that is common to all abilities that are interconnected by the tetrad equation. (Spearman, 1927, p. 75–76)

This did not immediately clean up the definitional muddle Spearman so deplored in the concept of *intelligence*. To find g, one had to find "the abilities that are interconnected by the tetrad equation" and identify "that constituent—whatever it may be—common to all" those abilities. Most important, one had to distinguish the g common factor from the specific factors that also account for individual differences in mental abilities. The specific factor of each measure of mental ability had to be identified because the tetrad difference test of Spearman's theory required that there be no duplication of such factors in a battery of measures designed to test the theory. The muddle remained because investigators had different ideas about the abilities that should be interconnected by the tetrad equation; they had different ideas about the essential constituents of g; and they had different ideas about what constituted *a specific factor*. There was still much wrangling about where to point to find g.

Nevertheless, the Spearman definition of g provided a way clean up the definitional mess. It required experiments. Measurement devices had to be assembled in accordance with hypotheses that they intercorrelated in a manner such that the tetrad differences be zero. To meet Burt's criticism, the devices would have to measure abilities that were accepted as indicating human intelligence. A single experiment, such as Spearman's (1904a) study, would not prove the point, but it would be evidence in support of the point, and if more studies answering to Burtlike criticisms also proved the point, the theory of g would gain acceptance in the scientific community. In the process, the constituents of g would become clear. Spearman's definition of g was thus a call to action that could end the wrangling about the meaning of intelligence. Experiments would indicate g, the constituents of g, and the nature of specific abilities that are independent of g.

Laying Out the Structural Evidence

Spearman (1927) answered that call. And he presented

proof that g and s (specific abilities) exist. ... To the question, whether the divisibility of abilities into g and s (with s throughout independent) really occurs to any large extent ... our evidence appears to have answered convincingly in the affirmative. Such two independent factors have been demonstrated for at any rate a great number of sets of tests commonly used for 'general intelligence.' (Spearman, 1927, p. 150)

The evidence to which Spearman referred was, first, intercolumnar correlations calculated on the correlation matrices of 14 studies conducted between 1889 and 1914; these correlations ranged between 1.16 and .89 and averaged .99.

> All this evidence lies beyond reasonable doubt ... the intercolumnar correlation shows itself to be excellently satisfied. On the other hand, we must remember that this criterion itself leaves much to be desired ... Let us turn to the genuine criterion, the tetrad difference ... (Spearman, 1927, p. 140)

He then presented evidence indicated by the distributions of tetrad differences calculated for correlation matrices originally obtained by Simpson (14 measurement devices; 37 persons); Brown (8 devices; 66 persons); Bonser (5 devices; 757 persons); Holzinger (9 devices; 50 persons); and Magson (7 devices; 149 persons). In each case, the median observed tetrad difference was nearly as small as, or smaller than, the probable error of the tetrad differences. The agreement of observed with theoretical errors of sampling the tetrad differences was, Spearman said, "nearly perfect" and, moreover, the results obtained by in applying this correct criterion have fully corroborated the results obtained with the earlier intercolumnar correlation criterion.

So he concluded, first with a caution: "Science knows no finality ... all conclusions drawn in the present work are subject to 'inevitable eventual corrections and limitations.'" But then with confidence, given

> ... the degree of exactness attained already, the agreement of the observed values with those required by theory must be admitted by any unbiased person to have been surprisingly close. In general, it seems quite as good as, if not better than, that usually reached in determining the mechanical equivalent of heat and thus establishing the law of conservation of physical energy. (Spearman, 1927, pp. 159–160)

Dealing With Discrepancies at Hand

There were problems, however. Some of these were in the data Spearman presented. For example, the Simpson matrix was not positive definite; it had two negative roots. Given only the computing capability available to Spearman, this probably could not have been noticed. There were two common factors, not one, in the Holzinger data. The reported correlation matrix of Magson was asymmetrical. Three of the eight factor coefficients of the Brown data were too small to reach statistical significance; the near-zero correlations for the variables would have contributed small tetrad differences, but these would mainly indicate the smallness of the correlations.

But again, these were procedures problems—not attended to much at the time. Most of the problems with Spearman's claims resulted because other investigators carefully applying his test did not find what he found. He faced some of these problems head-on in his 1927 presentation of "proof that g and s exist." To explain why others testing his hypothesis did not get results consistent with his theory, he identified a number of conditions that could produce specific factor overlap, and thus yield results that would falsely falsify his hypothesis.

For results obtained on about 1,000 army recruits with the eight measurement devices of the Army Alpha, he argued that because the measures were obtained at nine different camps, then if "... in any camp the testing or marking happened to be more generous than in others with respect to any of these tests, the men here would tend to shine in these particular tests; the result must be to generate additional correlation between these tests quite independently of any psychological connection between them" (Spearman, 1927, p. 157).

For results obtained on 2,599 members of the British Civil Service with seven devices intended to measure general intelligence, he argued that because some of the devices required selecting an answer from among several choices and some required "inventing" an answer, these two response forms produced specific factor overlap; thus test of the tetrad differences seemed to invalidate the g-factor hypotheses when it was valid. He calculated the tetrad differences separately for the devices that had the same response form and found "... the agreement of observation with theory at once becomes admirable" (Spearman, 1927, p. 154).

For results obtained with six successive measurements with the Binet test series at intervals of 6 months, he argued the "... tests change in nature as the age of the testee increases. Consequently, the tests for any two neighboring ages will have much in common that does not extend to ages farther apart" (Spearman, 1927, p. 151).

In these ways, Spearman mounted a general argument that whenever there were differences in test-battery administers or scorers, or diversity in age or training or gender or other such factors within the samples of testees, or diversity in measurement devices in respect to item form (as the above-mentioned selective or inventive response requirement), then specific factor overlap would occur, the distribution of the calculated tetrad differences would not match the theoretical distribution, and the one common factor hypothesis would be falsely rejected.

Downfall of the Theory

In describing conditions under which the tetrad-difference test might fail when the one common factor hypothesis was valid, Spearman's did not deal with the results of Burt (1909, 1911, 1924) and others who were presenting similar findings at about the same time (Carter, 1928; Cox, 1928; Kelley, 1928). Prominent critics of his theory did not accept his post hoc arguments that the theory was correct even when the results of well-conducted tests did not support it. Faced with this dissention and recognizing the many, many ways in which the tetrad difference test might fail, Spearman (1927) set forth a different theory. He argued that g entered into every kind of ability measure and this was indicated by positive intercorrelations among these measures "... for the purpose of indicating the amount of g possessed by a person, any test will do ... the most ridiculous 'stunts' will measure the self-same g as will the highest exploits of logic or flights of imagination" (Spearman, 1927, p. 197). He referred to this argument for the "universality of g" as "the theorem of indifference of the indicator" (p. 197). In accordance with this theorem, evidence of positive correlations among abilities was sufficient to support his theory. This evidence was, and is, prevalent.

Spearman's argument from the "theorem of indifference of indicator" has been embraced by a preponderance of prominent scientists studying human abilities. For example, Jenson (1998) in his widely praised book (Beaujean, 2002; Detterman, 1998; Miele, 2003; Nyborg, 2003) made the "theorem" the centerpiece of his claim that Spearman discovered general intelligence. He used it to explain why different ability tests are positively correlated, why positive intercorrelations among ability tests are prevalent, why a g factor must be found at the top in higher order multiple factor analysis, and why, therefore, the theory of general intelligence is basically correct. These arguments have been put forth by other prominent investigators (e.g., Carroll, 1993; Eysenck, 1982; Gottfredson, 1997).

But this theory is a step down from the scientific theory of g. Indeed, it is, at best, barely a scientific theory. It is true that in broad samples of people, almost all tests regarded as measuring any aspect of human intelligence are positively correlated, and the rare exceptions—for samples of very young children (Bayley, 1969) and for the correlations between highly speeded tests at low levels of difficulty and unspeeded tests at high levels of difficulty (Guilford, 1964)—might be written off as unimportant or explained as in some way compatible with the hypothesis. But it is true, also, that practically every variable that in any sense indicates the good things in life—health, money, education, and so forth, and athletic and artistic abilities, as well as cognitive abilities—correlate positively with every other such thing.[9] Granted that some (Herrnstein & Murray, 1994) might take such findings evidence that general intelligence is truly universal, there is no falsifiable test that distinguishes this theory of the "good things" from the theory of g. There is no way to identify the constituents of g and distinguish them from what is not g—the specific factors. The theory has the same character as the theories Spearman had earlier so roundly and soundly criticized; g has so many meanings that finally it has none.

Indeed, the so-called "theorem of indifference of indicator" is not a theorem at all. If it were true that when all intercorrelations among variables are positive, there must be one common factor—a factor that might have to be found at the top of the order in higher order multiple factor analysis—it could be said that this was proof of the theorem. But this is not true. This was demonstrated by Thomson (1919) a few years after Spearman's theory came into prominence.

The Thomson–Thorndike Theory

Positive intercorrelations among all of a set of variables can be indicative of two or three or four or more common factors; it need not be indicative a single higher

---

[9]The same positive correlation obtains when things are measured at the opposite pole of the not so good things in life—poor health, little money, lousy education, and lack of abilities, as discussed at some length in Herrnstein and Murray (1994).

order common factor. Indeed, Thomson argued that positive intercorrelations among abilities is just as compatible with a theory of many common factors as it is with a theory of one common factor. He showed that if a measurement device—Device 1, say—involves elementary processes *a, b, c,* and *d,* for example, then if Device 2 involves processes *a, e, f,* and *h* it can correlate with Device 1 in virtue of sharing process *a* (but not *b, c, d, e, f,* or *h*). Similarly, if Device 3 involves processes *b, e, i, j,* and *k,* it can correlate with Device 1 in virtue of sharing process *b,* and it can correlate with Device 2 in virtue of sharing process *e,* (and not sharing any other processes with Test 1 or Jest 2). Device 4 can share process *c* with Device 1, process *f* with Device 2, and process *h* with Device 3 and thus be positively correlated with all three tests without sharing any processes common to all four tests. Continuing in this way Thomson showed that all the devices of a battery of measurement devices can be positively correlated and not involve a single common factor.

Thomson's demonstration was prompted by a theory of many factors of intelligence that was put forth by E. L. Thorndike in 1903, the year before Spearman's theory was first presented. In line with Thorndike's thinking, Thomson argued that performance on any cognitive measure can be seen to involve many processes of perception, apprehension, retention, association, reasoning, reflection, retrieval, and so forth, and that such processes can be configured—organized, called forth, applied, and expressed—in a great variety of different ways, and these different configurations can overlap and be shared in an even larger number of ways to produce the performances on the different measures that make up a battery of positively correlated cognitive devices.

Two conditions observed in many studies of cognitive abilities—positive manifold of the intercorrelations among samples of ability variables and the varying composition of a general factor among these variables—are consistent with Thomson's theory of human abilities, but not with Spearman's theory of one common factor. Thomson's theory does not claim that there is one general factor that pervades all cognitive abilities.[10] Several investigators of the last century, Humphreys (1971) most prominent among them, favored this kind of theory of human cognitive capabilities.

ATTEMPTS TO RETAIN g THEORY

Note that *g* theory did not go quietly into the night. There were many efforts to retain it. Recognizing the validity of Spearman's argument that overlapping specifics would spoil tests of the one common factor hypothesis, Alexander (1935), Brown (1933), Brown and Stephenson, (1933), El Koussy (1935), and Rimoldi (1948) designed studies in which the assembled tests were thought to at once measure the important abilities of intelligence and not introduce specific factor overlap. These efforts failed. In each case, several common factors were required

---

[10]Nor does it call for a theory of mass action of neural activity underlying all cognitive behavior.

to fit the data. This was the verdict of almost all factor analytic studies conducted from the 1930s onward (summarized in Carroll, 1993; Ekstrom, French, & Harman, 1979; Hakstian & Cattell, 1974).

Such evidence did not end the matter in Spearman's day and it has not ended the matter even today. A theory that humans differ in an innately determined general intelligence is widely and strongly believed. Belief in the theory is entrenched in our culture and language. It is not simply Spearman's theory; it is the theory of many. Such belief in the basic correctness of the theory has charged efforts to retain it even in the face of mounting evidence of its inadequacy. It is instructive to consider these salvage attempts.

The High Correlations Argument

It is sometimes argued that the correlations among different devices said to measure intelligence are large and this indicates that g is operating throughout the devices.

There is no merit to this argument. It is merely a version of the correlations are positive argument. It is consistent with Thomson's theory, not g theory. The test of g theory does not require that correlations be large. What constitutes a "large" correlation is a question for debate or for practical need to predict, not a question required of g theory. By almost any reasonable criterion, correlations between devices thought to measure intelligence are not always large, even when adjusted to estimate attenuation due to unreliability; they are in the neighborhood of from .15 to .80. The only refutable hypothesis of the argument—that a correlation can not be smaller than, say, x—is arbitrary. Different sum of abilities measures of intelligence—the Binet and Wechsler devices, for example—correlate highly because they measure the same things, not because they measure the same thing. The so-called "high correlation" argument is baseless.

The Higher Order Common Factor Argument

It has been argued that if positively correlated ability measures are factored to yield common factors at a primary level, and the primary common factors are factored to yield second-order factors, and these are factored to yield third-order factors and factoring continues in this manner until only one factor is indicated at some even higher order that one factor is evidence of g.

This again is merely a version of the correlations are positive argument. There is no refutable hypothesis; a higher order factor can always be computed. In practice, the one factor determined in this manner in one study is not the same as the one factor found in other studies. If a battery contains many reliable tests measuring spatial abilities, for example, the one factor calculated at the highest order has its highest correlations with spatial abilities. If the battery is comprised largely of reliable measures requiring verbal comprehension, the one factor at the higher order is a verbal comprehension factor.

This is well illustrated in Carroll's (1993) *tour de force* reanalysis of some 477 batteries of ability measuring devices. In his monograph, Carroll (1993) identified "... 53 factors, in 146 datasets, classified as measuring 'general intelligence' or possibly Spearman's factor *g*" (p. 591; see Table 15.4). Inspection of these results indicates that often the general factors of different analyses contained no measurement devices (no abilities) that are the same; the factors were thus "general" in respect to entirely different sets of variables. When the batteries contained some of the same variables, the general factors were different; one was a general visualization factor; another was a general verbal comprehension factor; and so on. Even when batteries were made up of the same measurement devices, the order of the correlations with the general factor were notably different; the factors did not pass the test of metric invariance (Meredith & Horn, 2001). To argue that these kinds of results indicate general intelligence, one must appeal to the discredited "theorem of indifference of indicator"—essentially, assume what one is trying to prove. Carroll's findings do not support a theory of *g*.

Hierarchical Analysis With Test for One Common Factor.   A higher order factor analysis converging on one factor at the top would provide evidence in support of Spearman's theory if three conditions were met: (a) the factor intercorrelation at the next to highest order satisfied the one common factor (rank one) requirements of the Spearman model, (b) the factor at the highest order was invariant across different samples of people and different occasions of measurement, and (3) the set of analyzed variables—hence the factors at the various levels—included a good complement of the abilities indicating human intelligence. If these conditions were met, there could still be questions about whether important indicators of intelligence were left out of the sample of abilities, but one would need to identify such indicators to give credence to the claim and discount the evidence. Until then, the results would be supportive of a general factor theory.

A study reported by Thurstone and Thurstone (1941) seemed to have met these conditions. This study was based on research in which Thurstone (1935, 1938) put forth a multiple factor theory to describe the cognitive abilities of intelligence. Rather than specifying a single common ability (Spearman) or overlapping bondings of many, many abilities (Thomson), Thurstone specified a relatively small number of primary abilities, each of which could be identified as a common factor among several (three or four) different exemplar measures of the ability. A test of one major hypothesis of the theory was in principle the same as the test of Spearman's theory; the rank of the matrix of intercorrelations had to equal the number of hypothesized common factors. In these landmark studies, Thurstone gathered broad samples of the abilities of intelligence and, in multiple factor analyses, identified primary abilities of verbal comprehension (V), word fluency (W), number facility (N), spatial thinking (S), associative memory (M), perceptual speed (P), general reasoning (R), inductive reasoning (I), and deductive reasoning (D).

In the study that seemed to support Spearman's theory Thurstone and Thurstone (1941) tested the one common factor hypothesis at the second order among primary abilities. The rank of the matrix of intercorrelations among the V, W, N, S, M, and I primary factors was found to be very close to unity. This was consistent with Spearman's theory. Unfortunately, the results were obtained for a trimmed battery—only six of the nine primary abilities had been analyzed. When another—or other—primary abilities were included in the battery, the rank-one condition no longer obtained. Thus, the finding was that the general factor was not truly general.

Another well-known higher order study (Gustafsson & Undheim, 1996) is often cited as indicating support for Spearman's theory of g. The study was well designed to represent a broad sampling of the abilities accepted as indicating human intelligence. The findings indicated that at the second order in analysis among primary abilities, there were several broad factors representing different forms of intelligence. Gustafsson and Undheim interpreted one of these second-order factors as indicating fluid intelligence, Gf, an ability we describe in some detail in later sections of this chapter. Gustafsson and Undheim allowed the second-order factors to be correlated, and calculated a single factor at what they regarded as the third order. They found, however, that they could rotate this third-order factor into perfect alignment (correlation = 1.0) with the second-order Gf factor. The third-order factor was interpreted as g.

Thus, the finding seemed to be that g is equivalent to Gf and, because the third-order factor accounts for the correlations among the second-order factors, the factor interpreted as g accounts for the components held in common by all the abilities and thus is a general factor consistent with Spearman's theory. There are several problems with this interpretation of the findings.

First, because the third-order factor correlates perfectly with a second-order factor, there really is no need for a third-order factor. The second-order factors account for the primary factor intercorrelations just as well without, as with, the third-order factor. Rotation of the second-order factors could just as well have been orthogonal, for example. The third-order factor is simply a different way of summarizing the second-order findings (e.g., for details, see McArdle, 1989).

Second, granted that it is informative to describe the second-order factors with an oblique solution and to condense the intercorrelations thereby introduced into a third-order factor, that third-order factor could be aligned with any one of the second-order factors, not simply Gf. It could just as well be aligned with a second-order factor Gustafsson and Undheim (1996) interpreted as *crystallized intelligence*, Gc, for example.[11]

---

[11]It is reasonable that Gustafsson and Undheim (1996) chose to align their g factor with Gf—because the indicator variables of Gf are most similar to the process variables that Spearman described as indicating g (as we point out in another section of this chapter). But such alignment should not be taken

Third, any second-order factor chosen to absorb (summarize) the intercorrelations would still be independent of the other second-order factors. Such a factor is identical to the third-order factor, but not identical to the other second-order factors; it does not account for them. The evidence thus indicates that several second-order factors are required to account for the primary factor intercorrelations. One factor will not do it. The findings indicate that Gf, or g if we prefer that label, is not a general factor; it is but one among several second-order factors required to describe the correlations among primary ability indicators of human intelligence.

Thus, we learn from the Gustafsson and Undheim (1996) study what we learned from the Thurstone and Thurstone (1941) study—namely, that one common factor does not describe the intercorrelations among primary abilities of human intelligence. There is another lesson we can learn from Gustafsson and Undheim that we do not learn from Thurstone and Thurstone. This is that there are several intelligence-like factors at the second-order among primary factors. Only two such factors were required in Thurstone and Thurstone, but the Gustafsson and Undheim results indicate that more than two "intelligences" are needed to describe broad samples of the human abilities. We look into this matter in a later section, after we consider other major parts of Spearman's theory.

SPEARMAN'S THEORY OF PROCESSES

Although he railed against doing it in some of his writings, Spearman developed several important ideas about processes of intelligence. Indeed, second only to his development of a test for a common factor hypothesis, these ideas have most influenced research on human cognitive capabilities. It is interesting, too, that these ideas contradict some of Spearman's most forceful criticisms of the theorizing of his contemporaries (for recent details, see Deary, Bell, Bell, Campbell, & Fazal, 2004).

In his work on processes, Spearman went well beyond merely pointing to where g can be found. He put thought into identifying the particular behavior that indicates g and distinguishes it from specific factors. He tried to define g by declaring what it is like, contrary to what he advised when he criticized others' theories of intelligence.

Spearman described "what g is like" with what he called "laws of behavior." By "laws," he meant regularities established by experiments. The laws he was concerned with were intended to describe "the entire range of possible operations of knowing." Although the laws were presented as statements of fact, we would see them today as hypotheses about processes such as are analyzed in studies of cognitive psychology. The laws called for operational definitions of constructs that should, if g theory is correct, relate to each other in the manner described in the theory.

---

as proof of the equivalence of g and Gf; it is merely a statement that the abilities that define Gf appear to be the same as the processes Spearman identified as indicating g.

The "noegenetic[12] laws" were at the core of the theory. Under this heading, Spearman referred to capacity for creating understanding and building knowledge out of what is sensed, perceived, and comprehended. Three noegenetic laws were said to account for this capacity: the law of apprehension of experience, the law of eduction of relations, and the law of eduction of correlates.

In the law of apprehension of experience Spearman argued that in order to think in a way that would indicate g—and show it in the behavior of attempting to solve a problem—one must first sense and perceive the fundamental features (the fundaments) of the problem. With the law of eduction of relations, Spearman argued that there are relations among the fundaments of a problem, and one must comprehend these in order to make a response (in attempt to solve the problem) that can indicate a magnitude of g. With the law of eduction of correlates, he argued that for a person to make a response that indicates a quantity of g, that person must extrapolate or interpolate or generalize to infer a not immediately educed relation from the evidence of the extant relations.

The laws of eduction of relations and correlates were said to operate with all of several different kinds of relations—relations of conjunction, space, and time; relations of causation, constitution, attribution, and identity; relations of evidence, likeness, and conjunction; and relations among psychological concepts. To illustrate operations of measurement that would indicate g, test items were constructed, or taken from the constructions of others, to show each of the relations of eduction and to indicate how the relations operated in eduction of correlates.

An Important Departure From Earlier Theory

The law of apprehension of experience fell by the wayside in Spearman's definitive statements of his theory; individual differences in g were said to be primarily a function of the two eductive processes. Deemphasizing the apprehension law in his definitive theory is a major departure from Spearman's original theory. In this, as mentioned earlier, he argued strenuously for Galton's hypothesis that keenness of sensory discrimination indicates quality of intellect. He had reported in 1904, for example, ". . . we arrive at the remarkable result that the common and essential element in the Intelligences wholly coincides with the common and essential element in the Sensory Functions" (Spearman, 1904a, p. 269). But this "remarkable result" was obtained only after many adjustments of the data and corrections of correlations for attenuation due to unreliability of the measures. The raw, uncorrected correlations were small, as they had been in Galton's study, and as they were usually found to be in the studies of others. In his corrections of correlations Spearman "arbitrarily assumed observational errors" (his words) that gave him low reliabilities, which in the denominator of corrections for unreliability, gave him unrealistically

---

[12]As from *noesis*, to stand for purely intellectual apprehension.

large and mathematically impossible "corrected" correlations. Spearman probably would have noticed such unbelievable results. This, plus the persistent finding of near-zero correlations for the apprehension of experience measures, very possibly led him away from his earlier conclusion that sensory discrimination is a major feature of intelligence.

In any case, in his later writings, Spearman relegated apprehension of experience and keenness of sensory discrimination to minor roles in the theory of g. Apprehension was still seen to be part of the processing of g—it provided a foundation for educing relations and correlates—but the level of apprehension achieved by most people, excluding only the retarded, was sufficient for exercise of the other noegenetic processes; these other processes were seen as the essential processes that indicated individual differences in magnitudes of g in studies of normal people.

Further Contributions

This account of how apprehension of experience relates to abilities regarded as central to human intelligence is accepted in contemporary theory. Elementary sensory processes relate at only a low level to the reasoning, acquisition, and retention processes of human intellect. Other features of Spearman's theory also have become part of contemporary scientific theory of human cognitive capability.

Notable among these "other features" are Spearman's ideas about the speed of thinking. Spearman had found that quickness in educing relations and correlates, when measured in a particular person and problem, is in competition with the quality of that thinking; slower and more thoughtful thinking usually is associated with better and more nearly correct thinking. But Spearman found, also, that in analyses of between-person differences, quickness in educing relations and correlates was often positively, although only lowly, correlated with quality of that thinking.

> On the whole ... g has shown itself to measure a factor both in goodness and in speed of cognitive process. The connection between the goodness and the speed is that of being interchangeable. If the conditions ... eliminate the influence of speed, then g measures goodness, and vice versa. When—as is most usual—both influences are at play, then g measures the efficiency compounded of both. (Spearman, 1927, p. 138)

It is now generally recognized that a speed-accuracy trade-off operates within a person and that individual differences in speed and quality of thinking are usually positively, though lowly, correlated (e.g., see Salthouse, 1985, 1991, for reviews).

Also imbedded in contemporary theory is Spearman's account of a relationship between what he called "intensity of thinking"—which today is referred to as the level of difficulty of problems solved—and "extensity of thinking," which today is called working memory span; that is, the ability to hold information in awareness while doing other things such as solving a problem that requires the retained information. According to Spearman, "both the intensity and extensity of cognitive operations depend on g . . . the two constitute alternative dimensions of the same constant cognitive output characterizing each individual" (Spearman, 1927 p. 269). It is now generally recognized that working memory span is closely related to ability to solve reasoning problems of a high level of difficulty (e.g., Baddeley, 1994).

Spearman's findings and theory in regard to recall memory have also become a part of contemporary thinking about *short-term memory*—the ability to remember for a few seconds items for which one has no organizational scheme. The human can retain for a short time (less than 60 seconds without rehearsal) only about seven unrelated items, with individual differences ranging generally from about nine items to about five items. If there is a momentary distraction, the memory is lost. Usually, for example, we can retain a 7-digit telephone number long enough to dial it, provided no one asks us a question when we are trying to do the dialing (also see Sperling, 1960).

Spearman recognized in his studies that such memory is a lower order process relative to the eductive processes of g—in his words,

> . . . memory correlates with measures of g to an amount close upon .30 . . . the memorizing even of sentences and passages has only a medium correlation with g. And in proportion as the material to be learnt becomes either unrelated or sensory—so that the influence of eduction whilst learning diminishes—the correlation with g dwindles down towards the point of disappearance. (Spearman, 1927, p. 280)

This is essentially the modern-day view of the way short-term memory is related to what is known as fluid reasoning (Flanagan, Genshaft, & Harrison, 1997; McArdle & Woodcock, 1998; McGrew, Werder, & Woodcock, 1991).

RESTRUCTURING THE THEORY

The Thurstone and Thurstone (1941) study showed that a set of important abilities of intelligence can be found to fit the one common factor model. This was indicated, also, in the Spearman studies to which we have referred. In these studies, Spearman and his co-workers carefully selected variables that would fit a one common factor model, and they sometimes explicitly dropped from their analyses variables that spoiled such a fit (Brown & Stephenson, 1933; Hart & Spearman, 1912; Spearman, 1927). The findings thus suggested that for some sets of abilities, Spearman's test of his theory applies, but for other sets of abilities, it does not.

Spearman's Unintentional Two Common Factor Theory

The sets abilities found to fit the model in Spearman's work were well accepted as indicating human intelligence. But some of the abilities that did not fit were also abilities that at least some who were studying human abilities regarded as indicative of human intelligence. For example, Spearman found

... general information turns out to measure intelligence very badly indeed ... [and] ... scholastic tests do not appear to have manifested any correlation with *g* except insofar as they involve eduction, either at the actual testing, or during the antecedent learning. ... there is nothing to indicate that *g* has any correlation with pure retentivity ... the available evidence indicates that *g* is exclusively involved in eduction and not at all in bare retention ... Spearman, 1927, pp. 277, 278, 290)

Thus, Spearman, in effect, reduced his claims for *g*; it was not truly general, for it did not account for "pure retentivity," "bare retention," and "general information"—surely activities requiring mental effort. Indeed, activities that some investigators regarded as among the best indicators of human intelligence. For example, general information is a principal component of the Stanford-Binet, Wechsler, and other measures of intelligence.

Thus, with these kinds of observations, Spearman introduced a theory of two intelligences, although, granted, the introduction was rather oblique and unintentional. A theory of this form was later developed by Raymond Cattell, who, as a student, had worked closely with Spearman.

Other Evidence of a Two Common Factor Theory

At about the time Spearman was noticing a distinction between *g* and "pure retentivity," other investigators in entirely different lines of research were noticing that some abilities of intelligence—what I now call Gf abilities—declined irreversibly with brain damage and with aging in adulthood, but other abilities of intelligence—which I will call Gc abilities—did not show this decline pattern. Interestingly, the Gf abilities were described in much the same way as Spearman described the processes of *g*; and the Gc abilities were those of retained general information and scholastic knowledge, very much like the "pure retentivity" abilities that Spearman said were not good indicators of *g*.

In studies of brain damage, for example, Bianchi (1922), Feuchtwanger, (1923), Kubitschek (1928), Dandy (1933), Weisenberg and McBride (1935) and Rowe (1937) reported that pathology (stroke) and surgery in the adult brain produced very little or no enduring loss of abilities of knowledge, verbal facility, fluency, and everyday judgment—even after an entire hemisphere of the brain had been removed (Rowe, 1937)—but in the same person, the pathology or surgery produced profound and lasting, seemingly irreversible, loss of ability to understand and reason with complex novel relationships. Similarly, in studies of aging, Willoughby (1927), Jones, Conrad, and Horn (1928), Babcock (1930), Miles (1934), and Christian and Paterson (1936) reported that older adults did as well as, or better than, younger adults on tests that measured knowledge and verbal facility, but performed more poorly than younger adults on measures of logical reasoning when the relations that had to be comprehended were not such that the person could have studied and used them at prior times.

TABLE 11–2
A Description of Current Gf Tasks and Their Relation to Spearman's Process Theory

Variable Description	Spearman Process
Span of apprehension. Measured with an adaptation of the Sperling (1960) paradigm.	Immediate apprehension span—awareness of fundaments.
Primacy memory. Measured as recall of first two elements of a series of elements.	Retaining fundaments in awareness.
Working memory. Measured as recall in reverse order of a series of elements.	Maintaining awareness. Required to educe relations.
Comprehension of conjunctions Measured with power letter series.	Eduction of relations among fundaments.
Drawing inferences. Measured with remote associations.	Eduction of correlates.
Focused attention. Measured with slow tracing.	??? Capacity for concentration.
Carefulness, Measured with few incorrect answers on several tests.	Pervasiveness of capacity for apprehending experience.

Note. The intercorrelations among these indicators of Gf satisfy the requirements of the one-common-factor model (RMSEA = .067). We have found comparable approximations to the model with other combinations of tasks designed to indicate Gf.

These findings led Cattell (1941), looking primarily at the age-differences research, and Hebb (1941), reviewing the brain-injury findings, to propose that there must be two broad intelligences—neither a general intelligence. Cattell coined the term *fluid intelligence* to describe the Gf abilities that declined with age and brain damage, and *crystallized intelligence* to describe the Gc abilities that did not irreversibly decline with brain damage and improved with age in adulthood. He developed a comprehensive theory to describe the development and effects of these two intelligences (Cattell, 1963).

Gf and Spearman's Process Theory of g

Cattell's concept of fluid intelligence borrowed heavily from Spearman's process theory of *g*. The close similarity between these two concepts can be seen in the following descriptions of variables sampled to indicate Gf in a series of factor analytic and developmental studies (Horn, Donaldson & Engstrom, 1981; see Table 11–2).

Thus, Gf and *g* are similar constructs. This is suggested in other work. For example, in citing evidence in support of *g* theory, researchers often refer to evidence indicating Gf (e.g., Jensen, 1998). Devices that are referred to as providing good measures of *g*—matrices and topology—are found to be good marker variables for identifying the Gf factor (but not good indicators of the Gc factor).

EMERGENCE OF MULTIPLE-ABILITIES THEORY

Our discussion up to this point suggests that a theory of two common factors of intelligence emerged, partly as a result of Spearman's work. But the accumulating evidence often suggested even more than two factors.

We have seen that from Burt's (1909) efforts onward, results from attempts to validate Spearman's theory repeatedly indicated several common factors among indicators of human intelligence. In this early work, there was first an attempt to fit Spearman's model and when that failed, group factors were calculated to account for the residuals left after the general factor was partialed out. As investigators learned about centroid analysis and principal component analysis, these methods were used in place of Spearman's methods. In any case, the method of calculating factors begged the question of a general ability factor by simply calculating it; and the method required that other abilities—group factors—be leftovers, residuals of what was not accounted for by a general factor.

The results of such studies were highly unstable. Not only was the general factor of one study not the same as, and often very different from, the general factor of other studies, the residual factors were contrasts between different sets of abilities and the contrasts were often very different from one study to another.

The contrasts, necessitated by the methods,[13] sometimes seemed to make pretty good sense. For example, the variables correlating positively with the second factor could be verbal abilities when the variables correlating negatively were mathematical abilities, and one could reason that in school, after the general factor was taken into account, students tended to get sorted into those who liked and studied literature (history, etc.)—hence showed well on measures of verbal abilities—and those who liked and studied mathematics (the physical sciences, etc.), thus evinced good mathematical abilities. The problem was that the factoring methods that produced results were not replicable. In studies in which there were somewhat different samplings of variables, instead of getting the interpretable result of verbal abilities contrasted with mathematical abilities, for example, the results would indicate a second factor in which verbal abilities were contrasted with spatial abilities or a factor in which mathematics abilities were contrasted with speeded abilities. There was little stability in the results of different studies.

There were attempts to rectify these problems, while retaining the idea that a general factor had to be calculated. The bi-factor theory and method of Holzinger (1934), particularly, in which the group factors were specified and calculated, tended to remedy the problem of the instability of the group factors, but it compounded the problem of the instability of the first factor.

---

[13]In centroid analysis, the positive and negative correlations had to sum to zero, and these were approximately the conditions imposed by Spearman's method; in principal components analysis, the sum of squares of the positive correlations had to equal the sum of squares of the negative correlations.

Tryon (1932) with cluster analysis and Thurstone (1931, 1947) with simple-structure rotation developed methods that did deal with the instability problem. Their methods simply did not require a first, general factor. Thurstone's method became the method of choice of most researchers. Results from use of these methods were often stable from study to study under conditions in which the results from using unrotated centroid and truncated principal components analyses were quite unstable.

Thurstone's method served a new theory of human intelligence—a theory of multiple primary mental abilities. This theory had two principal tests. It required, first, as mentioned before, that the rank of the matrix of intercorrelations be equal to the number of common factors specified in theory; and, second, that a particular structure be specified for the factor coefficients, and that this structure be found for the factors rotated to meet the separately defined criteria of simple structure.

The concept of *simple structure* stemmed from reasoning that no influence in nature affects everything; hence no factor should affect all variables. And no variable is affected by all the influences in nature; indeed, most variables should be affected by only a few factors. As with Spearman's theory, Thurstone's theory required experiments that were well designed to pass the two tests.

The simple-structure test was particularly difficult to formulate. In any particular study there could be a number of common factors each expected (by hypothesis) to influence particular specified sets of variables. The sets, that is, a relatively small number of variables affected by a factor, could vary; communalities of the variables could vary; the number of factors could vary; and the factors need not be orthogonal. This made it very difficult—perhaps impossible—to write general mathematical requirements for simple structure for all cases. Several mathematical and/or statistical procedures for attaining approximations to simple structure were developed (e.g., Varimax, Oblimax, Equamax, Promax).

The beauty of these methods as seen from a scientific perspective was that they defined particular structures, each different from the other, quite independently of any substantive theory. They specified mathematical models—metatheories—a scientist could attempt to fit by appropriate sampling of variables and subjects. For example, the Varimax model required one fairly broad factor (but not a factor as broad as the general factor of a centroid and principal axis models) along with several less-broad factors, whereas the Equamax model required that all factors be equally broad.

The main problem with the models was that they did not restrict just how broad was broad or how equal was equal with a statistical test that indicated departure from chance. For this reason, they came to be called "exploratory" methods, although, as noted, they were distinctly not exploratory in requiring experimenters to design studies in accordance with an objectively defined model. With the advent of "confirmatory" methods, the hypotheses of a specified simple structure (or any other structure) could be tested and regarded as either tenable or not at a designated alpha test level (e.g., Horn & McArdle, 1980, 1992).

Thurstone's theory of cognitive abilities required specifying how each sampled variable was affected by each primary ability, and how each primary ability was distinguished from other primary abilities, from specific factors and from error. Ideally in most cases, variables were expected (by hypothesis) to relate primarily to only one primary ability factor, although in some well designed cases, a variable was selected to indicate the influence of two primary abilities. Thus, the factor structure would be simple because most of the correlations between variables and factors would zero (chancelike); variables would correlate primarily only with one factor, and factors would correlate primarily with only the few variables.

Chaos Rendered by a Plethora of Primary Abilities

The promise when Thurstone's theory first appeared was that experiments would establish a boundary for the number of primary abilities needed to describe and understand human intellectual capacities. As we have noted, Thurstone's (1935, 1938) initial experiments suggested that this number might be about nine. To the dismay of many, however, further applications of Thurstone's logic and methods with different batteries of variables turned up many more than nine primary abilities. From the 1940s onward, dozens of studies of the common factors among tests thought to measure important features of human intelligence produced dozens of factors regarded as indicating primary mental abilities.

Summary studies identified replications of, first, over 40 such abilities (e.g., Ekstrom, French, & Harman 1979; Hakstian & Cattell, 1974), and then, as results from more studies rolled in, over 120 primary mental abilities (Carroll, 1993; Guilford, 1964). It came to be recognized (Humphreys, Ilgen, McGrath, & Montanelli, 1969) that, depending only on the number and ingenuity of scientists who might construct mental ability tests—and most could make up a new test every morning before breakfast—the number of primary abilities is arbitrarily large. Thus, it seemed that research on the nature of human intellectual abilities had come a full circle, back to where it was before Spearman (1927) moaned "chaos itself can go no farther."

Salvation Through Construct Validation at the Second Order

Thurstone (1947) pointed out that identifying a common factor is only an initial form of the evidence that is needed to build scientific understanding; it is necessary also to establish a network of lawful relationships a factor has with other variables. These relationships form the basis for the explanatory framework that defines a scientific theory. This network of relationships prescribes the construct validity of a factor.

There appeared to be little hope of building construct validities for the multitude of primary ability factors that grew up in the aftermath of Thurstone's research. But the distinctly different relationships to brain damage and aging in adulthood that had been found for Gf and Gc factors suggested that construct validities might be established for factors identified at this broader, second-order level. Evidence has gradually accumulated to support this supposition. It indicates that second-order factors among primary abilities relate not only to the Gf and Gc distinctions, but also to distinctions between visual and hearing processes, and to concepts of *immediate memory* and *consolidation in memory* for which relationships have been established through the controlled, manipulative, experimental research of cognitive psychology. Second-order factors thus appear to provide at least a beginning basis of operational definitions of constructs for building a scientific theory of human cognitive functioning.

The second-order factors were first identified in studies largely aimed at indicating the nature of the Gf and Gc factors. However, as we indicated earlier in discussing Gustafsson and Undheim (1996), the findings from these studies suggested that the two common factor theory of intelligence needed to be extended to a several common factor theory. The results from such studies came to be referred to as indicating an extended Gf–Gc theory. Usually eight or nine such factors were indicated. In analyses based on practically all the factor analytic studies done up to about 1990—some 477 batteries of cognitive ability measures— Carroll (1993) identified eight factors at the second order. These factors have now been described, and their construct validities discussed, in wide variety of articles and books (e.g., Carroll, 1993; Flanagan et al., 1997; Flanagan & Harrison, 2005; Horn, 1968; McArdle & Woodcock, 1998; McGrew et al., 1991; Perfect & Maylor, 2000; Schaie, 1996; Woodcock, 1995). Here we will describe the factors only briefly in what follows immediately, and then, in later sections, review some major indications of their distinct construct validities.

> *Fluid reasoning* (Gf). The factor that most resembles Spearman's concept of *g*. It indicates capacities for identifying relationships, comprehending implications, and drawing inferences in novel content.
>
> *Acculturation knowledge* (Gc). The factor that represents Spearman's ideas about variables that do not provide good indications of *g*, particularly "general information" and "bare retention." It indicates breadth of knowledge.
>
> *Fluency of retrieval from long-term storage* (TSR). A factor that indicates consolidation in memory and association memory over long periods of time.
>
> *Short-term apprehension and retrieval* (SAR). This factor indicates a capacity for maintaining awareness stimulus elements for a span of a minute or so.
>
> *Visual processing* (Gv). Abilities of visual closure, maintaining visual constancy and fluency in recognizing the way objects appear in space as they are rotated and reoriented in various ways.
>
> *Auditory processing* (Ga). Abilities of perception of sound patterns under distraction or distortion, maintaining awareness of order and rhythm among sounds, and comprehending groupings of sounds.

Processing speed (Gs). Although involved in almost all intellectual tasks, this factor is indicated most purely in rapid scanning and comparisons in intellectually simple tasks in which almost all people would get the right answer if the task were not highly speeded.

Correct decision speed (CDS). Measured in quickness in providing answers in tasks that are not of trivial difficulty.

Also, although broad quantitative knowledge was not identified as a separate second-order factor in Carroll's (1993) large-scale secondary analysis, such a factor has construct-validity relationships that indicate that it is quite distinct from Gc and other second-order factors.

These broad factors, including quantitative knowledge, although positively correlated, are operationally independent and have predictive independence, as well as independence in virtue of having distinct construct validities. Predictive independence is indicated by evidence that a best-weighted linear combination of any set of eight of the factors does not account for the reliable covariance among the elements of the ninth factor. This means that the beta-weight for each of the nine factors can be significant in the prediction of complex criteria.

Although there are suggestions that some of the second-order factors are more related to genetic influences than others, the broad patterns do not represent a clean distinction between genetic and environmental determinants. Such distinctions appear to be better made at the primary level or below.

EVIDENCE PERTAINING TO CONSTRUCT VALIDITY

In previous sections of this chapter we considered details of the factor analytic evidence pertaining to Spearman's *g* theory. We did this because claims for support for that theory have appealed primarily to structural (i.e., correlational, factor analytic) evidence. But the evidence that most surely indicates the there is not one general factor that pervades all cognitive abilities is really a lack of construct validity for a general factor and the presence of at least some construct validity for the second-order factors. That is, studies of development throughout the lifespan, of neural function and brain damage, of behavior genetics and environmental influences, and of prediction of criteria most often indicate that clumping abilities together in a single general composite intended to represent IQ or *g* obscures distinct relationships that can be seen if second-order factor measurements are used in place of general-factor composites. There is space here to provide only a brief view of this evidence.

Developmental Evidence

The evidence we referred to earlier—indicating that Gf and Gc abilities have quite different relationships to age in adulthood—is dramatically indicative of how considering only a general factor obscures relationships that can be made clear; Gf declines while Gc increases over age; if the two are clumped together in a general factor, these distinct relationships are not seen.

Studies of childhood development also indicate a distinction between the two forms of intelligence. Gf and Gc can be identified as distinctly different abilities as early as in the third year of life, at which age the correlation between the two is approximately .65 when the internal consistency reliabilities of the factors are approximately .90. The correlation between the two becomes smaller at successively later stages of development. In adulthood, the correlation is found to be in a range of about .40 to .50 with factor internal consistency reliabilities in a range of .80 to .90 (for reviews, see Horn, 1991).

Gc correlates in a range of .40 to .60 with the educational or economic level of one's parents and with one's own educational or economic level at later ages. It correlates also with other indicators of social class. Gf, in contrast, correlates in a range of .20 to .45 with these same indicators of social class (Cattell, 1971). Such findings suggest that the development of Gc abilities is promoted by acculturation.

Individual differences in the Gc abilities are associated with individual differences in the quality and amount of formal education—*explicit acculturation*. This, in turn, is related to child-rearing that promotes a valuing of formal education and the attainment of the knowledge of the dominant culture. These educational and child-rearing conditions are positively associated with socioeconomic level. They are also correlated with a cluster of factors that point to secure home, neighborhood, and school environments (Bohlin, Hagekul, & Rydell, 2000).

Other second-order factors have trajectories over age that are different from those of either Gf or Gc. The averages for the abilities of short-term working memory (SAR) memory decline at a different rate than the averages for the abilities of Gf; the averages for the abilities of TSR (the broad factors of capacity to consolidate new information and retrieval) from stored knowledge increase at a different rate than the averages for the abilities of Gc.

In several of our own recent longitudinal studies (e.g., McArdle & Woodcock, 1997; McArdle, Hamagami, Meredith, & Bradway, 2000; McArdle, Ferrer-Caja, Hamagami, & Woodcock, 2002; McArdle, chap. 7 in this volume) found repeated-measures age differences of the same general form as have been found in cross-sectional studies.

Brain Function and Malfunction

A good candidate for a construct validity link between neural function and a general factor is the spike potential of the neuron, for this operates in all neurons and thus all the neural functioning that underlies human behavior. It has not yet been shown that individual differences in any aspect of the spike potential are related to cognitive ability differences in humans. Similarly, the evidence does not indicate any other single neural function—neural speed or neural energy or neural mass action—accounts for a part of the variability in all of the cognitive abilities regarded as indicating human intelligence.

Indeed, the findings suggest the opposite. Different abilities relate to different brain functions. With respect to the buildup of memories, for example (the buildups become part of cognitive abilities), there appear to be at least three—perhaps four—distinct neural functions. One system is centered in the cerebellum; one is largely associated with the function of the hippocampus; one is related to function of the amygdala; and one is characterized by protein synthesis, perhaps mainly in the frontal lobes (Thompson, 1998).

There is direct evidence linking classical-conditioning learning to neural function in the cerebellum. It is shown, specifically, that selectively disabling and enabling the interpositus nucleus with freezing techniques first wipes out and then restores classical conditioning association learning (Lavond & Kanzawa, 2000). Function in this area of the brain thus affects an elementary form of learning. Some elementary language learning, for example, is clang association—that is, classical conditioning—learning. Language acquisition is, of course, part of what is regarded as the most unique aspects of all human intelligence.

The hippocampus plays a different role than the cerebellum in memory, learning, and consolidation. The hippocampus is in quite a different part of the brain than the interpositus nucleus, and there are no direct pathways between the two. The hippocampus is essential for retaining the outcomes of instrumental learning in long-term memory. It seems not to be heavily involved in long-term memory storage, as such. Several lines of evidence lead to these conclusions.

The most dramatic of this kind of evidence has derived from studies of a person known a HM, a person whose hippocampus became entirely nonfunctional in consequence of surgical removal of approximately two thirds of the tissue (Corkin, 2002; Scoville & Milner, 1957). After the surgery, some of HM's abilities appeared to be quite normal, but the ability to consolidate in learning—to commit what was learned to memory—was completely gone. In conversation, HM could recall information learned and stored in the past. This indicated that Gc knowledge was intact. HM could remember a telephone number long enough to dial it, which indicated that SAR apprehension and/or retrieval was normal. HM could learn a complex motor skill as well as most people, which suggested that he normal functioning of classical conditioning learning mediated through the interpositus nucleus. But HM's intermediate association memory was lost. HM could carry on an intelligent conversation, but he could not remember that he had the conversation. He could remember a telephone number long enough to dial it, but couldn't commit the number to memory. HM was quite unable to remember experiences just a few minutes prior to a test for recall. Removal of the hippocampus removed this ability to consolidate learning.

This relationship between consolidation in learning and hippocampus function has been documented in studies of other people who have had lesions in the hippocampus area, and analogous effects have been found in controlled experiments with monkeys (Thompson, 1998). The relationship has also been indicated in studies of injuries other than ablation. For example, heavy use of alcohol (drinking to the point of passing out) has been found to result in loss of neural function in the mammilary bodies and nearby hippocampus, and this loss, too, is associated with loss of intermediate-term memory and consolidation in learning—a condition known as Korsakoff's syndrome.

Although checks and balances work to ensure that all areas of the brain receive an adequate supply of blood, still conditions such as illnesses, high fever, exhaustion, and poisoning bring about decreases in blood flow. The hippocampus area of the brain is particularly vulnerable to such diminutions (Hachinski, 1980). The arteries that supply blood to the hippocampus branch at right angles from the main trunks and terminate as end arteries in the area, unlike the Y branches from the main trunks that supply other parts of the brain. This means that any drop in blood flow can result in "drying up" at the end arteries, death of neurons, and loss of neural function. Infarcts occur more frequently in the hippocampus than in comparison structures (Corsellis, 1976). Again, what is lost in cognitive ability is consolidation in learning, recorded as poor memory over time periods of more than a few minutes.

Thus, consolidation in learning, an ability that surely is part of what is referred to as *intelligence*, is associated primarily with neural function operating in and around the hippocampus, and this function is not much related to Gc and SAR. The hippocampus function is different from the cerebellum function of the interpositus nucleus, which supports another form of learning. There is little reason to suppose that these functions of different parts of the brain are merely parts of a unitary brain function such as proposed in the theory of *g*.

These are simply examples. However, such examples add up to suggest that there is no single, unitary function that could represent a principle of mass action process of the kind hypothesized by Lashley (1938) and Spearman (1927) in his theory of *g*. The evidence indicates instead that different neural functions support different cognitive abilities. The neural functions are affected by events such as those illustrated in the extreme in the case of HM, a case of Korsakoff's syndrome, and diminutions of blood flow. Less extreme versions of these extreme conditions likely occur for different people at different points of development—before birth, at birth, in infancy, childhood, adolescence, adulthood, old age—and result in individual differences in measures of the various abilities that depend on different neural functions.

Genetic Influences

There seems to be very little direct evidence linking particular genes and genetic factors to particular abilities of reasoning, learning, retention, and retrieval. Such evidence as there is suggests that different sets of genes produce different brain structures and functions, which in turn support and help determine different cognitive abilities. But it is clear that brain structure and function are determined in part by genes; so, since different neural structures and functions are associated with different cognitive abilities of human intelligence, different genes most likely are as well (for review, see McArdle & Prescott, 1996).

Individual differences in brain structures are rather like individual differences in the faces of people; when you see different faces, you can visualize different brain structures behind those faces. Just as there are separate genetic factors affecting ear shape and nose length, so there are separate genetic factors affecting the size and shape and function of the right and left hemispheres of the brain, the cerebellum, the limbic brain, the hippocampus, and so on. Different sets of genes also affect neurotransmitter systems and the pathways joining regions of the brain. Different structures, determined by different combinations of genes, enable different reactions to environmental stimulations. Different environmental stimulations affect separate brain functions differently. Such combinations of genetic and environmental influences, huge in number, produce great variety in the patterns of abilities we can measure (see Humphreys, 1971; McArdle, Prescott, Hamagami, & Horn, 1998).

It is possible, of course, that a single set of genes operate in unison throughout the separate neural systems, and thus operate throughout all human abilities, but on the face of it, this seems unlikely. If it is true, it would seem that it must be a gene or a set of genes that affect some elementary function of all neurons, such as the spike potential function of each individual neuron. If such a feature does indeed affect all human abilities, that influence is very likely small relative to the influences of the separate functions of different parts of the neural system.

EMERGING THEORY

The results we have reviewed in previous sections of this chapter provide glimmerings of the nature of adult human intelligence, but they are dim glimmerings. Some of the information is incorrect. The big picture is not in focus.

Problems With Current Theory of Cognitive Capabilities

What we see as intelligence in the theory and research findings reviewed in previous sections is not consistent with what we see when see adults doing the jobs they do in our society. The current theory points to adulthood aging declines Gf, SAR and Gs—major abilities of intelligence. But decline does not characterize what we see in everyday observations of adults. In the research, we see adolescents and young adults more intelligent than older adults, but in life we do not see increasing deficits of reasoning and memory at least not through the main period of adulthood, from the 30s into the 70s. We see advanced-age adults doing most of the intellectual work of maintaining and advancing the culture; we see older people who are the intellectual leaders in science, politics, business, and academics, people who are in their positions of responsibility largely because (we think) they are—in some sense we need to define—more intelligent than younger adults and adolescents.

So, there's something out of kilter here. Are we measuring the wrong things in the research thus far done? The answer appears to be "yes." It may be yes both in regards to abilities that are regarded as not declining in adulthood—Gc and TSR—as well as in regards to the abilities for which the research does indicate decline—Gf, SAR, and Gs.

Consider Gc first. As defined, this is supposed to indicate the depth of the knowledge of the culture, as well as breadth of this knowledge. In the practice of measurement, however, we get only breadth, no depth. The primary abilities that indicate the factor are surfacelike—the beginning course—not what one who seriously studies a domain of knowledge comes ultimately to understand. Instead of measuring understanding of science or literature, for example, we measure vocabulary, information, and reasoning sampled only at the elementary level of introduction to these domains of knowledge. Our measures provide only indications of knowledge of a culture that would be expressed by persons with a wide sampling of knowledge bases (i.e., a dilettante). A person flitting over many areas of knowledge in his or her study will score higher on these measures of Gc than a person who has devoted intensive study to developing truly profound understanding in an area of knowledge. But we recognize this latter, not the dilettante, as the most intelligent—the one most likely to make significant contributions to the culture, the one who becomes CEO, the one to whom we award the Nobel Prize. Such persons are referred to as *expert*. Experts best exemplify the capabilities that indicate the nature and limits of human intelligence.

Consider next the reasoning we measure in the primary abilities that define Gf, fluid intelligence, and equate with Spearman's *g*, the *sine qua non* of intelligence. This is a measure of reasoning with a made-up problem that really is no problem. The reasoning is inductive, requiring, in the device used to measure it, as little knowledge as possible. In contrast, the reasoning we regard as indicating intelligence (e.g., in the CEO) is reasoning with relevant information. It is deductive reasoning employing knowledge. It is the kind of reasoning identified in descriptions of the thinking of experts—in chess, financial planning, and medical diagnosis (Charness, 1991; de Groot, 1978; Ericsson, 1996; Walsh & Hershey, 1993).

The expert is able to construct a framework within which to organize and effectively evaluate presented information, while novices, with no expertise basis for constructing a framework, search for patterns and do reasoning by trial-and-error evaluations—inductive reasoning. The expert apprehends large amounts of organized information, comprehends many relationships among elements of this information, infers possible continuations and extrapolations, and, as a result, is able to select the best path from among many possibilities in deciding on the most likely outcome, consequence, or extension of relationships. The expert goes from the general comprehension of relations and knowledge of principles to most likely specifics.

The person able to do this kind of reasoning is regarded as intelligent, and what is recognized as intelligence in adults. This is not to argue that the inductive reasoning of Gf is not an aspect of what is also called intelligence. However, it is to argue that the reasoning of Gf may not be a central characteristic of intelligence, but expertise reasoning may be.

A Glimpse at Findings From Research on Expertise

To summarize: (a) abilities that come to fruition in adulthood best represent the quintessential expression of human intellectual capacity; (b) the measures currently used to estimate intelligence do not assess these abilities, they do not assess all the important abilities of human intelligence; (c) when measures currently used do assess these abilities, they do not assess them at a depth sufficient to indicate the essential character of intelligence; (d) the abilities not measured and not among the abilities currently used to estimate intelligence are in-depth abilities of expertise.

The principal problems of design of research for describing adult human intelligence are problems of circumscribing domains of expertise and constructing measures of the abilities of the highest levels of expertise in these domains. The research should identify the relationships between these measures and other measures thought to indicate human intelligence. The research should show the relationships these measures have with variables that help indicate causes and effects, that is, variables that indicate the validity of the expertise–ability constructs.

Horn and Masunaga (2000) have studied expertise in playing the game of GO. We have designed research in accordance with the stipulations I outline. I do not have the space here to provide much of a summary of what we have discovered so far (see Masunaga & Horn, 2000, 2001). One principal conclusion we draw from review of the results of research by others is that intensive practice is required to attain and maintain high levels of expertise. This practice must extend into adulthood, which means that there can be increases in expertise abilities of intelligence in adulthood. If there is such practice, expertise abilities do not decline. Intensive practice is not simply practice; it is practice focused on attaining ever higher levels of expertise.

Also important for this research, we found that research on expertise pointed to some of the abilities that, it appeared, would be important features of adult intelligence. Charness (1991) identified expertise deductive reasoning as one such ability. Ericsson and Kintsch (1995) had identified a wide-span working memory that also appeared to be important. These two abilities, it seemed, were not sampled in the research on primary mental abilities and the second-order factors of extended Gf–Gc theory, but the abilities characterized high levels expertise that indicated high levels of human intelligence.

Following these leads, we found in our studies that a form of expertise deductive reasoning (EDR) that is quite separate from Gf reasoning, and a wide-span working memory (WSWM) that is quite separate from short-term working memory (SAR). The span for WSWM is several times as wide as the span of SAR. An hypothesis stipulating that a factor of expertise speed is separate from cognitive speed (Gs) was not supported: expertise speed and cognitive speed were collinear. Gf, SAR Gs were found to decline with age in adulthood. EDR and WSWM were found to decline as a function lack of intensive practice and lack of expertise. Advanced levels of EDR and WSWM were maintained throughout adulthood in people who worked to advance their level of expertise. Expertise abilities of older high-level experts exceeded the abilities of younger persons at lower levels of expertise.

These conclusions flow from few studies. There have been no longitudinal follow-up studies of broad samples of adults that could help indicate the extent to which the findings apply to people in general. There is particular need for developmental research on expertise.

CLOSING COMMENTS AND CONCLUSIONS

One can question whether a study ever has been adequately designed to test Spearman's model of one common factor pervading all expressions of human intelligence; the possibility of specific factor overlap has never been entirely ruled out. But granting that uncertainty, most of the factor analytic evidence does not support the single g theory. A wide array of evidence from research on development, education, neurology, and genetics suggests that it is unlikely that a factor general to all abilities produces individual differences in all of what are regarded as indicators of human intelligence. There have been many efforts to discredit and counteract this evidence; they have not altered the conclusion—no general factor has been found. The evidence suggests that if there is such a factor—a behavioral concomitant of neural spike potential, for example—it accounts for no more than a miniscule part of the variance in human intellectual abilities.

But while his theory of a general factor has not found support, Spearman's model for testing that theory, and his ideas about processes that indicate important features of a general factor, have been very important for the development of scientific theory of human cognitive capabilities over the last century. His idea of testing a hypothesis stipulating that a latent variable may underlie many manifest indicators, and his mathematical and statistical methods for accomplishing this test, are the core concepts of the theory of *common factors*. That theory is a fundamental part of the current theory of multiple factors and structural equation modeling, which theory, in turn, is not only the basis for modern theory of human capabilities, but also the basis for a very large amount of other substantive theory in psychology. Spearman's concept of g is in major respects the concept of Gf, fluid reasoning, in modern theory. His ideas about what g is not became—in modern theory—ideas about what Gc, crystallized knowledge, is. He described *apprehension of experience, cognitive speed–power trade-off and individual differences*, and *short-term memory* in much the same way as these concepts are described in modern theory. Spearman's influence on present-day scientific thinking has been large. His ideas are well embedded in that thinking.

Thurstone's theory of simple structure for multiple common factors of cognitive abilities also was very important. Current theory of human intellectual capacities derives directly and mainly from the work of Spearman and Thurstone.

That current theory is described under the heading of extended Gf–Gc theory. This is an account of evidence indicating that individual differences in behaviors characterizing human intelligence can, to a considerable extent, be described in terms of broad factors of capacity to consolidate new information and retrieve it (TSR), capacity to retain information in accessible storage (Gc), capacity for reasoning in novel situations (Gf) capacity for holding unorganized information in immediate awareness over short periods of time (SAR), capacity for organizing and retaining visual information (Gv), capacity for organizing and retaining auditory information (Ga), capacity for quantitative thinking (Gq), and capacity for speedy thinking (Gs). The theory organizes evidence of the relationships these broad constructs have with other variables, principally variables pertaining to development and neurological functioning, but also variables pointing to achievements in school and work and variables representing genetic variations. Gf, SAR and Gs are found to decline with age and brain damage in the same people in which Gc and TSR increase with age and are less affected by brain damage. Evidence from several sources indicates links between the separate broad factors and separate brain functions.

Extended Gf–Gc theory does not adequately describe abilities that appear to be quintessential expressions of human intelligence—in particular, abilities that reach their peaks of development in adulthood. Research on expertise has pointed to two of these abilities, one a factor expertise deductive reasoning (EDR) that is distinct from Gf reasoning, the other a factor of wide-span working memory (WSWM) for which the span is considerably larger and more flexible than for SAR. It appears that these two expertise abilities do not decline over the period of adulthood if there is continued intensive practice to improve—unlike the findings for the comparable Gf and SAR abilities. Spearman's seminal work paved the way in research on human intelligence, but research over the past 100 years has done much to alter our views about the original theory. Although we may not see new changes in our lifetime, the next 100 years of good scientific thinking promises to reveal much more about the true essence of these critical human characteristics.

ACKNOWLEDGMENTS

We thank Hiromi Masunaga, Robert Sternberg, and Kevin McGrew for their very helpful comments.

REFERENCES

Alexander, W. P. (1935). Intelligence, concrete and abstract [Monograph Suppl.]. *British Journal of Psychology*, 9–177.

Babcock, E. (1930). An experiment in the measurement of mental deterioration. *Archives of Psychology, 18*, 105.

Baddeley, A. (1994). Memory. In A. M. Colman (Ed.), *Companion encyclopedia of psychology* (Vol. 1, pp. 281–301). London: Routledge.

Bayley, N. (1969). *Manual for the Bayley Scales of Infant Development*. New York: Psychological Corporation.

Beaujean, A. A. (2002). On the life and scholarship of Arthur R. Jensen. In Proceedings of the SASP Convention, London.

Bianchi, L. (1922). *The mechanism of the brain and the function of the frontal lobes*. Edinburgh, Scotland: Oliver & Boyd.

Binet, A., & Simon, T. (1905). Sur le necessite d'etablit un diagnostic scientifique des etats inferieurs de l'intelligence [On the necessity of establishing a scientific diagnosis of inferior states of intelligence]. *L'Annee Psychologique, 11*, 163–190, 191–244, 245–366.

Bohlin, G., Hagekul, B., & Rydell, A. M. (2000). Attachment and social functioning: A longitudinal study from infancy to middle childhood. *Social Development, 9*, 24–39.

Brown, W. A. (1933). The mathematical and experimental evidence for the existence of a central intellective factor. *British Journal of Psychology, 23*, 171–179.

Brown, W. A., & Stephenson, W. (1933). A test of the theory of the two factors. *British Journal of Psychology, 23*, 352–370.

Browne, M. A. & Cudeck, R. (1993). Alternative ways of assessing model fit. In K. A. Bollen & J. S. Long (Eds.), *Testing structural equation models* (pp. 136–162). Newbury Park, CA: Sage.

Burt, C. (1909). Experimental tests of general intelligence. *British Journal of Psychology, 3*, 94–177.

Burt, C. (1911). Experimental tests of higher mental processes and their relation to general intelligence. *Journal of Experimental Pedagogy and Training, 1*, 93–112.

Burt, C. (1924). *Report of consultive committee on psychological tests of educable capacity*. London: H. M. Stationery Office.

Carroll, J. B. (1993). *Human cognitive abilities: A survey of factor-analytic studies*. New York: Cambridge University Press.

Carter, H. D. (1928). The organization of mechanical intelligence. *Journal of Genetic Psychology, 35*, 270–285.

Cattell, R. B. (1941). Some theoretical issues in adult intelligence testing. *Psychological Bulletin, 38*, 592.

Cattell, R. B. (1963). Theory for fluid and crystallized intelligence: A critical experiment. *Journal of Educational Psychology, 54*, 1–22.

Cattell, R. B. (1971) *Abilities: Their structure, growth and action*. Boston: Houghton-Mifflin.

Charness, N. (1991). Expertise in chess: the balance between knowledge and search. In K. A. Ericsson & J. Smith (Eds.), *Toward a general theory of expertise* (pp. 39–63). New York: Cambridge University Press.

Christian, A. M. & Paterson, D. G. (1936). Growth of vocabulary in later maturity. *Journal of Psychology, 1*, 167–169.

Corkin, S. (2002). What's new with the amnesic patient H.M. *Nature Reviews Neuroscience, 3*(2), 153–60.

Corsellis, J. A. N. (1976). Aging and the dementias. In W. Blackwood & J. A. N. Corsellis (Eds.), *Greenfield's neuropathology* (pp. 796–848). London: Arnold.

Cox, G.W. (1928). *Mechanical aptitude*. London: Methuen.

Dandy, W. S. (1933). Physiologic studies following extirpation of the right cerebral hemisphere in man. *Bulletin: Johns Hopkins Hospital, 53*, 31–51.

Deary, I. J., Bell, P. J., Bell, A. J., Campbell, M. L., & Fazal, N. D. (2004). Sensory discrimination and intelligence: Testing Spearman's other hypothesis. *American Journal of Psychology, 117* (1), 1–18.

de Groot, A. D. (1978). *Thought and choice and chess*. The Hague: Mouton.

Detterman, D. K. (Ed.). (1998). Kings of men: A special issue of the journal intelligence about Arthur Jensen [Special issue]. *Intelligence, 26* (3).

Ekstrom, R. B., French, J. W. & Harman, H. H. (1979). Cognitive factors: Their identification and replication. *Multivariate Behavioral Research Monographs, 79*.

El Koussy, A. A. H. (1935). The visual perception of space. *British Journal of Psychology*, Monograph Supplement, No. 20.

Ericsson, K. A. (1996). The acquisition of expert performance. In K. A. Ericsson (Ed.), *The road to excellence* (pp. 1–50). Mahwah, NJ: Lawrence Erlbaum Associates.

Ericsson, K. A., & Kintsch, W. (1995). Long-term working memory. *Psychological Review, 105*, 211–245.

Eysenck, H. J. (Ed.). (1982). *A model for intelligence*. Berlin: Springer-Verlag.

Feuchtwanger, E. (1923). Funktionen des Stiruhirns ihre Pathologie und Psycholgic. *Monograph Gesalk Neurologia Psychiatri, 38*, 194–206.

Flanagan, D. P., Genshaft, P. I., & Harrison, P. L. (Eds.). (1997). *Contemporary intellectual assessment*. New York: Guilford Press.

Flanagan, D. P., & Harrison, P. L. (Eds.). (2005). *Contemporary intellectual assessment: theories, tests and kssues*. New York: Guilford Press.

Galton, F. (1952). *Hereditary genius: An inquiry into its laws and consequences*. New York: Horizon Press. (Original work published 1869)

Galton, F. (1883). *Inquiries into human faculty and its development*. London: Dent.

Gottfredson, L. S. (1997). Why *g* matters: The complexity of everyday life. *Intelligence, 24*, 79–132.

Grattan-Guinness, I., & Ledermann, W. (1994). Matrix theory. In I. Grattan-Guinness (Ed.), *Companion encyclopedia of the history and philosophy of the mathematical sciences* (pp. 775-786). London: Routledge.

Guilford, J. P. (1964). Zero intercorrelations among tests of intellectual abilities. *Psychological Bulletin, 61*, 401–404.

Gulliksen, H. (1950). *Theory of mental tests*. New York: Wiley

Gustafsson, J. E., & Undheim, J. O. (1996). Individual differences in cognitive functions. In D. C. Berliner & R. C. Calfee (Eds.), *Handbook of educational psychology* (pp. 186–242). New York: Simon & Schuster.

Hachinski, V. (1980). Relevance of cerebrovascular changes in mental function. *Mechanisms of Aging and Development, 10*, 1–11.

Hakstian, A. R., & Cattell, R. B. (1974). The checking of primary ability structure on a broader basis of performances. *British Journal of Educational Psychology, 44*, 140–154.

Hart, B., & Spearman, C. E. (1912). General ability, its existence and nature. *British Journal of Psychology, 5*, 51–81.

Hebb, D. O. (1941). The clinical evidence concerning the nature of normal adult test performance. *Psychological Bulletin, 38*, 593.

Herrnstein, R., & Murray, C. (1994). *The bell curve: Intelligence and class structure in American life*. New York: Free Press.

Holzinger, K. J. (1934). *Preliminary reports on the Spearman-Holzinger unitary trait study* (Rep. Nos. 1–9). Chicago: University of Chicago, Statistical Laboratory, Department of Education.

Horn, J. L. (1968). Organization of abilities and the development of intelligence. *Psychological Review, 75*, 242–259.

Horn, J. L. (1991). Measurement of intellectual capabilities: A review of theory. In K. S. McGrew, J. K. Werder, & R. W. Woodcock (Eds.), *Woodcock-Johnson technical manual* (pp. 197–245). Allen, TX: DLM Teaching.

Horn, J. L., Donaldson, G., & Engstrom, R. (1981). Apprehension, memory, and fluid intelligence decline in adulthood. *Research in Aging, 3*(1), 33–84.

Horn, J. L. & Masunaga, H. (2000). New directions for research on aging and intelligence. In T. J. Perfect & E. A. Maylor (Eds.), *Models of cognitive aging* (pp. 125–159). Oxford, UK: Oxford University Press.

Horn, J. L., & McArdle, J. J. (1980). Perspectives on mathematical and statistical model building (MASMOB) in research on aging. In L. Poon (Ed.), *Aging in the 1980s: Psychological issues* (pp. 503–541). Washington, D C: American Psychological Association.

Horn, J. L., & McArdle, J. J. (1992). A practical guide to measurement invariance in research on aging. *Experimental Aging Research, 18*(3), 117–144.

Humphreys, L. G. (1971). Theory of intelligence. In R. Cancro (Ed.), *Intelligence: Genetic and environmental influences* (pp. 31–42). New York: Grune & Stratton.

Humphreys, L. G., Ilgen, D., McGrath, D., & Montanelli, R. (1969). Capitalization on chance in rotation of factors. *Educational and Psychological Measurement, 29*, 259–271.

Jensen, A. R. (1998). *The g factor: The science of mental ability.* London: Praeger.

Johnson, R. C., McClearn, G. E., Yuen, S., Nagoshi, C. T., Ahern, F. M., & Cole, R. E. (1985). Galton's data a century later. *American Psychologist, 40*(8), 875–892.

Jones, H. H., Conrad, A. S., & Horn, A. (1928). Psychological studies of motion pictures, II. Observation and recall as a function of age. *University of California Publications in Psychology, 3*, 225–243.

Kelley, T. L. (1928). *Crossroads in the mind of man.* Stanford, CA: Stanford University Press.

Kendall, M. G. (1961). *Rank correlation methods.* New York: Hafner Publishing Co.

Kubitscheck, P. S. (1928). The symptomatology of tumors of the frontal lobe based on a series of twenty-two cases. *Archives of Neurology in Psychiatry, 20*, 559–579.

Lashley, K. S. (1929). *Brain mechanisms and intelligence: A quantitative study of injuries to the brain.* Chicago: University of Chicago Press.

Lashley, K. S. (1938). Factors limiting recovery after central nervous system lesion. *Journal of Nervous and Mental Diseases, 78*, 733–755.

Lawley, D. N. (1943–1944). A note on Karl Person's selection formula. *Proceedings of the Royal Society of Edinburgh (Section A), 28*–30.

Lavond, D. G., & Kanzawa, S. A. (2000). Inside the black box. In J. E. Steinmetz, M. Gluck, & P. Solomon (Eds.), *Model systems and the neurobiology associative learning: A festschrift in honor of Richard F. Thompson* (pp. 245–269). Hillsdale, NJ: Lawrence Erlbaum Associates.

Masunaga, H., & Horn, J. L. (2000). Characterizing mature human intelligence: Expertise development. *Learning and Individual Differences, 12*, 5–33.

Masunaga, H., & Horn, J. L. (2001). Expertise and age-related changes in components of intelligence. *Psychology and Aging, 16*(2), 293–311.

McArdle, J. J. (1989). Comments on Gustaffson's Paper. In P. Ackerman, R. Kanfer, & R. Cudeck (Eds.), *Learning and individual differences: Abilities, motivation, and methodology* (pp. 229–230). Hillsdale, NJ: Lawrence Erlbaum Associates.

McArdle, J. J., Ferrer-Caja, E., Hamagami, F., & Woodcock, R. W. (2002). Comparative longitudinal multilevel structural analyses of the growth and decline of multiple intellectual abilities over the life-span. *Developmental Psychology, 38*(1), 115–142.

McArdle, J. J., Hamagami, F., Meredith, W., & Bradway, K. P. (2000). Modeling the dynamic hypotheses of Gf-Gc theory using longtitudinal life-span data. *Learning and Individual Differences, 12*(1), 53–79.

McArdle, J. J., & Prescott, C. A. (1997). Contemporary models for the biometric genetic analysis of intellectual abilities. In D. P. Flanagan, J. L. Genshaft, & P. L. Harrison (Eds.), *Contemporary intellectual assessment: Theories, tests and issues* (pp. 403–436). New York: Guilford Press.

McArdle, J. J., Prescott, C. A., Hamagami, F., & Horn, J. L. (1998). A contemporary method for developmental—genetic analyses of age changes in intellectual abilities. *Developmental Neuropsychology, 14*(1), 69–114.

McArdle, J. J., & Woodcock, J. R. (1997). Expanding test-rest designs to include developemental time-lag components. *Psychological Methods, 2*(4), 403–435.

McArdle, J. J., & Woodcock, R. (Eds.). (1998), *Human cognitive abilities in theory and practice.* Chicago, IL: Riverside Press.

McGrew, K. S., Werder, J. K., & Woodcock, R. W. (1991). *Woodcock–Johnson technical manual.* Allen, TX: One DLM Park.

Meredith, W. (1964). Notes on factorial invariance. *Psychometrika, 29*, 177–185.

Meredith, W., & Horn, J. L. (2001). The role of factorial invariance in modeling growth and change. In A. G. Sayer & L. M. Collins (Eds.), *New methods for the analysis of change* (pp. 203–240). Washington, DC: American Psychological Association.

Miele, F. (2003). *Intelligence, race and genetics: Conversations with Arthur R. Jensen.* Boulder, CO: Westview.

Miles, C. C. (1934). The influence of speed and age on intelligence scores of adults. *Journal of Genetic Psychology, 10*, 208–210.

Neale, M. C., Boker, S. M., Xie, G., & Maes, H. H. (1999). *Mx: Statistical Modeling* (5th ed.). Richmond, VA: Medical College of Virginia.

Nyborg, H. (Ed.). (2003). *The scientific study of general intelligence—Tribute to Arthur R. Jensen.* New York: Pergamon.

Paterson, D. G., & Elliot, R. N. (1930). *Minnesota Mechanical Ability Tests.* Minneapolis, MN: University of Minnesota Press.

Pearson, K. (1901). On lines and planes of closest fit to systems of points in space. *Philosophical Magazine, 6*, 559–572.

Perfect, T. J., & Maylor, E. A. (Eds.). (2000). *Models of cognitive aging.* Oxford, UK: Oxford University Press.

Rimoldi, H. J. (1948). Study of some factors related to intelligence. *Psychometrika, 13*, 27–46.

Rowe, S. N. (1937). Mental changes following the removal of the right cerebral hemisphere for brain tumor. *American Journal of Psychiatry, 94*, 605–614.

Salthouse, T. A. (1985). Speed of behavior and its implications for cognition In J. E. Birren & K. W. Schaie (Eds.), *Handbook of the psychology of aging* (2nd ed. pp. 400–426) New York: Van Nostrand Reinhold.

Salthouse, T. A. (1991). *Theoretical perspectives on cognitive aging.* Mahwah, NJ: Lawrence Erlbaum Associates.

Schaie, K. W. (1996). *Intellectual development in adulthood: The Seattle longitudinal study.* Cambridge, MA: Cambridge University Press.

Scoville, W., & Milner, B. (1957). Loss of recent memory after bilateral hippocampal lesions. *Journal of Neurology, Neurosurgery and Psychiatry, 20*, 11.

Spearman, C. E. (1904a). "General intelligence," objectively determined and measured. *American Journal of Psychology, 15,* 201–293.

Spearman, C. E. (1904b). The proof and measurement of association between two things. *American Journal of Psychology, 15,* 72–101.

Spearman, C. E. (1914) Theory of two factors. *Psychological Review, 21,* 101–115.

Spearman, C. E. (1923). *The nature of intelligence and the principles of cognition.* London: Macmillan.

Spearman, C. E. (1927). *The abilities of man: Their nature and measurement.* New York: Macmillan.

Sperling, G. (1960). The information available in brief visual presentations. *Psychological Monographs, 74,* 498.

Steiger, J. H. (1990). Structural model evaluation and modification: An interval estimation approach. *Multivariate Behavioral Research, 25,* 173–180.

Thompson, R. F. (1998). *The brain: A neuroscience primer.* New York: Freeman.

Thomson, G. A. (1919). On the cause of hierarchical order among correlation coefficients. *Proceedings of the Royal Society, A, 95,* 400–408.

Thorndike, E. L. (1903). Intelligence. *Educational Psychology.*

Thurstone, L. L. (1931). Multiple factor analysis. *Psychological Review, 38,* 406–427.

Thurstone, L. L. (1935). *The vectors of mind.* Chicago: University of Chicago Press.

Thurstone, L. L. (1938). Primary mental abilities. *Psychometric Monographs, 1,* 1–121.

Thurstone, L. L. (1947). *Multiple factor analysis.* Chicago: University of Chicago Press.

Thurstone, L. L., & Thurstone, T. G. (1941). Factorial studies of intelligence. *Psychometric Monographs.*

Tryon, R. C. (1932). Multiple factors vs. two factors as determiners of abilities. *Psychological Review, 39,* 324–351.

Walsh, D. A., & Hershey, D. A. (1993). Mental models and the maintenance of complex problem solving skills in old age. In J. Cerella, J. Rybash, W. Hoyer, & M. Commons (Eds.), *Adult information processing: Limits on loss* (pp. 553–584). San Diego: Academic Press.

Weisenberg, T., & McBride, K. E. (1935). *Aphasia: A clinical and psychological study.* New York: Commonwealth Fund.

Willoughby, R. R. (1927). Family similarities in mental test abilities. *Genetic Psychology Monographs, 2,* 235–277.

Woodcock, R. W. (1995). Theoretical foundations of the WJ–R measures of cognitive ability. *Journal of Psychoeducational Assessment, 8,* 231–258.

CHAPTER 12

Factoring at the Individual Level: Some Matters for the Second Century of Factor Analysis

John R. Nesselroade
The University of Virginia

INDIVIDUAL LEVEL FACTOR ANALYSIS

The place of the individual in a science of behavior aspiring to establish general lawful relationships is somewhat ambiguous (Carlson, 1971; Magnusson, 2003; Molenaar, 2004). Tucker (1966), in his presentation of the generalized learning curve analysis model, wrote "... one traditional approach attempts to discover and delineate the general attributes of psychological phenomena as applicable to all individuals, while the alternate approach deals with individual differences in the extent or quality of selected aspects of behavior" (p. 479). What I want to underscore is not the two disciplines of scientific psychology to which Tucker was referring (see also Cronbach, 1957) but to a distinction Tucker made, but did not elaborate, within the individual differences tradition when he explicitly mentioned extent of individual differences and quality of individual differences. I start with the question, "Taking account of both genetic and experiential factors, are any two of us so nearly alike that we can be considered mere replicates of each other in the same manner as we would regard two bars of iron?" That is to say, are we essentially replicates of each other differing only quantitatively, if at all, according to some Gaussian dictate? Or are we qualitatively different in key respects? The scientific use of factor analysis at the individual level is intimately bound to these questions, I believe.

Within the broad context of qualitative versus quantitative interindividual differences, the concerns of this chapter are some conceptual and/or substantive matters regarding the application of factor models to individual, multivariate time series. Descriptions of promising models, including some of their history, and technical aspects of fitting them to empirical data are presented in chapter 13 by Browne and Zhang. My discussion of related topics will include: (a) aspects of the so–called idiographic and/or nomothetic debate as it bears on factor analyzing multivariate time series; (b) some reflections concerning the adequacy of the "received" view of factorial invariance for the individual level context; and (c) the key role that I believe extensions of individual level factor analysis will play in the future of behavioral research. Before concluding, I identify what I believe to be another fruitful application for the early part of factor analysis's next 100 years.

When the P-technique factor analysis—applying the common factor model to single case, multivariate time series—was presented more than 50 years ago (Cattell, Cattell, & Rhymer, 1947), Cattell believed that basic or fundamental personality traits were detectable both intraindividually and interindividually and that averaging enough P-technique solutions would yield a structure similar to what one would obtain by averaging enough R-technique (cross–sectional data) solutions. This level of unitariness of traits was one criterion by which one would know that a basic personality trait had been identified whether in intraindividual variation or in interindividual differences. In this vein, R. B. Cattell (1966) asserted, "... we should be very surprised if the growth pattern in a trait bore no relation to its absolute pattern, as an individual difference structure, and this would throw doubt on the scientific usefulness of the concept of unitariness for the trait" (p. 358).

But, Cattell (1966) also registered some misgivings:

> ... whereas in the case of traits, the nature of the growth process may well be such that the growth weight pattern at level x is significantly different from the individual difference pattern at level x, denoting that growth has previously occurred in a different way. For example, the height of the head (and presumably individual differences therein) contributes much more to the general stature factor in a young child than in an older child, and this is an important fact in the biology of growth. (p. 358)

The P-technique factor analysis application was subject to criticism for technical reasons (e.g., Anderson, 1963; Holtzman, 1963), which we will not go into here. Indeed, Cattell (1963) himself was concerned about the model's failure to account for lagged relationships between factors and manifest variables.

More recently, the notion of establishing unitariness of traits by means of convergent information from interindividual differences and intraindividual variability analyses has been challenged by Molenaar and colleagues (see, e.g., Molenaar, 2004; Molenaar, Huizenga, & Nesselroade, 2003), especially in regard to nonergodic processes[1] such as developmental ones. Molenaar (2004) asserted "... no asymptotic equivalence relationship between the structures of (interindividual differences) and (intraindividual variability) exists" (p. 203) for nonergodic processes. Even in the limiting conditions of infinite participants (in the case of interindividual differences approaches), and infinite time points (in the case of intraindividual change approaches), structures defined in one arena do not merge with structures of the other arena. These are different kinds of information and having many, many instances of either kind does not make them "average out" to the same structure.

At roughly the same time that Cattell was arguing for possible convergence between interindividual differences and intraindividual variability information, Bereiter (1963) suggested, "A necessary and sufficient proof of the statement that two tests "measure the same thing" is that they yield scores which vary together over changing conditions. P technique is the logical technique for studying the interdependencies of measures" (p. 15) and warned "... correlations between measures over individuals should bear some correspondence to correlations between measures for the same or randomly equivalent individuals over varying occasions, and the study of individual differences may be justified as an expedient substitute for the more difficult P-technique" (p. 15). Bereiter went on to say, "... however, the fact that measures on the same individuals may not correlate the same way on different occasions must be taken as evidence for the inadequacy of individual differences analysis as a substitute for P-technique analysis" (p. 15).

Although Bereiter did not use the terminology, he too seemed to be alluding to the differences between ergodic and nonergodic systems of variables. Clearly, some of the basis for distinguishing between what could be learned from structuring interindividual differences and intraindividual variability was being laid down by thoughtful psychometricians a half century ago.

Accepting that the two kinds of information—interindividual differences and intraindividual variation—are different, it is a small step to accept that both are potentially valuable and therefore worth exploring further. Thus, in the case of nonergodic processes, the Molenaar argument is not an either–or situation so much as it is "some of both." For students of "process," such as developmentalists, the primary focus is on intraindividual variation and the key role of the differential approach is to identify individual differences (and similarities) in the patterns of intraindividual

---

[1]Nesselroade and Molenaar (1999) used the statistical mechanics concept *ergodicity* to characterize behavioral systems for which the dynamics based on averages along a single trajectory were equivalent to those based on averages over the density of multiple trajectories in phase space. They pointed out the parallel in classical test theory of estimating true scores based on one-occasion group data instead of one-person, multioccasion data. A similar notion is encountered in scaling methods that substitute the single responses of many judges for the many responses of a single judge.

change rather than individual differences in putatively stable attributes (Baltes, Reese, & Nesselroade, 1977; Nesselroade, 2002).

THE PLACE OF THE INDIVIDUAL IN A SCIENCE OF BEHAVIOR

As was noted earlier, the place of the individual in a science of behavior has been rather ambiguous. On one hand, the individual is simply one of many replicates needed to provide variability, drive down the magnitude of standard errors, and generally satisfy sample size requirements—replicates viewed as differing in amount but not in kind, whose scores provide the basis for inferring structures and defining relationships that characterize the organization of variables. On the other hand, the individual is not a replicate but, rather, a unique entity, the repeated measurements of which provide the basis for inferring structures that define the organization of variables across occasions of measurement for that person.

Tension between the idiosyncratic and the common has played on the choices of behavioral scientists and has influenced the development of our field for a long time. Although a science of behavior cannot tolerate a different set of laws for each individual, if we ignore the uniqueness of the individual and attend only to observable features that all individuals have in common, we are forced to concentrate on a very limited subset of the interesting behaviors.

The literature contains an old distinction between idiographic and nomothetic concerns (e.g., Allport, 1937; Lamiell, 1981, 1988; Rosenzweig, 1958, 1986; van Kampen, 2000; Zevon & Tellegen, 1982). Harré (2001), for example, noted

> There are studies of individuals as such, an idiographic science. There are studies of people in groups or collectives, a nomothetic science. The analogue of a law of nature had no place in idiographic science while, perhaps with the help of statistical analysis, it could have a place in nomothetic science. The distinction is related to but not identical to that between two kinds of empirical inquiry. There is the intensive design, the study of a group by the study of a typical member and there is the extensive design, the aggregation of information about the members of a population into a statement about the population as a whole. (p. 7309)

A version of the two kinds of relationships used elsewhere to illustrate their differences (Nesselroade & Ritter, 2001) is depicted in Figure 12–1. The point here is that nomothetic relationships bear a major burden of "overriding" and "synthesizing" idiographic relationships which, if indeed the latter exist, will tend to weaken or even suppress the former.

Thus, idiographic concerns center on the uniqueness of the individual whereas nomothetic concerns emphasize the generality of lawfulness in behavior. These two

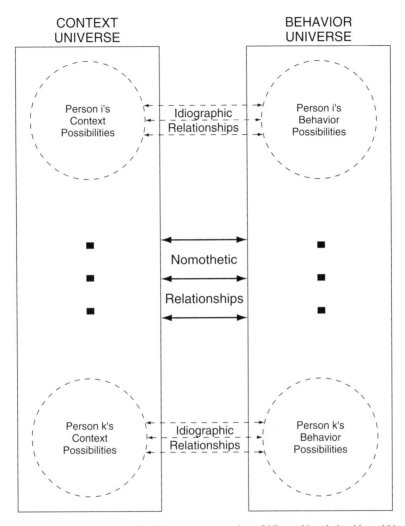

FIGURE 12–1. Nomothetic relationships as an aggregation of idiographic relationships within a generalized S–R paradigm.

orientations generally have been regarded as antithetical but attempts at rapprochement, some of them involving the use of P-technique factor analysis, can be found in the literature of the past two decades or so (Lamiell, 1981; Nesselroade & Ford, 1985; Zevon & Tellegen, 1982).

For me, the excitement is no longer the debate per se as much as it is the awareness that there are compelling rationales for how the idiographic orientation can complement the nomothetic one (see, e.g., Lamiell, 1981; Nesselroade & Ford, 1985; Zevon & Tellegen, 1982) and seeing the development of more and more powerful methods for harnessing idiographic information in the service of constructing lawful relationships.

In my view, one of the obvious linchpins in capitalizing on idiographic information in building nomothetic laws from a multivariate perspective is the concept of *factorial invariance*. But, I believe this is a much more complicated matter than it might at first seem and try to explore it more fully in the following sections.

FACTOR INVARIANCE

The concept of factor invariance has played a major and venerated role in the literature for well over 50 years (Meredith, 1964a, 1964b, 1993; Thurstone, 1947, see also chap. 8, this volume, by Millsap & Meredith). The concept has been prominent in both the factor analysis literature and, more recently, in the structural equation modeling literature involving latent variables. It is the "holy grail" that drove pursuit of simple structure (Thurstone, 1947) and confactor rotation (Cattell 1944; McArdle & Cattell, 1994) which, in turn, were the primary motivation for the development of countless graphical, topographical, and analytical rotation procedures. In developmental research, for example, factorial invariance has been used to make the critical distinction between quantitative and qualitative changes that allows for testing of theoretical formulations such as the differentiation hypothesis of cognitive development (see, e.g., Olsson & Bergman, 1977; Reinert, 1970).

Thurstone (1947) defined factor invariance on the loading pattern but its specification has sometimes included other elements of a factorial representation, including factor intercovariances, uniquenesses, and so forth (see, e.g, Nesselroade & Thompson, 1995; Olsson & Bergman, 1977, see also chap. 8, this volume, by Millsap & Meredith). Both metric invariance and the less restrictive configural invariance are intimately involved in the production of convincing, theoretically driven empirical research (Horn, McArdle, & Mason, 1983). The more or less routine use of these concepts in traditional individual differences research abounds in the literature and has been instrumental in evaluating measurement instruments as well as many kinds of comparisons in modeling multivariate data.

Factor loading patterns are our worldly windows into latent space. By means of these links between the unobserved factors and the observed, manifest variables, we can see the extent to which the latter are "influenced" by the former. One of the central arguments developed by analysts of changes and differences regarding the evaluation of invariance is that it can be used to find out if we are "measuring the same thing" in different instances, whether in a repeated measures or a group comparison situation. The presumption is that if the loading pattern is invariant, the nature of the variables remains intact across comparisons. An illustration (Nesselroade, 1970) I have used for a long time to convey these ideas is to define two factor specification equations:

$$z_{ji} = a_{j1}f_{1i} + a_{j2}f_{2i} + \cdots + a_{jk}f_{ki} + u_{ji} \qquad \text{(Equation 12.1)}$$

$$z'_{ji} = a_{j1}f'_{1i} + a_{j2}f'_{2i} + \cdots + a_{jk}f'_{ki} + u'_{ji} \qquad \text{(Equation 12.2)}$$

where z_{ji} represents an observed score for person i on variable j at some point in time. z'_{ji} represents an observed score for person i on variable j at some subsequent point in time. The a_{jq} represent the loading of factor q on variable j, the f_{qi} and f'_{qi} represent factor scores for person i at the two different times, and the u_{ji} and u'_{ji} represent the unique factor scores for variable j at the two times. Loading invariance allows the subtraction and rearrangement of terms into:

$$z'_{ji} - z_{ji} = a_{j1}(f'_{1i} - f_{1i}) + a_{j2}(f'_{2i} - f_{2i}) + \cdots + a_{jk}(f'_{ki} - f_{ki}) + (u'_{ji} - u_{ji})$$
$$\text{(Equation 12.3)}$$

thus expressing the observed change as a parsimonious function of changes in the factor scores. Here, invariance renders the interpretation of changes simple and straightforward. A similar demonstration holds for between-group differences.

But, when we enter the world of individual level factor analysis with the hope of finding a meaningful basis for aggregating information across multiple individuals as advocated, for instance, by Zevon and Tellegen (1982) and by Nesselroade and Ford (1985), I am uneasy about this line of argument for reasons now presented. I propose that there are some serious limitations in the concept of factorial invariance as it has been implemented in the study of intraindividual variability, and change and explore some of the implications of these limitations as well as a modified way to think about factor invariance that I believe will make it more useful to a science that I hope is on the verge of a productive resolution of the idiographic–nomothetic debate. First, however, let us look more closely at a couple of matters of aggregation of information across individuals.

AGGREGATION OF INFORMATION ACROSS INDIVIDUALS NEEDS TO BE INFORMED AS MUCH AS POSSIBLE

Molenaar (2004), for example, has made clear, and I am in agreement, that the blind aggregation of information across individuals—even across many individuals—is not necessarily appropriate when the objective involves the study of individual level processes. Related arguments have been advanced by Lamiell (1981, 1988, 1997). One of our primary scientific aims is the articulation of general lawful relationships but the cost of accomplishing that will be greater than simply amassing large samples of participants and aggregating information over the totality. It will have to include the careful, intensive examination of the individual so that aggregation over individuals can be informed.

Thus, from the standpoint of building a nomothetic science, factoring at the individual level is not an end in itself but rather a means to an end as has been illustrated by, for example Lebo and Nesselroade (1978) and Zevon and Tellegen (1982) in multiple individual P-technique studies. In addition to the fundamental concerns of generalizability, there are matters of theory building and testing that can be more precisely evaluated with individual level factor analytic data than within the traditional interindividual paradigm (Bereiter, 1963). There are two matters on which I want to touch briefly that fall under the concerns of aggregation across individuals.

First, there is the question of the level at which aggregation should occur. Nesselroade and Molenaar (1999), for example, devised an algorithm for making an informed pooling of individual lagged covariance patterns that rested on the Bartlett-type notions of homogeneity of covariance matrices. But, as is argued, there are reasons for pushing the aggregation back to the level of the individual factor solutions and beyond because of measurement concerns.[2]

Second, related to the next topic, informed aggregation of information across individuals has to be somewhat "creative" because traditional criteria and procedures may not be appropriate. This is illustrated in consideration of the matter of factor pattern invariance within an individual level factoring context. This leads us back to the matter of factor invariance and its use within the context of individual level factor analyses.

INVARIANCE NEED NOT ALWAYS BE DEFINED AT THE PRIMARY FACTOR LEVEL TO BE CRITICAL

The problem comes to a head in individual level analyses (e.g., Cattell's P-technique, dynamic factor analysis). We have learned from experience, especially in the context of self-report, but I argue that the matter is more general, that in comparing intraindividual variability outcomes across individuals in the service of identifying more general relationships that the nature of a manifest variable can differ in surprising, qualitative ways from one person to another. For example, two participants in the P-technique studies by Mitteness and Nesselroade (1987) explained their use of the adjective rating scale, *Anxious versus Not Anxious*, during postdata collection debriefing. One participant had responded in terms of her self-perceived anxiety and the other in terms of her self-perceived eagerness. The earlier quote by Cattell (1966) that "the height of the head (and presumably individual differences therein) contributes much more to the general stature factor in a young child than in an older child" (p. 358) illustrates a fundamental difference in meaning of what is ostensibly the same variable height in two different individuals. My concern is that, more generally, genetic differences as well as unique life

---

[2]John Horn has persistently argued for this position in our discussions over the past decade or so.

histories impinge on a wide variety of potential measures used in individual level factor analyses. For example, indicators such as respiration rate, blood pressure, perspiration rate, and so forth, although they are in large part "driven" by the autonomic nervous system, are to some degree subject to conditioning and function, in part, in ways that reflect the individual's unique life history.

Thus, even though the measurement instruments are ostensibly the same across different individuals, to the extent that the kinds of uniqueness already described prevails, at the primary factor level, one cannot expect the results of individual level factor analyses to be commensurate from one participant to another. Said another way, one cannot rely on the traditional conceptions of factor invariance to provide a basis for informed aggregation of individual level analysis results into nomothetic relationships. This is a very real dilemma. How does one proceed with building a nomothetic science when the information contributed from different individuals cannot be regarded as on the same footing?

PRIMARY FACTOR LOADING PATTERNS AS IDIOGRAPHIC FILTERS

I suggest that even though manifest variables are not necessarily the "same" variables from one person to another, it can still make theoretical sense for factors to be thought of as the same from one person to another. Consider disease states such as cancer, for instance.[3] The person with cancer A manifests one set of symptoms whereas the person with cancer B displays another set of symptoms. Although there may be some overlapping symptoms, there are others that are unique to the individual case, but this does not deter our referring to both individuals as cancer victims nor our seeking a common, underlying mechanism.

At a more psychological level, the concept, *state anxiety*, connotes intraindividual variability. As a theoretical concept, state anxiety applies to many, if not all, individuals, but it is likely that the relationship of the concept to a set of manifest indicators (e.g., autonomic nervous system manifestations, self-reported symptoms, etc.) differs from one person to another due, in part, to "accidents" of personal history and experience or, in the case of self-report, idiosyncratic language usage. In such cases, the usual conception of factor invariance may create problems if one is trying to establish that state anxiety is a factor accounting for occasion-to-occasion variation in different persons, each analyzed at the individual level.

In fact, it seems that more useful here is the idea that primary factors can be the same across different individuals even though the loading patterns are not invariant. That is to say, factor loading patterns can be construed in the role of "filters" at the first order level and allow for idiosyncrasies at the individual person-measures interface.

---

[3]I am grateful to Donald H. Ford for this example.

TABLE 12–1

Correlations Among Factors For Five Individuals: Cell Entries Are Individual Outcomes When the Two Factors Were Identified for a Given Subject.

	Energy	Well-Being	Fatigue	Social Affection	Well-Being (2)
Energy	—				
Well-Being	+.35, +.60, +.76, −.35, +.66	—			
Fatigue	−50, −.58, —, −.58, −.56	−.18, −.31, —, +.37 −.42	—		
Social-Affection	+.48, −.04, +.32, —, —	+.65, +.25, +.46, —, —	−.08, +.15, —, —, —	—	
Well-Being(2)	+.31, +.68, +.30, +.70, —	+.52, +.61, +.53, −.02, —	−.30, −.39 —, −.50, —	+.49, +.14, +.32, — —	—

Note. Inconsistencies are italicized.

However, one needs some convincing empirical evidence to make this line of argument seem plausible. Although I do not have convincing evidence as yet, I want to illustrate the idea with empirical data from the multiple individual P-technique study by Lebo and Nesselroade (1978) that involved P techniques of five young women, each experiencing their first pregnancy. In Table 12.1 are presented the factor intercorrelations as they appeared in the original article. The factors were rotated graphically to simple structure, separately for each individual, with no effort to enhance similarities across persons at either the factor pattern or factor intercorrelation levels. In conducting these analyses, variables with little or no variability were dropped for that individual. Factors were identified and labeled separately for each individual.

The point is that despite all the "individuality" of the loading patterns, there is enough consistency in the factor intercorrelations to warrant the suggestion that the pattern of factor interrelations might be very similar despite factor patterns at that level not being so similar. To what extent such agreement might be deliberately enhanced using the technologies available today remains to be seen, but trying it is clearly possible. In Figure 12–2 an interpretation is schematized that emphasizes the following two points:

1. An ostensibly common measurement space that is not upheld at the primary factor level.

2. Individual-level factors that, although they have different primary loading patterns for different people, manifest the possibility of similar patterns of

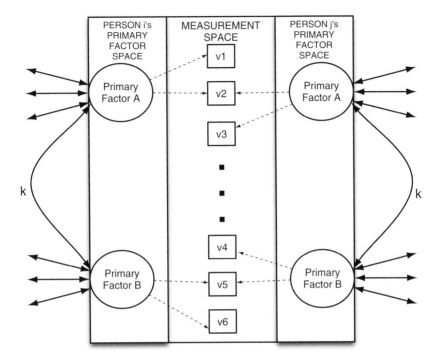

FIGURE 12–2.   Schematic representation of primary factor patterns as idiographic filters coupling measures to theoretical space.

relationships at the interfactor level and similar patterns of relationships with other external variables.

Consider two matters that these possibilities raise. First, from the standpoint of a more traditional factorial invariance emphasis, if we are willing to use variations in the factor-loading patterns from person to person to "filter" out idiosyncrasies, as it were, and find that the factor interrelations are similar across people, it implies that the second–order (or perhaps higher order) factor patterns might be fitted as invariant, in the traditional sense (i.e., configural or metric invariance), across people. In other words, factorial invariance in the usual sense can remain a key conception in individual-level analyses at a higher order level by using the factor-loading patterns to "filter out" the idiosyncratic nature of the manifest variables.

Second, and even less concrete, is the notion that a structure can be invariant at a level other than the primary factor level and asking the question, "Does this suffice to claim 'the same concept'?" In their presentation of *construct validity*, Cronbach and Meehl (1955) argued that a necessary condition for a construct to be scientifically admissible was that it occur in a nomological net, at least some of whose laws involve observables. Thus, from a construct validity perspective, the

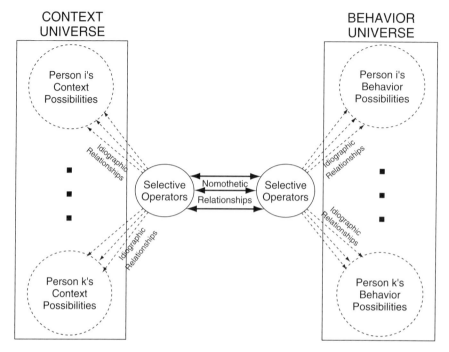

FIGURE 12–3.   Complementary idiographic and nomothetic systems with selective operators in a generalized S–R paradigm.

possibility exists to amass sufficient evidence to turn these idiosyncratic "mavericks" into respectable elements of theory.

Nesselroade and Ritter (2001) tried to cast the situation in terms of selective operators and their possible mathematical group structure as shown in Figure 12–3 but, for our purposes here, individual level factor analysis of time series information seems a more immediately available path to identifying such patterns. Elsewhere (Nesselroade, 2004), I also raised the possibility that invariance might be sought at the process level by focussing on patterns of auto– and cross–regression of latent factors, for example, in individual level dynamic factor models. As mentioned, this would allow for idiosyncratic patterns of factor loadings at the first–order factor level.

CONCLUDING REMARKS

Factor analysis and some of its most esteemed concepts, such as factorial invariance, have been instrumental in propelling the study of behavior to its present-day level. Included among the important innovations is the adaptation of the factor model to individual level analyses. Such applications have been critical, for example, to the rigorous establishment of the trait–state distinction in personality theory (e.g., Cattell & Scheier, 1961; J. L. Horn, 1972) and to a more productive framing of the so–called idiographic and/or nomothetic debate into one more suggestive of cooperation than of competition. As the study of process becomes more and more salient, the merits of, and potential gains from, further, more sophisticated modeling of intraindividual change and variability cannot be ignored. As Browne and Zhang (chap. 13, this volume) have amply demonstrated, an array of modeling applications for individual level factor analyses is waiting to serve these purposes.

Unfortunately, or fortunately, depending upon one's viewpoint, there is substantial justification for critically evaluating the appropriateness of slavishly applying the factor model as it has evolved over the past 100 years, primarily in the environment of differential psychology, to the study of intraindividual variability and change. Attention was called to this matter by Bereiter (1963) over 40 years ago but his arguments seem largely to have been disregarded although they clearly were not discredited. His essential argument, which seems to me to run counter to prevailing thought, was that, in studying relationships among variables, covariation within individuals over occasions was superior to covariation within occasions over individuals and that the latter needed to be justified as a substitute for the former rather than the converse.

What Bereiter (1963) did not deal with is the matter of *generalizability* and how one might usefully aggregate information from many different individual level analyses. This is where the idiographic–nomothetic debate seems to be centered with regard to factor analyzing individual level multivariate time series. But the adequacy of simply working toward an "average" individual level factor representation has been challenged with regard to modeling the kind of change processes represented by development and learning (e.g., Molenaar, 2004).

In my view, the most promising attempts so far at resolving the idiographic–nomothetic debate in a constructive manner and being able to capitalize on the strengths of both individual level analyses and the more traditional interindividual differences approaches involve the use of individual level analyses such as P technique and derivatives as preliminary to aggregating information across multiple individuals for the purpose of developing and testing theory as has been suggested by Zevon and Tellegen (1982; see also Lebo & Nesselroade, 1978; Nesselroade & Ford, 1985). But, I have attempted to point out that this is likely not a straightforward task of merely applying the tools of interindividual differences study to lots of intraindividual variation data sets. Rather, acknowledging the idiosyncrasies of individuals without letting those idiosyncrasies wreck the search for general lawfulness will require some innovation in our applications of basic notions of measurement and analysis. Until something better comes along, it is my belief that factor analysis at the individual level along with expanded versions of key concepts such as *factor invariance* can be a powerful and productive way to begin the method's second century.

ACKNOWLEDGMENTS

This work was supported by The Institute for Developmental and Health Research Methodology at the University of Virginia. Although they are in no way responsible for the content of this chapter, I am grateful to Paul Baltes, Michael Browne, Don Ford, John L. Horn, Bill Meredith, and Jack McArdle for decades of discussion of the issues. I dedicate this chapter to the memory of John L. Horn, critical friend and friendly critic for nearly 50 years.

REFERENCES

Allport, G. W. (1937). *Personality: A psychological interpretation.* New York: Holt, Rinehart, & Winston.

Anderson, T. W. (1963). The use of factor analysis in the statistical analysis of multiple time series. *Psychometrika, 28,* 1–24.

Baltes, P. B., Reese, H. W., & Nesselroade, J. R. (1977). *Life-span developmental psychology: Introduction to research methods.* Monterrey, CA: Brooks/Cole.

Bereiter, C. (1963). Some persisting dilemmas in the measurement of change. In C. W. Harris (Ed.), *Problems in measuring change* (pp. 3–20). Madison, WI: University of Wisconsin Press.

Carlson, R. (1971). Where is the person in personality research? *Psychological Bulletin, 75*(3), 203–219.

Cattell, R. B. (1944). 'Parallel proportional profiles' and other principles for determining the choice of factors by rotation. *Psychometrika, 9,* 267–283.

Cattell, R. B. (1963). The structuring of change by P–technique and incremental R–technique. In C. W. Harris (Ed.), *Problems in measuring change* (pp. 167–198). Madison, WI: University of Wisconsin Press.

Cattell, R. B. (1966). Patterns of change: Measurement in relation to state dimension, trait change, lability, and process concepts. In R. B. Cattell (Ed.), *Handbook of multivariate experimental psychology* (1st ed., pp. 355–402). Chicago, IL: Rand McNally.

Cattell, R. B., Cattell, A. K. S., & Rhymer, R. M. (1947). P-technique demonstrated in determining psychophysical source traits in a normal individual. *Psychometrika, 12,* 267–288.

Cattell, R. B., & Scheier, I. H. (1961). *The meaning and measurement of neuroticism and anxiety.* New York: Ronald Press.

Cronbach, L. J. (1957). The two disciplines of scientific psychology. *American Psychologist, 12,* 71–84.

Cronbach, L. J., & Meehl, P. E. (1955). Construct validity in psychological tests. *Psychological Bulletin, 52,* 281–302.

Harré, R. (2001). Individual/Society: History of the concept. In N. J. Smelser & P. B. Baltes (Eds.), *International encyclopedia of the social and behavioral sciences* (Vol. 11, pp. 7306–7310). Oxford: Elsevier Science.

Holtzman, W. H. (1963). Statistical models for the study of change in the single case. In C. W. Harris (Ed.), *Problems in measuring change* (pp. 199–211). Madison, WI: University of Wisconsin Press.

Horn, J., McArdle, J. J., & Mason, R. (1983). When invariance is not invariant: A practical scientist's view of the ethereal concept of factorial invariance. *The Southern Psychologist, 1,* 179–188.

Horn, J. L. (1972). State, trait, and change dimensions of intelligence. *The British Journal of Educational Psychology, 42*(2), 159–185.

Lamiell, J. T. (1981). Toward an idiothetic psychology of personality. *American Psychologist, 36*, 276–289.

Lamiell, J. T. (1988). *Once more into the breach: Why individual differences research cannot advance personality theory.* Paper presented at the annual meeting of the American Psychological Association, Atlanta, GA.

Lamiell, J. T. (1997). Individuals and the differences between them. In R. Hogan, J. A. Johnson, & S. Briggs (Eds.), *Handbook of personality psychology* (pp. 117–141). New York: Academic Press.

Lebo, M. A., & Nesselroade, J. R. (1978). Intraindividual differences dimensions of mood change during pregnancy identified in five P–technique factor analyses. *Journal of Research in Personality, 12*, 205–224.

Magnusson, D. (2003). The person approach: Concepts, measurement models, and research strategy. In S. C. Peck & R. W. Roeser (Eds.), *New directions for child and adolescent development* (pp. 3–23). New York: Wiley Periodicals, Inc.

McArdle, J. J., & Cattell, R. B. (1994). Structural equation models of factorial invariance in parallel proportional profiles and oblique confactor problems. *Multivariate Behavioral Research, 29*(1), 63–113.

Meredith, W. (1964a). Notes on factorial invariance. *Psychometrika, 29*(2), 177–185.

Meredith, W. (1964b). Rotation to achieve factorial invariance. *Psychometrika, 29*(2), 186–206.

Meredith, W. (1993). Measurement invariance, factor analysis and factor invariance. *Psychometrika, 58*, 525–543.

Mitteness, L. S., & Nesselroade, J. R. (1987). Attachment in adulthood: Longitudinal investigation of mother–daughter affective interdependencies by P–technique factor analysis. *The Southern Psychologist, 3*, 37–44.

Molenaar, P. C. M. (2004). A manifesto on psychology as idiographic science: Bringing the person back into scientific psychology—this time forever. *Measurement: Interdisciplinary Research and Perspectives, 2*, 201–218.

Molenaar, P. C. M., Huizenga, H. M., & Nesselroade, J. R. (2003). The relationship between the structure of interindividual and intraindividual variability: A theoretical and empirical vindication of developmental systems theory. In U. M. Staudinger & U. Lindenberger (Eds.), *Understanding human development: Dialogues with lifespan psychology* (pp. 339–360). Norwell, MA: Kluwer Academic.

Nesselroade, J. R. (1970). Application of multivariate strategies to problems of measuring and structuring long–term change. In L. R. Goulet & P. B. Baltes (Eds.), *Life–span developmental psychology: Research and theory* (pp. 193–207). New York: Academic Press.

Nesselroade, J. R. (2002). Elaborating the different in differential psychology. *Multivariate Behavioral Research, 37*(4), 543–561.

Nesselroade, J. R. (2004). *Optimizing the contributions of individual level analyses—another look at the idiographic/nomothetic debate.* Paper presented at the annual meeting of the Society of Multivariate Experimental Psychology, Naples, FL.

Nesselroade, J. R., & Ford, D. H. (1985). P–technique comes of age: Multivariate, replicated, single–subject designs for research on older adults. *Research on Aging, 7*, 46–80.

Nesselroade, J. R., & Molenaar, P. C. M. (1999). Pooling lagged covariance structures based on short, multivariate time–series for dynamic factor analysis. In R. H. Hoyle (Ed.), *Statistical strategies for small sample research* (pp. 224–250). Newbury Park, CA: Sage.

Nesselroade, J. R., & Ritter, R. (2001). *Optimizing the contributions of individual level analyses to establishing generalizability across individuals: A new look at the idiographic–nomothetic debate.* Unpublished manuscript, Department of Psychology, University of Virginia.

Nesselroade, J. R., & Thompson, W. (1995). Selection and related threats to group comparisons: An example comparing factorial structures of higher and lower ability groups of adult twins. *Psychological Bulletin, 117,* 271–284.

Olsson, U., & Bergman, L. R. (1977). A longitudinal factor model for studying change in ability structure. *Multivariate Behavioral Research, 12,* 221–242.

Reinert, G. (1970). Comparative factor analytic studies of intelligence throughout the human life span. In L. R. Goulet & P. B. Baltes (Eds.), *Life–span developmental psychology: Research and theory* (pp. 467–484). New York: Academic Press.

Rosenzweig, S. (1958). The place of the individual and of idiodynamics in psychology: A dialogue. *Journal of Individual Psychology, 14,* 3–20.

Rosenzweig, S. (1986). Idiodynamics vis–á–vis psychology. *The American Psychologist, 41,* 241–245.

Thurstone, L. L. (1947). *Multiple factor analysis.* Chicago: University of Chicago Press.

Tucker, L. R. (1966). Learning theory and multivariate experiment: Illustration by determination of generalized learning curves. In R. B. Cattell (Ed.), *Handbook of multivariate experimental psychology* (pp. 476–501). Chicago: Rand McNally.

van Kampen, V. (2000). Idiographic complexity and the common personality dimensions of insensitivity, extraversion, neuroticism, and orderliness. *European Journal of Personality, 14,* 217–243.

Zevon, M., & Tellegen, A. (1982). The structure of mood change: Idiographic/nomothetic analysis. *Journal of Personality and Social Psychology, 43*(1), 111–122.

CHAPTER 13

Developments in the Factor Analysis of Individual Time Series

Michael W. Browne
Guangjian Zhang
The Ohio State University

HISTORICAL INTRODUCTION

The factor analysis of a single multivariate time series dates back to Cattell's P technique (Cattell, Cattell, & Rhymer, 1947). The original P technique involves the collection of multivariate measurements on a single subject at a substantial number of time points. The data obtained are then factor analyzed in exactly the same way as multivariate measurements on a substantial number of different subjects at the same time. Thus the original P technique requires no special purpose methodology or computational techniques.

Since the first empirical application of the P technique by Cattell, it has been used to a considerable extent. Reviews of applications of Cattell's P technique have been given by Luborsky & Mintz (1972) and by Jones and Nesselroade (1990). The original P technique provided the information in which Cattell was most interested, namely the extent to which factor patterns differ between individuals and the extent to which intraindividual factor patterns differ from the interindividual factor pattern. This information is interesting and continues to be used up to the present time. For example, a careful study of intraindividual and interindividual factor patterns was carried out by Borkenau and Ostendorf (1998). In this work, intraindividual factor matrices were rotated to a least squares fit to an interindividual factor

265

matrix obtained from a preceding large study, which included the same variables. Substantial differences were found between intraindividual factor matrices among themselves and between intraindividual factor matrices and the interindividual factor matrix. Borkenau and Ostendorf also found, however, that when intraindividual correlation matrices were averaged across individuals and submitted to a factor analysis, a similar factor pattern was obtained to that of the interindividual study on a different sample.

Early observations were made that the method of factor analysis proposed by Cattell does not make full use of information contained in the data collected. Holtzman (1963) pointed out that the information contained in autocorrelation matrices obtained from the same data was being disregarded. Anderson (1963) also pointed out that information about change over time was being neglected in the Cattell P technique. He suggested that available time series methodology be applied to factor scores for studying time effects on the data. Thus these two early authors both felt that the P technique should be supplemented by an analysis of time effect with Holtzman (1963) suggesting the analysis of autocorrelations for this purpose and Anderson (1963) suggesting the analysis of factor scores using time series methodology.

Anderson's suggestions were followed up by subsequent authors who analyzed the data matrix to investigate the effect of a latent time series on the observations but without the explicit calculation of factor scores. These approaches made use of Kalman filter techniques operating directly on the data matrix to obtain maximum normal likelihood estimates, not only of factor loadings, but also of parameters in a latent autoregressive time series with moving average residuals (ARMA). Engle and Watson (1981) considered a single factor model following an autoregressive time series but also allowed for the influence of an exogenous variable. The Engle–Watson approach was generalized to several independent factors, each following an ARMA time series by Immink (1986). Recent applications of a computer program suitable for fitting a multiple factor model to the data matrix assuming a vector ARMA (VARMA) latent time series have been reported by Hamaker, Dolan, and Molenaar (2005). This program employs the Kalman filter and may be downloaded from the Internet (cf. Hamaker et al., 2005, p. 218).

Holtzman (1963) had suggested that autocorrelations be used to supplement information employed in Cattell's P technique. Two different methods for factor analyzing autocorrelation matrices were proposed subsequently. One was a method for confirmatory factor analysis proposed by Nesselroade, McArdle, Aggen, and Meyers (2002) that assumed the autocorrelation matrix structure implied by an autoregressive time series data model. It involved a single factor matrix, as in Cattell's P technique. Their data model resembled that of Engle and Watson (1981) but their estimation procedure was different. The Nesselroade et al. (2002) chapter demonstrated the effectiveness of using autocorrelation matrices for estimating a latent autoregressive process and motivated our present research. The other method, proposed by Molenaar (1985), was an adaptation of a data model of Geweke and

Singleton (1981) to the situation where estimates are derived from autocorrelation matrices. It involved multiple factor matrices, and no autoregressive or moving average coefficients. Both the single factor matrix model and the multiple factor matrix model have been referred to as *Dynamic Factor Analysis* models by their proponents. Browne and Nesselroade (2005, pp. 441–449) compared these two models and considered relationships between them. The single factor matrix model was referred to as the *Process Factor Analysis* model because the factors are endogenous variables following a VARMA process. Because the factors in the multiple factor matrix model are exogenous random shocks that are uncorrelated across time, this model was referred to as the *Shock Factor Analysis* model.

Cattell's original P technique was exploratory and involved a rotation to simple structure. Subsequent methods have been primarily confirmatory, although one (Hamaker et al., 2005) has employed an initial exploratory step with rotation to locate small factor loadings, followed by a second confirmatory step where factor loadings are reestimated with previously small factor loadings restricted to be zero.

The present chapter suggests a simple enhancement of Cattell's P technique to take the interdependence of observations over time into account. An exploratory factor analysis with a rotation to simple structure is carried out first as in the P technique. Then the same factor matrix is used in conjunction with manifest variable autocorrelation matrices to obtain estimates of factor autocorrelation matrices. Finally a transformation of the factor autocorrelation matrices to VARMA time series weight matrices and the corresponding shock covariance matrix is carried out. No restrictions are imposed on parameters so that the enhanced P technique, like Cattell's original method, is exploratory.

THE PROCESS FACTOR ANALYSIS MODEL

This section will be concerned with a special case of the process factor analysis model (Browne & Nesselroade, 2005, pp. 442–444) that will be used to provide an extension of Cattell's P technique. First of all, the data model is considered. Subsequently, the autocorrelation structure implied by the data model is examined, and finally, moment estimators of the time series parameters in the model are presented.

The Data Model

We consider a situation where one individual has taken the same battery of n_v tests at T equally spaced points in time. Let the T vector variates $\mathbf{y}_1, \mathbf{y}_2, \dots, \mathbf{y}_T$, each of order $n_v \times 1$, represent these scores.

The process factor analysis (PFA) model (cf. Browne & Nesselroade, 2005, Equation 19) consists of two parts. The first part is similar to the standard factor analysis model with n_v manifest variables and k factors:

$$\mathbf{y}_t = \boldsymbol{\mu} + \boldsymbol{\Lambda}\mathbf{f}_t + \mathbf{u}_t$$

where $\mathbf{y}_t$ represents the $n_v \times 1$ vector of manifest variables measured at time t, $\boldsymbol{\mu}$ is a mean vector, $\boldsymbol{\Lambda}$ is a $n_v \times k$ factor matrix that remains *invariant* over time, $\mathbf{f}_t$ is a $k \times 1$ vector of common factors at time t, and $\mathbf{u}_t$ is a $n_v \times 1$ vector of unique factors at time t. In the usual manner the unique factor vector, $\mathbf{u}_t$, is decomposed into a vector of specific factors, $\mathbf{s}_t$, and a vector of measurement errors, $\mathbf{e}_t$:

$$\mathbf{u}_t = \mathbf{s}_t + \mathbf{e}_t.$$

As is the case in the standard factor analysis model, the measurement errors are uncorrelated across time as well as being contemporaneously uncorrelated, being distributed according to a multivariate distribution with a mean vector of $\mathbf{0}$ and a diagonal covariance matrix $\mathbf{D}_\varepsilon$. This will subsequently be represented in abbreviated notation as $\mathbf{e}_t \sim (\mathbf{0}, \mathbf{D}_\varepsilon)$. In contrast to the standard factor analysis model, where specific factors are uncorrelated with all other latent variables, a specific factor may be correlated across time. The same specific factor will recur at each time point and may also be assumed to follow a time series (cf. Engle & Watson, 1981).

The second part of the PFA model specified in Browne and Nesselroade (2005, Equation 20) is a time series model relating the common factor vectors, $\mathbf{f}_t$, at different time points. This time series is the VARMA(p, q) process,

$$\mathbf{f}_t = \sum_{i=1}^{p} \mathbf{A}_i \mathbf{f}_{t-i} + \mathbf{z}_t + \sum_{j=1}^{q} \mathbf{B}_j \mathbf{z}_{t-j}, \qquad \text{(Equation 13.1)}$$

where $\mathbf{z}_t \sim (\mathbf{0}, \boldsymbol{\Psi})$ is a random shock vector, the $\mathbf{A}_i$ are autoregressive weight matrices and the $\mathbf{B}_j$ are moving average weight matrices. This part of the PFA model bears little resemblance to the standard factor analysis model. In Equation 13.1 the factors are endogenous and correlated across time whereas they are exogenous and uncorrelated between subjects in the standard factor analysis model.

Two simplifications of the PFA model are introduced to facilitate a simple and computationally robust extension of Cattell's P technique. Firstly the unique factor vector is assumed to consist of pure measurement error, $\mathbf{u}_t = \mathbf{e}_t \sim (\mathbf{0}, \mathbf{D}_\varepsilon)$, and be uncorrelated across time. Consequently the factor analysis component of the PFA model becomes

$$\mathbf{y}_t = \boldsymbol{\mu} + \boldsymbol{\Lambda}\mathbf{f}_t + \mathbf{e}_t \qquad \text{(Equation 13.2)}$$

where

$$\text{Cov}\left(\mathbf{e}_t, \mathbf{e}_t'\right) = \mathbf{D}_\varepsilon$$
$$\text{Cov}\left(\mathbf{e}_{t+\ell}, \mathbf{e}_t'\right) = \mathbf{0}, \text{ for all } t, \ell \neq 0 \qquad \text{(Equation 13.3)}$$
$$\text{Cov}\left(\mathbf{e}_t, \mathbf{z}_{t*}'\right) = \mathbf{0}, \text{ for all } t, t^*.$$

This will make a simple estimation procedure possible. Inspection of residuals has suggested that this assumption is usually reasonable for adjective rating data of the type used in our example. Secondly, the moving average part of the model in

Equation 13.1 is omitted to yield the latent vector autoregressive latent process, $\text{VAR}(p) = \text{VARMA}(p, 0)$:

$$\mathbf{f}_t = \sum_{i=1}^{p} \mathbf{A}_i \mathbf{f}_{t-i} + \mathbf{z}_t \quad t = 1, 2, \ldots, T \qquad \text{(Equation 13.4)}$$

Generalized Yule–Walker moment estimates (e.g., Lütkepohl, 1993, section 8.6) are used for the autoregressive parameters. These involve the solution of a system of linear equations. For moving average parameters, moment estimates would require the iterative solution of a system of nonlinear equations that often yields convergence difficulties and estimates that are problematical (cf. Wei, 1990, p. 137). Furthermore $\text{VARMA}(p, q)$ processes have identification difficulties that are not present with $\text{VARMA}(p, 0)$ processes (e.g., Lütkepohl, 1993, section 8.6). Consequently $\text{VARMA}(p, 0)$, or equivalently $\text{VAR}(p)$, processes are easier to estimate and are less prone to identification difficulties. In the present chapter a $\text{VARMA}(p, 0)$ latent process is assumed and the corresponding PFA model is referred to as a $\text{PFA}(p, 0)$ model.

Inspection of the right-hand side of the latent time series model in Equation 13.4 shows that the factor vectors, $\mathbf{f}_{t-i}$, with nonpositive subscripts, $0, -1, -2, \ldots, -(p-1)$ only occur when $t \leq p$. Consequently only the first p factor vectors, $\mathbf{f}_1, \ldots, \mathbf{f}_p$, are influenced by factor vectors that occur before the data are collected. To account explicitly for these influences of the latent time series prior to the first time point, Equation 13.4 may be written as

$$\mathbf{f}_1 = \mathbf{x}_1 + \mathbf{z}_1$$

$$\mathbf{f}_t = \mathbf{x}_t + \sum_{\ell=1}^{t-1} \mathbf{A}_\ell \mathbf{f}_{t-\ell} + \mathbf{z}_t \quad \text{when} \quad t = 2, \ldots p, \, p \geq 2 \qquad \text{(Equation 13.5)}$$

$$\mathbf{f}_t = \sum_{\ell=1}^{p} \mathbf{A}_\ell \mathbf{f}_{t-\ell} + \mathbf{z}_t \qquad \text{when} \quad t = p+1, \ldots T$$

where

$$\mathbf{x}_1 = \mathbf{A}_1 \mathbf{f}_0 + \mathbf{A}_2 \mathbf{f}_{-1} + \cdots + \mathbf{A}_p \mathbf{f}_{1-p}$$

$$\mathbf{x}_2 = \mathbf{A}_2 \mathbf{f}_0 + \mathbf{A}_3 \mathbf{f}_{-1} + \cdots + \mathbf{A}_p \mathbf{f}_{2-p}$$

$$\qquad \text{(Equation 13.6)}$$

or, in general,

$$\mathbf{x}_t = \sum_{\ell=t}^{p} \mathbf{A}_\ell \mathbf{f}_{t-\ell}, \quad t = 1, \ldots, p. \qquad \text{(Equation 13.7)}$$

Thus $\mathbf{x}_1$ encapsulates the effect of the preceding time series on the first factor vector $\mathbf{f}_1$, $\mathbf{x}_2$ its effect on the second factor vector $\mathbf{f}_2$ and, in general, $\mathbf{x}_t$, $t \leq p$, its effect on the tth factor vector, $\mathbf{f}_t$. Factor $\mathbf{f}_{p+1}$ and subsequent factors are not directly affected by the time series that precedes the first time point. The $pk \times 1$

vector

$$\mathbf{x} = \begin{bmatrix} \mathbf{x}_1 \\ \mathbf{x}_2 \\ \vdots \\ \mathbf{x}_p \end{bmatrix}$$

is known as an initial state[1] vector (du Toit & Browne, 2001, p. 284.)

The covariance matrix of the initial state vector,

$$\underset{pk \times pk}{\mathbf{\Theta}} = \text{Cov}\left(\mathbf{x}, \mathbf{x}'\right) = \begin{bmatrix} \mathbf{\Theta}_{11} & \mathbf{\Theta}_{12} & \cdots & \mathbf{\Theta}_{1p} \\ \mathbf{\Theta}_{21} & \mathbf{\Theta}_{22} & \cdots & \mathbf{\Theta}_{2p} \\ \vdots & \vdots & & \ddots \\ \mathbf{\Theta}_{p1} & \mathbf{\Theta}_{p2} & & \mathbf{\Theta}_{pp} \end{bmatrix}, \text{ where } \mathbf{\Theta}_{ij} = \text{Cov}\left(\mathbf{x}_i, \mathbf{x}'_j\right),$$

(Equation 13.8)

influences the implied covariance structure of the endogenous vector variates, $\mathbf{f}_t$. If stationarity is assumed, this initial state covariance matrix, $\mathbf{\Theta}$, is a function, $\mathbf{\Theta}\left(\mathbf{A}_1, \ldots, \mathbf{A}_p, \mathbf{\Psi}\right)$, of the parameters of the latent time series (du Toit & Browne, 2001). This function is defined by

$$\text{vec}\left(\mathbf{\Theta}\right) = \left(\mathbf{I} - \mathbf{A} \otimes \mathbf{A}\right)^{-1} \text{vec}\left(\mathbf{G}\mathbf{\Psi}\mathbf{G}'\right) \qquad \text{(Equation 13.9)}$$

where vec($\mathbf{\Theta}$) is a $p^2k^2 \times 1$ vector formed by stacking (e.g., Harville, 1997, pp. 339–340) columns of the $pk \times pk$ matrix $\mathbf{\Theta}$, $\otimes$ stands for the Kronecker product (e.g., Harville, 1997, p. 133) of two matrices, and the two matrices

$$\mathbf{A} = \left[\begin{array}{c|cccc} \mathbf{A}_1 & \mathbf{I} & \mathbf{0} & \cdots & \mathbf{0} \\ \mathbf{A}_2 & \mathbf{0} & \mathbf{I} & \cdots & \mathbf{0} \\ \vdots & \vdots & \vdots & \ddots & \vdots \\ \mathbf{A}_{p-1} & \mathbf{0} & \mathbf{0} & \cdots & \mathbf{I} \\ \mathbf{A}_p & \mathbf{0} & \mathbf{0} & \cdots & \mathbf{0} \end{array}\right] \text{ and } \mathbf{G} = \begin{bmatrix} \mathbf{A}_1 \\ \mathbf{A}_2 \\ \vdots \\ \mathbf{A}_{p-1} \\ \mathbf{A}_p \end{bmatrix} \qquad \text{(Equation 13.10)}$$

are functions of the autoregressive weights. The $pk \times pk$ matrix $\mathbf{\Theta}$ is reconstituted from the elements of the $(pk)^2 \times 1$ vector, vec($\mathbf{\Theta}$), after it has been calculated using Equation 13.9.

A path diagram of a stationary PFA$(2, 0)$ model with six manifest variables and two factors is shown in Figure 13–1. Standard path diagram conventions are used. Manifest variables are represented by rectangles and latent variables by circles. Regression weights (factor loadings or autoregressive coefficients) are represented by unidirectional arrows. Bidirectional arrows stand for variances or covariances.

---

[1]This state vector is associated with a particular state-space representation of a VAR(p) time series. Other state–space representations of the same time series exist together with different state vectors.

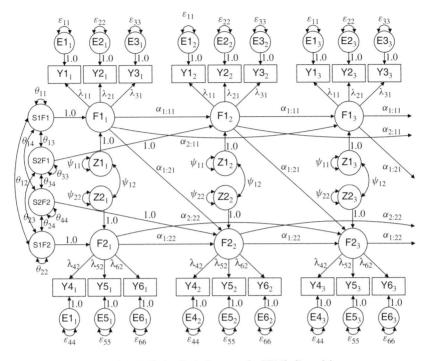

FIGURE 13–1.   Path diagram of a PFA(2, 0) model.

The six manifest variables are named Y1, Y2, . . . ,Y6. Subscripts, for example, $Y1_2$, indicate the time, $t = 2$, of measurement. A measurement error associated with variable $Y1_2$ is represented by $E1_2$. The two factors are represented by F1 and F2. A random shock associated with $F1_2$ is represented by $Z1_2$.

In order to avoid many intersecting lines in the path diagram, a confirmatory PFA(2, 0) model is shown with some parameters restricted to be zero, despite the fact that this chapter is concerned primarily with exploratory dynamic factor analysis.

In matrix notation the factor analysis part of the model depicted in Figure 13–1 is

$$\mathbf{y}_t = \boldsymbol{\mu} + \boldsymbol{\Lambda}\mathbf{f}_t + \mathbf{e}_t, \quad t = 1, 2, 3, \ldots$$

where

$$\boldsymbol{\Lambda} = \begin{bmatrix} \lambda_{11} & 0 \\ \lambda_{21} & 0 \\ \lambda_{31} & 0 \\ 0 & \lambda_{32} \\ 0 & \lambda_{42} \\ 0 & \lambda_{52} \end{bmatrix}$$

and $\mathrm{Var}(e_{tt}) = \varepsilon_{tt}$, $t = 1, \ldots, 6$. The time series part of the model in Figure 13–1 is

$$\mathbf{f}_t = \mathbf{A}_1 \mathbf{f}_{t-1} + \mathbf{A}_2 \mathbf{f}_{t-2} + \mathbf{z}_t, \quad t = 1, 2, 3, \ldots$$

where

$$\mathbf{A}_1 = \begin{bmatrix} \alpha_{1:11} & 0 \\ \alpha_{1:21} & \alpha_{1:22} \end{bmatrix}, \quad \mathbf{A}_2 = \begin{bmatrix} \alpha_{2:11} & 0 \\ 0 & \alpha_{2:22} \end{bmatrix},$$

$$\mathrm{Cov}\left(\mathbf{z}_t, \mathbf{z}_t'\right) = \mathbf{\Psi} = \begin{bmatrix} \psi_{11} & \psi_{12} \\ \psi_{12} & \psi_{22} \end{bmatrix}.$$

Zero elements of $\mathbf{\Lambda}$, $\mathbf{A}_1$, $\mathbf{A}_2$ represent parameters constrained to be zero with no associated paths in the path diagram. Nonzero elements appear as labels of single headed arrows indicating directional influences in Figure 13–1. This path diagram shows that factor loadings, λ_{ij}, error variances, ε_{ii}, autoregressive weights, $\alpha_{i:jk}$, and shock variances and covariances, ψ_{ij}, remain constant as time, t, varies. Although the measurement errors, E, and random shocks, Z, in the path diagram appear to be similar, there is an important difference (Browne & Nesselroade, 2005, pp. 419, 442–423). The measurement error EI_1, influences YI_1 and has no influence on any other variable in the diagram. On the other hand, the random shock, ZI_1, not only directly influences FI_1 but indirectly influences the process thereafter; ZI_1 has an indirect influence on FI_2, FI_3 and subsequent terms.

The effects of the initial state vector

$$\mathbf{x} = \begin{bmatrix} \mathbf{x}_1 \\ \mathbf{x}_2 \end{bmatrix} = \begin{bmatrix} x_1 \\ x_2 \\ x_3 \\ x_4 \end{bmatrix} = \begin{bmatrix} \mathrm{S1F1} \\ \mathrm{S1F2} \\ \mathrm{S2F1} \\ \mathrm{S2F2} \end{bmatrix} \qquad \text{(Equation 13.11)}$$

are shown prior to $t = 1$ in Figure 13–1. In order to minimize the crossing of paths, the order of state variables in the figure differs from that in Equation 13.11.

There are two state subvectors, $\mathbf{x}_1$ and $\mathbf{x}_2$, because the order of the autoregressive process is $p = 2$. Each has two elements because there are $k = 2$ factors. The two elements of $\mathbf{x}_1$ are labeled $\mathrm{S1F1}$ (State 1 Factor 1) and $\mathrm{S1F2}$ in Figure 13–1 and influence the latent time series at $t = 1$. The two elements of $\mathbf{x}_2$, $\mathrm{S2F1}$ and $\mathrm{S2F2}$, influence the latent time series at $t = 2$. Elements of the initial state covariance matrix

$$\mathrm{Cov}\left(\mathbf{x}, \mathbf{x}'\right) = \mathbf{\Theta} = \begin{bmatrix} \mathbf{\Theta}_{11} & \mathbf{\Theta}_{12} \\ \mathbf{\Theta}_{21} & \mathbf{\Theta}_{22} \end{bmatrix} = \left[\begin{array}{cc|cc} \theta_{11} & \theta_{12} & \theta_{13} & \theta_{14} \\ \theta_{21} & \theta_{22} & \theta_{23} & \theta_{24} \\ \hline \theta_{31} & \theta_{32} & \theta_{33} & \theta_{34} \\ \theta_{41} & \theta_{42} & \theta_{43} & \theta_{44} \end{array} \right]$$

represent variances and covariances of initial state variables and are used to label two-headed arrows in the initial state part of the model on the left of the path diagram in Figure 13–1.

The current model in Figure 13–1 is related to an earlier model suggested by Nesselroade et al. (2002, Figure 9.2), but the two models are not equivalent. The difference is that the earlier model made allowances for the direct influence of the $p = 2$ time points preceding the first observation, whereas the current model uses initial state variables to encapsulate both direct and indirect effects from the infinity of preceding time points. This makes a stationary latent process possible. Although both the earlier model and the current model are fitted to autocorrelation matrices, the methods used for estimating parameters differ substantially.

The Manifest Variable Autocorrelation Structure Implied by the PFA$(p, 0)$ Model

The model defined by Equation 13.2 and Equation 13.3 implies the following structure for the manifest variable autocovariance matrices, $\text{Cov}(\mathbf{y}_{t+\ell}, \mathbf{y}_t')$, $\ell = 0, 1, 2, \ldots$:

$$\text{Cov}\left(\mathbf{y}_{t+\ell}, \mathbf{y}_t'\right) = \begin{cases} \boldsymbol{\Lambda} \text{Cov}\left(\mathbf{f}_{t+\ell}, \mathbf{f}_t'\right) \boldsymbol{\Lambda}' + \mathbf{D}_\varepsilon, & \ell = 0 \\ \boldsymbol{\Lambda} \text{Cov}\left(\mathbf{f}_{t+\ell}, \mathbf{f}_t'\right) \boldsymbol{\Lambda}', & 1 \le \ell \le L \end{cases} \qquad \text{(Equation 13.12)}$$

where L is the maximum lag to be employed[2] with $p \le L \le T - p$. We assume that the latent time series in Equation 13.4 is covariance stationary:

$$\text{Cov}\left(\mathbf{f}_{t+\ell}, \mathbf{f}_t'\right) = \boldsymbol{\Phi}_\ell \quad \ell = 0, 1, 2, \ldots, \quad -\infty \le t < \infty, \qquad \text{(Equation 13.13)}$$

so that $\text{Cov}\left(\mathbf{f}_{t+\ell}, \mathbf{f}_t'\right)$ remains the same at all possible t. The autocovariance structure in Equation 13.12 then becomes

$$\begin{aligned} \boldsymbol{\Sigma}_0 &= \text{Cov}\left(\mathbf{y}_t, \mathbf{y}_t'\right) = \boldsymbol{\Lambda} \boldsymbol{\Phi}_0 \boldsymbol{\Lambda}' + \mathbf{D}_\varepsilon, & \ell = 0 \\ \boldsymbol{\Sigma}_\ell &= \text{Cov}\left(\mathbf{y}_{t+\ell}, \mathbf{y}_t'\right) = \boldsymbol{\Lambda} \boldsymbol{\Phi}_\ell \boldsymbol{\Lambda}', & 1 \le \ell \le L \end{aligned} \qquad \text{(Equation 13.14)}$$

so that the manifest time series implied by the latent time series is also covariance stationary.

The requirement of covariance stationarity of the latent time series in Equation 13.13 is essential for the autocovariance structure in Equation 13.14 to be appropriate. This will be true when (Hamilton, 1994, Proposition 10.1) the largest modulus

---

[2]Lags from $0, \ldots, p$ only will be used for estimation. Lags $> p$ will be used for fit assessment only.

of a complex eigenvalue, $\lambda_i(\mathbf{A})$, $i = 1, \ldots, kp$, of the square nonsymmetric matrix $\mathbf{A}$ in Equation 13.10 is less than one:

$$\max\{|\lambda_i(\mathbf{A})|\} < 1. \qquad \text{(Equation 13.15)}$$

The autocovariance structure in Equation 13.14, will not be valid, even if the data model in Equation 13.2 and Equation 13.4 is true, if the autoregressive weight matrices, $\mathbf{A}_1, \ldots, \mathbf{A}_p$ yield a matrix $\mathbf{A}$ that that does not satisfy the stationarity condition in Equation 13.15. Consequently it is advisable to verify that the inequality in Equation 13.15 is satisfied by estimated autoregressive coefficients whenever the PFA$(p, 0)$ model is fitted.

As is the case in the standard exploratory factor analysis model, the exploratory PFA model is invariant under changes of scale.[3] Consequently the covariance matrices, $\boldsymbol{\Sigma}_\ell$, in Equation 13.14 may be replaced by correlation matrices, $\mathbf{P}_\ell$, without loss of generality. In the standard factor analysis model, the factor covariance matrix is constrained to have unit diagonals for identification purposes so that the factor covariance matrix and factor correlation matrix coincide. Similar identification conditions are also appropriate in the exploratory PFA model where no restrictions are imposed either on the shock covariance matrix, $\boldsymbol{\Psi}$, (beyond symmetry) or on the autoregressive weight matrices, $\mathbf{A}_\ell$, in Equation 13.5. Diagonal elements of the lag zero covariance matrix, $\boldsymbol{\Phi}_0$, are constrained to be equal to one for identification purposes so that it is a correlation matrix and the elements of the square nonsymmetric matrices $\boldsymbol{\Phi}_\ell$, $\ell = 1, 2, \ldots$, are autocorrelation coefficients. The manifest variable autocorrelation structure implied by the exploratory PFA$(p, 0)$ model then is

$$\begin{aligned}
\mathbf{P}_0 &= \operatorname{Corr}\left(\mathbf{y}_t, \mathbf{y}_t'\right) = \boldsymbol{\Lambda}\boldsymbol{\Phi}_0\boldsymbol{\Lambda}' + \mathbf{D}_\varepsilon, \quad \ell = 0 \\
\mathbf{P}_\ell &= \operatorname{Corr}\left(\mathbf{y}_{t+\ell}, \mathbf{y}_t'\right) = \boldsymbol{\Lambda}\boldsymbol{\Phi}_\ell\boldsymbol{\Lambda}', \quad \ell = 1, 2, \ldots L,
\end{aligned} \qquad \text{(Equation 13.16)}$$

noting that $\boldsymbol{\Lambda}$ and $\mathbf{D}_\psi$ do not have the same values in Equation 13.14 and Equation 13.16. The remainder of this chapter is concerned only with the autocorrelation structure in Equation 13.16 so that no confusion will result.

The Latent Variable Autocorrelation Structure Implied by the PFA$(p, 0)$ Model

For Equation 13.16 to represent a fully specified manifest variable autocorrelation structure, the latent variable autocorrelation structure is required, that is, the autocorrelation matrices $\boldsymbol{\Phi}_\ell$, $\ell = 0, \ldots, L$, need to be expressed as functions of the shock covariance matrix, $\boldsymbol{\Psi}$, and the autoregressive weight matrices, $\mathbf{A}_1, \ldots, \mathbf{A}_p$.

---

[3]If the manifest variable vector, $\mathbf{y}_t$, is rescaled to $\mathbf{D}\mathbf{y}_t$, where $\mathbf{D}$ is diagonal with non-null diagonal elements, free elements of $\boldsymbol{\Lambda}$ and $\mathbf{D}_\varepsilon$ in Equation 13.14 change in value but the fit of the model is not affected.

A result for the covariance matrix of a stationary VARMA time series given by du Toit and Browne (2001) will now be adapted for this purpose.

Let $L^+ = L + 1$ be the number of distinct lags considered, including lag 0, and let

$$\mathbf{f} = \begin{bmatrix} \mathbf{f}_1 \\ \mathbf{f}_2 \\ \mathbf{f}_3 \\ \vdots \end{bmatrix}$$

be the $L^+ k \times 1$ vector formed by stacking L^+ factor vectors. Then the correlation matrix of $\mathbf{f}$ is the symmetric block Toeplitz matrix

$$\underset{L^+k \times L^+k}{\boldsymbol{\Phi}} = \text{Corr}\left(\mathbf{f}, \mathbf{f}'\right) = \begin{bmatrix} \boldsymbol{\Phi}_0 & \boldsymbol{\Phi}_1' & \boldsymbol{\Phi}_2' & \cdots \\ \boldsymbol{\Phi}_1 & \boldsymbol{\Phi}_0 & \boldsymbol{\Phi}_1' & \ddots \\ \boldsymbol{\Phi}_2 & \boldsymbol{\Phi}_1 & \boldsymbol{\Phi}_0 & \ddots \\ \vdots & \ddots & \ddots & \ddots \end{bmatrix} \qquad \text{(Equation 13.17)}$$

because the stationarity requirement in Equation 13.13 implies that if $i \geq t$ and $\ell = i - t$ then

$$\text{Corr}\left(\mathbf{f}_i, \mathbf{f}_t'\right) = \text{Corr}\left(\mathbf{f}_{t+\ell}, \mathbf{f}_t'\right) = \boldsymbol{\Phi}_\ell \quad \text{and} \quad \text{Corr}\left(\mathbf{f}_t, \mathbf{f}_i'\right) = \text{Corr}\left(\mathbf{f}_t, \mathbf{f}_{t+\ell}'\right) = \boldsymbol{\Phi}_\ell'.$$

The first block column of $\boldsymbol{\Phi}$ will therefore provide the L^+ required $k \times k$ autocorrelation matrices $\boldsymbol{\Phi}_0, \boldsymbol{\Phi}_1, \dots, \boldsymbol{\Phi}_L$ for the latent time series. Some additional notation will be required to express $\boldsymbol{\Phi}$ as a function of the time series parameters. Let

$$\mathbf{T}_{-A} = \begin{bmatrix} \mathbf{I}_k & \mathbf{0} & \mathbf{0} & \cdots \\ -\mathbf{A}_1 & \mathbf{I}_k & \mathbf{0} & \ddots \\ -\mathbf{A}_2 & -\mathbf{A}_1 & \mathbf{I}_k & \ddots \\ \vdots & \ddots & \ddots & \ddots \end{bmatrix}$$

be the lower triangular block Toeplitz matrix formed from the negative autoregressive weight matrices, with inverse[4]

$$\mathbf{T}_C = \mathbf{T}_{-A}^{-1} = \begin{bmatrix} \mathbf{I}_k & \mathbf{0} & \mathbf{0} & \cdots \\ \mathbf{C}_1 & \mathbf{I}_k & \mathbf{0} & \ddots \\ \mathbf{C}_2 & \mathbf{C}_1 & \mathbf{I}_k & \ddots \\ \vdots & \ddots & \ddots & \ddots \end{bmatrix}.$$

---

[4] All blocks below $-\mathbf{A}_p$ in any block column of $\mathbf{T}_{-A}$ are null. This does not apply to $\mathbf{T}_C$.

Also let

$$\underset{L^+k \times L^+k}{\mathbf{\Theta}^*} = \begin{bmatrix} \mathbf{\Theta} & \mathbf{0} \\ \mathbf{0} & \mathbf{0} \end{bmatrix}$$

be the $pk \times pk$ initial state covariance matrix, $\mathbf{\Theta}$, defined by Equation 13.9 after augmentation by null matrices to yield a $L^+k \times L^+k$ matrix. The required expression for $\mathbf{\Phi}$ now is (cf. du Toit and Browne, 2001, Equation 14.9)

$$\underset{L^+k \times L^+k}{\mathbf{\Phi}} = \mathbf{T_C} \left(\mathbf{\Theta}^* + \mathbf{I}_{L^+} \otimes \mathbf{\Psi} \right) \mathbf{T'_C} . \qquad \text{(Equation 13.18)}$$

Simplification of the first block column of $\mathbf{\Phi}$ shows that the autocorrelation function of the latent time series is

$$\begin{bmatrix} \mathbf{\Phi}_0 \\ \mathbf{\Phi}_1 \\ \mathbf{\Phi}_2 \\ \mathbf{\Phi}_3 \\ \vdots \end{bmatrix} = \begin{bmatrix} \mathbf{I_k} & \mathbf{0} & \mathbf{0} \\ \mathbf{C}_1 & \mathbf{I_k} & \mathbf{0} \\ \mathbf{C}_2 & \mathbf{C}_1 & \mathbf{I_k} \\ \mathbf{C}_3 & \mathbf{C}_2 & \mathbf{C}_1 \\ \vdots & \ddots & \ddots \end{bmatrix} \begin{bmatrix} \mathbf{\Theta}_{11} + \mathbf{\Psi} \\ \mathbf{\Theta}_{21} \\ \mathbf{\Theta}_{31} \end{bmatrix}$$

when $p = 3$. In general

$$\mathbf{\Phi}_0 = \mathbf{\Theta}_{11} + \mathbf{\Psi} \qquad \text{(Equation 13.19)}$$

and[5]

$$\mathbf{\Phi}_\ell = \sum_{j=0}^{\min(\ell,p)} \mathbf{C}_{\ell-j} \left(\mathbf{\Theta}_{j+1,1} + \delta_{j,0}\mathbf{\Psi} \right), \quad \ell = 1, 2, \dots L, \qquad \text{(Equation 13.20)}$$

where $\delta_{j,0} = 1$ when $j = 0$, $\delta_{j,0} = 0$ otherwise, and $\mathbf{C}_0 = \mathbf{I}_k$.

Decomposition of the Implied Factor Correlation Matrix, $\mathbf{\Phi}_0$

Equation 13.19 is important because it contains information about the relative contribution of the preceding time series and the current shocks to factor variances and covariances.

To show this it is convenient to express the latent time series model in Equation 13.4 as

$$\mathbf{f}_t = \widetilde{\mathbf{f}}_t + \mathbf{z}_t \qquad \text{(Equation 13.21)}$$

---

[5]Only the first block column of $\mathbf{\Theta}$ in Equation 13.8 is required for this expression. Alternative expressions for the lagged correlation matrices, $\mathbf{\Phi}_\ell$, that involve other block columns of $\mathbf{\Theta}$ may be derived by considering block columns of $\mathbf{\Phi}$ after the first, but they are less straightforward.

where

$$\widetilde{\mathbf{f}}_t = \sum_{i=1}^{p} \mathbf{A}_i \mathbf{f}_{t-i} \qquad \text{(Equation 13.22)}$$

is the prediction of $\mathbf{f}_t$ from the preceding terms, $\mathbf{f}_{t-i}$, in the time series and the shock vector, $\mathbf{z}_t$, represents current influences on $\mathbf{f}_t$, at time t. Thus Equation 13.21 decomposes the factor vector into a predicted value from preceding variables and a current shock in a manner similar to linear regression.

Comparison of Equation 13.22 with Equation 13.6 shows that at time $t = 1$, $\widetilde{\mathbf{f}}_1$ and the initial state variable x_1 are the same. Stationarity implies that

$$\text{Cov}(\widetilde{\mathbf{f}}_t, \widetilde{\mathbf{f}}_t') = \text{Cov}(\widetilde{\mathbf{f}}_1, \widetilde{\mathbf{f}}_1') = \mathbf{\Theta}_{11} \text{ for all } t.$$

Thus another perspective on Equation 13.19 is that it decomposes $\mathbf{\Phi}_0 = \text{Corr}$ $(\mathbf{f}_t, \mathbf{f}_t') = \text{Cov}(\mathbf{f}_t, \mathbf{f}_t')$ into the sum of $\mathbf{\Theta}_{11} = \text{Cov}(\widetilde{\mathbf{f}}_t, \widetilde{\mathbf{f}}_t')$ and $\mathbf{\Psi} = \text{Cov}(\mathbf{z}_t, \mathbf{z}_t')$. The relative influence of the previous state of the process represented by $\widetilde{\mathbf{f}}_t$ and an independently distributed random shock, $\mathbf{z}_t$, in determining $\mathbf{f}_t$ may be evaluated by comparing these covariance matrices. The factor correlations in $\mathbf{\Phi}_0$ will be determined predominantly by the preceding part of the process when the elements of $\mathbf{\Theta}_{11}$ are large, and by the covariances among random shocks when the elements of $\mathbf{\Theta}_{11}$ are near zero. In particular, the diagonal elements of $\mathbf{\Theta}_{11}$,

$$[\mathbf{\Theta}_{11}]_{ii} = \frac{\text{Var}\left([\widetilde{\mathbf{f}}_t]_i\right)}{\text{Var}\left([\mathbf{f}_t]_i\right)} = \text{Corr}^2\left([\mathbf{f}_t]_i, [\widetilde{\mathbf{f}}_t]_i\right) \qquad \text{(Equation 13.23)}$$

are squared multiple correlations (coefficients of determination) analogous to the squared multiple correlations of linear regression and communalities of factor analysis. They are bounded below by 0 and above by 1 and reveal the proportion of variance in a factor at time t explained by the process before time t. If $[\mathbf{\Theta}_{11}]_{ii} = 0$ the i-th factor $[\mathbf{f}_t]_i$ is uncorrelated across time and is equal to the corresponding latent shock $[\mathbf{z}_t]_i$. If $[\mathbf{\Theta}_{11}]_{ii} = 1$ the i-th factor $[\mathbf{f}_t]_i$ is perfectly predictable from the preceding process and the shock term $[\mathbf{z}_t]_i$ is null. The latent time series will not be stationary.

PARAMETER ESTIMATION

The method that is used to estimate parameters in the PFA$(p, 0)$ model is an extension of Cattell's P technique. Factor analysis model parameters are estimated from the lag 0 manifest variable correlation matrix as is done in the P technique. The factor matrix is rotated obliquely to simple structure yielding a rotated factor matrix and associated lag 0 factor correlation matrix. In the extension, the factor autocorrelation matrices, at lag 1 or more, are estimated from the corresponding manifest variable autocorrelation matrices and the previously obtained factor matrix. Using the multivariate extension of the Yule–Walker method the factor autocorrelation matrices are then transformed into autoregressive weight matrices for the latent time series.

For clarity, the estimation process is broken down into stages in the following description.

Stage A: Estimation of Manifest Variable Autocorrelation Matrices.   Sample autocovariance matrices, are computed using

$$\mathbf{S}_\ell = \frac{1}{T} \sum_{t=1}^{T-\ell} (\mathbf{y}_{t+\ell} - \bar{\mathbf{y}})(\mathbf{y}_t - \bar{\mathbf{y}})', \quad \ell = 0, \ldots, p \qquad \text{(Equation 13.24)}$$

where L is the maximum lag to be employed with $p \le L \le T - p$ and

$$\bar{\mathbf{y}} = \frac{1}{T} \sum_{t=1}^{T} \mathbf{y}_t$$

The corresponding sample autocorrelation matrices are

$$\mathbf{S}_\ell = \mathrm{Diag}^{-\frac{1}{2}}[\mathbf{S}_0]\, \mathbf{S}_\ell\, \mathrm{Diag}^{-\frac{1}{2}}[\mathbf{S}_0], \quad \ell = 0, \ldots, p, \qquad \text{(Equation 13.25)}$$

where $\mathrm{Diag}[\mathbf{S}_0]$ represents the diagonal matrix formed from the diagonal elements of $\mathbf{S}_0$. Although use of the same divisor, T, in Equation 13.24 for lagged covariance matrices, $\mathbf{S}_\ell$, involving the summation of different numbers of terms is somewhat counterintuitive, this ensures (Brockwell & Davis, 1991, Proposition 5.2.1) a nonnegative definite block Toeplitz correlation matrix

$$\mathbf{R} = \widehat{\mathrm{Corr}}(\mathbf{y}, \mathbf{y}') = \begin{bmatrix} \mathbf{R}_0 & \mathbf{R}_1' & \mathbf{R}_2' & \cdots & \mathbf{R}_L' \\ \mathbf{R}_1 & \mathbf{R}_0 & \mathbf{R}_1' & \cdots & \mathbf{R}_{L-1}' \\ \mathbf{R}_2 & \mathbf{R}_1 & \mathbf{R}_0 & \cdots & \mathbf{R}_{L-2}' \\ \vdots & \vdots & \vdots & \ddots & \vdots \\ \mathbf{R}_L & \mathbf{R}_{L-1} & \mathbf{R}_{L-2} & \cdots & \mathbf{R}_0 \end{bmatrix} \qquad \text{(Equation 13.26)}$$

where

$$\mathbf{y} = \begin{bmatrix} \mathbf{y}_1 \\ \mathbf{y}_2 \\ \mathbf{y}_3 \\ \vdots \\ \mathbf{y}_{L^+} \end{bmatrix},$$

represents L^+ consecutive observations on the battery of tests. This correlation matrix is a sample estimate of the population correlation matrix of $\mathbf{y}$ and consequently must be nonnegative definite to be admissible.

The sample autocorrelation matrices, $\widehat{\mathbf{R}}_\ell$, in Equation 13.25 are estimates of population autocorrelation matrices, $\mathbf{P}_\ell$ in Equation 13.16, under the saturated model.

Stage B: Estimation of the Factor Matrix Λ, Error Covariance Matrix, $\mathbf{D}_\varepsilon$, and Lag 0 Factor Correlation Matrix, Φ_0.

The structure for the population lag 0 correlation matrix, $\mathbf{P}_0$, in Equation 13.16 is fitted to $\mathbf{R}_0$ to obtain estimates of the factor analysis parameters without yet assuming a latent time series. Since $\mathbf{S}_0$, defined in Equation 13.24 with $\ell = 0$, will not have a Wishart distribution because the $\mathbf{y}_t$ are not independently distributed, maximum Wishart likelihood estimates are not justified. Rather, the simple and robust (Briggs & MacCallum, 2003; MacCallum, Tucker, & Briggs, 2001) ordinary least squares (OLS) approach is used. This involves minimizing the sum of squared residuals, $\mathrm{tr}\!\left[\left(\mathbf{R}_0 - \Lambda^*\Lambda^{*\prime} - \mathbf{D}_\varepsilon\right)^2\right]$, to provide OLS estimates $\widehat{\mathbf{D}}_\varepsilon$ and $\widehat{\Lambda}^*$. The iterative principal factor method could be used for this purpose but the nested Newton–Raphson algorithm for OLS estimation, described by Jöreskog (1977), is computationally more efficient. An oblique rotation is carried out on $\widehat{\Lambda}^*$ to yield a rotated factor matrix, $\widehat{\Lambda}$, and a lag 0 factor correlation matrix, $\widetilde{\Phi}_0$. A number of suitable rotation methods are available (cf. Browne, 2001). If interest is centered on the extent to which various intraindividual factor patterns differ from an interindividual factor pattern an oblique rotation to a partially specified target (e.g., Browne, 2001, pp. 123–125) is helpful. Each intraindividual factor matrix is rotated obliquely to the same target. A meaningful comparison of the ways individual factor patterns differ from the target is then possible.

This part of the analysis is Cattell's P technique, updated with modern computational methods. The extension that follows involves the inclusion of information from autocorrelation matrices to estimate autoregressive weight matrices.

Stage C: Estimation of the Factor Autocorrelation Matrices, Φ_ℓ, $\ell \geq 1$.

The rotated factor matrix, $\widehat{\Lambda}$, obtained in Stage B, is now regarded as fixed. Each factor autocorrelation matrix, Φ_ℓ, in the structure for the population lag ℓ manifest autocorrelation matrix, $\mathbf{P}_\ell$, in Equation 13.16 is estimated by OLS from the corresponding $\mathbf{R}_\ell$. Minimization of the residual sum of squares $\mathrm{tr}\!\left[\left(\mathbf{R}_\ell - \widehat{\Lambda}\Phi_\ell\widehat{\Lambda}'\right)\left(\mathbf{R}_\ell - \widehat{\Lambda}\Phi_\ell\widehat{\Lambda}'\right)'\right]$ with respect to Φ_ℓ, given $\widehat{\Lambda}$, yields the estimate

$$\widetilde{\Phi}_\ell = \left(\widehat{\Lambda}'\widehat{\Lambda}\right)^{-1}\widehat{\Lambda}'\mathbf{R}_\ell\widehat{\Lambda}\left(\widehat{\Lambda}'\widehat{\Lambda}\right)^{-1} \qquad \ell = 1, 2, \ldots, L \qquad \text{(Equation 13.27)}$$

The correlation matrix $\widetilde{\Phi}_0$ *obtained by oblique rotation* in Stage B is symmetric, but the $\widetilde{\Phi}_\ell$, $\ell \geq 1$, in Equation 13.27 are nonsymmetric. Notice that the manifest variable correlation structure in Equation 13.16 has been used on its own in obtaining $\widetilde{\Phi}_\ell$ *without any reference to the autocorrelation structure of a latent VAR(p) time series* given in Equation 13.20. The only assumption made about the latent time series is that it is stationary.

Although the block Toeplitz manifest variable correlation matrix **R** in Equation 13.26 is nonnegative definite, the corresponding estimate of the block Toeplitz latent variable correlation matrix $\widetilde{\mathbf{\Phi}}$

$$\widetilde{\mathbf{\Phi}} = \widehat{\mathrm{Corr}}\left(\mathbf{f}, \mathbf{f}'\right) = \begin{bmatrix} \widetilde{\mathbf{\Phi}}_0 & \widetilde{\mathbf{\Phi}}'_1 & \widetilde{\mathbf{\Phi}}'_2 & \cdots & \widetilde{\mathbf{\Phi}}'_L \\ \widetilde{\mathbf{\Phi}}_1 & \widetilde{\mathbf{\Phi}}_0 & \widetilde{\mathbf{\Phi}}'_1 & \cdots & \widetilde{\mathbf{\Phi}}'_{L-1} \\ \widetilde{\mathbf{\Phi}}_2 & \widetilde{\mathbf{\Phi}}_1 & \widetilde{\mathbf{\Phi}}_0 & \cdots & \widetilde{\mathbf{\Phi}}'_{L-2} \\ \vdots & \vdots & \vdots & \ddots & \vdots \\ \widetilde{\mathbf{\Phi}}_L & \widetilde{\mathbf{\Phi}}_{L-1} & \widetilde{\mathbf{\Phi}}_{L-2} & \cdots & \widetilde{\mathbf{\Phi}}_0 \end{bmatrix}, \qquad \text{(Equation 13.28)}$$

where

$$\mathbf{f} = \begin{bmatrix} \mathbf{f}_1 \\ \mathbf{f}_2 \\ \mathbf{f}_3 \\ \vdots \\ \mathbf{f}_{L+} \end{bmatrix},$$

can be indefinite. Because a correlation matrix must be nonnegative definite, it is advisable as an admissibility check to see whether the smallest eigenvalue of $\widetilde{\mathbf{\Phi}}$ is negative, implying that $\widetilde{\mathbf{\Phi}}$ is indefinite.

Some understanding of the reason why $\widetilde{\mathbf{\Phi}}$ can be indefinite may be gained by considering the following alternative expression for the lag 0 factor correlation matrix,

$$\widetilde{\mathbf{\Phi}}_0 = \left(\widehat{\mathbf{\Lambda}}'\widehat{\mathbf{\Lambda}}\right)^{-1} \widehat{\mathbf{\Lambda}}' \left(\mathbf{R}_0 - \widehat{\mathbf{D}}_\varepsilon\right) \widehat{\mathbf{\Lambda}} \left(\widehat{\mathbf{\Lambda}}'\widehat{\mathbf{\Lambda}}\right)^{-1}, \qquad \text{(Equation 13.29)}$$

which yields the same result obtained from the oblique rotation procedure in Stage B. Suppose that $\left(\mathbf{R}_0 - \widehat{\mathbf{D}}_\varepsilon\right)$ in Equation 13.29 were replaced by $\mathbf{R}_0$, as in Equation 13.27, to give

$$\widetilde{\mathbf{\Phi}}_0^+ = \left(\widehat{\mathbf{\Lambda}}'\widehat{\mathbf{\Lambda}}\right)^{-1} \widehat{\mathbf{\Lambda}}' \mathbf{R}_0 \widehat{\mathbf{\Lambda}} \left(\widehat{\mathbf{\Lambda}}'\widehat{\mathbf{\Lambda}}\right)^{-1}.$$

If $\widetilde{\mathbf{\Phi}}_0^+$ were substituted for $\widetilde{\mathbf{\Phi}}_0$ in Equation 13.28, the resulting $\widetilde{\mathbf{\Phi}}^+$ would be nonnegative definite because

$$\widetilde{\mathbf{\Phi}}^+ = \left(\mathbf{I}_L \otimes \left(\widehat{\mathbf{\Lambda}}'\widehat{\mathbf{\Lambda}}\right)^{-1} \widehat{\mathbf{\Lambda}}'\right) \mathbf{R} \left(\mathbf{I}_L \otimes \widehat{\mathbf{\Lambda}} \left(\widehat{\mathbf{\Lambda}}'\widehat{\mathbf{\Lambda}}\right)^{-1}\right).$$

Consequently any indefinite $\widetilde{\mathbf{\Phi}}$ would be due to the inclusion of $\widehat{\mathbf{D}}_\varepsilon$ in Equation 13.29.

Stage D: Transformation of Factor Autocorrelation Estimates to Time Series Parameter Estimates.   During this stage, the time series parameter estimates, $\widehat{\boldsymbol{\Psi}}$, $\widehat{\mathbf{A}}_1, \ldots, \widehat{\mathbf{A}}_p$ are obtained from the factor autocorrelation estimates up to lag p, $\widetilde{\boldsymbol{\Phi}}_0$, $\widetilde{\boldsymbol{\Phi}}_1, \ldots, \widetilde{\boldsymbol{\Phi}}_p$. Available estimates, $\widetilde{\boldsymbol{\Phi}}_\ell$, with $p < \ell \le L$ are disregarded at this stage, but may be used later in Stage F when model fit is assessed. Because the number of distinct time series parameters to be estimated is equal to the number of distinct autocorrelations, the process involves zero degrees of freedom. Consequently a transformation from one set of parameter estimates to another equivalent set of parameter estimates is being carried out.

The retained factor autocorrelation matrix estimates are transformed to autoregressive weight matrix estimates, $\widehat{\mathbf{A}}_1, \ldots, \widehat{\mathbf{A}}_p$, and a shock covariance matrix estimate, $\widehat{\boldsymbol{\Psi}}$, by using the multivariate Yule–Walker (e.g. Lütkepohl, 1993) procedure[6]:

$$
\begin{bmatrix} \widehat{\mathbf{A}}_1 & \widehat{\mathbf{A}}_2 & \widehat{\mathbf{A}}_3 & \cdots & \widehat{\mathbf{A}}_p \end{bmatrix} =
$$

$$
\begin{bmatrix} \widetilde{\boldsymbol{\Phi}}_1 & \widetilde{\boldsymbol{\Phi}}_2 & \widetilde{\boldsymbol{\Phi}}_3 & \cdots & \widetilde{\boldsymbol{\Phi}}_p \end{bmatrix}
\begin{bmatrix}
\widetilde{\boldsymbol{\Phi}}_0 & \widetilde{\boldsymbol{\Phi}}_1 & \widetilde{\boldsymbol{\Phi}}_2 & \cdots & \widetilde{\boldsymbol{\Phi}}_{p-1} \\
\widetilde{\boldsymbol{\Phi}}_1' & \widetilde{\boldsymbol{\Phi}}_0 & \widetilde{\boldsymbol{\Phi}}_1 & \cdots & \widetilde{\boldsymbol{\Phi}}_{p-2} \\
\widetilde{\boldsymbol{\Phi}}_2' & \widetilde{\boldsymbol{\Phi}}_1' & \widetilde{\boldsymbol{\Phi}}_0 & \cdots & \widetilde{\boldsymbol{\Phi}}_{p-3} \\
\vdots & \vdots & \vdots & \ddots & \vdots \\
\widetilde{\boldsymbol{\Phi}}_{p-1}' & \widetilde{\boldsymbol{\Phi}}_{p-2}' & \widetilde{\boldsymbol{\Phi}}_{p-3}' & \cdots & \widetilde{\boldsymbol{\Phi}}_0
\end{bmatrix}^{-1}
$$

(Equation 13.30)

and

$$
\widehat{\boldsymbol{\Psi}} = \widetilde{\boldsymbol{\Phi}}_0 - \widehat{\mathbf{A}}_1 \widetilde{\boldsymbol{\Phi}}_1' - \widehat{\mathbf{A}}_2 \widetilde{\boldsymbol{\Phi}}_2' - \widehat{\mathbf{A}}_3 \widetilde{\boldsymbol{\Phi}}_3' - \cdots - \widehat{\mathbf{A}}_p \widetilde{\boldsymbol{\Phi}}_p' .
$$

(Equation 13.31)

It is advisable to verify that the autoregressive weight matrix estimates provided by Equation 13.30 satisfy the stationarity condition in Equation 13.15 and that the shock covariance matrix estimate provided by Equation 13.31 has no negative eigenvalues before interpreting the results of the analysis.

The key to the simplicity of the current estimation procedure is the use of a maximum lag of $\ell = p$ for the $\widetilde{\boldsymbol{\Phi}}_\ell$. A reparameterization is no longer possible if autocorrelation matrices, $\mathbf{R}_\ell$, with $\ell > p$ are to be used. Other more complicated iterative procedures are available for estimating the time series parameters immediately by OLS (Browne & Zhang, 2005), without an intermediate estimation of factor autocorrelations. These iterative procedures can employ sample autocorrelation matrices, $\mathbf{R}_\ell$, with lag $\ell > p$, thereby making use of more information from the data. In addition they are suitable for confirmatory dynamic factor analysis.

---

[6] A computationally efficient recursive algorithm for computing the same estimates has been given by Whittle (1963; also see Brockwell & Davis, 1991, Proposition 11.4.1.)

Stage E: Estimation of Implied Covariance Matrices.   After the parameter estimates $\widehat{\mathbf{A}}_1, \ldots, \widehat{\mathbf{A}}_p$ and $\widehat{\mathbf{\Psi}}$ have been obtained in Stage D, we require estimates of lagged factor covariance matrices, $\mathbf{\Phi}_\ell = \mathrm{Cov}(\mathbf{f}_{t+\ell}, \mathbf{f}_t')$, and the predicted-factor covariance matrix, $\mathbf{\Theta}_{11} = \mathrm{Cov}(\widetilde{\mathbf{f}}_t, \widetilde{\mathbf{f}}_t')$. These are functions of the time series parameters.

We consider general computing formulae for the estimates that are valid at any lag, ℓ, whether or not $\ell > p$. First of all estimates $\widehat{\mathbf{\Theta}}_{11}, \ldots, \widehat{\mathbf{\Theta}}_{p1}$ are obtained from Equation 13.9 and Equation 13.10 after the estimates $\widehat{\mathbf{A}}_1, \ldots, \widehat{\mathbf{A}}_p$ and $\widehat{\mathbf{\Psi}}$ have been substituted for population parameters. Estimates, $\widehat{\mathbf{\Phi}}_0, \ldots, \widehat{\mathbf{\Phi}}_p$, of the factor auto-correlation matrices are then obtained from Equations 13.19 and Equation 13.20.

When $\ell < p$, information from Stage C can be used in a simple manner to yield the same results (up to computer accuracy[7]) as those obtained using Equation 13.9 and Equation 13.19. We take

$$\widehat{\mathbf{\Phi}}_\ell = \widetilde{\mathbf{\Phi}}_\ell \quad \ell = 0, \ldots, p$$

where $\widetilde{\mathbf{\Phi}}_0$ is known from the rotation in Stage B and the $\widetilde{\mathbf{\Phi}}_\ell$, $\ell = 1, \ldots, p$, have been obtained in Stage C. The estimate of $\mathrm{Cov}(\widetilde{\mathbf{f}}_t, \widetilde{\mathbf{f}}_t')$ is given by

$$\widehat{\mathrm{Cov}}(\widetilde{\mathbf{f}}_t, \widetilde{\mathbf{f}}_t') = \widehat{\mathbf{\Theta}}_{11} = \widetilde{\mathbf{\Phi}}_0 - \widehat{\mathbf{\Psi}} \qquad \text{(Equation 13.32)}$$

As was discussed in the subsection titled "Decomposition of the Implied Factor Correlation Matrix," $\widehat{\mathbf{\Theta}}_{11}$ and $\widehat{\mathbf{\Psi}}$ provide important information concerning the relative strength of the contribution of the preceding time series and current random shocks to the factor variances and covariances. Further discussion is provided when the practical example is considered.

Stage F: Decomposition of Goodness of Fit.   A root mean square residual index may be used to assess fit of the PFA$(p, 0)$ model at each lag. This is defined as the square root of the ratio of the sum of squared residuals at lag ℓ and the number of residuals that are not zero by definition:

$$\mathrm{RMS}_0 = \sqrt{\frac{\mathrm{tr}\left[\left(\mathbf{R}_0 - \widehat{\mathbf{\Lambda}}\widehat{\mathbf{\Phi}}_0\widehat{\mathbf{\Lambda}}' - \widehat{\mathbf{D}}_\varepsilon\right)^2\right]}{n_v\,(n_{v-1})}},$$

$$\mathrm{RMS}_\ell = \sqrt{\frac{\mathrm{tr}\left[\left(\mathbf{R}_\ell - \widehat{\mathbf{\Lambda}}\widehat{\mathbf{\Phi}}_\ell\widehat{\mathbf{\Lambda}}'\right)\left(\mathbf{R}_\ell - \widehat{\mathbf{\Lambda}}\widehat{\mathbf{\Phi}}_\ell\widehat{\mathbf{\Lambda}}'\right)'\right]}{n_v^2}}, \quad \ell = 1, \ldots, L.$$

$$\text{(Equation 13.33)}$$

---

[7]A numerical verification showed that in the practical example with 30 variables, 5 factors and 90 time points, given in the next section, the values of elements of $\widehat{\mathbf{\Phi}}_\ell$, $\ell = 0, \ldots, p$, yielded by Equation 13.20 agreed with the $\widetilde{\mathbf{\Phi}}_\ell$ yielded by Equation 13.29 and Equation 13.27 to 8 decimal places.

The number of new free parameter estimates at a particular lag, ℓ, is defined to be the number of free parameters not estimated at a preceding lag. It follows that the number of new free parameters at lag 0 is the number of elements of $\widehat{\boldsymbol{\Phi}}$ plus the number of free elements of $\boldsymbol{\Lambda}$, corrected for rotational indeterminacy. The number of new free parameters at lags $1 \leq \ell \leq p$ is the number of elements of $\widetilde{\boldsymbol{\Phi}}_\ell$ defined by Equation 13.27. No new parameters are estimated at any lag $\ell > p$ and $\widehat{\boldsymbol{\Phi}}_\ell$ in Equation 13.20 is a function of estimates from preceding lags. The number of new free parameters estimated at each lag is

$\ell = 0$	$1 \leq \ell \leq p$	$p < \ell \leq L$
$n_v k - \frac{1}{2} k\,(k-1)$	k^2	0

The n_v error variances have not been included in the number of free parameters at $\ell = 0$ because they are perfectly predictable from the other parameter estimates,

$$\widehat{\mathbf{D}}_\varepsilon = \mathrm{Diag}\left[\mathbf{I} - \widehat{\boldsymbol{\Lambda}}\widehat{\boldsymbol{\Phi}}_0\widehat{\boldsymbol{\Lambda}}'\right],$$

and result in diagonal residuals being zero by definition and not counted for RMS_0. Because more parameters are estimated at lag 0 it can be expected that RMS_0 will be smaller than any RMS_ℓ, $\ell > 0$. Also, because no parameters are estimated at any $\ell > p$, it is to be expected that higher values of RMS_ℓ, $\ell > p$, will be obtained. Any RMS_ℓ, $\ell > p$, is not a fit index, but rather is a forward-validation index that measures how well parameter estimates obtained from lags $0, \ldots, p$ account for manifest variable autocorrelations at lag $\ell > p$.

Summary of the Parameter Estimation Procedure

A summary of the essential steps of the computational procedure follows. We assume that $L = p$ for simplicity:

- *Compute the sample* autocorrelation matrices $\mathbf{R}_0, \mathbf{R}_1, \ldots, \mathbf{R}_p$ using Equation 13.24 and Equation 13.25.
- *Apply a standard exploratory factor* analysis with oblique rotation to $\mathbf{R}_0$ to yield the factor matrix, $\widehat{\boldsymbol{\Lambda}}$, factor correlation matrix, $\widetilde{\boldsymbol{\Phi}}_0$ and error covariance matrix, $\widehat{\mathbf{D}}_\varepsilon$ (P-technique).
- *Compute* $\widetilde{\boldsymbol{\Phi}}_1, \cdots, \widetilde{\boldsymbol{\Phi}}_p$ using Equation 13.27.
- *Compute* $\widehat{\mathbf{A}}_1, \ldots, \widehat{\mathbf{A}}_p$ using Equation 13.30 and $\widehat{\boldsymbol{\Psi}}$ using Equation 13.31.
- *Compute* $\widehat{\boldsymbol{\Theta}}_{11}$ using Equation 13.32.
- *Calculate the root mean square measures* of model fit using Equation 13.33.

ILLUSTRATIVE EXAMPLE

In a well-planned study of similarities and differences between intraindividual and interindividual factor analyses of indicators of the Big Five personality factors, Borkenau and Ostendorf (1998) employed the general framework of Cattell's P technique. They used an interindividual factor analysis based on a large sample to select six marker variables for each of the five factors. These variables were 7-point ratings of adjectives that were judged to be suitable for interpretation not only as traits in the interindividual factor analysis, but also as states in an intraindividual factor analysis. The resulting 30-item scale was administered daily over 90 days to each of 22 subjects. A principal components analysis was carried out on each within-subject correlation matrix, $\mathbf{R}_0$. Each resulting 30×5 matrix of component loadings was rotated orthogonally to a least squares fit to a common fully speci-fied target. This target was derived, using a Varimax rotation, from the preceding interindividual investigation. Because a fully specified target was employed, the analysis provided information on metric invariance of factor matrices (cf. Millsap & Meredith, chap. 8, this volume).

The data from the first Borkenau–Ostendorf subject[8], referred to henceforth as B-O#1, are used here to provide an illustration of the present methodology for fitting a PFA(2, 0) model. Ways in which the present analysis differs from the original Borkenau–Ostendorf analysis are: (a) OLS factor analysis is employed; (b) Oblique rotation to a partially specified target is used thereby providing information on configural invariance of factor matrices (cf. Millsap & Meredith, chap 8, this volume); and (c) sample autocorrelation matrices, $\mathbf{R}_\ell$, $\ell \geq 1$, are used to estimate parameters in a latent time series.

Table 13–1 shows the obliquely rotated factor matrix, $\widehat{\mathbf{\Lambda}}$ and the error vari-ances. The pattern of the partially specified target was based on the interindividual factor matrix in Borkenau and Ostendorf (1998, Table 13–1). Loadings correspond-ing to unspecified target elements denoted by the symbol "?" (in Browne, 2001, pp. 123–125), are shown in bold face in our Table 13–1. Target elements for the remaining factor loadings were all specified to be equal to 0. The target therefore represented a perfect cluster solution with six marker variables, selected by Borke-nau and Ostendorf (1998), for each of the Big Five personality factors. Because the marker variable target elements were unspecified, neither the magnitude nor the sign of the corresponding elements (in boldface) of the rotated factor matrix, $\widehat{\mathbf{\Lambda}}$, were influenced by the choice of target.

Variable names and factor names in our Table 13–1 are the same, and in the same order, as in Borkenau and Ostendorf (1998, Table 13–1). In the intraindividual

---

[8]Another PFA(2, 0) analysis of the data from this subject is reported by Hamaker et al. (2005, Table 4) using a different estimation procedure. Results appear to differ substantially between their analysis and the current analysis.

TABLE 13–1

Factor Matrix After Oblique Target Rotation, and Error Variances

Variable	N	E	A	C	I	EV
Irritable	**.86**	−.16	.02	−.03	.10	.26
Bad-tempered	**.39**	.19	−.27	−.27	−.23	.41
Vulnerable	**.89**	−.25	−.01	−.09	.25	.23
Emotionally Stable	**−.73**	.20	.14	.04	.13	.25
Calm	**−.64**	.13	.35	−.23	.24	.34
Resistant	**−.72**	.06	.18	−.04	.07	.41
Dynamic	.11	**.67**	.31	.13	.00	.50
Sociable	−.37	**.35**	−.23	−.04	.32	.38
Lively	−.24	**.54**	−.17	.00	.20	.42
Shy	.47	**−.31**	.27	−.17	−.28	.28
Silent	.13	**−.69**	.05	.03	−.03	.45
Reserved	.26	**−.48**	.30	−.06	−.21	.40
Good-natured	−.06	.11	**.65**	.12	.11	.47
Helpful	.06	.15	**.49**	.41	−.11	.46
Considerate	−.18	−.34	**.07**	.51	.29	.34
Selfish	.30	.18	**−.39**	−.30	.00	.47
Domineering	.47	.32	**−.56**	.01	.04	.35
Obstinate	.23	.18	**−.64**	−.01	.16	.45
Industrious	.20	.52	.21	**.54**	−.03	.44
Persistent	−.24	−.09	−.36	**.70**	−.01	.44
Responsible	−.03	.04	.05	**.69**	−.11	.51
Lazy	−.23	−.08	−.38	**−.50**	−.14	.45
Reckless	−.13	.16	−.21	**−.63**	.08	.42
Changeable	.28	.12	−.30	**−.24**	−.36	.44
Witty	.00	.16	−.16	−.05	**.68**	.43
Knowledgeable	.11	−.11	.03	.03	**.82**	.42
Prudent	.16	.10	.11	.00	**.69**	.54
Unresourceful	.02	−.20	.12	.07	**−.66**	.42
Uninformed	.04	.05	−.04	−.12	**−.70**	.44
Unimaginative	.07	−.27	.03	.02	**−.66**	.33

Note. N = Neuroticism; E = Extraversion; A = Agreeableness; C = Conscientiousness; I = Intellect; EV = Error Variance. Factor loadings in bold face correspond to unspecified target elements. Remaining elements are required to be close to 0 in a least squares sense.

state factor analysis for B-O#1, there are five clearly defined factors. Factor names, originally intended for interindividual traits, seem reasonable for B-O#1 states, and most of the marker adjectives chosen for trait factors are appropriate for the corresponding B-O#1 state factor. In all five sets of intended marker variables, a pattern of three positive loadings followed by three negative loadings, that was observable in the Borkenau–Ostendorf trait factor analysis, also occurred in the present B-O#1 state factor analysis. This pattern occurred for each factor although no information about the signs of loadings was provided in the target. Some cases do occur, however, where a marker adjective intended for a particular interindividual trait factor is less appropriate for the corresponding B-O#1 state factor. For example:

- The adjective, *Considerate*, intended as a marker for the trait factor, *Agreeableness*, is inappropriate for the intended factor but is a reasonable marker for the B-O#1 state factor, *Conscientiousness*.
- The adjective, *Shy*, intended as a negative marker for the trait factor *Extraversion* is a stronger positive marker for the B-O#1 state factor *Neuroticism*.
- The adjectives, *Sociable* and *Selfish*, intended as markers for the trait factors *Extraversion* and *Agreeableness* respectively, are not clear markers for any of the B-O#1 state factors.

It is to be expected that a factor analysis of a battery of Likert items applied to a number of different individuals should differ somewhat from a factor analysis of the same battery of Likert items applied to one individual on a number of consecutive occasions. A factor analysis over a random sample of individuals investigates covariances between traits over individuals whereas a factor analysis of one individual's responses over time investigates covariances between states of that individual over occasions. A target rotation chooses the pattern of the intraindividual factor matrix to be as close as possible to the interindividual factor matrix, so that any differences that occur are unavoidable and truly present. On the other hand a blind analytic rotation procedure could move an intraindividual factor matrix away from the interindividual factor matrix and thereby introduce artifactual differences.

Error variance estimates are shown in the last column of Table 13–1. They lie between .23 and .54 so that there are no estimates on the lower bound of zero and none are unacceptably large.

The estimate of the lag 0 factor correlation/covariance matrix, Φ_0, is shown in Table 13–2. This correlation matrix is implied by the latent time series. There is a moderate negative correlation between factors *Neuroticism* and *Intellect* and a moderate positive correlation between *Agreeableness* and *Conscientiousness*. Other correlation coefficients are smaller in magnitude.

TABLE 13–2

Lag 0 Factor Correlation Matrix:
Correlation (f_t, f_t') $\forall t$

	N	*E*	*A*	*C*	*I*
N	1.00	−.10	.00	−.24	−.43
E	−.10	1.00	−.14	−.11	.27
A	.00	−.14	1.00	.39	−.02
C	−.24	−.11	.39	1.00	.21
I	−.43	.27	−.02	.21	1.00

Note. N = Neuroticism; E = Extraversion; A = Agreeableness; C = Conscientiousness; I = Intellect.

It is helpful to assess the relative contribution of the time series that precedes the current time point, $\tilde{\mathbf{f}}_t$, and the random shock at the time point, $\mathbf{z}_t$, to the current factor, $\mathbf{f}_t$, in the relationship (see Equation 13.21) $\mathbf{f}_t = \tilde{\mathbf{f}}_t + \mathbf{z}_t$. This may be accomplished by considering the corresponding relationship (see Equation 13.19) $\mathrm{Cov}(\mathbf{f}_t, \mathbf{f}_t') = \mathrm{Cov}(\tilde{\mathbf{f}}_t, \tilde{\mathbf{f}}_t') + \mathrm{Cov}(\mathbf{z}_t, \mathbf{z}_t')$.

The estimate $\hat{\boldsymbol{\Theta}}_{11}$ of $\mathrm{Cov}(\tilde{\mathbf{f}}_t, \tilde{\mathbf{f}}_t')$ is shown in Table 13–3. Each diagonal element is an estimate of a squared multiple correlation (coefficient of determination) and indicates the proportion of variation in a factor explained by the preceding time series (see Equation 13.23). The proportion of variation explained by the concurrent random shock is indicated by the corresponding diagonal element of the estimate, $\hat{\boldsymbol{\Psi}}$, of $\mathrm{Cov}(\mathbf{z}_t, \mathbf{z}_t')$ shown in Table 13–4. Comparison of diagonal elements of Tables 13–3 and Table 13–4 suggest that random shocks account primarily for the variation in the factors *Neuroticism, Extraversion, Conscientiousness* and *Intellect,* and that the preceding time series and the random shock account approximately equally for variation in *Agreeableness.* Also the moderate negative correlation between *Neuroticism* and *Intellect* and the moderate positive correlation between *Agreeableness* and *Conscientiousness* in Table 13–2 are both explained approximately equally by the preceding time series and the random shock. There is a noticeable tendency for the shock variance estimates in the diagonal of $\hat{\boldsymbol{\Psi}}$ in Table 13–4 to be larger than the error variance estimates in the last column of Table 13–1.

The two autoregressive weight matrices, $\mathbf{A}_1$ and $\mathbf{A}_2$ are shown in Table 13–5. The only large weight is that of *Agreeableness* on itself at lag 1 which is .82. For the other factors there do not seem to be clear causal patterns[9].

Root mean square residuals (see Equation 13.33) at lags 1 to 4 are shown in Table 13–6. As can be expected from the earlier discussion of root mean square

TABLE 13–3

Predicted-Factor Covariance Matrix,

$$\hat{\boldsymbol{\Theta}}_{11} = \widehat{\mathrm{Cov}}\left(\tilde{\mathbf{f}}_t, \tilde{\mathbf{f}}_t'\right) \forall t$$

	N	E	A	C	I
N	.33	.04	.20	−.04	−.22
E	.04	.26	−.19	−.09	−.12
A	.20	−.19	.53	.19	.01
C	−.04	−.09	.19	.36	.03
I	−.22	−.12	.01	.03	.32

Note. N = Neuroticism ; E = Extraversion; A = Agreeableness; C = Conscientiousness; I = Intellect.

---

[9]Interpretation would be easier here if standard errors were available. Bootstrap methodology for providing this information is currently being developed.

TABLE 13–4
Shock Covariance Matrix: $\widehat{\Psi} = \widehat{\text{Cov}}\left(z_t, z_t'\right) \forall t$

	N	E	A	C	I
N	.67	−.14	−.21	−.21	−.21
E	−.14	.74	.04	−.02	.40
A	−.21	.04	.47	.20	−.03
C	−.21	−.02	.20	.64	.18
I	−.21	.40	−.03	.18	.68

Note. N = Neuroticism; E = Extraversion; A = Agreeableness; C = Conscientiousness; I = Intellect.

TABLE 13–5
Autoregressive Weight Matrices

$\widehat{A}_1$	\multicolumn{5}{c}{Time $t-1$}
Time t	N	E	A	C	I
N	0.28	0.14	0.43	-0.04	0.47
E	0.13	-0.23	-0.28	0.07	0.47
A	0.37	-0.07	0.82	-0.40	0.22
C	-0.07	-0.31	0.23	0.10	0.09
I	-0.04	-0.05	-0.25	0.00	-0.51

$\widehat{A}_2$	\multicolumn{5}{c}{Time $t-2$}
Time t	N	E	A	C	I
N	-0.21	-0.07	0.00	-0.18	0.33
E	0.02	0.05	0.28	-0.24	0.15
A	-0.39	-0.38	-0.33	0.33	0.28
C	-0.10	-0.18	-0.23	0.38	0.16
I	0.29	0.08	0.01	0.26	-0.07

Notes. (1) N, Neuroticism ; E, Extraversion; A, Agreeableness; C, Conscientiousness; I, Intellect. (2) Stationarity condition is satisfied: $\text{Max}\left|\lambda\left(A\right)\right| = 0.59 < 1$

TABLE 13–6
Root Mean Squared Residuals at Different Lags

Lag	0	1	2	3	4
RMR	0.043	0.076	0.083	0.097	0.103
NNP	140	25	25	0	0

Note. RMR = $\sqrt{\text{Average squared non-null residual}}$ NNP: Number of new free parameters at lag ℓ.

residual indices, the RMR is smaller at lag 0 than at later lags because 140 free parameters are involved at lag 0 and only 25 at lags 1 and 2. Since $p = 2$ the RMR indices at lags 3 and 4 are forward-validation indices and are a little larger than the RMR indices at lags 1 and 2. Since the differences between RMR indices at lags greater than p and those at lags $1, \ldots, p$ are fairly small, they indicate reasonably good predictions at higher lags not used for estimation processes.

CONCLUDING COMMENTS

The enhancement of Cattell's P technique described here is easily implemented and provides additional information that will help the user to decide on the extent to which factors on preceding occasions affect factors on the current occasion. The only iterative computations required are for estimating the factor matrix and rotating it to an interpretable pattern. Similar computations are involved in Cattell's P technique. All additional computations required for estimating parameters of the latent time series are noniterative.

A requirement of this noniterative approach is that the maximum lag for the autocorrelation matrices, $\mathbf{R}_\ell$, $\ell = 0, \ldots, L$, should be equal to the order of the latent VAR(p) process, $L = p$. This limits the amount of information used but the method appears to be effective.

A computer program (Browne & Zhang, 2005) is available for carrying out the analyses described here. It can also carry out additional analyses where OLS estimates of latent time series parameters are obtained iteratively without intermediate estimates of factor autocorrelations. This makes the inclusion of autocorrelation matrices at lags greater than p possible, and also allows for confirmatory dynamic factor analyses with factor loadings or autoregressive weights fixed to zero.

ACKNOWLEDGMENT

The authors are indebted to Peter Borkenau for making his 22 intra-individual data sets available to us. Only the first is used as an example in the present chapter, but all 22 were helpful for developing our dynamic factor analysis methodology and testing our computer program. We are greatful to Marieke Timmerman for bringing these data to our attention and helping us to obtain them. Our grateful thanks also go to Robert Cudeck, Emilio Ferrer and Jing Zhu for reading a preliminary version of the chapter and providing helpful comments.

REFERENCES

Anderson, T. W. (1963). The use of factor analysis in the statistical analysis of time series. *Psychometrika, 28*, 1–25.

Borkenau, P., & Ostendorf, F. (1998). The Big Five as states: How useful is the five factor model to describe intraindividual variations over time? *Journal of Research in Personality, 32,* 202–221.

Briggs, N. E., & MacCallum, R. C. (2003). Recovery of weak common factors by maximum likelihood and ordinary least squares estimation. *Multivariate Behavioral Research, 38,* 25–56.

Brockwell, P. J., & Davis, R. A. (1991). *Time series: Theory and methods* (2nd ed.). New York: Springer.

Browne, M. W. (2001). An overview of analytic rotation in exploratory factor analysis. *Multivariate Behavioral Research, 36,* 111–150.

Browne, M. W., & Nesselroade, J. R. (2005) Representing psychological processes with dynamic factor models: Some promising uses and extensions of ARMA time series models. In A. Maydeu-Olivares & J. J. McArdle (Eds.), *Advances in psychometrics: A festschrift to Roderick P. McDonald* (pp. 415–451). Mahwah, NJ: Lawrence Erlbaum Associates.

Browne, M. W., & Zhang, G. (2005). DyFA: Dynamic factor analysis of lagged correlation matrices, version 2.03. [WWW document and computer program]. Available from http://faculty.psy.ohio-state.edu/browne/

Cattell, R. B., Cattell, A. K. S., & Rhymer, R. M. (1947). P-technique demonstrated in determining psycho-physiological source traits in a normal individual. *Psychometrika, 12,* 267–288.

du Toit, S. H. C., & Browne, M. W. (2001). The covariance structure of a vector ARMA time series. In R. Cudeck, S. H. C. du Toit, & D. Sörbom (Eds.), *Structural equation modeling: Present and future* (pp. 279–314). Chicago: Scientific Software International, Inc.

Engle, R., & Watson, M. (1981). A one-factor multivariate time series model of metropolitan wage rates. *Journal of the American Statistical Association, 76,* 774–781.

Geweke, J., & Singleton, K. (1981). Maximum likelihood confirmatory factor analysis of economic time series, *International Economic Review, 22,* 37–54.

Hamaker, E. L., Dolan, C. V., & Molenaar, P. C. M. (2005). Statistical modeling of the individual: Rationale and application of multivariate stationary time series analysis. *Multivariate Behavioral Research, 40,* 207–234.

Hamilton, J. D. (1994). *Time series analysis.* Princeton, NJ: Princeton University Press.

Harville, D. A. (1997). *Matrix algebra from a statistician's perspective.* New York: Springer-Verlag.

Holtzman, W. (1963). Statistical models for the study of change in the single case. In C. W. Harris (Ed.), *Problems in measuring change* (pp. 199–211). Madison: The University of Wisconsin.

Immink, W. (1986). *Parameter estimation in Markov models and dynamic factor analysis.* Unpublished doctoral dissertation, University of Utrecht.

Jones, C. J., & Nesselroade, J. R. (1990). Multivariate, replicated, single-subject, repeated measures designs and P-technique factor analysis: A review of intraindividual change studies. *Experimental Aging Research, 16,* 171–183.

Jöreskog, K. G. (1977). Factor analysis by least squares and maximum likelihood methods. In K. Enslein, R. Ralston, & S. W. Wilf (Eds.), *Statistical methods for digital computers* (Vol. 3, pp. 125–153). New York: Wiley.

Luborsky, L., & Mintz, J. (1972). The contribution of P-technique to personality, psychotherapy, and psychosomatic research. In R. M. Dreger (Ed.), *Multivariate personality research: Contributions to the understanding of personality in honor of Raymond B. Cattell* (p. 387–410). Baton Rouge, LA: Claitor's Publishing Division.

Lütkepohl, H. (1993). *Introduction to multiple time series analysis* (2nd. ed.). Berlin: Springer-Verlag.

MacCallum, R. C., Tucker, L. R., & Briggs, N. E. (2001). An alternative perspective on parameter estimation in factor analysis and related methods. In R. Cudeck, S. du Toit, & D. Sörbom (Eds.), *Structural equation modeling: Present and future* (pp. 39–57). Lincolnwood, IL: SSI.

Molenaar, P. C. M. (1985). A dynamic factor model for the analysis of multivariate time series. *Psychometrika, 50*, 181–202.

Nesselroade, J. R., McArdle, J. J., Aggen, S. H., & Meyers, J. M. (2002). Alternating dynamic factor models of multivariate time-series analysis. In D. M. Moscowitz & S. L. Hershberger (Eds.), *Modeling intraindividual variabilility with repeated measures data* (pp. 235–265). Mahwah, NJ: Lawrence Erlbaum Associates.

Wei, W. S. (1990). *Time series analysis: Univariate and multivariate methods*. New York: Addison-Wesley.

Whittle, P. (1963). On the fitting of multivariate autoregressions and the approximate canonical factorization of a special density matrix. *Biometrika, 40*, 129–134.

CHAPTER 14

Factor Analysis and Latent Structure of Categorical and Metric Data

Irini Moustaki
Athens University of Economics and Business

The chapter discusses generalized linear latent variable models for metric and categorical responses including nominal, ordinal, and discrete time survival variables. The classical factor analysis model is a special case of the general model presented here. The models include a measurement part where latent variables and observed covariates affect a function of the expected value of a response directly and a structural part that links latent variables and covariates with a linear function.

There are two main approaches in the literature for fitting models with latent variables and covariate effects, namely the structural equation modeling (SEM) approach that uses univariate and bivariate data information and the full information modeling approach that uses all p-variate data information, where p is the number of manifest variables. In this chapter, we consider only the full information approach. The theoretical formulation of the general model discussed here is based on the work done by Bartholomew (1987) and Bartholomew and Knott (1999).

In the SEM approach, important contributions have been made for both single and mixtures of types of variables by Muthén (1984), Arminger and Küsters (1988), Lee, Poon, and Bentler (1990a, 1990b), Jöreskog (1990, 1994). SEM is supported by commercial software such as LISREL (Jöreskog & Sörbom, 1999), EQS (Bentler, 1992) and Mplus (Muthén & Muthén, 2000). Jöreskog and Moustaki (2001) and Moustaki, Jöreskog, and Mavridis (2004) compared some limited information approaches with the full information approach for the case of ordinal manifest variables with respect to parameter estimates and goodness of fit.

The models discussed here are presented within a generalized linear framework that allows for metric, categorical variables and a mixture of those. In addition, covariate effects that affect the latent variables and covariates that affect directly the manifest variables are included. The work presented in the chapter is a review of the work discussed in Moustaki and Knott (2000) for categorical and metric variables, Moustaki (1996) for mixed (binary and metric) manifest variables, Moustaki (2003) for ordinal variables, and Moustaki and Steele (2005) for discrete time survival variables. All models presented here are extended to allow for covariate effects.

Within that generalized linear latent variable framework, one could also consider any of the models developed within the psychometric literature known also as *item response theory approach*. For example, these are the two parameter logistic model (Birnbaum, 1968, Bock & Aitkin, 1981), the three parameter model (Birnbaum, 1968), the model for nominal responses (Bock, 1972), the partial credit model (Masters, 1982), the graded response model (Samejima, 1969), and the generalized partial credit model (Muraki, 1992). Samejima's work on the graded response model for ordinal responses originated a lot of research activity in the area of latent variable models for ordinal variables. A review of those models and many more can be found in van der Linden and Hambleton (1997). We should note that the item response theory models for categorical responses developed in the last 50 years have extended in a multivariate setup, models for a single dependent variable developed mainly within the areas of psychophysics and biometrics. More specifically, the original idea of the probit model was introduced in Thurstone (1927) and then used in work by Mosier (1940, 1941) and Ferguson (1942) with the most complete treatment given in Lord (1952). Finally, Berkson (1951) adopted the logistic link over the probit.

Very important are also the recent advances in estimation methods such as the E–M algorithm (Dempster, Laird, & Rubin, 1977) and Bayesian estimation methods as well as advances in computers that made latent variable models with many factors and complex structures easier to estimate than 30 years ago.

The chapter is organized as follows. We begin with the theoretical framework that has been used to model latent variables and we also discuss the models within a generalized linear latent variable framework. We then discuss model estimation, problems encountered with model fit, and ways of obtaining latent scores. Finally, we present two applications of mixed metric and categorical variables with and without covariate effects.

THEORETICAL FRAMEWORK

Let us denote with $\mathbf{y}$ the $p \times 1$ vector of manifest variables, with $\mathbf{x}$ and $\mathbf{w}$ the $r \times 1$ and $k \times 1$ vectors of observed covariates and with $\mathbf{z}$ the $q \times 1$ vector of latent variables. As only $\mathbf{y}$ can be observed any inference must be based on the joint distribution of **y**:

$$f(\mathbf{y} \mid \mathbf{x}, \mathbf{w}) = \int_{R_\mathbf{z}} g(\mathbf{y} \mid \mathbf{z}, \mathbf{x}) \varphi(\mathbf{z} \mid \mathbf{w}) d\mathbf{z} \qquad \text{(Equation 14.1)}$$

where $\varphi(\mathbf{z} \mid \mathbf{w})$ is the distribution of the latent variables $\mathbf{z}$ that depend on the covariates $\mathbf{w}$, $g(\mathbf{y} \mid \mathbf{z}, \mathbf{x})$ is the conditional distribution of $\mathbf{y}$ given $\mathbf{z}$ and $\mathbf{x}$. Note that the density functions $\varphi(\mathbf{z} \mid \mathbf{w})$ and $g(\mathbf{y} \mid \mathbf{z}, \mathbf{x})$ are not uniquely determined.

Modeling manifest variables as functions of latent variables and covariates implies that if correlations among the ys can be explained by a set of latent variables and a set of explanatory variables, then when all zs and the xs are accounted for, the ys will be independent (local independence). Therefore, q and x must be chosen so that:

$$g(\mathbf{y} \mid \mathbf{z}, \mathbf{x}) = \prod_{i=1}^{p} g(y_i \mid \mathbf{z}, \mathbf{x})$$

If this condition holds then (14.1) is written:

$$f(\mathbf{y} \mid \mathbf{x}, \mathbf{w}) = \int_{R_\mathbf{z}} \prod_{i=1}^{p} g_i(y_i \mid \mathbf{z}, \mathbf{x}) \varphi(\mathbf{z} \mid \mathbf{w}) d\mathbf{z} \qquad \text{(Equation 14.2)}$$

GENERALIZED LINEAR LATENT VARIABLE MODELS

One can adopt a generalized linear model framework to specify latent variable models for categorical and metric responses (see Moustaki, 2003; Moustaki & Knott, 2000). A generalized linear model consists of three components:

1. The random component in which each of the p random response variables, $(y_1, \ldots, y_p)$ has a distribution from the exponential family, (such as Bernoulli, Poisson, Multinomial, Normal, Gamma).

2. The systematic component in which latent variables and covariates, $\mathbf{z}' = (z_1, \ldots, z_q)$, $\mathbf{x}' = (x_1, \ldots, x_r)$ produce a linear predictor η_i corresponding to each y_i:

$$\eta_i = \alpha_{i0} + \sum_{j=1}^{q} \alpha_{ij} z_j + \sum_{l=1}^{r} \beta_{il} x_l, \quad i = 1, \ldots, p. \qquad \text{(Equation 14.3)}$$

3. The links between the systematic component and the conditional means of the random component distributions:

$$\eta_i = v_i(\mu_i(\mathbf{z}, \mathbf{x}))$$

   where

$$\mu_i(\mathbf{z}, \mathbf{x}) = E(y_i \mid \mathbf{z}, \mathbf{x})$$

and $v_i(.)$ is called the link function which can be any monotonic differentiable function and may be different for different manifest variables y_i, $i = 1, \ldots, p$.

We shall, in fact, assume that $(y_1, y_2, \ldots, y_p)$ denotes a vector of p manifest variables where each variable has a distribution in the exponential family taking the form:

$$g_i(y_i; \theta_i, \phi_i) = \exp\left\{\frac{y_i\theta_i - b_i(\theta_i)}{\phi_i} + d_i(y_i, \phi_i)\right\}, \quad i = 1, \ldots, p,$$

(Equation 14.4)

where $b_i(\theta_i)$ and $d_i(y_i, \phi_i)$ are specific functions taking a different form depending on the distribution of the response variable y_i. All the distributions discussed in this chapter have canonical link functions with $\theta_i = \eta_i$ except the case of ordinal manifest variables; ϕ_i is a scale parameter.

We now give several different types of responses to the three components of the generalized model.

Binary Responses

Let y_i take values 0 and 1. Suppose that the manifest binary variable has a Bernoulli distribution with expected value $\pi_i(\mathbf{z}, \mathbf{x})$. The link function is defined to be the logit, that is:

$$v(\pi_i(\mathbf{z}, \mathbf{x})) = \theta_i(\mathbf{z}, \mathbf{x}) = \text{logit}\,\pi_i(\mathbf{z}, \mathbf{x}) = \ln\left(\frac{\pi_i(\mathbf{z}, \mathbf{x})}{1 - \pi_i(\mathbf{z}, \mathbf{x})}\right)$$

$$= \alpha_{i0} + \sum_{j=1}^{q}\alpha_{ij}z_j + \sum_{l=1}^{r}\beta_{il}x_l, \qquad \text{(Equation 14.5)}$$

where

$$\pi_i(\mathbf{z}, \mathbf{x}) = P(y_i = 1 \mid \mathbf{z}, \mathbf{x}) = \frac{\exp^{\theta_i(\mathbf{z}, \mathbf{x})}}{(1 + \exp^{\theta_i(\mathbf{z}, \mathbf{x})})}.$$

Then

$$b_i(\theta_i(\mathbf{z}, \mathbf{x})) = \log(1 + \exp^{\theta_i(\mathbf{z}, \mathbf{x})}),$$

$$d_i(y_i, \phi_i) = 0,$$

$$\phi_i = 1,$$

and the conditional probability of y_i is:

$$g_i(y_i \mid \mathbf{z}, \mathbf{x}) = \pi_i(\mathbf{z}, \mathbf{x})^{y_i}(1 - \pi_i(\mathbf{z}, \mathbf{x}))^{1-y_i}. \qquad \text{(Equation 14.6)}$$

An alternative model is derived by replacing the logit link with the probit. The probit model is closer to the classical factor analysis model. It is assumed that binary items are manifestations of some continuous underlying variable. The observed binary variable is merely an indicator of whether the underlying continuous variable is above or below a threshold. The probit model is written as:

$$v(\pi_i(\mathbf{z}, \mathbf{x})) = \text{probit}\,\pi_i(\mathbf{z}, \mathbf{x}) = \Phi^{-1}(\pi_i(\mathbf{z}, \mathbf{x})) = \alpha_{i0} + \sum_{j=1}^{q} \alpha_{ij} z_j + \sum_{l=1}^{r} \beta_{il} x_l,$$

(Equation 14.7)

where Φ^{-1} is the inverse of the normal distribution function. The relationship between the logit and the probit has been noted by Lord and Novick (1968):

$$\text{logit}(u) \doteq (\pi/\sqrt{3})\Phi^{-1}(u), \quad \text{for all } u.$$

The probit link lacks the simple interpretation of the logit link as well as the sufficiency principle explained in the section where the scoring methods are presented.

Nominal Responses

In the polytomous nominal case, the indicator variable y_i is replaced by a vector-valued indicator function with its s'th element defined as:

$$y_{i(s)} = \begin{cases} 1, & \text{if the response falls in category } s, \text{ for } s = 1, \ldots, c_i \\ 0, & \text{otherwise} \end{cases}$$

where c_i denotes the number of categories of variable i and $\sum_{s=1}^{c_i} y_{i(s)} = 1$. The response pattern of an individual is written as $\mathbf{y}' = (\mathbf{y}'_1, \ldots, \mathbf{y}'_p)$ of dimension $\sum_i c_i$.

The single response function of the binary case is now replaced by a set of functions $\pi_{i(s)}(\mathbf{z}, \mathbf{x})$ $(s = 1, \ldots, c_i)$ where $\sum_{s=1}^{c_i} \pi_{i(s)}(\mathbf{z}, \mathbf{x}) = 1$.

In the binary case, both y_i and θ_i are scalars where in the polytomous case, they are vectors. The first category of the polytomous variable is arbitrarily selected to be the *reference* category. The vector $\theta_i(\mathbf{z}, \mathbf{x})$ is written as:

$$\boldsymbol{\theta}'_i(\mathbf{z}, \mathbf{x}) = \left\{ 0, \ln \frac{\pi_{i(2)}(\mathbf{z}, \mathbf{x})}{\pi_{i(1)}(\mathbf{z}, \mathbf{x})}, \ldots, \ln \frac{\pi_{i(c_i)}(\mathbf{z}, \mathbf{x})}{\pi_{i(1)}(\mathbf{z}, \mathbf{x})} \right\}, \quad i = 1, \ldots, p$$

The canonical parameter $\theta_i(\mathbf{z}, \mathbf{x})$ remains a linear function of the latent variable:

$$\boldsymbol{\theta}_i(\mathbf{z}, \mathbf{x}) = \alpha_{i0} + \sum_{j=1}^{q} \alpha_{ij} z_j + \sum_{l=1}^{r} \beta_{il} x_l$$

where $\boldsymbol{\alpha}'_{ii'} = (\alpha_{ii'}(1) = 0, \alpha_{ii'}(2), \ldots, \alpha_{ii'}(c_i)),\quad \boldsymbol{\beta}'_{il} = (\beta_{il}(1) = 0, \beta_{il}(2), \ldots,$ $\beta_{il}(c_i)), i' = 0, 1, \ldots, q, l = 1, \ldots, r$, and

$$\pi_{i(s)}(\mathbf{z}, \mathbf{x}) = \frac{\exp^{\alpha_{i0}(s)+\sum_{j=1}^{q}\alpha_{ij}(s)z_j+\sum_{l=1}^{r}\beta_{il}(s)x_l}}{\left(\sum_{h=1}^{c_i}\exp^{\alpha_{i0}(h)+\sum_{j=1}^{q}\alpha_{ij}(h)z_j+\sum_{l=1}^{r}\beta_{il}(h)x_l}\right)},$$

$$b_i(\boldsymbol{\theta}_i(\mathbf{z}, \mathbf{x})) = \log\left(\sum_{h=1}^{c_i}\exp^{\alpha_{i0}(h)+\sum_{j=1}^{q}\alpha_{ij}(h)z_j+\sum_{l=1}^{r}\beta_{il}(h)x_l}\right),$$

$$\phi_i = 1.$$

The conditional distribution of $\mathbf{y}_i$ is taken to be the multinomial distribution:

$$g_i(\mathbf{y}_i \mid \mathbf{z}, \mathbf{x}) = \prod_{s=1}^{c_i}(\pi_{i(s)}(\mathbf{z}, \mathbf{x}))^{y_{i,s}}, \qquad \text{(Equation 14.8)}$$

where $y_{i,s} = 1$ if the response y_i is in category s and $y_{i,s} = 0$ otherwise.

Ordinal Responses

Let y_i denote an ordinal variable with c_i ordered response categories. To take into account the ordinality properties of the variable, we model the cumulative probabilities instead of the response category probabilities using for example the logit link:

$$\text{logit}[\gamma_{is}(\mathbf{z}, \mathbf{x})] = \text{logit}\,P(y_i \leq s \mid \mathbf{z}, \mathbf{x}) = \alpha_{i0}^{(s)} - \sum_{j=1}^{q}\alpha_{ij}z_j + \sum_{l=1}^{r}\beta_{il}x_l,$$

$$i = 1, \ldots, p; s = 1, \ldots, c_i$$

$$\text{(Equation 14.9)}$$

where $\gamma_{is}(\mathbf{z}, \mathbf{x})$ is the cumulative probability of a response in category s or lower of item y_i, written as:

$$\gamma_{is}(\mathbf{z}, \mathbf{x}) = \pi_{i1}(\mathbf{z}, \mathbf{x}) + \pi_{i2}(\mathbf{z}, \mathbf{x}) + \cdots + \pi_{is}(\mathbf{z}, \mathbf{x})$$

It follows that the probability of a randomly selected individual responding in category s can be derived from the cumulative probabilities as:

$$\pi_{is} = \gamma_{is} - \gamma_{i,s-1}, \quad i = 1, \ldots, p; s = 1, \ldots, c_i \quad \text{(Equation 14.10)}$$

The parameters $\alpha_{i0}^{(s)}$ are referred as "cut-points" on the logistic scale where $\alpha_{i0}^{(1)} < \alpha_{i0}^{(2)} < \cdots < \alpha_{i0}^{(c_i)}$, $\alpha_{i0}^{(0)} = -\infty$ and $\alpha_{i0}^{(c_i)} = +\infty$.

It can be shown that:

$$\theta_{i,s}(\mathbf{z}, \mathbf{x}) = \log \frac{\gamma_{i,s}}{\gamma_{i,s+1} - \gamma_{i,s}}, \quad s = 1, \dots, c_i - 1 \quad \text{(Equation 14.11)}$$

and

$$b(\theta_{i,s}(\mathbf{z}, \mathbf{x})) = \log \frac{\gamma_{i,s+1}}{\gamma_{i,s+1} - \gamma_{i,s}} = \log\{1 + \exp(\theta_{i,s}(\mathbf{z}, \mathbf{x}))\}, \quad s = 1, \dots, c_i - 1$$

$$\text{(Equation 14.12)}$$

As can be seen from (14.11), the parameter $\theta_{i,s}$ is not a linear function of the latent variables.

The conditional density of y_i is given by:

$$g_i(y_i \mid \mathbf{z}, \mathbf{x}) = \prod_{s=1}^{c_i} \pi_{i,s}(\mathbf{z}, \mathbf{x})^{y_{i,s}}$$

$$= \prod_{s=1}^{c_i} (\gamma_{i,s} - \gamma_{i,s-1})^{y_{i,s}}, \quad \text{(Equation 14.13)}$$

where $y_{i,s} = 1$ if the response y_i is in category s and $y_{i,s} = 0$ otherwise.

Poisson Distribution

Let y_i denote a Poisson random variable. The link function is defined through

$$v(\mu_i(\mathbf{z}, \mathbf{x})) = \theta_i(\mathbf{z}, \mathbf{x}) = \ln \mu_i(\mathbf{z}, \mathbf{x}) = \alpha_{i0} + \sum_{j=1}^{q} \alpha_{ij} z_j + \sum_{l=1}^{r} \beta_{il} x_l,$$

$$b_i(\theta_i(\mathbf{z}, \mathbf{x})) = \exp(\theta_i(\mathbf{z}, \mathbf{x})) = \mu_i(\mathbf{z}, \mathbf{x}),$$

$$\phi_i = 1,$$

$$g_i(y_i \mid \mathbf{z}, \mathbf{x}) = \frac{\mu_i(\mathbf{z}, \mathbf{x})^{y_i}}{y_i!} \exp^{-\mu_i(\mathbf{z}, \mathbf{x})}, \quad y_i \geq 0.$$

Discrete Time Survival Variables

As has been discussed by Moustaki and Steele (2005), latent variable models can also accommodate both uncensored and censored discrete time survival variables. The uncensored case implies that survival times are completely observed for all individuals, while the censored case allows for right-censored survival times.

Uncensored discrete-time survival variables may be treated as ordinal responses. The cumulative probability γ_{is} denotes the probability that a randomly selected individual will have the event of interest measured with variable y_i by time s, that is $\gamma_{is} = Pr(y_i \leq s)$. The cumulative probability can be modeled with

(14.9). Other link functions more common in the area of survival analysis can be also used (see McCullagh, 1980).

In the presence of censoring, we observe y, the minimum of the survival time and the censoring time, t, together with a censoring indicator u which takes the value 1 if the event occurred within the observation period and 0 otherwise. Prior to analysis, for each individual m, y_m is converted to a sequence of binary responses $\{\delta_{mt}\}$, $t = 1, 2, \ldots, y_m$, where

$$\delta_{mt} = \begin{cases} 0 & t < y_m \\ 0 & t = y_m \text{ and } u_m = 0 \\ 1 & t = y_m \text{ and } u_m = 1. \end{cases}$$

By creating the binary responses the modeling for this function of y_m can be done in the same way as with binary data. For example, an individual m who had the event during the fourth discrete time interval ($y_m = 4$) would have a response vector $\delta'_m = (0, 0, 0, 1)$, while for an individual who was censored during the same interval $\delta'_m = (0, 0, 0, 0)$. Taking the δ_{mt} as a set of binary responses, the "success" probability is modeled as a function of the latent variables and covariates. Here, the success probability is the probability that an individual experiences an event at time t given that they have survived to t. This is simply the hazard function

$$h_{mt} = Pr(\delta_{mt} = 1 | \delta_{m,t-1} = 0). \qquad \text{(Equation 14.14)}$$

The hazard function can be modeled using any link function appropriate for binary response data, including the logit and the probit functions (see [14.5] for the logit link).

The conditional density function for a randomly selected individual m is:

$$g(\delta_m \mid z_m, \mathbf{x}_m) = \prod_{t=1}^{y_m} (1 - h_{mt})^{1 - \delta_{mt}} h_{mt}^{\delta_{mt}}, \qquad \text{(Equation 14.15)}$$

where δ_m is the vector of binary responses $(\delta_{m1}, \ldots, \delta_{y_m})$.

Normal Distribution

Let y_i have a normal distribution with marginal mean α_{i0} and variance σ_{ii}. The link function of the conditional distribution $(y_i \mid \mathbf{z}, \mathbf{x})$ is the identity:

$$v(\mu_i(\mathbf{z}, \mathbf{x})) = \theta_i(\mathbf{z}, \mathbf{x}) = \alpha_{i0} + \sum_{j=1}^{q} \alpha_{ij} z_j + \sum_{l=1}^{r} \beta_{il} x_l \qquad \text{(Equation 14.16)}$$

Also,

$$b_i(\theta_i(\mathbf{z}, \mathbf{x})) = \frac{[\theta_i(\mathbf{z}, \mathbf{x})]^2}{2}$$

$$\phi_i = \sigma_{ii},$$

$$g_i(y_i \mid \mathbf{z}, \mathbf{x}) = \frac{1}{\sqrt{2\pi\sigma_{ii}}} \exp\left\{-\frac{1}{2\sigma_{ii}}\left(y_i - \alpha_{i0} - \sum_{j=1}^{q}\alpha_{ij}z_j - \sum_{l=1}^{r}\beta_{il}x_l\right)^2\right\}.$$

(Equation 14.17)

Gamma Distribution

Suppose y_i has a Gamma distribution. The link function is the reciprocal:

$$v(\mu_i(\mathbf{z}, \mathbf{x})) = \theta_i(\mathbf{z}, \mathbf{x}) = -\frac{1}{\psi_i(\mathbf{z}, \mathbf{x})} = \alpha_{i0} + \sum_{j=1}^{q}\alpha_{ij}z_j + \sum_{l=1}^{r}\beta_{il}x_l,$$

(Equation 14.18)

and

$$b_i(\theta_i(\mathbf{z}, \mathbf{x})) = -\log(-\theta_i(\mathbf{z}, \mathbf{x})) = -\log\left(\frac{1}{\psi_i(\mathbf{z}, \mathbf{x})}\right),$$

$$\phi_i = \frac{1}{v_i},$$

$$d_i(y_i; \phi_i) = v_i \log(v_i y_i) - \log y_i - \log \Gamma(v_i).$$

Hence,

$$g_i(y_i \mid z) = \frac{\exp\left\{-\frac{v_i}{\psi_i(\mathbf{z}, \mathbf{x})} y_i\right\} y_i^{v_i-1}}{\left(\frac{\psi_i(\mathbf{z}, \mathbf{x})}{v_i}\right)^{v_i} \Gamma(v_i)} \psi_i(z) > 0, \quad y_i > 0, \quad v_i > 0.$$

(Equation 14.19)

The shape parameter for the Gamma distribution is $v_i = \frac{1}{\phi_i}$ and the dispersion parameter is $\frac{\psi_i(\mathbf{z}, \mathbf{x})}{v_i} = \psi_i(\mathbf{z}, \mathbf{x})\phi_i$. Now, the requirement that the $\psi_i(\mathbf{z}, \mathbf{x})$ is positive imposes restrictions on the values of the parameter estimates, which imply that $\theta_i(\mathbf{z}, \mathbf{x})$ is negative.

The Structural Model

In the structural part of the model, the latent variable z_{jm} for an individual m is related to a set of observed covariates $\mathbf{w}_m$ in a simple linear form:

$$z_{jm} = \sum_{d=1}^{k}\lambda_{dj}w_{md} + \epsilon_m, \quad j = 1, \dots, q \qquad \text{(Equation 14.20)}$$

where λ_{dj} are the regression coefficients and ϵ_m is a standard normal residual. It follows that, conditional on the covariates $\mathbf{w}$, the distribution of the latent variable z_{jm} is normal with mean $\sum_{d=1}^{k} \lambda_{dj} w_{md}$ and variance one. The covariates $\mathbf{w}$ are assumed to be fixed and nonstochastic. The structural parameters can be written in a vector valued form as $\boldsymbol{\lambda}' = (\boldsymbol{\lambda}_1', \ldots, \boldsymbol{\lambda}_q')$, where the jth element of $\boldsymbol{\lambda}'$ is $\boldsymbol{\lambda}_j' = (\lambda_{1j}, \lambda_{2j}, \ldots, \lambda_{kj})$.

MODEL ESTIMATION

For a random sample of size n the complete log-likelihood is written as:

$$L = \sum_{m=1}^{n} \log f(\mathbf{y}_m, \mathbf{z}_m \mid \mathbf{x}_m, \mathbf{w}_m)$$

$$= \sum_{m=1}^{n} \left[\log g(\mathbf{y}_m \mid \mathbf{z}_m, \mathbf{x}_m) + \log \varphi(\mathbf{z}_m \mid \mathbf{w}_m, \boldsymbol{\lambda}) \right] \quad \text{(Equation 14.21)}$$

where $\mathbf{y}'_m$ is a $p \times 1$ vector of manifest variables of any type. Because $\mathbf{z}$ is unknown the log-likelihood given in (14.21) is maximized using an E–M algorithm. The expectation is with respect to the posterior distribution of $\mathbf{z}$ given the observations $(\varphi(\mathbf{z} \mid \mathbf{y}, \mathbf{x}))$.

Estimation of the structural parameters λ

From (14.21) we see that the estimation of the structural parameters $\boldsymbol{\lambda}_j' = (\lambda_{1j}, \ldots, \lambda_{kj})$ does not depend on the first component of the complete log-likelihood. Therefore, the estimation can be done separately from the parameters related with the measurement part of the model. In addition, the latent variables are assumed to be independent conditional on $\mathbf{w}$ so that

$$\varphi(\mathbf{z} \mid \mathbf{w}) = \varphi(z_1 \mid \mathbf{w}, \boldsymbol{\lambda}_1') \times \cdots \times \varphi(z_q \mid \mathbf{w}, \boldsymbol{\lambda}_q').$$

The expected score function with respect to the parameter vector $\boldsymbol{\lambda}_j$; $j = 1 \ldots, q$ takes the form:

$$ES_m(\boldsymbol{\lambda}_j) = \int \cdots \int S_m(\boldsymbol{\lambda}_j) \varphi(\mathbf{z} \mid \mathbf{y}_m, \mathbf{x}_m) d\mathbf{z} \quad \text{(Equation 14.22)}$$

where $\varphi(\mathbf{z} \mid \mathbf{y}_m, \mathbf{x}_m)$ denotes the posterior distribution of the latent variables given what has been observed and

$$S_m(\boldsymbol{\lambda}_j) = \frac{\partial \log \varphi(z_j \mid \mathbf{w}_m, \boldsymbol{\lambda}_j)}{\partial \boldsymbol{\lambda}_j} = \mathbf{w}_m(z_j - \mathbf{w}_m' \boldsymbol{\lambda}_j); \quad j = 1, \ldots, q$$

Therefore (14.22) becomes:

$$ES_m(\boldsymbol{\lambda}_j) = \int \cdots \int \mathbf{w}_m(z_j - \mathbf{w}_m' \boldsymbol{\lambda}_j) \varphi(\mathbf{z} \mid \mathbf{y}_m, \mathbf{x}_m) d\mathbf{z} \quad \text{(Equation 14.23)}$$

Solving $\sum_{m=1}^{n} E S_m(\boldsymbol{\lambda}_j) = 0$ and approximating the integrals over $\mathbf{z}$ by a weighted summation over a finite number of points and weights, we get an explicit solution for the maximum likelihood estimator of $\boldsymbol{\lambda}_j$. The points for the integral approximations are the Gauss-Hermite quadrature points given in Straud and Sechrest (1966). This approximation in effect treats each latent variable as discrete with values $z_{t_1}, \ldots, z_{t_v}$ and their corresponding probabilities $\varphi(z_{t_1} \mid \mathbf{w}, \boldsymbol{\lambda}), \ldots, \varphi(z_{t_v} \mid \mathbf{w}, \boldsymbol{\lambda})$. Other approximations can be used such as Monte Carlo, adaptive quadrature points, and Laplace approximation.

Estimation of the Measurement Model Parameters

The estimation of the parameters α_{i0}, α_{ij} and β_{il} depends on the first component of (14.21) where $j = 1, \ldots, q; l = 1, \ldots, k; i = 1, \ldots, p$.

Let denote $\mathbf{a}'_i = \left(\alpha_{i0}, \alpha_{i0}^{(s)}, \boldsymbol{\alpha}_{i0}, \alpha_{i1}, \ldots, \alpha_{iq}, \beta_{i1}, \ldots, \beta_{ir}, \phi_i \right)$, $i = 1, \ldots, p$, $s = 1, \ldots, c_i$ where $\mathbf{a}'_i$ is a vector of parameters.

The expected score function of the parameter vector $\mathbf{a}_i$ where the expectation is taken with respect to $\varphi(\mathbf{z} \mid \mathbf{y}, \mathbf{x})$ is:

$$E S_m(\mathbf{a}_i) = \int \cdots \int S_m(\mathbf{a}_i) \varphi(\mathbf{z} \mid \mathbf{y}_m, \mathbf{x}_m) d\mathbf{z}, \quad m = 1, \ldots, n$$

(Equation 14.24)

where

$$S_m(\mathbf{a}_i) = \frac{\partial \log g(\mathbf{y}_m \mid \mathbf{z}, \mathbf{x}_m)}{\partial \mathbf{a}_i}, \quad i = 1, \ldots, p$$

where $g(\mathbf{y}_m \mid \mathbf{z}, \mathbf{x}_m)$ takes its form from the exponential family in (14.4). Eventually, the unknown parameters are in the functions $b_i(\theta_i(\mathbf{z}, \mathbf{x}))$ and in the parameter $\theta_i(\mathbf{z}, \mathbf{x})$. Therefore the derivatives of those functions need to be computed. Detailed results can be found in Moustaki and Knott (2000) and Moustaki (2003).

The maximization of the log-likelihood (14.21) is done by an E–M algorithm. The steps of the algorithm are defined as follows:

Step 1:   Choose initial estimates for all model parameters.

Step 2:   E-step: Compute the expected score functions with respect to model parameters (14.22 and 14.24).

Step 3:   M-step: Obtain improved estimates for the parameters by solving the non-linear maximum likelihood equations for Bernoulli, Multinomial, Gamma and Poisson distributed variables and using the explicit equations for Normal distributed variables.

Step 4:   Return to step 2 and continue until convergence is attained.

Alternative maximization methods have been used such as Newthon-Raphson in the software GLAMM (Rabe-Hesketh, Pickles, & Skrondal, 2001) as well as Bayesian estimation methods (Patz & Junker, 1999a, 199b; Moustaki & Knott, 2004).

Sampling Properties of the Maximum Likelihood Estimates

From the first order asymptotic theory, the maximum likelihood estimates have a sampling distribution which is asymptotically normal. Asymptotically the sampling variances and covariances of the maximum likelihood estimates of the parameters λ' and $\mathbf{a}'$ and the scale parameters are given by the elements of the inverse of the information matrix at the maximum likelihood solution.

GOODNESS OF FIT

Testing how well a latent variable model fits the data is one of the most difficult problems in evaluating a model. In principle, one could use overall goodness-of-fit statistics such as the Pearson X^2 or the likelihood ratio statistic G^2 given by:

$$X^2 = \sum_{i=1} \frac{(O_i - E_i)^2}{E_i}$$

$$G^2 = 2 \sum_{i=1} O_i \log \frac{O_i}{E_i}$$

where O_i and E_i are the observed and expected frequency of response pattern i. When the sample size n is large and p small the statistics under the hypothesis that the model fits follow a chi-square distribution with degrees of freedom the number of response patterns minus the number of independent parameters minus one. As the number of items increases, the chi-square approximation to the distribution of either goodness-of-fit statistic ceases to be valid. Parameter estimates are still valid but it is difficult to assess the model. Problems arising from the sparseness of the multiway contingency tables in the binary case are discussed in Reiser and VandenBerg (1994). Bartholomew and Tzamourani (1999) proposed alternative ways for assessing the goodness-of-fit of the model for binary variables based on Monte Carlo methods and parametric bootstrapping.

Bartholomew and Tzamourani (1999), Jöreskog and Moustaki (2001) and Moustaki et al. (2004) used as a measure of fit the differences in the one-, two- and three-way margins between the observed and expected frequencies under the model. The differences were computed using a X^2 or a G^2 statistic. If these differences are small, it means that the associations between all pairs of responses are well predicted by the model. The given discrepancy measures can be used to measure discrepancies in the margins. Those statistics, also known as residuals, are not independent and so no formal testing can be done. However, if for example in the binary case, we consider the distribution of each residual as a chi-square with 1 degree-of-freedom then a residual with a X^2 or G^2 value greater than 4 will indicate a poor fit. Residuals analysis of that type can be used as a diagnostics procedure for identifying a pair of variables that the model does not fit well and suggest ways in which the scales constructed through the model may be improved.

In addition, one can compute for a given response pattern, standardized residuals (Cochran, 1954) or adjusted residuals (Haberman, 1973). The latter under certain regularity conditions follows the standard normal distribution.

Formal limited information tests that are based on the univariate and bivariate margins have been developed by Christoffersson (1975), Muthén (1978), Reiser and VandenBerg (1994), Bartholomew and Leung (2002), Maydeu-Olivares and Joe (2005). In those tests, the null hypothesis is stated as $H_0 : \epsilon = 0$ where ϵ can be a vector of first- and second-order margins with elements:

$$\epsilon_i = \sqrt{n}(p_i - \pi_i) \quad \text{and} \quad \epsilon_{ij} = \sqrt{n}(p_{ij} - \pi_{ij}),$$

where p_i and p_{ij} are the true first- and second-order proportions and π_i and π_{ij} are the ones under the model.

Most tests are based on a Wald type statistic defined as:

$$W = \mathbf{e}' \hat{\Sigma}^{-1} \mathbf{e}$$

where $\hat{\Sigma}$ is the estimated covariance matrix of ϵ and

$$e_i = \sqrt{n}(\hat{p}_i - \hat{\pi}_i) \quad \text{and} \quad e_{ij} = \sqrt{n}(\hat{p}_{ij} - \hat{\pi}_{ij}),$$

where $\hat{p}_i$ and $\hat{p}_{ij}$ are the observed first- and second-order proportions and $\hat{\pi}_i$ and $\hat{\pi}_{ij}$ are the estimated ones under the model.

Differences among the tests are with respect to the way the covariance matrix is estimated, whether they account for first- and second-order margins or even higher order margins, whether they use standardized or unstandardized residuals, and finally, whether the parameters are taken to be known or not.

Finally, instead of testing the goodness-of-fit of a specified model, we could alternatively use a criterion for selecting among a set of different models. This procedure gives information about the goodness-of-fit for each model in comparison with other models. This is particularly useful for the determination of the number of factors required. Sclove (1987) gives a review of some of the model selection criteria used in multivariate analysis such as those due to Akaike, Schwarz, and Kashap. These criteria take into account the value of the likelihood at the maximum likelihood solution and the number of parameters estimated.

SCORING METHODS FOR THE GENERALIZED LATENT VARIABLE MODEL

Social scientists are particularly interested in locating individuals on the dimensions of the latent factor space according to their response patterns. The latent scores can be substituted for the manifest variables in analysis with other independent variables of interest (though with some risk of bias).

Bartholomew (1980, 1981) argues that as latent variables in the model are random, Bayes's theorem provides the logical link between the data and the latent variables. Hence, the mean of the posterior distribution of z_j given $\mathbf{y}$, ($E(z_j \mid \mathbf{y})$) can be used to score $\mathbf{y}$ where $j = 1, \ldots, q$.

An alternative method uses the component scores (Bartholomew, 1984). That method avoids the integrations required in the calculation of the posterior mean. From the posterior distribution of the latent variable given the observed response pattern, it is clear that the posterior distribution depends on y only through $Y_j = \sum_{i=1}^{p} \frac{\alpha_{ij}}{\phi_i} y_i$; Y thus is a Bayesian sufficient statistic for $\mathbf{z}$. The sufficiency depends on the choice of the link function, it holds for the logit link but not for the probit. Sufficient statistic does not exist in the ordinal variables case.

The component score has an obvious intuitive appeal because of its linearity and the fact that it weights the manifest variables in proportion to their contribution to the common factor.

APPLICATION

We present here two applications of latent variable models with different types of responses. In the first example, a welfare index is constructed from a total of five indicators, three of which are binary and two metric. The second example measures the degree of family planning among women in Bangladesh using a combination of binary, ordinal, and survival time indicators.

Example 1: Some Variables on Welfare

Five welfare indicators have been analyzed in Moustaki and Knott (1997) in order to construct a welfare or poverty index. The five items are from the *Swiss Enquête sur la Consommation* survey in 1990. Information is collected from 1,963 households. Outliers have been removed from the data. For each metric variable, observations that lie well above the rest of the data are excluded from the analysis. That leaves us with 1923 households. The variables are:

> Presence of a dishwasher in the home.
> Presence of a video recorder in the home.
> Members of the household own a car.

Amount of money spend on food.

Amount of money spent on clothing.

The selected items were selected from a pool of welfare indicators. Some of the items in that pool such as hot water, cooker, fridge, color TV and washing machine were present in the majority of households. These items are expected to have small discrimination power. In an attempt to use all the mentioned items, together with disposable income and amount of money spent on leisure to construct the welfare index, both the one- and two-factor models gave a bad fit. Our initial aim is to find a set of items that can be explained by one factor the welfare factor. Therefore, we removed the indicators that were positively answered by the majority of the households (85% to 99%), the indicator income that is defined as a function of different types of expenditures, and the equivalent leisure expenditures. The last item was removed after we found that the two-factor model fitted on the indicators. Dishwasher, video recorder, car, food expenditures, clothing expenditures and leisure expenditures was marginally preferred to the one-factor model, according to Akaike's criterion.

The first three items are binary and item 4 and item 5 are metric. The coding used for the binary items is 1 for a *yes* response and 0 *otherwise*. The three binary items are fitted using the model defined in (14.5). Judging from their frequency distributions, it is reasonable that item 4 is treated as normally distributed and item 5 as gamma distributed. The models fitted to items 4 and 5 are given in (14.16) and (14.18) respectively. All the metric variables are standardized so that item 4 has mean zero and variance one, and item 5 variance one. The one-factor model gave a good fit judging from the one-, two-, and three-way margins of the binary items and Akaike's information cuterion (AIC). The AIC is 16546 for the one-factor model and 16544 for the two-factor model.

The parameter estimates are given in Table 14–1. From the last column of the table, we see that the median individual is very likely to have a car ($\pi_3 = 0.91$) and less likely to have a dishwasher ($\pi_3 = .40$) and video recorder ($\pi_3 = .38$) Scores

TABLE 14–1
Estimates and Standard Errors for the One-Factor Model

Binary	$\hat{\alpha}_{i0}$	$\hat{\alpha}_{i1}$	$P(y_i = 1 \mid z = 0)$
Presence of dishwasher	−.43 (0.07)	1.49 (0.15)	.40
Presence of video	−.51 (0.05)	.74 (0.08)	.38
Own a car	2.30 (0.15)	1.72 (0.18)	.91
Normal	$\hat{\alpha}_{i0}$	$\hat{\alpha}_{i1}$	$\hat{\sigma}_{ii}$
Food expenditures	.00 (0.02)	.50 (.03)	.75 (.03)
Gamma	$\hat{\alpha}_{i0}$	$\hat{\alpha}_{i1}$	$\hat{\phi}_{ii}$
Cloth expenditures	−.74 (0.02)	.18 (0.01)	.39 (.01)

based on the responses on the five items can be computed and rank households on the identified "welfare" factor.

Example 2: Family Planning

The data set analyzed here has been thoroughly discussed in Moustaki and Steele (2005). The data come from the Bangladesh Demographic and Health Survey of 1996 (Mitra, Al-Sabir, Cross, & Jamil, 1997), a nationally representative survey of women who were ever married, aged 10 to 49 years. A total of 9,127 women were successfully interviewed. A sample of 800 women was initially selected. After omitting six cases with missing data, the final analysis sample contains 794 women. The manifest variables are four indicators of a woman's preferences and behavior regarding fertility and family planning:

> Ever use of contraception [at any time].
> Son preference in ideal family size.
> Ideal family size.
> Second birth interval.

The variable *Ever use of contraception* is coded as 1 for a *yes* response and 0 *otherwise*. The *son preference* variable is coded *1* if the ideal number of sons exceeded the number of daughters, and *0 otherwise*. The *ideal family size* variable refers to the preferred total number of children and it is treated as an ordinal variable with one or two children taken as the lowest category and *Up to God* as the highest category. The duration variable, is the length of time between the birth of the first child and the conception of the second. In defining the timing of the second birth, discrete time intervals of 1 year were used and an observation period not exceeding 5 years was considered. We modeled the hazard of a second conception within yearly intervals for a 5-year period after the first birth. For women who had not conceived within 5 years, pregnancy outcomes other than live births were treated as censored. Of the 794 women in the analysis sample, 21.9% had a censored second-birth interval. The ordinal variable and the duration variable are fitted using (14.9) and (14.14) respectively.

We considered the following covariates, which are commonly found to be associated with reproductive health outcomes in Bangladesh and in many other developing countries: woman's age at survey in years [Age], highest level of education achieved [Educ], coded as none (reference category), primary and secondary or higher and type of region of residence [Urban], coded as rural (reference) and urban.

Table 14–2 gives the maximum likelihood estimates for the latent variable model without covariate effects. Taking into account the factor loadings lead us to interpret z as a summary measure of attitudes toward family planning, ranging from liberal (low values of z) to traditional (high values).

TABLE 14–2
ML Estimates for the One-Factor Measurement Model Without Covariates

		$\hat{\alpha}_{i0}$	$\hat{\alpha}_{i1}$	st.$\hat{\alpha}_{i1}$
Binary items				
Ever use of contraception		.88	−.67	−.56
Son preference		−1.78	1.08	.73
Ordinal item				
Ideal family size	No. of children			
	3	1.06	−2.94	−0.95
	4+	3.15		
	"Up to God"	5.47		
Survival item				
Second birth interval	Year			
	1	−2.03	.03	
	2	−1.06		
	3	−1.04		
	4	−1.21		
	5	1.20		

Next, covariates were introduced in the model. We found that the best fitted model according to the AIC and BIC (Bayesian Information Criterion) criteria is the one that allows age and education to have direct effects on each of the manifest variables, after controlling for the latent variable and variable residence to have an effect on the latent variable. From the estimates of the covariate effects shown in Table 14–3, we see that older and uneducated women are more likely than younger and educated women to have never used contraception, to have a preference for sons and large families, and a short interval between their first and second births. Finally, women who live in urban areas tend to have lower values on the latent variable than rural women, that is, they have more liberal attitudes toward family planning.

TABLE 14–3
ML Estimates of Covariate Effects for the Selected Model

	Age	Education (ref. = none)		Urban
		Primary	Secondary	
Manifest indicators				
Ever use of contraception	−.29	.25	1.35	—
Son preference	.22	.22	−.37	—
Ideal family size	−.98	1.16	2.18	—
Second birth interval	.21	.04	−.30	—
Latent variable	—	—	—	−.38

CONCLUSION

Surveys collect information on variables deÞned on different scales of measurement such as ordinal, nominal, metric, and so forth. When one variable is analyzed as a function of observed covariates, models such as the logistic, probit, multinomial logistic, proportional hazards models, and so on have been used to account for the nature of the variables involved. In multivariate analysis, it has been common and still is to analyze categorical variables using the standard factor analysis model for continuous responses that makes the assumption of multivariate normality. That might lead to biased estimates as well as wrong standard errors and goodness-of-Þt tests. In addition, Pearson correlations underestimate the true correlations among variables.

In structural equation modeling, ordinal and binary variables are assumed to be generated by underling continuous variables usually assumed to follow standard normal distributions. The classical factor analysis model is Þtted on the underling continuous variables. However, this assumption cannot be made for nominal variables.

Item response theory has generalized the regression models for categorical variables to deal with more than one dependent categorical variable and with covariates that are nonobserved (latent variables). Item response theory models have been primarily used in educational testing and psychometrics, where emphasis was given primarily to unidimensional models.

The last decade is devoted to develop a general model framework for any type of responses including categorical, metric, survival type variables, mixed type variables and covariate effects (see Mellenbergh, 1992; Moustaki, 2003; Moustaki & Knott, 2000; Skrondal & Rabe-Hesketh, 2004). The progress made in computing and estimation methods have made those developments possible. However, reducing computing time, availability of fast commercial software, efÞciency of numerical calculations required, goodness-of-Þt tests are still issues of great concern and under development.

REFERENCES

Arminger, G., & Kusters, U. (19). atent trait models with indicators of mixed measurement level. In R. angeheine & . Rost (ds.), *Latent trait and latent class models* (pp. 1 3). ew ork Plenum Press.

artholomew, . . (19 0). actor analysis for categorical data. *Journal of the Royal Statistical Society B, 42* (3), 293 321.

artholomew, . . (19 1). Posterior analysis of the factor model. *British Journal of Mathematical and Statistical Psychology, 434*, 93 99.

artholomew, . . (19 4). Scaling binary data using a factor model. *Journal of the Royal Statistical Society, Series B, 46*, 120 123.

artholomew, . . (19). *Latent variable models and factor analysis* GrifÞn statistical monographs and courses, ol. 40 . ondon harles GrifÞn & ompany td.

Bartholomew, D. J., & Knott, M. (1999). *Latent variable models and factor analysis* (Vol. 7, 2nd ed.). London: Arnold.

Bartholomew, D. J., & Leung, S. O. (2002). A goodness-of-fit test for sparse 2^p contingency tables. *British Journal of Mathematical and Statistical Psychology, 55*, 1–15.

Bartholomew, D. J., & Tzamourani, P. (1999). The goodness-of-fit of latent trait models in attitude measurement. *Sociological Methods and Research, 27*, 525–546.

Bentler, P. M. (1992). *EQS: Structural equation program manual*. Los Angeles: BMDP Statistical Software.

Berkson, J. A. (1951). Why I prefer logits to probits. *Biometrics, 7*, 327–329.

Birnbaum, A. (1968). Some latent trait models and their use in inferring an examinee's ability. In F. M. Lord & M. R. Novick (Eds.), *Statistical theories of mental test scores* (pp. 425–435). Reading, MA: Addison-Wesley.

Bock, R. D. (1972). Estimating item parameters and latent ability when responses are scored in two or more nominal categories. *Psychometrika, 37*(1), 29–51.

Bock, R. D., & Aitkin, M. (1981). Marginal maximum likelihood estimation of item parameters: application of an EM algorithm. *Psychometrika, 46*(4), 443–459.

Christoffersson, A. (1975). Factor analysis of dichotomized variables. *Psychometrika, 40*(1), 5–31.

Cochran, G. (1954). Some methods for strengthening the common χ^2 tests. *Biometrics, 10*, 417–451.

Dempster, A. P., Laird, N. M., & Rubin, D. B. (1977). Maximum likelihood from incomplete data via the EM algorithm. *Journal of The Royal Statistical Society, Series B, 39*, 1–38.

Ferguson, G. A. (1942). Item selection by the constant process. *Psychometrika, 7*, 19–29.

Haberman, S. (1973). The analysis of residuals in cross-classification tables. *Biometrics, 29*, 205–220.

Jöreskog, K. G. (1990). New developments in LISREL: Analysis of ordinal variables using polychoric correlations and weighted least squares. *Quality and Quantity, 24*, 387–404.

Jöreskog, K. G. (1994). On the estimation of polychoric correlations and their asymptotic covariance matrix. *Psychometrika, 59*, 381–389.

Jöreskog, K. G., & Moustaki, I. (2001). Factor analysis of ordinal variables: A comparison of three approaches. *Multivariate Behavioral Research, 36*, 347–387.

Jöreskog, K. G., & Sörbom, D. (1999). *LISREL 8 user's reference guide*. Chicago: Scientific Software International.

Lee, S. Y., Poon, W. Y., & Bentler, P. M. (1990a). Full maximum likelihood analysis of structural equation models with polytomous variables. *Statistics and Probability Letters, 9*, 91–97.

Lee, S. Y., Poon, W. Y., & Bentler, P. M. (1990b). A three-stage estimation procedure for structural equation models with polytomous variables. *Psychometric, 55*, 45–51.

Lord, F. M. (1952). A theory of test scores *Psychometric Monograph, No. 7*.

Lord, F. M., & Novick, M. R. (Eds.). (1968). *Statistical theories of mental test scores*. Reading, MA: Addison-Wesley.

Masters, G. N. (1982). A Rasch model for partial credit scoring. *Psychometrika, 47*, 149–174.

Maydeu-Olivares, A., & Joe, H. (2005). Limited- and full-information estimation and goodness-of-fit testing in 2^n contingency tables: A unified framework. *Journal of the American Statistical Association, 100*, 1009–1020.

McCullagh, P. (1980). Regression models for ordinal data. *Journal of the Royal Statistical Society, Series B, 42*, 109–142.

Mellenbergh, G. J. (1992). Generalized linear item response theory. *Psychological Bulletin, 115*, 300–307.

Mitra, S., Al-Sabir, A., Cross, A., & Jamil, K. (1997). *Bangladesh demographic and health survey, 1996–97*. Dhaka and Calverton, MD: National Institute of Population Research and Training (NIPORT), Mitra and Asso., & Macro International, Inc.

Mosier, C. I. (1940). Psychophysics and mental test theory: Fundamental postulates and elementary theorems. *Psychological Review, 47*, 355–366.

Mosier, C. I. (1941). Psychophysics and mental test theory II: The constant process. *Psychological Review, 48*, 235–249.

Moustaki, I. (1996). A latent trait and a latent class model for mixed observed variables. *British Journal of Mathematical and Statistical Psychology, 49*, 313–334.

Moustaki, I. (2003). A general class of latent variable models for ordinal manifest variables with covariate effects on the manifest and latent variables. *British Journal of Mathematical and Statistical Psychology, 56*, 337–357.

Moustaki, I., Jöreskog, K. G., & Mavridis, D. (2004). Factor model for ordinal variables with covariate effects on the manifest and latent variables: A comparison LISREL and IRT approaches. *Structural Equation Modeling, 11*(4), 487–513.

Moustaki, I., & Knott, M. (1997). Generalized latent trait models [Statistics Research Rep. no. 36]. London: Statistics Department, London School of Economics.

Moustaki, I., & Knott, M. (2000). Generalized latent trait models. *Psychometrika, 65*, 391–411.

Moustaki, I., & Knott, M. (2004). Computational aspects of the E–M and Bayesian estimation in latent variable models. In A. van der Ark, M. Croon, & K. Sijtsma (Eds.), *New developments in categorical data analysis for the social and behavioral sciences* (pp. 103–124). Mahwah, NJ: Lawrence Erlbaum Associates.

Moustaki, I., & Steele, F. (2005). Latent variable models for mixtures of categorical and duration responses, with an application to fertility preferences and family planning in Bangladesh. *Statistical Modelling, 5(4)*, 327–342.

Muraki, E. (1992). A generalized partial credit model: Application of an EM algorithm. *Applied Psychological Measurement, 16*, 159–176.

Muthén, B. O. (1978). Contributions to factor analysis of dichotomous variables. *Psychometrika, 43*(4), 551–560.

Muthén, B. O. (1984). A general structural model with dichotomous, ordered categorical and continuous latent variable indicators. *Psychometrika, 49*(1), 115–132.

Muthén, B. O., & Muthén, L. (2000). *Mplus: The comprehensive modeling program to applied researchers*. Los Angeles: Muthén and Muthén.

Patz, R. J., & Junker, B. W. (1999a). Applications and extensions of MCMC in IRT: Multiple item types, missing data, and rated responses. *Journal of Educational and Behavioral Statistics, 24*, 342–366.

Patz, R. J., & Junker, B. W. (1999b). A straightforward approach to Markov chain Monte Carlo methods for item response models. *Journal of Educational and Behavioral Statistics, 24*, 146–178.

Rabe-Hesketh, S., Pickles, A., & Skrondal, A. (2004). *GLAAM Manual* (Working paper series, working paper 160). U.C. Berkeley Division of Biostatistics.

Reiser, M., & VandenBerg, M. (1994). Validity of the chi-square test in dichotomous variable factor analysis when expected frequencies are small. *British Journal of Mathematical and Statistical Psychology, 47*, 85–107.

Samejima, F. (1969). Estimation of latent ability using a response pattern of graded scores. *Psychometrika Monograph Supplement No. 17*.

Sclove, S. (1987). Application of model-selection criteria to some problems of multivariate analysis. *Psychometrika, 52*, 333–343.

Skrondal, A., & Rabe-Hesketh, S. (2004). *Generalized latent variable modelling*. Boca Raton, FL: Chapman & Hall/CRC.

Straud, A. H., & Sechrest, D. (1966). *Gaussian quadrature formulas*. Englewood Cliffs, NJ: Prentice-Hall.

Thurstone, L. L. (1927). A law of comparative judgement. *Psychological Review, 34*, 273–286.

van der Linden, W., Hambleton, R. K. (1997). *Handbook of modern item response theory*. New York: Springer.

CHAPTER 15

Rotation Methods, Algorithms, and Standard Errors

Robert I. Jennrich
University of California at Los Angeles

Rotation represents the primary distinction between exploratory and confirmatory factor analysis. An attempt is made to overview the main components of rotation from the work of Thurstone to the present. These components are rotation methods, rotation algorithms, and standard errors for rotated factor loadings. For simplicity of presentation, only oblique rotation is considered.

The methods review begins with the graphical methods of Thurstone and proceeds to indirect and direct analytic methods. There is a renewed interest in the old, almost abandoned, hyperplane distance methods. In the context of direct rotation, these are component loss methods. Component loss and the popular quartic methods are considered in some detail. Basic properties including conditions that lead to the recovery of perfect simple structure are given. A number of rotation algorithms, including general closed form pairwise algorithms for quartic criteria and general pairwise and gradient projection algorithms for arbitrary criteria, are discussed.

Standard errors for rotated loadings using linear approximation methods are reviewed. These include methods using the asymptotic distribution of the initial loadings, constrained maximum likelihood methods, nonparametric constrained minimum deviance methods, and nonparametric pseudovalue methods.

The *factor analysis model* considered has the form

$$x = \Lambda f + u \qquad \text{(Equation 15.1)}$$

where x is a vector of observed responses, f is a vector of common factors, and u is a vector of unique factors defined on a population. The matrix Λ is a p by k

matrix of factor loadings. It is assumed that the vectors f and u have mean zero and are uncorrelated, that the components of f have variance one, and that the components of u are uncorrelated.

Then the covariance matrix Σ of x has the structure

$$\Sigma = \Lambda \Phi \Lambda' + \Psi$$

where $\Phi = \text{cov}\, f$, $\Psi = \text{cov}\, u$, and Ψ is diagonal.

If there are no further constraints that affect Σ, (15.1) is called an *exploratory model*. If there are enough constraints to uniquely identify Λ and Φ it is called a confirmatory model. Models that are neither exploratory nor confirmatory do not seem to have a name. The two named models represent a major division in the study and application of factor analysis. Often an exploratory analysis is used to help formulate a confirmatory analysis. Here only exploratory analysis is considered.

For exploratory analysis there are two steps. The first is estimating

$$\Omega = \Lambda \Phi \Lambda' \qquad \text{(Equation 15.2)}$$

and Ψ from a sample of values of x. This is called *extraction*. The second is estimating Λ and Φ from the estimate of Ω. This is called *rotation* for reasons that will become clear later. The rotation problem is the major component of exploratory factor analysis and is the problem considered here.

Given Ω there are many Λ and Φ that satisfy (15.2). The usual approach to estimating Λ and Φ, that is to the rotation problem, is to find a Λ that looks nice or slightly more specifically has a simple form or structure. The main problem is what does this vague statement mean? One case is clear. If each row of Λ has at most one nonzero element, Λ is said to have *perfect simple structure* an example of which is displayed in Table 15–1. The difficulty is that among all factorizations (15.2) of Ω there may not be a Λ with perfect simple structure and that is the usual case. Thurstone (1935) proposed a less demanding definition of simple structure. The second loading matrix in Table 15–1 has *Thurstone simple structure*. Thurstone simple structure requires a fair number of zeros, but far fewer than perfect simple structure. The complexity of a row of Λ is the number of nonzero elements in the

TABLE 15–1

Examples of Perfect and Thurstone Simple Structure

Perfect			Thurstone		
1	0	0	1	0	0
1	0	0	0	1	0
1	0	0	0	0	1
0	1	0	.89	.45	0
0	1	0	.89	0	.45
0	0	1	0	.71	.71

row. Thurstone simple structure can allow row complexities of 1, 2, 3, or more. As with perfect simple structure, however, there may be no factorization (15.2) of Ω that has a Λ with Thurstone simple structure and this is the usual case. It may, however, be possible to find a Λ that approximates Thurstone simple structure or even perfect simple structure.

Rather than attempting to define simple structure, one might attempt to identify simpler structure. That is, given two Λ, decide which is simpler. This might be done by just looking at them. Sometimes one is clearly simpler than the other. Rather than just looking, one might also consider the context of the problem. Perhaps in context one is clearly simpler. The trouble with this approach is it doesn't tell how to estimate Λ and Φ. This is usually done by choosing a *rotation criterion* Q that assigns a numerical complexity $Q(\Lambda)$ to Λ. The Λ that satisfies (15.2) for some Φ and minimizes Q is the rotated value of Λ corresponding to Q. Unfortunately there are many choices for Q. Most rotation research is centered on finding a useful choice. This problem is addressed in the next section, Oblique Rotation for Estimating Λ and Φ.

A special version of the classical factor analysis model assumes the factors are uncorrelated. Then Φ is an identity matrix and (15.2) becomes

$$\Omega = \Lambda\Lambda'$$

This form is called the *orthogonal factor analysis* model. When the factors may be correlated, it is called the *oblique factor analysis model*. Because of its greater generality, the oblique model can produce significantly simpler loading matrices. To simplify our presentation, we consider only the oblique case.

OBLIQUE ROTATION FOR ESTIMATING Λ AND Φ

It is helpful to parameterize Λ and Φ in (15.2) appropriately. Choose an A so

$$\Omega = AA'$$

This may be done by using a principal components factorization of Ω. The extraction step usually presents Ω in this form. The matrix A is called an *initial loading matrix*, which we assume has full column rank. When this is the case, Λ and Φ satisfy (15.2) if and only if

$$\Lambda = AT^{-1} \quad \text{and} \quad \Phi = TT' \qquad \text{(Equation 15.3)}$$

for some matrix T with rows of length one. Thus T provides a parameterization for Λ and Φ. The rows of T correspond to the factors f.

In the case of the orthogonal factor analysis model $\Phi = I$, T is an orthogonal matrix, and the rows of Λ are rotations of the rows of A. This motivates calling the problem of finding a specific Λ that satisfies (15.2) a rotation problem in the orthogonal case. Although it makes less sense, this terminology is also used in the oblique case. Thus the Λ that satisfy (15.3) are called the oblique rotations of A.

Finding an oblique rotation Λ of A to minimize a criterion $Q(\Lambda)$ reduces to finding a T with rows of length one to minimize

$$f(T) = Q(AT^{-1}) \qquad \text{(Equation 15.4)}$$

Graphical Methods

The original rotation methods were graphical. The first term $c = \Lambda f$ in the factor analysis model (15.1) is called the common part of x. The ith component of c has the form

$$c_i = \lambda_{i1} f_1 + \cdots + \lambda_{ik} f_k$$

This is plotted in Figure 15–1 for the case of two factors. The result of plotting all c_i is displayed in Figure 15–2. The two factor solution is obtained by choosing new factors $\tilde{f}_1$ and $\tilde{f}_2$ through the clusters of c_i and updating the λ_{ir}.

For more than two factors one cycles through pairs of factors making similar plots. One can have the computer automate the plotting and updating so that all that is required is choosing the new factors. Fifteen lines of computer code are

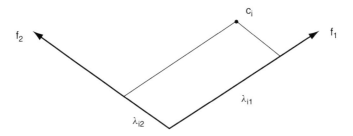

FIGURE 15–1.   Plot of the factors f_1 and f_2 and a single c_i in the case $k = 2$.

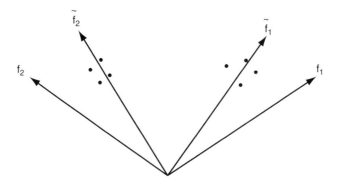

FIGURE 15–2.   Plot of the factors f_1 and f_2, the new factors $\tilde{f}_1$ and $\tilde{f}_2$, and all of the c_i for the case $k = 2$.

sufficient for this. Because it is better to actually do it than simply talk about doing it, the author attempted to graphically rotate the well-known Thurstone 26 variable box data (Thurstone, 1947, p. 371). Table 15–2 shows Thurstone's result and that of the author.

To aid in comparing these solutions, their *sorted absolute loading plots* (Jennrich, 2006) are given in Figure 15–3. The author did not do as well as Thurstone. A proper solution is known to have 27 small values. Thurstone got 27 small values. The author also got 27 small values but clearly not as small. It is also known that a proper solution has three pure indicators and these should produce three large values. Thurstone found three distinct large values. The author failed to find these. The only conclusion one can draw from Figure 15–3 is that Thurstone is much better at graphical rotation than Jennrich.

Although this may be the case, with the reader's indulgence, the author would like a rematch. Thurstone's 26 variable box problem is known as a hard problem.

TABLE 15–2
Graphical Solutions to Thurstone's 26 Variable Box Problem

Formula	Thurstone			Jennrich		
x_1	.95	.01	.01	.98	.02	.02
x_2	.02	.92	.01	.04	.97	−.02
x_3	.02	.05	.91	−.02	−.07	1.02
$x_1 x_2$	.59	.64	−.03	.62	.69	−.05
$x_1 x_3$	.60	.00	.62	.58	−.07	.70
$x_2 x_3$	−.04	.60	.58	−.05	.55	.63
$x_1^2 x_2$	.81	.38	.01	.81	.43	−.00
$x_1 x_2^2$	.35	.79	.01	.36	.85	−.02
$x_1^2 x_3$	.79	−.01	.41	.77	−.05	.46
$x_1 x_3^2$	.40	−.02	.79	.42	−.07	.92
$x_2^2 x_3$	−.04	.74	.40	−.04	.73	.42
$x_2 x_3^2$	−.02	.41	.74	−.05	.35	.80
x_1/x_2	.74	−.77	.06	.75	−.83	.09
x_2/x_1	−.74	.77	−.06	−.75	.83	−.09
x_1/x_3	.74	.02	−.73	.82	.15	−.85
x_3/x_1	−.74	−.02	−.73	−.82	−.15	.85
x_2/x_3	−.07	.80	−.76	−.01	.99	−.91
x_3/x_2	.07	−.80	.76	.01	−.99	.91
$2x_1 + 2x_2$	.51	.70	−.03	.53	.76	−.06
$2x_1 + 2x_3$	.56	−.04	.69	.54	−.10	.74
$2x_2 + 2x_3$	−.02	.60	.58	−.03	.55	.62
$(x_1^2 + x_2^2)^{1/2}$	.50	.69	−.03	.52	.74	−.05
$(x_1^2 + x_3^2)^{1/2}$	.52	−.01	.68	.51	−.08	.74
$(x_2^2 + x_3^2)^{1/2}$	−.01	.60	.55	−.01	.56	.59
$x_1 x_2 x_3$	.43	.46	.45	.43	.45	.47
$(x_1^2 + x_2^2 + x_3^2)^{1/2}$	.31	.51	.46	.32	.49	.48

Note. The formulas on the left were used to generate values for the 26 variables from the dimensions x_1, x_2, and x_3 of Thurstone's boxes.

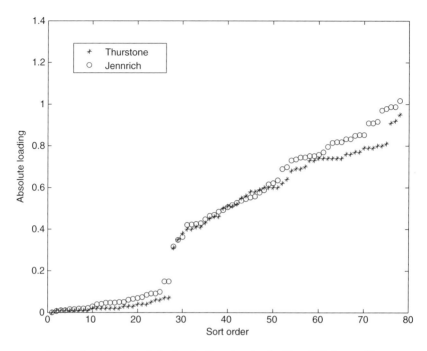

FIGURE 15–3.   Sorted absolute loading plots for the 26 variable box problem.

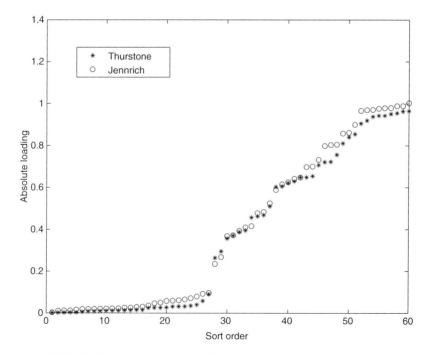

FIGURE 15–4.   Sorted absolute loading plots for the 20 variable box problem.

Many rotation methods fail on this problem. Thurstone's 20 variable box problem, on the other hand, is much simpler. It is used to train students. Figure 15–4 shows the author's and Thurstone's results on this problem. Again a proper solution should have 27 small values. The author found these almost as well as Thurstone. A proper solution to this problem is known to have nine pure indicators. The author found nine large values as did Thurstone, but those of the author are a little more distinct. The author would like to declare this contest a tie.

Actually the author rotated loadings while Thurstone rotated reference coefficients. More precisely, the author plotted rows of the loading matrix using an oblique coordinate system whereas Thurstone plotted rows of the corresponding reference structure using an orthogonal coordinate system. As is shown in the next subsection, these approaches are closely related; too closely to explain the difference in the graphical talents of the author and Thurstone.

Reference Structure and Early Analytic Methods

The analytic oblique rotation problem was not originally formulated as described by (15.4) because the required optimization, which involves T^{-1}, seemed too difficult. Using T^{-1} can be avoided by using reference structures. Following Thurstone (1947) and Harman (1976), let the rows of a nonsingular matrix U be *biorthogonal* to the rows of T and have length one. Biorthogonal means the rth row of U is orthogonal to the sth row of T whenever $r \neq s$. Let

$$R = AU'$$

This is called the *reference structure* corresponding to U. Note that

$$R = AT^{-1}TU' = \Lambda D$$

where D is diagonal because the rows of T and U are biorthogonal. This result is of interest because it means the columns of R are rescaled versions of the columns of Λ and this suggests that R is simple when Λ is simple and conversely. Rather than apply a complexity criterion to Λ one can apply it to R. The analytic rotation problem is then to minimize

$$Q(R) = Q(AU')$$

over all nonsingular U with rows of length one. Here U' has replaced the T^{-1} in (15.4). Harman (1976) calls making R simple an *indirect method* and making Λ simple a *direct method* because it simplifies the loadings directly.

Carroll (1953) has shown that when Q is the quartimin criterion, $Q(AU')$ viewed as a function of a single row of U is a constant plus a homogeneous quadratic function of the row. Because the row must have length one, an optimal value is the eigenvector of the matrix defining the quadratic function that corresponds to its smallest eigenvalue. Cycling through the rows of U gives a relatively simple algorithm for minimizing $Q(R)$. Actually this can be generalized to the entire orthomin family of criteria. It does not, however, seem to generalize to other criteria. For some time, indirect orthomin was the standard method of oblique analytic rotation.

Direct Methods

Indirect methods based on rotating reference structures were eventually replaced by methods that rotated loading matrices directly. The first such method was introduced by Jennrich and Sampson (1966) for direct quartimin rotation. Today direct methods are standard. Algorithms for these will be discussed under Analytic Oblique Rotation Algorithms. Before discussing algorithms, however, we identify some oblique rotation criteria.

Quartic Criteria. By *quartic criteria* we mean criteria like quartimin, biquartimin, covarimin, and more generally, the oblimin and Crawford-Ferguson families. When applied to loading matrices, these are quartic functions of the factor loadings. The oblimin criteria, for example, have the form

$$Q(\Lambda) = \sum_{r \neq s} \sum \left(\sum_i \lambda_{ir}^2 \lambda_{is}^2 - \frac{\gamma}{p} \sum_i \lambda_{ir}^2 \sum_i \lambda_{is}^2 \right)$$

The quartimin, biquartimin, and covarimin criteria correspond to $\gamma = 0, .5, 1$ respectively.

Quartimin criteria have been used for both indirect and direct rotation. In the direct case, Jennrich (1979) has shown that for every $\gamma > 0$ there is an initial loading matrix A such that the oblimin criterion with parameter γ is unbounded below over oblique rotations of A and as a consequence Φ approaches singularity and Λ approaches infinity when attempting to minimize the criterion. Although there always exists such an initial loading matrix, this need not happen for a specific initial loading matrix. Nevertheless Harman (1976) recommends using only values of $\gamma \leq 0$ for direct quartimin rotation.

Among quartic criteria, Browne (2001), in a paper that is a bible for analytic rotation, recommends the Crawford-Ferguson family

$$Q(\Lambda) = (1 - \kappa) \sum_i \sum_{r \neq s} \sum \lambda_{ir}^2 \lambda_{is}^2 + \kappa \sum_{i \neq j} \sum_r \sum \lambda_{ir}^2 \lambda_{js}^2$$

The first term of this criterion is a multiple of the quartimin criterion and can be viewed as a measure of column complexity. The second term is a similar measure of row complexity. The parameter κ weights the two complexities.

Component Loss Criteria. Using terminology introduced by Jennrich (2006), *component loss criteria* (CLC) for oblique rotation have the form

$$Q(\Lambda) = \sum \sum h(|\lambda_{ir}|)$$

The function h is called the defining *component loss function* (CLF). Criteria of this form have a long history going back to the hyperplane count criteria of Thurstone (1947). These were applied to reference structures rather than loading matrices.

Although hyperplane count criteria were used fairly successfully with graphical methods, attempts to apply analytic methods (Eber, 1966) failed because the CLF defining the criterion is very discontinuous. Indeed it wasn't even recognized that the hyperplane count criterion was a CLC. A breakthrough came when Katz and Rohlf (1974) recognized this and replaced the discontinuous CLF by a continuous approximation. The resulting CLC is much easier to optimize using analytic methods and in some standard examples produced nice results. The next advance came when Rozeboom (1991) recommended applying the CLC directly to the loading matrix rather than the reference structure matrix.

It is surprising that a method so simple and simply motivated has been mostly ignored. The author believes this is because until recently there has been no serious attempt to discover what form the CLF h that defines Q should have. Jennrich (2006) has shown:

Theorem 1:   If h is concave and nondecreasing and if Λ is a rotation of A that has perfect simple structure, then Λ minimizes Q over all rotations of A. Moreover, if h is strictly concave, any minimizer of Q must have perfect simple structure.

Strictly speaking, this theorem applies only to perfect simple structure cases, but it motivates using concave CLF more generally. Indeed, one might argue that any proper rotation method should produce perfect simple structure whenever it exists.

Jennrich (2006) has shown that concave CLF methods can work quite well much more generally. Moreover, as long as the CLF is concave, it does not seem to matter what specific concave CLF is used. For example, the very simple linear CLF has no trouble producing a proper solution to the 26 variable box problem that is almost identical to Thurstone's graphical solution and the best analytic solutions.

Other Criteria.   We have considered only two basic classes of oblique rotation criteria, quartic and CLC. There are many others, for example Yates's (1987) Geomin criterion, Bentler's (1977) Invariant Pattern Simplicity criterion, McCammon's (1966) Minimum Entropy criterion, and McKeon's (1968) Infomax criterion. There is a cottage industry producing papers on new criteria. A criterion is proposed. An algorithm is found to optimize it. Rotations for several standard examples are produced. There may be some comparisons with other methods, but this is difficult because there is no gold standard to use for this. For a very nice overview of rotation criteria and rotation methods in general, see Browne (2001).

ANALYTIC OBLIQUE ROTATION ALGORITHMS

As noted, the first analytic oblique rotation algorithms were for indirect methods. Here we consider only direct methods that rotate loading matrices rather than reference structures.

Closed Form Pairwise Algorithms for Quartic Criteria

Let f_1 and f_2 be a pair of factors and consider rotating f_1 in the plane of f_1 and f_2. More precisely let the new f_1 factor have the form

$$\tilde{f}_1 = \alpha_1 f_1 + \alpha_2 f_2$$

and have variance of one. Jennrich and Sampson (1966) have shown the values of the quartimin criterion under such rotations can be expressed as a fourth-degree polynomial $Q(\delta)$ in $\delta = \alpha_1/\alpha_2$. This may be minimized in closed form by solving the cubic equation $Q'(\delta) = 0$. Cycling through all ordered pairs of factors gives a pairwise algorithm for minimizing the criterion. This method generalized to the oblimin family of criteria is used in a number of major software systems.

Although to date no formal proof has been given, this approach also works when the quartimin criterion is replaced by any quartic criterion $Q(\Lambda)$ that is invariant under sign changes in the columns of Λ. These include essentially all quartic criteria and in particular the orthomin and Crawford-Ferguson families of criteria. Because five values determine a quartic polynomial, $Q(\delta)$ can be found by evaluating Q at five loading matrices corresponding to five values of δ. As a consequence, the only specific information required to implement these methods is a formula for $Q(\Lambda)$.

General Pairwise Line Search Algorithms

Browne and Cudeck have developed a pairwise line search algorithm for minimizing arbitrary rotation criteria. Let $Q(\Lambda)$ be any rotation criterion that is invariant under sign changes in the columns of Λ. These include all criteria known to the author. As was done by Jennrich and Sampson, Browne and Cudeck let f_1 and f_2 be an arbitrary pair of factors and consider rotating f_1 in the plane of f_1 and f_2. For pairwise rotations of this form, they have shown that the values of the criterion Q can be expressed as a function $Q(\delta)$ of the parameter δ used by Jennrich and Sampson. In general $Q(\delta)$ will not be quartic, but it can be minimized using a general line search algorithm. This forms a basis for a pairwise algorithm for minimizing Q. This is a remarkable algorithm.

- It works for almost any rotation criterion $Q(\Lambda)$.
- All that is required is a formula for $Q(\Lambda)$.
- It is remarkably simple.
- It has been used successfully for many different criteria.

Unfortunately, Browne and Cudeck have not published an account of their method and observations on its performance. Their method is used, however, by Browne, Cudeck, Tateneni, and Mels (2002) in the CEFA (comprehensive exploratory factor analysis) software. This free software deals with almost every aspect of exploratory factor analysis including a broad variety of methods for extraction and rotation, factoring correlation matrices, and providing standard errors for the estimates produced. It has a graphical user interface and a nice manual. The software and manual may be downloaded.[1]

Gradient Projection Algorithms

Jennrich (2002) gave a general gradient method that does not require cycling through pairs of factors. The oblique rotation problem is to minimize

$$f(T) = Q(AT^{-1})$$

over all T in the manifold $\mathcal{M}$ of nonsingular T with rows of length one. This is a slightly more precise expression of the problem than that given earlier. The gradient projection (GP) algorithm proceeds as follows.

Given a $T \in \mathcal{M}$ and an arbitrary scalar $\alpha > 0$, compute the gradient G of f at T and project $X = T - \alpha G$ onto $\mathcal{M}$. See Figure 15–5. The algorithm moves T in a negative gradient direction and then projects the result back onto $\mathcal{M}$. At first it seems like the required projection may be difficult to find because projecting onto a nonlinear manifold is a nonlinear regression problem and these generally require complex iterative procedures. For the manifold $\mathcal{M}$, however, projection is very easy and this is what motivates this method. The projection $\tilde{T}$ of X onto $\mathcal{M}$ is simply X scaled to have rows of length one.

The GP algorithm uses the following basic theorem.

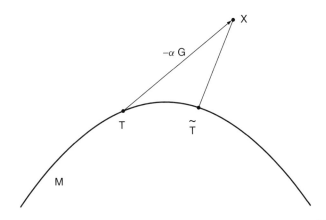

FIGURE 15–5.   Graphical representation of the gradient projection algorithm.

---

[1]http://quantrm2.psy.ohio-state.edu/browne/

Theorem 2:   If T is not a stationary point of f restricted to $\mathcal{M}$, then

$$f(\tilde{T}) < f(T)$$

for all $\alpha > 0$ and sufficiently small.

Using Theorem 2, the GP algorithm halves an initial value of α until $f(\tilde{T}) < f(T)$. Replacing T by $\tilde{T}$ gives a strictly monotone iterative algorithm for minimizing f over $\mathcal{M}$ and hence Q over all rotations of the initial loading matrix A. Strictly monotone algorithms are desirable because they must converge to stationary points. Moreover, because the only points of attraction of a strictly monotone algorithm are local minima, strictly monotone algorithms are almost guaranteed to converge to a local minimum.

This approach requires a formula for the gradient of Q in addition to a formula for Q. Jennrich (2004b) has shown that this problem-specific requirement can be removed with almost no loss of precision by using numerical gradients. Using these, the gradient projection algorithm has the same nice properties as the Browne and Cudeck line search algorithm without the need to cycle through pairs of factors.

Free SAS, SPSS, R/S, and Matlab code for GP rotation can be downloaded.[2] Thus for almost any computing environment one is working in, one can find code written specifically for that environment and hence code that may be used immediately without any need for translation. There is code for both orthogonal and oblique rotation using analytic and numerical gradients. The analytic gradients tend to be quite simple. They are given for the most popular and some less popular but promising criteria.

Advantages and Disadvantages

The pairwise quartic algorithms have the advantage that no line search is required and they are probably the fastest of the algorithms discussed. Their main disadvantage is that they are restricted to quartic criteria.

The main advantage of the pairwise line-search algorithm is that it applies to arbitrary criteria and the only method specific code required is that for evaluating the criterion. Also it is a very simple algorithm. Minor disadvantages are that it requires cycling through pairs and requires a line-search subalgorithm.

The main advantages of the GP algorithm are that it applies to arbitrary rotation problems, it does not require stepping through pairs of factors, and when using numerical gradients, it is very simple. When using analytic gradients, it appears to be significantly faster than the general pairwise algorithm, at least in the limited experience of the author. Its main disadvantage is that when used with analytic gradients, it requires method-specific code to produce these. Although this can be

---

[2]http://www.stat.ucla.edu/research/gpa

avoided with almost no loss of precision by using numerical gradients, their use significantly slows the algorithm.

STANDARD ERRORS FOR ROTATED LOADINGS

Measured in terms of actual computer usage, exploratory factor analysis is one of the most frequently used methods of statistical analysis. Among these, it is somewhat unique in that popular computer implementations fail to produce standard errors for the parameter estimates. For many forms of statistical analysis, standard errors are a by-product of the fitting procedure. Consider, for example, regression analysis and the many forms of analysis related to it. This is the case for confirmatory factor analysis as well, but because of the rotation problem, it is not the case for exploratory factor analysis. Other methods are required. Here we outline a number of methods that may be used to produce standard errors for rotated loadings. For the most part, these are asymptotic methods based on linear approximations. As is discussed next, little progress seems to have been made using less linear methods such as the jackknife, the bootstrap, and Markov-chain-Monte-Carlo (MCMC) methods. Cudeck and O'Dell (1994) discuss a variety of uses for standard errors in exploratory factor analysis.

Methods Using the Asymptotic Distribution of the Initial Loadings

Let $\hat{A}$ be an estimate for an initial loading matrix A based on a sample of size n. This is usually asymptotically normally distributed. More precisely let $\hat{a}$ and a be vector forms of $\hat{A}$ and A. Then as $n \to \infty$

$$\sqrt{n}(\hat{a} - a) \to N(0, \operatorname{acov} \hat{a})$$

where $\operatorname{acov} \hat{a}$ is the asymptotic covariance matrix for $\hat{a}$.

Results of this form have been given by

- Anderson and Rubin (1956) for principal component loadings and normal sampling.
- Lawley (1967) for canonical loadings and normal sampling.
- Joreskog (1969) for confirmatory factor analysis and normal sampling.
- Browne (1984) for confirmatory factor analysis and non-normal sampling.
- Gitshick (1939) for principal component analysis and normal sampling.

Actually Lawley's formula for $\operatorname{acov} \hat{a}$ has an error that was corrected by Jennrich and Thayer (1973).

The confirmatory factor analysis approach is particularly attractive. It assumes the upper diagonal part of A is zero. A standard confirmatory factor analysis then produces an estimate for acov($\hat{a}$) as a by-product of the extraction procedure.

Consider any analytic rotation method. Let A be an initial loading matrix and let Λ be the corresponding rotated loading matrix that is a function of A. In vector form let

$$\lambda = h(a)$$

Differentiating gives

$$d\lambda = \frac{dh}{da} da$$

where dh/da is the Jacobian of h at a.

Assuming $\hat{a}$ is asymptotically normally distributed, it follows from the delta method that $\hat{\lambda}$ is also and that

$$\text{acov } \hat{\lambda} = \frac{dh}{da} \text{acov}(\hat{a}) \frac{dh'}{da}$$

Thus the problem of finding the asymptotic distribution for rotated loadings given this is known for the corresponding initial loadings reduces to finding the Jacobian of the function that defines the rotation.

One can find dh/da by implicit differentiation. For this begin with the equalities

$$\Lambda = AT^{-1}$$

$$\text{dg}(TT') = I \qquad\qquad \text{(Equation 15.5)}$$

$$\text{ndg}\left(\Lambda' \frac{dQ}{d\Lambda} (TT')^{-1} \right) = 0$$

Here dg and ndg are operators that extract the diagonal and nondiagonal parts of a matrix and $dQ/d\Lambda$ is the gradient of an arbitrary rotation criterion Q at Λ. The last equation is a stationary condition for the oblique rotation defined by Q. This may be found in Jennrich (1973). The idea is to implicitly differentiate these equations. More specifically let t be the vector form of T and

$$f(a, t) = \text{vec}(AT^{-1})$$

$$\varphi(\lambda, t) = \text{vec}\left(\text{ndg}\left(\Lambda' \frac{dQ}{d\Lambda} (TT')^{-1} \right) + \text{dg}(TT') - I \right)$$

where vec is an operator that writes a matrix in vector form. Then the equalities (15.5) can be written in the form

$$f(a, t) = \lambda$$

$$\varphi(\lambda, t) = 0$$

Implicit differentiation gives

$$\dot{f}_1 da + \dot{f}_2 dt = d\lambda$$

$$\dot{\varphi}_1 d\lambda + \dot{\varphi}_2 dt = 0$$

where $\dot{f}_1$ is the partial Jacobian of f with respect to a and $\dot{f}_2$, $\dot{\varphi}_1$, and $\dot{\varphi}_2$ are defined similarly.

Solving for $d\lambda$ in terms of da gives

$$\frac{dh}{da} = \dot{f}_1 - \dot{f}_2 (\dot{\varphi}_1 \dot{f}_2 + \dot{\varphi}_2)^{-1} \dot{\varphi}_1 \dot{f}_1$$

The proceeding is a simplification of the derivation given by Jennrich (1973). To use this, one needs a way to compute the derivatives for f and ϕ. Those for f are simple.

$$\dot{f}_1 = I \otimes (T')^{-1}$$

$$\dot{f}_2 = -\Lambda \otimes (T')^{-1}$$

where $\otimes$ is the Kronecker matrix product. Jennrich (1973) gave the derivatives for φ when using criteria from the generalized Crawford Ferguson family. In general, however, these can be quite complex and it might be best to proceed numerically by letting

$$\dot{\varphi}_1 = \text{ numerical derivative of } \varphi \text{ w.r.t. } \lambda$$

$$\dot{\varphi}_2 = \text{ numerical derivative of } \varphi \text{ w.r.t. } t$$

Using these provides a reasonably simple and quite general way to produce standard errors for rotated loadings. Numerical derivatives work very well here. When printed to two decimal places, standard errors computed with exact and numerical derivatives agree exactly in almost every case.

Constrained Optimization Methods

In the last subsection, we expressed the asymptotic covariance matrix for rotated loadings in terms of that for the corresponding initial loadings. Here we express it in terms of the information matrix when using maximum likelihood estimation and for more general forms of estimation in terms of the asymptotic covariance matrix for the sample covariance matrix S. This is done using constrained optimization methods.

Maximum Likelihood Methods.   As an alternative to the method of the previous section, Methods Using the Asymptotic Distribution of the Initial Loadings, Jennrich (1974) used a result of Silvey (1971) on constrained maximum likelihood estimation to find the asymptotic distribution of the rotated loadings $\hat{\Lambda}$.

Let the observed responses $x_1, \cdots, x_n$ be a sample from a normal population. Let S be their sample covariance matrix, ϕ be the upper diagonal part of Φ written as a vector, ψ be the diagonal of Ψ written as a vector, $\theta = (\lambda', \phi', \psi')'$ be the complete parameter vector, and $\ell(\theta)$ be the likelihood of θ given the observed responses.

This likelihood is over parameterized. Recall, however, that for oblique rotation Λ and Φ must satisfy the stationary condition

$$\text{ndg}\left(\Lambda' \frac{dQ}{d\Lambda} \Phi^{-1}\right) = 0$$

Write this as

$$\varphi(\theta) = 0$$

Let $\dot\varphi$ be the Jacobian of φ at θ and $\mathcal{I}$ be the information matrix at θ. Using Silvey's (1971) result on constrained maximum likelihood estimation

$$\begin{pmatrix} \mathcal{I} & \dot\varphi' \\ \dot\varphi & 0 \end{pmatrix}^{-1} = \begin{pmatrix} \text{acov}(\hat\theta) & * \\ * & * \end{pmatrix}$$

That is when the augmented information matrix on the left is inverted what is in the upper left hand corner of the inverse is the asymptotic covariance matrix for the constrained maximum likelihood estimate $\hat\theta$ and in particular for $\hat\lambda$. If $\dot\varphi$ is computed numerically, this is a very simple approach when using maximum likelihood factor analysis.

About 25 years later, a massive generalization of this approach appeared in the CEFA program. This is discussed next.

Minimum Deviance Methods.   We consider here estimates obtained by minimizing functions that measure the discrepancy between S and Σ. More specifically, this means minimizing a function of the form

$$F(S, \Sigma) = F(S, \Lambda\Phi\Lambda' + \Psi)$$

with respect to Λ, Φ, and Ψ. Without constraints on Λ, however, this has many minima. If the loadings Λ also minimize a rotation criterion, they must satisfy the corresponding stationary constraint. Define θ and the constraint function $\varphi(\theta)$ as in the previous subsection and let s be a vector whose components are the upper diagonal elements of S. Then the estimator $\hat\theta$ of θ minimizes

$$f(\theta, s) = F(S, \Lambda\Phi\Lambda' + \Psi)$$

under the constraint $\varphi(\theta) = 0$. Note that $\hat\theta$ is a function of s. More specifically let

$$\hat\theta = g(s)$$

Let σ be the upper diagonal part of Σ written as a vector and let $dg/d\sigma$ be the Jacobian of g at σ. Because s is asymptotically normally distributed, $\hat\theta$ is also and using the delta method

$$\mathrm{acov}\,\hat{\theta} = \frac{dg}{d\sigma}\mathrm{acov}(s)\frac{dg}{d\sigma}{'}$$

This reduces the problem of finding the asymptotic distribution of $\hat{\theta}$ to finding $dg/d\sigma$.

These are essentially the methods used by Browne and Cudeck in CEFA (R. Cudeck, personal communication, August 2005).

The asymptotic covariance matrix for $\hat{\lambda}$ is found from the asymptotic covariance matrix for s. For normal samples, the asymptotic covariance matrix for s is a simple function of Σ. In the nonparametric case, it is a function of the fourth moments of the distribution sampled and may be estimated from the fourth sample moments of the observed responses. (See, e.g., Browne, 1984).

Pseudovalue Methods

Jennrich and Clarkson (1980) suggested using pseudovalues to estimate standard errors for rotated loadings. This approach has the advantage that it is nonparametric and does not require estimating fourth moments of the population sampled.

As before let λ be the vector form of Λ and let $\hat{\lambda}$ be an estimator of λ that is a function of the sample covariance matrix S. Jennrich and Clarkson define pseudo values $\tilde{\lambda}_t$ for λ, one for each of the n observed values x_t of x. The sample covariance matrix for these pseudo values is an asymptotically consistent estimate of the asymptotic covariance matrix for $\hat{\lambda}$.

More specifically let

$$\hat{\lambda} = h(S)$$

and let $\widehat{dh}$ be the differential of h at S. The "hat" is to indicate that dh is evaluated at S rather than at Σ. For each $t = 1, \cdots, n$ define a "pseudo value"

$$\tilde{\lambda}_t = \widehat{dh}((x_t - \bar{x})(x_t - \bar{x})') \qquad \text{(Equation 15.6)}$$

Let $S_{\tilde{\lambda}}$ be the sample covariance matrix for the vectors $\tilde{\lambda}_1, \cdots, \tilde{\lambda}_n$. Then

$$S_{\tilde{\lambda}} \to \mathrm{acov}(\hat{\lambda})$$

This method has several advantages.

- It is a nonparametric method. One can sample from any distribution, use any method of extraction, and any method of rotation.
- 4th sample moments of the x_t are not required.
- Except for finding $\widehat{dh}$, this is a very simple method.

Computing the pseudo values $\tilde{\lambda}_t$ defined in (15.6) requires finding $\widehat{dh}$. Jennrich and Clarkson show how to do this for normal theory maximum likelihood extraction with orthomax rotation. This needs to be extended to other extraction and rotation methods.

One approach may be to use the minimum deviance methods from the previous subsection Minimum Deviance Methods. For minimum deviance estimation $\widehat{dh}$ is given by

$$\widehat{dh}(M) = \frac{dg}{ds}\mathrm{vecs}(M)$$

where dg/ds is $dg/d\sigma$ from the Minimum Deviance Methods subsection evaluated at s rather than at σ, M is an arbitrary symmetric matrix, and $\mathrm{vecs}(M)$ is the upper diagonal part of the symmetric matrix M written as a vector.

The author believes this is a very promising method that deserves further investigation. To the author's knowledge, there has been no comparison of the pseudovalue methods and methods based on estimating the fourth moments of the distribution sampled.

Less Linear Methods

By less linear methods, we mean things like the jackknife, the bootstrap, and for Bayesian estimation MCMC methods. Pennell (1972) and Clarkson (1979) have used the jackknife to produce standard errors for rotated loadings. The basic jackknife uses n jackknife values, each of which requires carrying out a factor analysis, extraction and rotation. Doing this n times makes this an expensive procedure. Jackknifing by groups helps to reduce this expense, but the main problem with using the jackknife concerns alignment. In exploratory factor analysis the rotated loading matrix Λ is determined only up to column permutation and column sign change. To make the jackknife work, the generated loading matrices must be aligned. Doing this in an automated way that is good enough for jackknifing is pretty much an unsolved problem. Alignment failures have devastating effects on jackknife standard error estimates. Similar problems arise when using the bootstrap. There is considerable expense associated with analyzing a bootstrap sample and again alignment is the main problem. MCMC methods face these problems as well and require a parametric form for the sampling distribution of x. At present, the only feasible estimates for standard errors of rotated loadings seem to be linearization methods like those in the previous subsections.

COMMENTS

We have attempted to overview the main components of exploratory factor analysis, rotation methods, rotation algorithms, and producing standard errors for rotated loadings.

For the most part, choosing a rotation method means choosing a complexity criterion. Choosing a good criterion is a difficult problem. Many criteria have been proposed, but little progress has been made in attempting to compare them and recommending a specific choice. The problem is that there is no gold standard and hence no definitive way to make comparisons. The best we have at present are a few examples for which desirable solutions have been identified, for example, Thurstone's box problem. Another problem is that very little theory has been developed to point to a desirable method. The problem of choosing a good rotation method appears to be stalled. Some new ideas are needed.

In contrast we seem to have done very well on the algorithm problem. In a sense the problem is solved. The very general, simple, and reasonably fast pairwise line search algorithm of Browne and Cudeck and gradient projection algorithm of Jennrich allow one to optimize almost any rotation criterion. There is always room for improvement, but the need at present is not pressing.

The standard error problem needs work, but unlike the criterion problem, there are promising ways to proceed. A first step would be to have Browne and Cudeck publish their standard error results. Another would be to extend the pseudovalue methods of Jennrich and Clarkson beyond maximum likelihood extraction and orthomax rotation. And then, if possible, compare these methods. Another approach, though less promising in the view of the author, may be to find an alignment algorithm that is good enough to support jackknife, bootstrap, and MCMC methods.

Psychometricians and more generally statisticians seem to fear numerical derivatives. What they should fear are the consequences of failing to use them. The work described here suggests they produce accurate results and greatly simplify what would otherwise be very complicated methods. Cudeck and O'Dell (1994) have gone further. Rather than using numerical derivatives as a step in the process of differentiating a rotation algorithm $\lambda = h(a)$ they suggest numerically differentiating the algorithm itself. That is running the rotation algorithm multiple times making small changes in its argument a one component at a time and using differences in the values of λ to estimate dh/da. Doing this takes a good deal more courage than numerically differentiating the value of a simple matrix expression that is computed with great accuracy. Their approach, however, and its application also to algorithms of the form $\theta = g(\sigma)$ has the potential to greatly simplify the use of derivatives to produce standard errors in exploratory factor analysis. It deserves further investigation.

REFERENCES

Anderson, T. W., & Rubin, H. (1956). Statistical inference in factor analysis. *Proceeding of the Third Berkeley Symposium on Mathematical Statistics and Probability, 5,* 111–150.

Bentler, P. M. (1977). Factor simplicity index and transformations. *Psychometrika, 42,* 277–295.

Browne, M. W. (1984). Asymptotically distribution-free methods for the analysis of covariance structures. *British Journal of Mathematical and Statistical Psychology, 37,* 62–83.

Browne, M. W. (2001). An overview of analytic rotation in exploratory factor analysis. *Multivariate Behavioral Research, 36,* 111–150.

Browne, M. W., Cudeck, R., Tateneni, K., & Mels, G. (2002). CEFA: Comprehensive Exploratory Factor Analysis, Version 1.10 [Computer software and manual]. Retrieved from http://quantrm2.psy.ohio-state.edu/browne/

Carroll, J. B. (1953). An analytical solution for approximating simple structure in factor analysis. *Psychometrika, 18*, 23–28.

Clarkson, D. B. (1979). Estimating the standard errors of factor loadings by jackknifing. *Psychometrika, 44*, 297–314.

Cudeck, R., & O'Dell, L. L. (1994). Application of standard error estimates in unrestricted factor analysis: Significance tests for factor loadings and correlations. *Psychological Bulletin, 115*, 475–487.

Eber, H. W. (1966). Toward oblique simple structure: Maxplane. *Multivariate Behavioral Research, 1*, 112–125.

Girshick, M. A. (1939). On the sampling theory of roots of determinental equations. *Annals of Mathematical Statistics, 10*, 203–224.

Harman, H. H. (1976). *Modern factor analysis* (3rd ed.). Chicago: University of Chicago Press.

Jennrich, R. I. (1973). Standard errors for obliquely rotated factor loadings. *Psychometrika, 38*, 593–604.

Jennrich, R. I. (1974). Simplified formulae for standard errors in maximum likelihood factor analysis. *British Journal of Mathematical and Statistical Psychology, 27*, 122–131.

Jennrich, R. I. (1979). Admissible values of γ in direct oblimin rotation. *Psychometrika, 44*, 173–177.

Jennrich, R. I. (2002). A simple general procedure for oblique rotation. *Psychometrika, 66*, 289–306.

Jennrich, R. I. (2004a). Rotation to simple loadings using component loss functions: The orthogonal case. *Psychometrika, 69*, 257–273.

Jennrich, R. I. (2004b). Derivative free gradient projection algorithms for rotation. *Psychometrika, 69*, 475–480.

Jennrich, R. I. (2006). Rotation to simple loadings using component loss functions: The oblique case. *Psychometrika, 71*, 173–191.

Jennrich, R. I., & Clarkson, D. B. (1980). A feasible method for standard errors of estimate in maximum likelihood factor analysis. *Psychometrika, 45*, 237–247.

Jennrich, R. I., & Sampson, P. F. (1966). Rotation for simple loadings. *Psychometrika, 31*, 313–323.

Jennrich, R. I., & Thayer, D. T. (1973). A note on Lawley's formulas for standard errors in maximum likelihood factor analysis. *Psychometrika, 38*, 571–580.

Jöreskog, K. G. (1969). A general approach to confirmatory maximum likelihood factor analysis. *Psychometrika, 34*, 183–202.

Katz, J. O., & Rohlf, F. J. (1974). FUNCTIONPLANE—A new approach to simple structure rotation. *Psychometrika, 39*, 37–51.

Lawley, D. N. (1967). Some new results on maximum likelihood factor analysis. *Proceedings of the Royal Society of Edinburgh, A67*, 256–264.

McCammon, R. B. (1966). Principal component analysis and its application in large-scale correlation studies. *Journal of Geology, 74*, 721–733.

McKeon, J. J. (1968). *Rotation for maximum association between factors and tests*: Unpublished manuscript, Biometric Laboratory, George Washington University.

Pennell, R. (1972). Routinely computable confidence intervals for factor loadings using the "jackknife." *British Journal of Mathematical and Statistical Psychology, 25*, 107–114.

Rozeboom, W. W. (1991). Theory and practice of analytic hyperplane optimization. *Multivariate Behavioral Research, 26*, 179–197.

Silvey, D. S. (1971). *Statistical inference*. Baltimore: Penguin Books.
Thurstone, L. L. (1935) *Vectors of the mind*. Chicago: University of Chicago Press.
Thurstone, L. L. (1947) *Multiple factor analysis*. Chicago: University of Chicago Press.
Yates, A. (1987). *Multivariate exploratory data analysis: A perspective on exploratory factor analysis*. Albany: State University of New York Press.

CHAPTER 16

A Review of Nonlinear Factor Analysis
and Nonlinear Structural Equation
Modeling

Melanie M. Wall
University of Minnesota

Yasuo Amemiya
IBM Thomas J. Watson Research Center

According to a general interpretation, factor analysis explores, represents, and analyzes a latent lower dimensional structure underlying multivariate observations, in scientific investigations. In this context, factors are those underlying concepts or variables that define the lower dimensional structure, or that describe an essential and/or systematic part of all observed variables. Then, the use of a model is natural in expressing the lower dimensional structure or the relationship between observed variables and underlying factors. To define what is a scientifically relevant or interesting essential and/or systematic structure, the concept of conditional independence is often used. That is, the underlying factor space explored by factor analysis has the conditional independence structure where the deviations of observed variables from the systematic part are mutually unrelated, or where all interrelationships among observed variables are explained entirely by factors. This interpretation of the factor analysis concept does not limit the underlying factor space to be a linear space, nor the relationships between observations and factors to be linear. Hence, the idea of nonlinear factor analysis should not be treated as an extension of the basic factor analysis concept, but should be considered as an inherent effort to make factor analysis more complete and useful.

In the history of factor analysis practice, analysis with a linear structure or a linear model has been used almost exclusively, and the use of nonlinear analysis has started only recently. One possible reason for this delay in the use of nonlinear analysis is that, for many years, the relationships among variables were understood and represented only through correlations and/or covariances, that is, measures of linear dependency. Another reason may be the technical difficulty in development of statistical methods appropriate for nonlinear or general factor analysis. The proper model formulation facilitating methodological development has been part of the difficulty. Considering the fact that appropriate statistical methods for linear analysis were not established or accepted widely for 60 years, the rather slow development of statistical methods for nonlinear factor analysis is understandable. This chapter is intended to review such development of nonlinear factor analysis statistical methods.

Because different types of analysis may be interpreted as special cases of nonlinear factor analysis, it should be helpful to clearly define the scope of this chapter. The focus of this chapter is to cover nonlinear factor analysis methods used to explore, model, and analyze relationships or lower dimensional structure that underlies continuous (or treated as such) observed variables, and that can be represented as a linear or nonlinear function of continuous latent factors. A type of nonlinearity that is outside of this chapter's focus is that dictated by the discreteness of the observed variables. Factor analysis for binary or polytomous observed variables has been discussed and used for a number of years. Two popular approaches to such a situation are the use of threshold modeling and the generalized linear model with a link function as the conditional distribution of an observed variable given factors. The nature of nonlinearity in these approaches are necessitated by the observed variable types, and is not concerned with the nonlinearity of the factor space. Another kind of analysis similar to factor analysis, but not covered here, is the latent class analysis, where the underlying factor is considered to be unordered categorical. This can be interpreted as a nonlinear factor structure, but its nature differs from this chapter's main focus of exploring and/or modeling underlying nonlinear relationships. Another type of nonlinearity occurs in heteroscedastic factor analysis, where the error variances depend on factors; see Lewin-Koh and Amemiya (2003). Being different from addressing nonlinear relations among variables directly, heteroscedastic factor analysis is not covered here.

Within this chapter's scope with continuous observations and latent variables, one topic closely related to factor analysis is the structural equation analysis or the so-called LISREL modeling. As the name LISREL suggests, the models used traditionally in this analysis have been linear in latent variables. Restricting to linear cases, close relationships exist between the factor analysis model and the structural equation model (SEM). The factor analysis can be considered a part of the SEM corresponding to the measurement portion, or a special case of the SEM with no structural portion. Alternatively, the full SEM can be considered a special case of the factor analysis model with possible nonlinearity in parameters. But, for methodological research in these two areas, different aspects of analyses tend to be emphasized. Structural equation analysis methods usually focus on estimation of a structural model with an equation error with minimal attention to factor space exploration, and measurement instrument development. For the structural model fitting or estimation, it is natural to consider models possibly nonlinear in latent variables. Accordingly, a number of important methodological contributions have occurred in estimation for some types of nonlinear structural models. The review of this methodological development is included in this chapter, although some proposed methods may not be directly relevant for factor analytic interest of exploring nonlinear structure. It should be pointed out that the special-case relationship between the linear factor analysis model and the linear structural equation model may not extend to the nonlinear case, depending on the generality of nonlinear models being considered. The discussion on this point is also included at the end of section, General Nonlinear Structural Equation Analysis.

Consider the traditional linear factor analysis model for continuous observed and continuous factors,

$$\mathbf{Z}_i = \boldsymbol{\mu} + \boldsymbol{\Lambda}\mathbf{f}_i + \boldsymbol{\epsilon}_i \qquad \text{(Equation 16.1)}$$

where $\mathbf{Z}_i$ is a $p \times 1$ observable vector for individuals $i = 1 \ldots n$, $\mathbf{f}_i$ is a $q \times 1$ vector of "latent" factors for each individual, and the $p \times 1$ vector $\boldsymbol{\epsilon}_i$ contains measurement error. The traditional factor analysis model (16.1) is linear in the parameters (i.e., $\boldsymbol{\mu}$ and $\boldsymbol{\Lambda}$) and is linear in the factors. Unlike ordinary regression where the inclusion of functions of observed variables (e.g., x and x^2) would not be considered a nonlinear model as long as the regression relationship was linear in the coefficient parameters, with factor analysis, the inclusion of nonlinear function of the factors will be distinguished as a kind of nonlinear factor analysis model.

The idea of including nonlinear functions of factors is briefly mentioned in the first chapter of Lawley and Maxwell (1963). While drawing a contrast between principal component and factor analysis, they give reference to Bartlett's (1953) for the idea of including nonlinear terms in (16.1):

> The former method [principal component analysis] is by definition linear and additive and no question of a hypothesis arises, but the latter [factor analysis] includes what he [Bartlett (1953)] calls a *hypothesis of linearity* which, though it might be expected to work as a first approximation even if it were untrue, would lead us to reject the linear model postulated in eq (16.1) if the evidence demanded it. Since correlation is essentially concerned with linear relationships it is not capable of dealing with this point, and Bartlett briefly indicates how the basic factor equations would have to be amended to include, as a second approximation, second order and product terms of the postulated factors to improve the adequacy of the model ... While the details of this more elaborate formulation have still to be worked out, mention of it serves to remind us of the assumptions of linearity

implied in eq (16.1), and to emphasize the contrast between factor analysis and the empirical nature of component analysis. (p. 32)

The nonlinearity that Bartlett (1953) was indicating involved a nonlinearity in the factors, yet it was still restricted to additive linearity in the parameters. Very generally, a nonlinear factor analysis model could be considered where the linear relationship between $\mathbf{Z}_i$ and $\mathbf{f}_i$ is extended to allow for any relationship $\mathbf{G}$ thus

$$\mathbf{Z}_i = \mathbf{G}(\mathbf{f}_i) + \boldsymbol{\epsilon}_i. \qquad \text{(Equation 16.2)}$$

This general model proposed by Yalcin and Amemiya (2001) takes the p-variate function $\mathbf{G}(\mathbf{f}_i)$ of $\mathbf{f}$ to represent the fact that the true value (or systematic part) of the p-dimensional observation $\mathbf{Z}_i$ lies on some q-dimensional surface ($q < p$). Model (16.2) is very general and so a specific taxonomy of different kinds of nonlinear factor analysis models will be useful to help guide the historical review of methods. We consider the following taxonomy for nonlinear factor analysis models depending on how $\mathbf{f}_i$ enters $\mathbf{G}$:

- Additive parametric model:

$$\mathbf{G}(\mathbf{f}_i; \boldsymbol{\Lambda}) = \boldsymbol{\Lambda}\mathbf{g}(\mathbf{f}_i),$$

  where each element of $\mathbf{g}(\mathbf{f}_i)$ is a known specific function of $\mathbf{f}_i$ not involving any unknown parameters. Note that $\mathbf{G}$ is in an additive form being a linear combination of known functions, and that the coefficient $\boldsymbol{\Lambda}$ can be nonlinearly restricted. An example of the jth element of an additive $\mathbf{G}$ is a polynomial

$$G_j(\mathbf{f}_i) = \lambda_1 + \lambda_2 f_i + \lambda_3 f_i^2 + \lambda_4 f_i^3.$$

- General parametric model:

$$\mathbf{G}(\mathbf{f}_i; \boldsymbol{\Lambda})$$

  does not have to be in an additive form. For example,

$$G_j(\mathbf{f}_i) = \lambda_1 + \frac{\lambda_2}{1 + e^{\lambda_3 - \lambda_4 f_i}}.$$

- Nonparametric model:

$$\mathbf{G}(\mathbf{f}_i)$$

  is a nonparametric curve satisfying some smoothness condition. Examples include principal curves, blind source separation, and semiparametric dynamic factor analysis.

This chapter will focuses on the development of nonlinear factor analysis models of the first two types where some specific parametric functional form is specified. The third type of nonlinear factor analysis models relying on nonparametric or semiparametric relationships (which often but not always are used for dimension reduction or forecasting) will not be examined in detail here. Some starting places for examining the third type of models are, for example, for principal curves (Hastie & Stuetzle, 1989), for blind source separation in signal processing (Jutten & Karhunen, 2004; Taleb, 2002), for pattern recognition including speech recognition using neural networks (Honkela, 2004).

Methodological development for nonlinear factor analysis with continuous observations and continuous factors is reviewed and described in the next section, Development of Nonlinear Factor Analysis, followed by the section on Development of Nonlinear Structural Equation Analysis.

DEVELOPMENT OF NONLINEAR FACTOR ANALYSIS

The Difficulty Factor

Referencing several papers with Ferguson (1941) as the earliest, Gibson (1960) writes of the following dilemma for factor analysis: "When a group of tests quite homogeneous as to content but varying widely in difficulty is subjected to factor analysis, the result is that more factors than content would demand are required to reduce the residuals to a random pattern" (p. 381).

These additional factors had come to be known as "difficulty factors" in the literature. Ferguson (1941) writes

> The functional unity which a given factor is presumed to represent is deduced from a consideration of the content of tests having a substantially significant loading on that factor. As far as I am aware, in attaching a meaningful interpretation to factors the differences in difficulty between the tests in a battery are rarely if ever given consideration, and, since the tests used in many test batteries differ substantially in difficulty relative to the population tested, factors resulting from differences in the nature of tasks will be confused with factors resulting from differences in the difficulty of tasks. (p. 329)

Gibson (1960) points out specifically that it is nonlinearities in the true relationship between the factors and the observed variables which is in conflict with the linearity assumption of traditional linear factor analysis:

> Coefficients of linear correlation, when applied to such data, will naturally underestimate the degree of nonlinear functional relation that exists between such tests. Implicitly, then it is nonlinear relations among tests that lead to difficulty factors. Explicitly, however, the factor model rules out, in its fundamental linear postulate, only such curvilinear relations as may exist between tests and factors. (p. 381)

As a solution to this problem, Gibson (1951) who worked on latent structure analysis for his dissertation at University of Chicago, proposes to drop the continuity assumption for the underlying factor and instead discretize the latent space and perform a kind of latent profile analysis (Lazarsfeld, 1950). Gibson (1955, 1956) gives two presentations at the Annual Convention of the APA proposing this method for nonlinear factor analysis in the "single factor case", and "in two dimensions". The method is first described in the literature in Gibson (1959) where he writes of a method considering "what to do with the extra linear factors that are forced to emerge when nonlinearities occur in the data" (p. 229). The basic idea of Gibson can be seen in Figure 16–1, where the top three figures represent the true relationship between the score on three different variables and the underlying factor being measured. The middle plot represents the linear relationship assumed by the traditional linear factor analysis model (16.1). The variable $z1$ represented on the left is a variable that discriminates the factor mostly on the low end (e.g., low difficulty test) whereas the variable $z3$ on the right describes variability in the factor mostly at the high end (e.g., a difficult test). The fact that the observed variables are not linearly related to the underlying factor is a violation of the assumption for model (16.1). Gibson's idea (represented by the lower plots in Figure 16–1) was to forfeit modeling the continuous relationship and deal only with the means of the different variables $z1$–$z3$ given a particular latent class membership. This allowed for nonlinear relationships very naturally.

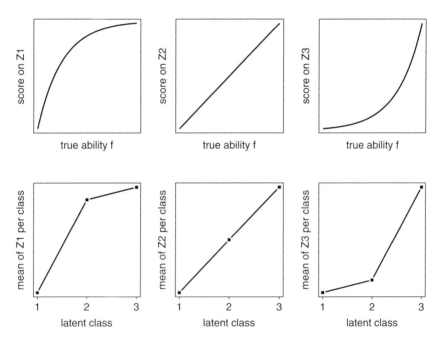

FIGURE 16–1.   Representation of true relationship between latent factor "true ability f" and score on three different variables, Z1–Z3 (Top); Gibson's proposal of categorizing the latent space to fit nonlinear relationships (Bottom).

First Parametric Model

Unsatisfied with Gibson's ad hoc nature of discretizing the continuous underlying factor in order to fit a nonlinear relation between it and the observed variables, McDonald (1962) developed a nonlinear functional relationship between the underlying continuous factors and the continuous observed variables.

Following our taxonomy described in the introduction, McDonald's model would be of the first type, that is, an additive parametric model, in particular, nonlinear in the factors but linear in the parameters. That is, given a vector $\mathbf{Z}_i$ of p observed variables for individuals $i = 1 \ldots n$, McDonald (1962, 1965, 1967a, 1967b) considered

$$\mathbf{Z}_i = \boldsymbol{\mu} + \boldsymbol{\Lambda}\mathbf{g}(\mathbf{f}_i) + \boldsymbol{\epsilon}_i \qquad \text{(Equation 16.3)}$$

$$\text{where } \mathbf{g}(\mathbf{f}_i) = (g_1(\mathbf{f}_i), g_2(\mathbf{f}_i), \ldots g_r(\mathbf{f}_i))'$$

$$\text{and } \mathbf{f}_i = (f_{1i} \ldots f_{qi})'.$$

The basic estimation idea of McDonald (1962) and the procedure described in more detail in McDonald (1967b) for pure polynomials was to fit a linear factor analysis with r underlying factors and then look to see if there was a nonlinear functional relationship between the fitted factor scores.

> We obtain factor scores on the two factors and plot them, one against the other. If there is a significant curvilinear relation (in the form of a parabola) we can estimate a quadratic function relating one set of factor scores to the other; this relation can then be put into the specification equation to yield the required quadratic functions for the individual manifest variates." (McDonald, 1962, p. 399)

McDonald was very prolific with regard to producing computer programs (usually Fortran) that were made available for users to implement his methods. For example, he developed COPE (corrected polynomials, etc.) and POSER for (polynomial series program) to be used for models with pure polynomial functions of the underlying factors $\mathbf{g}(\mathbf{f})$ in (16.3). Then FAINT (factor analysis interactions) was developed for the interaction models described in McDonald (1967a).

Despite the availability of programs, Etezadi-Amoli and McDonald (1983) write "programs for the methods were shown to be quite usable ... but the methods proposed do not seem to have been widely employed" (p. 315). A thorough search of the literature generally agrees with this, although later, Molenaar and Boomsma (1987) specifically use the work of McDonald (1967a) to estimate a genetic–environment interaction underlying at least three observed phenotypes. Etezadi-Amoli and McDonald (1983) deals with the same nonlinear factor analysis model (16.3) but proposes a different estimation method. They use the estimation method proposed in McDonald (1979), which treats the underlying factors as fixed and minimizes

$$l = \frac{1}{2}(\log |diag\mathbf{Q}| - \log |\mathbf{Q}|)$$

$$\mathbf{Q} = \frac{1}{n}\sum_{i=1}^{n}(\mathbf{Z}_i - \mathbf{\Lambda}\mathbf{g}(\mathbf{f}_i))(\mathbf{Z}_i - \mathbf{\Lambda}\mathbf{g}(\mathbf{f}_i))'$$

which is a kind of likelihood-ratio discrepancy function. One advantage of this method, which is implemented in a program called NOFA, is that now the dimension of $\mathbf{g}()$ is not restricted to be less than or equal to the number of linear factors that could be fit. This model can be considered to be an unrestricted nonlinear model within a certain class of nonlinear models for example, models with all second-order terms in a given number of factors. In this sense, it might be called an *exploratory nonlinear factor analysis*. However, it should be noted that identifiability problems introduced by the complexity of factor and nonlinear function indeterminacy limit this technique from being a panacea for general nonlinear exploratory factor analysis. Some problems of identifiability are discussed in Etezadi-Amoli and McDonald (1983) and it is claimed that polynomial factor models (without interaction terms) are not subject to rotational indeterminacy and should be meaningfully identifiable.

Additive Model With Normal Factors

While providing a very nice introduction to the previous nonlinear factor analysis work by both McDonald and Gibson, Mooijaart and Bentler (1986) propose a new method for estimating models of the form (16.3) when there is one underlying factor and the functions $\mathbf{g}$ are pure power polynomials. Mooijaart and Bentler (1986) write, "The differences with earlier work in this field are: (1) it is assumed that all variables (manifest and latent) are random variables; (2) the observed variables need not be normally distributed" (p. 242). Unlike McDonald who considered the underlying factors to be fixed and used factor scores for estimating relationships, Mooijaart and Bentler (1986) assume the underlying factor is normally distributed, in particular $f_i \sim N(0, 1)$. They point out that if $r > 1$, then $\mathbf{Z}_i$ is necessarily nonnormal. Because $\mathbf{Z}_i$ is not normally distributed, they propose to use the ADF method, which had been recently developed (Browne, 1984). That is they minimize

$$\frac{1}{n}(s - \sigma(\boldsymbol{\theta}))'\mathbf{W}(s - \sigma(\boldsymbol{\theta}))$$

w.r.t $\boldsymbol{\theta}$ containing $\mathbf{\Lambda}$ and $\mathbf{\Psi} = diag(var(\epsilon_{1i}), \ldots, var(\epsilon_{pi}))$, where s is a vector of the sample second- and third-order cross products and $\sigma(\boldsymbol{\theta})$ the population expectation of the cross products. Assuming $f_i \sim N(0, 1)$ it is possible to explicitly calculate the moments $E(\mathbf{g}(f_i)\mathbf{g}(f_i)')$ and $E\{(\mathbf{g}(f_i) \otimes \mathbf{g}(f_i))\mathbf{g}(f_i)'\}$ for $\mathbf{g}(f_i) = (f_i, f_i^2, \ldots, f_i^r)'$. These moments are then treated as fixed and known for the estimation. The method proposed also provided a test for overall fit and considered standard errors.

In order to show how the technique works, Mooijaart and Bentler (1986) gave an example application to an attitude scale:

> Not only in analyzing test scores a nonlinear model may be important, also in analyzing attitudes this model may be the proper model. Besides finding an attitude factor, an intensity-factor is also often found with linear factor analysis. Again, the reason here is that subjects on both ends of the scale (factor) are more extreme in their opinion than can be expected from a linear model. (p. 241)

They showed that when a traditional linear factor analysis model was used to fit an eight-item questionnaire about attitudes toward nuclear weapons that a one- and two-linear factor model do not fit well while a three-linear factor model did fit well. The researchers had no reason to believe that the questions were measuring three different constructs, instead they hypothesized only one. When a third-degree polynomial factor model was fit using the Mooijaart and Bentler (1986) method, it did fit well (with one factor).

General Nonlinear Factor Analysis

As reviewed in the previous subsections, a number of model fitting methods specifically targeting low-order polynomial models (or models linear in loading parameters) have been proposed over the years. However, attempts to formulate a general nonlinear model and to address statistical issues in a broad framework did not start until the early 1990s. In particular, a series of papers Amemiya (1993a, 1993b) and Yalcin and Amemiya (1993, 1995, 2001) introduced a meaningful model formulation, and statistical procedures for model fitting, model checking, and inferences for general nonlinear factor analysis.

Formulation of general nonlinear factor analysis should start with an unambiguous interpretation of factor analysis in general. One possible interpretation from a statistical point of view is that, in the factor analysis structure, all interrelationships among p observed variables are explained by $q(< p)$ underlying factors. For continuous observation, this interpretation can be extended to imply that the conditional expectation of the p-dimensional observed vector lies in a q-dimensional space, and that the p components of the deviation from the conditional expectation are conditionally independent. Then, the model matching this interpretation for an $p \times 1$ observation from the ith individual is

$$\mathbf{Z}_i = \mathbf{G}\left(\mathbf{f}_i; \mathbf{\Lambda}_0\right) + \boldsymbol{\epsilon}_i, \qquad \text{(Equation 16.4)}$$

where $\mathbf{G}$ is a p-valued function of a $q \times 1$ factor vector $\mathbf{f}_i$, $\mathbf{\Lambda}_0$ is the relationship or loading parameter indexing the class of functions, and the p components of the error vector $\boldsymbol{\epsilon}_i$ are mutually independent as well as independent of $\mathbf{f}_i$. This is a parametric version of model (16.2). The function $\mathbf{G}\left(\mathbf{f}_i; \mathbf{\Lambda}_0\right)$ defines an underlying p-dimensional manifold, or a q-dimensional curve (surface) in the p-dimensional space. This is one way to express a very general nonlinear factor analysis model for continuous measurements.

For a general nonlinear factor analysis model, it is difficult to uniquely define an unrestricted model even if the number of factors are set to a constant, unless the class of allowed nonlinear functions is specified and restricted in a certain way. This can be seen from the nonlinear surface interpretation, the factor $\mathbf{f}_i$ and the functional form $\mathbf{G}(\cdot; \Lambda_0)$ are not uniquely specified in model (16.4). That is, the same q-dimensional underlying structure given by the range space of $\mathbf{G}(\mathbf{f}_i; \Lambda_0)$ can be expressed as $\mathbf{G}^* \left(\mathbf{f}_i^*; \Lambda_0^*\right)$ using $\mathbf{G}^*$, $\mathbf{f}_i^*$, and Λ_0^* different from $\mathbf{G}$, $\mathbf{f}_i$, and Λ_0. This is the general or nonlinear version of the factor indeterminacy. In the linear model case where the indeterminacy is due to the existence of linear transformations of a factor vector (referred to as rotation), the understanding and removal by placing restriction on the model parameters were straightforward. For the general model (16.4), it is not simply linear transformations of the factor vector that lead to factor indeterminacy, but nonlinear functional transformation of the factor vector, which can lead to the same q-dimensional underlying structure. Hence, it is not immediately apparent how to express the structure imposed by the model unambiguously or to come up with a parameterization allowing a meaningful interpretation and estimation.

In their series of papers, Yalcin and Amemiya introduced an errors-in-variables parameterization for the general nonlinear model that readily removes the indeterminacy, and that is a generalization of the errors-in-variables or reference-variable approach commonly used for the linear model. In contrast to the linear case, where the errors-in-variables parameterization does not limit the space of possible linear models, it is noted that not all nonlinear surfaces $\mathbf{G}(\cdot)$ can be parameterized within the errors-in-variables framework. However, many practical and interpretable nonlinear functional forms can be and Yalcin and Amemiya (2001) emphasized the practical advantages of the errors-in-variables parameterization providing a simple and unified way to remove the factor indeterminacy in the nonlinear model, and matching naturally with a graphical model exploration and/or examination based on a scatter-plot matrix.

For the linear model case, the errors-in-variable parameterization places restrictions of being zeros and ones on the relationship or loading parameters, and identifies factors as the "true values" corresponding to the reference observed variables. Besides expressing linear model parameters uniquely and providing a simple interpretation, the errors-in-variables parameterization allowed meaningful formulation of a multipopulation and/or multisample model, and led to development of statistical inference procedures that are asymptotically valid regardless of the distributional forms for the factor and error vectors. For the general model (16.4), Yalcin and Amemiya proposed to consider models that can be expressed, after reordering of observed variables, in the errors-in-variables form

$$\mathbf{Z}_i = \left(\begin{array}{c} \mathbf{g}\left(\mathbf{f}_i; \Lambda\right) \\ \mathbf{f}_i \end{array} \right) + \epsilon_i. \qquad \text{(Equation 16.5)}$$

Here, as in the linear model case, the factor $\mathbf{f}_i$ is identified as the true value underlying the last q components (denoted $\mathbf{X}_i$) of the observed vector $\mathbf{Z}_i = \left(\mathbf{Y}_i', \mathbf{X}_i'\right)'$, and the function $\mathbf{g}(\mathbf{f}_i; \boldsymbol{\Lambda})$ gives a representation of the true value of the $(p - q) \times 1$ vector $\mathbf{Y}_i$ in terms of the true value $\mathbf{f}_i$. The explicit reduced form functional form $\mathbf{g}(\mathbf{f}_i; \boldsymbol{\Lambda})$ provides a unique parameterization of the nonlinear surface (given the choice of the reference variable $\mathbf{X}_i$). But, the identification of the relationship/loading parameter $\boldsymbol{\Lambda}$ and the error variances depend on the number of observed variables, p, in relation to the number of factors q, and on the avoidance of inconsistency and redundancy in expressing the parameterization $\mathbf{g}(\cdot; \boldsymbol{\Lambda})$.

Yalcin and Amemiya (2001) discussed a number of statistical issues relevant for factor analysis using the general models (16.4-16.5). First, the distributional assumption on the underlying factor $\mathbf{f}_i$ can be tricky. For example, if $\mathbf{g}(\mathbf{f}_i)$ is nonlinear, then the observation $\mathbf{Y}_i$ and the factor $\mathbf{f}_i$ cannot both be normal. In general, the relationship between the distributions of observations and latent variables can be nontrivial with nonlinear structure. Thus, statistical methods relying on a specific distributional assumption on the factor may not be practical or applicable broadly. This differs sharply from linear factor analysis, where it has been shown that the maximum normal likelihood estimators of the factor loadings and error variances are consistent and have nice properties for nearly any unspecified distribution of the factor vector. See, for example, Amemiya, Fuller, and Pantula (1987), Anderson and Amemiya (1988), and Browne and Shapiro (1988). The second issue is related to the use of nonlinear factor analysis in practice. An investigator or scientist may hypothesize the existence of a certain number of factors, but may not have a clear idea regarding a specific functional form for relationships. Then, the investigator should be interested in exploring various nonlinear models without changing the number of factors (and their reference variables), and in examining the fit and adequacy of each model (before increasing the number of factors). Hence, it would be useful to develop model fitting and checking procedures that can be applied to various models without worrying about the model identification and distributional assumption issues.

To address these statistical issues, Yalcin and Amemiya (2001) introduced two statistical approaches to nonlinear factor analysis using the errors-in-variables parameterization (16.5). The first approach called the extended linear maximum likelihood (ELM) method is an adaptation of a linear normal maximum likelihood algorithm with an adjustment for nonlinearity bias. This is an extension in the sense that, if the model happens to be linear, the method automatically reduces to the normal maximum likelihood known to have good properties without normality. If the model has any nonlinearity, the ELM requires computation of factor score estimates designed for nonlinear models, and evaluation of some terms at such estimates at each iteration. However, the method was developed to avoid the incidental parameter problem. In this sense, the ELM is basically a fixed-factor approach, and can be useful without specifying the distributional form for the factor. The computation of the factor score estimate for each individual at each iteration can lead to possible numerical instability and finite sample statistical inaccuracy, as evidenced in the paper's simulation study. This is a reason why Yalcin and Amemiya (2001) suggested an alternative approach.

Their second approach, the approximate conditional likelihood (ACL) method, uses the errors-in-variables parameterization (16.5), and an approximated conditional distribution of $\mathbf{Y}_i$ given $\mathbf{X}_i$. The method is also an application of the pseudolikelihood approach, and concentrates on obtaining good estimates for the relationship parameter $\mathbf{\Lambda}$ and error variances avoiding the use and full estimation of the factor distribution. Accordingly, the ACL method can be used also for a broad class of factor distributions, although the class is not as broad as that for the ELM. However, with the simpler computation, the ACL tends to be more stable numerically than the ELM.

A common feature for the ELM and ACL is that, given a specific errors-in-variables formulation with p and q (dimensions of the observed and factor vectors) satisfying

$$\frac{(p-q)(p-q+1)}{2} \geq p, \qquad \text{(Equation 16.6)}$$

almost any nonlinear model $\mathbf{g}(\mathbf{f}_i; \mathbf{\Lambda})$ can be fitted and its goodness of fit can be statistically tested. Note that the condition (16.6) is the counting-rule identification condition for the unrestricted (exploratory) linear factor analysis model (a special case of the general nonlinear model). Thus, given a particular number of factors, both methods can be used to explore different linear and nonlinear models and to perform statistical tests to assess and/or compare models. For both, the tests are based on error contrasts (defined differently for the two methods), and have an asymptotic chi-square distribution with degrees of freedom $\frac{(p-q)(p-q+1)}{2} - p$ under the model specification.

The overall discussion and approach in Yalcin and Amemiya (2001) are insightful for formulating nonlinear factor analysis and addressing statistical issues involved in the analysis. Their proposed model fitting and checking procedures are promising, but can be considered a good starting point in methodological research for nonlinear factor analysis. The issue of developing useful statistical methods for nonlinear factor analysis (addressing all aspects of analyses specific to factor analysis but not necessarily always relevant for the structural equation modeling) with minimal assumption on the factor distribution requires further investigation.

DEVELOPMENT OF NONLINEAR STRUCTURAL EQUATION ANALYSIS

With the introduction and development of LISREL (Jöreskog & Sörbom, 1981) in the late 1970s and early 1980s, came a dramatic increase in the use of structural models with latent or unmeasured variables in the social sciences (Bentler, 1980). There was an increased focus on modeling and estimating the relationship between variables in which some of the variables may be measured with error. But, as the name, "LISREL," transparently points out, it is a model and method for dealing with linear relationships thus limited in its ability to flexibly match complicated nonlinear theories.

Measurement Error Cross-Product Model

Focusing on a common nonlinear relationship of interest, Busemeyer and Jones (1983) pointed out in their introduction that "Multiplicative models are ubiquitous in psychological research" (p. 549). The kind of multiplicative model, Busemeyer and Jones (1983) were referring to is the following "interaction" or "moderator" model

$$f_3 = \alpha_0 + \alpha_1 f_1 + \alpha_2 f_2 + \alpha_3 f_1 f_2 + \delta \qquad \text{(Equation 16.7)}$$

where the latent variables (constructs) of interest f_1, f_2, and f_3 are possibly all measured with error. Busemeyer and Jones (1983) showed the serious deleterious effects of increased measurement error on the detection and interpretation of interactions, and show that multiplying variables measured with error amplifies the measurement error problem. They refer to Bohrnstedt and Marwell (1978) who provided a method for taking this amplified measurement error into account dependent on prior knowledge of the reliabilities of the measures for f_1 and f_2 and strong assumptions of their distributions. Feucht (1989) also demonstrates methods for "correcting" for the measurement error when reliabilities for the measures of latent variables were known outlining the strengths and drawbacks of the work of Heise (1986) and Fuller (1980, 1987). Lubinski and Humphreys (1990) further showed that not only could moderator effects (like the $f_1 f_2$ term in [16.7]) be missed, but that they could in some circumstances be incorrectly found when, in fact, there was some other nonmodeled nonlinear relationship in the structural model. McClelland and Judd (1993) provide a nice summary of the plentiful literature lamenting the difficulties of detecting moderator effects, giving earliest reference to Zedeck (1971). They go on to point out that one of the main problems is "field studies, relative to experiments, have non-optimal distributions of f_1 and f_2 and this means the efficiency of the moderator parameter estimate and statistical power is much lower" (p. 386).

It should be noted that additional work was also being done on more general nonlinear measurement error models than just the cross-product model (16.7). Fuller (1987) and Carroll, Ruppert, and Stefanski (1995) contain estimation methods for the nonlinear errors-in-variable model when the reliabilities for the measures of latent variables are known (or can be estimated in an obvious way). Consistent estimation of the parameters typically requires a sequence in which the error variances become small; see Wolter and Fuller (1982a, 1982b) and Amemiya and Fuller (1988). Although, for the general nonlinear measurement error model, a consistent estimator has been elusive, Fuller (1998) defines the types of conditions required to obtain one although admitting that in practice it will be difficult to verify.

Second-Order Structural Model With Linear Measurement Model Using Product Indicators

Responding to calls (e.g., by Busemeyer & Jones, 1983) for methods that could handle errors of measurement in structural models with nonlinear relations and that could deal with scenarios where reliabilities were not known but where multiple measurements of the latent variables existed, Kenny and Judd (1984) introduced a new method for estimating the coefficients of the nonlinear terms in the quadratic and cross product (interaction) structural equation model. Specifically, they dealt with the following models:

Interaction model:

$$Z_{1i} = \lambda_{11} f_{1i} + \lambda_{12} f_{2i} + \lambda_{13} f_{1i} f_{2i} + \epsilon_{1i}$$

$$Z_{2i} = \lambda_{21} f_{1i} + \epsilon_{2i}$$

$$Z_{3i} = f_{1i} + \epsilon_{3i}$$

$$Z_{4i} = \lambda_{42} f_{2i} + \epsilon_{4i}$$

$$Z_{5i} = f_{2i} + \epsilon_{5i}$$

Quadratic model:

$$Z_{1i} = \lambda_{11} f_{1i} + \lambda_{12} f_{1i}^2 + \epsilon_{1i}$$

$$Z_{2i} = \lambda_{21} f_{1i} + \epsilon_{2i}$$

$$Z_{3i} = f_{1i} + \epsilon_{3i}$$

Note that these models are, in fact, just special cases of $\mathbf{Z}_i = \boldsymbol{\mu} + \boldsymbol{\Lambda} \mathbf{g}(\mathbf{f}_i) + \boldsymbol{\epsilon}_i$ with some elements of $\boldsymbol{\Lambda}$ fixed to 1 or 0. Nevertheless, no reference was given in Kenny and Judd (1984) to any previous nonlinear factor analysis work. The basic idea of Kenny and Judd (1984) was to create new "observed variables" by taking products of existing variables and use these as additional indicators of the nonlinear terms in the model. For example, for the interaction model, consider

$$
\begin{pmatrix}
Z_{1i} \\
Z_{2i} \\
Z_{3i} \\
Z_{4i} \\
Z_{5i} \\
Z_{2i} Z_{4i} \\
Z_{2i} Z_{5i} \\
Z_{3i} Z_{4i} \\
Z_{3i} Z_{5i}
\end{pmatrix}
=
\begin{pmatrix}
\lambda_{11} & \lambda_{12} & \lambda_{13} \\
\lambda_{21} & 0 & 0 \\
1 & 0 & 0 \\
0 & \lambda_{42} & 0 \\
0 & 1 & 0 \\
0 & 0 & \lambda_{21}\lambda_{42} \\
0 & 0 & \lambda_{21} \\
0 & 0 & \lambda_{42} \\
0 & 0 & 1
\end{pmatrix}
\begin{pmatrix}
f_{1i} \\
f_{2i} \\
f_{1i} f_{2i}
\end{pmatrix}
+
\begin{pmatrix}
\epsilon_{1i} \\
\epsilon_{2i} \\
\epsilon_{3i} \\
\epsilon_{4i} \\
\epsilon_{5i} \\
u_{1i} \\
u_{2i} \\
u_{3i} \\
u_{4i}
\end{pmatrix},
$$

where

$$u_{1i} = \lambda_{21} f_{1i} \epsilon_{4i} + \lambda_{42} f_{2i} \epsilon_{2i} + \epsilon_{2i} \epsilon_{4i}$$

$$u_{2i} = \lambda_{21} f_{1i} \epsilon_{5i} + f_{2i} \epsilon_{2i} + \epsilon_{2i} \epsilon_{5i}$$

$$u_{3i} = f_{1i} \epsilon_{4i} + \lambda_{42} f_{2i} \epsilon_{3i} + \epsilon_{3i} \epsilon_{4i}$$

$$u_{4i} = f_{1i} \epsilon_{5i} + f_{2i} \epsilon_{3i} + \epsilon_{3i} \epsilon_{5i}.$$

Assuming $\mathbf{f}_i$ and $\boldsymbol{\epsilon}_i$ are normally distributed, Kenny and Judd (1984) construct the covariance matrix of $(f_{1i}, f_{2i}, f_{1i}f_{2i})'$ and $(\boldsymbol{\epsilon}', \mathbf{u}')'$. This results in many (tedious) constraints on the model covariance matrix. Despite the cumbersome modeling restrictions, this product indicator method of Kenny and Judd (1984) was possible to implement in existing linear structural equation modeling software programs (e.g., LISREL).

The Kenny and Judd (1984) technique attracted methodological discussions and alterations by a number of papers, including Hayduk (1987), Ping (1995, 1996a, 1996b, 1996c), Jaccard and Wan (1995, 1996), Jöreskog and Yang (1996, 1997), Li et al. (1998) as well as several similar papers within Schumacker and Marcoulides (1998), and within growth-curve modeling (Li, Duncan, & Acock, 2000; Wen, Marsh, & Hau, 2002). But, the method has been shown to produce inconsistent estimators when the observed indicators are not normally distributed (Wall & Amemiya, 2001). The generalized appended product indicator or GAPI procedure of Wall and Amemiya (2001) used the general idea of Kenny and Judd (1984) of creating new indicators, but stopped short of assuming normality for the underlying factors and instead allowed the higher order moments to be estimated directly rather than be considered functions of the first and second moments (as in the case when normality is assumed). The method produces consistent estimators without assuming any distributional form for the underlying factors or errors. Indeed this robustness to distributional assumptions is an advantage, yet still the GAPI procedure, like the Kenny Judd procedure entails the rather ad-hoc step of creating new product indicators and sorting through potentially tedious restrictions. Referring to Kenny and Judd (1984), MacCallum and Mar (1995) write

> Their approach is somewhat cumbersome in that one must construct multiple indicators to represent the nonlinear effects and one must determine nonlinear constraints to be imposed on parameters of the model. Nevertheless, this approach appears to be the most workable method currently available. An alternative method allowing for direct estimation of multiplicative or quadratic effects of latent variables without constructing additional indicators would be extremely useful. (p. 418)

Comparisons via simulation study between several different of the product indicator approaches for the interaction model were examined in Marsh, Wen, and Hau (2004).

Additive Nonlinear Structural Equation Model With Linear Measurement Model

The model motivating Busemeyer and Jones (1983), Kenny and Judd (1984) and those related works involved the product of two latent variables or the square of a latent variable in a single equation. Those papers proved to be the spark for a flurry of methodological papers introducing a new modeling framework and new estimation methods for the nonlinear structural equation model.

Partitioning $\mathbf{f}_i$ into endogenous and exogenous variables, i.e. $\mathbf{f}_i = (\boldsymbol{\eta}_i, \boldsymbol{\xi}_i)'$, the additive nonlinear structural equation model is

$$\mathbf{Z}_i = \boldsymbol{\mu} + \boldsymbol{\Lambda}\mathbf{f}_i + \boldsymbol{\epsilon}_i \qquad \text{(Equation 16.8)}$$

$$\boldsymbol{\eta}_i = \mathbf{B}\boldsymbol{\eta}_i + \boldsymbol{\Gamma}\mathbf{g}(\boldsymbol{\xi}_i) + \boldsymbol{\delta}_i.$$

Assuming the exogenous factors $\boldsymbol{\xi}_i$ and errors $\boldsymbol{\epsilon}_i$ and $\boldsymbol{\delta}_i$ are normally distributed, a maximum likelihood (ML) method should theoretically be possible. The nature of latent variables as "missing data" lends one to consider the use of the EM algorithm (Dempster, Laird, & Rubin, 1977) for ML estimation for (16.8). But because of the necessarily nonnormal distribution of $\boldsymbol{\eta}_i$ arising from any nonlinear function in $\mathbf{g}(\boldsymbol{\xi}_i)$, a closed form for the observed data likelihood is not possible in general. Klein, Moosbrugger, Schermelleh-Engel, and Frank (1997) and Klein and Moosbrugger (2000) proposed a mixture distribution to approximate the nonnormal distribution arising specifically for the interaction model and used this to adapt the EM algorithm to produce ML estimators. Then Lee and Zhu (2002) develop the ML estimation for the general model (16.8) using recent statistical and computational advances in the EM algorithms available for computing ML estimates for complicated models. In particular, owing to the complexity of the model, the E-step is intractable and is solved by using the Metropolis–Hastings algorithm. Furthermore the M-step does not have a closed form and thus conditional maximization is used (Meng & Rubin, 1993). Finally, bridge sampling is used to determine convergence of the MCECM algorithm (Meng & Wong, 1996). This same computational framework for producing ML estimates is then naturally used by S. Y. Lee, Song, and J. C. Lee (2003) in the case of ignorably missing data. The method is then further extended to the case where the observed variables $\mathbf{Z}_i$ may be both continuous or polytomous (Lee & Song, 2003a) assuming the underlying variable structure with thresholds relating the polytomous items to the continuous factors. Additionally a method for model diagnostics has been also proposed for the nonlinear SEM using ML (Lee & Lu, 2003).

At the same time that computational advances to the EM algorithm were being used for producing ML estimates for the parameters in model (16.8), very similar simulation-based computational algorithms for fully Bayesian inference were being applied to the same model. Given distributions for the underlying factors and errors and priors (usually noninformative priors) for the unknown parameters, Markov Chain Monte Carlo (MCMC) methods including the Gibbs sampler and Metropolis–Hastings algorithm can be relatively straightforwardly applied to (16.8). Wittenberg and Arminger (1997) worked out the Gibbs sampler for the special case cross-product model while Arminger and Muthén (1998) described the Bayesian method generally for (16.8). Zhu and Lee (1999) also present basically the same method as Arminger and Muthén (1998) but provide a Bayesian goodness-of-fit assessment. Lee and Zhu (2000) describe the fully Bayesian estimation for the model extended to include both continuous and polytomous observed variables $\mathbf{Z}_i$, like Lee & Song (2003a) do for ML estimation. Lee and Song (2003b) provide a method for model comparison within the Bayesian framework. Finally, the Bayesian method has further been shown to work for an extended model that allow for multigroup analysis (Song & Lee, 2002).

Although the ML and Bayesian methods provide appropriate inference when the distributional assumptions of the underlying factors and errors are correct, they may provide severely biased results when these noncheckable assumptions are incorrect. Moreover, there is a computational burden attached to both the ML and Bayesian methods for the nonlinear structural equation model, due to the fact that some simulation based numerical method is required.

Bollen (1995, 1996) developed a two-stage least squares method for fitting (16.8), which gives consistent estimation without specifying the distribution for $\mathbf{f}$ and additionally has a closed form. The method uses the instrumental variable technique where instruments are formed by taking functions of the observed indicators. One difficulty of the method comes from finding an appropriate instrument. Bollen (1995) and Bollen and Paxton (1998) show that the method works for the quadratic and interaction model but for general $\mathbf{g}(\boldsymbol{\xi}_i)$ it may be impossible to find appropriate instruments. For example, Bollen (1995) points out that the method may not work for the cubic model without an adequate number of observed indicators.

Wall and Amemiya (2000, 2003) introduced a two-stage method of moments (2SMM) procedure for fitting (16.8) when the nonlinear $\mathbf{g}(\boldsymbol{\xi}_i)$ part consists of general polynomial terms. Like Bollen's method, the 2SMM produces consistent estimators for the structural model parameters for virtually any distribution of the observed indicator variables where the linear measurement model holds. The procedure uses factor score estimates in a form of nonlinear errors-in-variables regression and produces closed-form method of moments type estimators as well as asymptotically correct standard errors. Simulation studies in Wall and Amemiya (2000, 2003) have shown that the 2SMM outperforms in terms of bias, efficiency, and coverage probability Bollen's two-stage least squares method. Intuition for this comes from the fact that the factor score estimates used in 2SMM are shown to be the pseudosufficient statistics for the structural model parameters in (16.8) and as such are using all the relevant information in the measurement model to estimate the structural model.

General Nonlinear Structural Equation Analysis

Two common features in the nonlinear structural equation models considered so far are the use of a linear measurement model and the restriction to additive structural models. (The linear simultaneous coefficient form in [16.8] gives only parametric nonlinear restrictions, and the reduced form is still additive in latent variables.) Also, many of the reviewed methods focus on estimation of a single structural equation, and may not be readily applicable in addressing some factor analytic issues. From the point of view that the factor analysis model is a special case of the structural equation model with no structural model, the methods already reviewed may not be considered to be nonlinear factor analysis methods. From another point of view, the structural equation system is a special case of the factor analysis model, when the structural model expressed in a reduced form is substituted into the measurement model, or when each endogenous latent variable has only one observed indicator in the separate measurement model and the equation and measurement errors are confounded. According to this, the nonlinear structural equation methods covered earlier in this section are applicable only for particular special cases of the general nonlinear factor analysis model. In this subsection, following the formulation in the subsection on general nonlinear factor analysis and related work by Amemiya and Zhao (2001, 2002), we present a general nonlinear structural equation system that is sufficiently general to cover or to be covered by the general nonlinear factor analysis model.

For a continuous observed vector $\mathbf{Z}_i$ and a continuous factor vector $\mathbf{f}_i$, the general nonlinear factor analysis model (16.4) or its form in the errors-in-variables parameterization (16.5) is a natural measurement model. A structural model can be interpreted as a set of relationships among the elements of $\mathbf{f}_i$ with equation errors. In practice, a structural model is proposed based on the subject-matter meaning or hypothesis. Each equation in the model represents a relationship with an equation error, which is assumed to have zero mean and to be independent of all the factor variables in the equation except for one (the "response" factor). For two factors f_{1i} and f_{2i}, consider a normal linear structural model

$$f_{1i} = \beta_0 + \beta_1 f_{2i} + \delta_{1i},$$

where f_{2i} and δ_{1i} are independent normal random variables, and β_0 and β_1 are unknown parameters. This model is equivalent to

$$f_{2i} = \alpha_0 + \alpha_1 f_{1i} + \delta_{2i},$$

where f_{1i} and δ_{2i} are independent normal random variables, and α_0 and α_1 are unknown parameters. But, without the normality condition or with nonlinearity, this type of equivalency no longer holds. For example, structural models

$$f_{1i} = \beta_0 \, e^{\beta_1 f_{2i}} + \delta_{1i}$$

and

$$f_{2i} = \alpha_0 + \alpha_1 \log f_{1i} + \delta_{2i}$$

are not equivalent, because of the presence of the equation error terms δ_{1i} and δ_{2i}. Hence, in expressing a nonlinear structural model, it is important to specify the way in which the equation error term enters the model. Emphasizing this point, a recursive nonlinear structural model can be specified, for example, as

$$f_{1i} - \beta_{10} - \frac{\beta_{11}}{1 + exp(\beta_{12}\, f_{2i} + \beta_{13}\, f_{3i})} = \delta_{1i}, \quad \text{(Equation 16.9)}$$

$$f_{2i} - \beta_{20} - \beta_{21}\, f_{3i} - \beta_{22}\, f_{3i}^2 = \delta_{2i}.$$

A model can be a simultaneous system without having a recursive nature, and can also be more implicit without an obvious response variable. But, any structural model can be written as a set of equations, each of which contains an equation error. Thus, one way to express a general structural model is

$$\mathbf{H}(\mathbf{f}_i; \boldsymbol{\beta}_0) = \boldsymbol{\delta}_i, \quad \text{(Equation 16.10)}$$

where $\boldsymbol{\delta}_i$ is a zero-mean $r \times 1$ equation error, and an r-valued function $\mathbf{H}(\cdot; \boldsymbol{\beta}_0)$ specifies relationships. Each row of (16.10) represent a single relationship that can be nonlinear in both $\mathbf{f}_i$ and $\boldsymbol{\beta}_0$. However, model (16.10) itself is not given in an identifiable form, in the sense that it is not written in an unambiguous way. For example, the multiplication of an $r \times r$ matrix does not alter the meaning of the model. One way to eliminate this indeterminacy is to consider an explicit reduced form. If (16.10) can be (at least theoretically) solved for r components of $\mathbf{f}_i$ in terms of other $q - r$ components, we obtain an explicit reduced form structural model

$$\boldsymbol{\eta}_i = \mathbf{h}(\boldsymbol{\zeta}_i; \boldsymbol{\beta}), \quad \text{(Equation 16.11)}$$

where

$$\mathbf{f}_i = \begin{pmatrix} \boldsymbol{\eta}_i \\ \boldsymbol{\xi}_i \end{pmatrix},$$

$$\boldsymbol{\zeta}_i = \begin{pmatrix} \boldsymbol{\xi}_i \\ \boldsymbol{\delta}_i \end{pmatrix}, \quad \text{(Equation 16.12)}$$

and $\boldsymbol{\delta}_i$ is the original equation error in (16.10). In general, solving a nonlinear implicit function (16.10) results in the equation error term $\boldsymbol{\delta}_i$ entering the explicit function $\mathbf{h}$ nonlinearly. If model (16.10) is recursive in $\mathbf{f}_i$ as in (16.9), then the explicit reduced model (16.11) can be obtained by recursive substitutions.

The explicit reduced model (16.11) is identiable as long as the parameter $\boldsymbol{\beta}$ has no redundancy. Thus, one can avoid the model ambiguity or identification problem by working only with structural models given in this explicit reduced form. Some structural models, for example, a recursive model, can be written in an unambiguous way without solving in an explicit reduced form. But, the explicit reduced form (16.11) provides a unified framework for the general nonlinear structural model.

By substituting the reduced form structural model (16.11) into the general nonlinear factor measurement model (16.5), we obtain an observation reduced form of the general nonlinear structural equation system

$$
\mathbf{Z}_i = \begin{pmatrix} \mathbf{g}\left(\mathbf{h}(\boldsymbol{\zeta}_i; \boldsymbol{\beta}), \boldsymbol{\xi}_i; \boldsymbol{\lambda}\right) \\ \mathbf{h}(\boldsymbol{\zeta}_i; \boldsymbol{\beta}) \\ \boldsymbol{\xi}_i \end{pmatrix} + \boldsymbol{\epsilon}_i . \qquad \text{(Equation 16.13)}
$$

This can be considered the general structural equation model in the measurement errors-in-variables parameterization and the structural reduced form. Written in this way, the general nonlinear structural equation system (16.13) is a nonlinear factor analysis model with a factor vector $\boldsymbol{\zeta}_i$ in (16.12). This model is similar to the errors-in-variables general nonlinear factor analysis model (16.5), except that $\boldsymbol{\delta}_i$, a part of the factor vector, does not have a reference observed variable but is restricted to have mean zero. The work of Amemiya and Zhao (2001, 2002) is being extended to develop statistical methods appropriate for the general nonlinear structural equation model (16.13).

CONCLUSION

In the last 100 years, the development of statistical methods for factor analysis has been motivated by scientific and practical needs, and has been driven by advancement in computing. This is also true for nonlinear factor analysis. As reviewed here, the needs for considering nonlinearity from scientific reasons were pointed out very early. But, the methodological research has become active only in recent years with the wide availability of the computing capabilities. Also, as in the linear case, the introduction of the LISREL or structural equation modeling was influential. The errors-in-variables (reference-variable) parameterization and the relationship-modeling approach, both made popular by LISREL, have been helpful in developing model formulation approaches and model fitting methods.

Nonlinear methodological research has broadened the scope and the applicability of factor analysis as a whole. The interdependency among multivariate observations are no longer assessed only through correlations and covariances, but can now be represented by complex relationship models. Important subject-matter questions involving nonlinearity, such as the existence of a cross-product or interaction effect, can now be addressed using nonlinear factor analysis methods.

As discussed in this chapter, the general formulation of nonlinear factor and structural equation analyses has emerged recently. This is an important topic for understanding the theoretical foundation and unification of such analyses. In this general context, there are a number of issues that can benefit from further development of statistical methods. One such issue is the basic factor analysis concern of determining the number of underlying factors or the dimensionality of nonlinear underlying structure. In general, more complete and useful methods for exploring multivariate data structure, rather than for fitting a particular model, are welcome. Another issue lacking proper methodology is the instrument assessment and development incorporating possibly nonlinear measurements. Also, the development of useful statistical procedures that are applicable without assuming a specific factor distributional form will continue to be a challenge in nonlinear factor analysis methodology. Nonlinear multipopulation and longitudinal data analyses need to be investigated as well. Nonlinear factor analysis methodological development is expected to be an active area of research for years to come.

REFERENCES

Amemiya, Y. (1993a). Instrumental variable estimation for nonlinear factor analysis. In C. M. Cuadras & C. R. Rao, (Eds.), *Multivariate Analysis: Future Directions 2* (pp. 113–129). Amsterdam: Elsevier.

Amemiya, Y. (1993b). On nonlinear factor analysis. *Proceedings of the Social Statistics Section, the Annual Meeting of the American Statistical Association*, 92–96, 290–294.

Amemiya, Y., & Fuller, W. A. (1988). Estimation for the nonlinear function relationship. *Annals of Statistics, 16,* 147–160.

Amemiya, Y., Fuller, W. A., & Pantula, S. G. (1987). The asymptotic distributions of some estimators for a factor analysis model. *Journal of Multivariate Analysis, 22,* 51–64.

Amemiya, Y., & Zhao, Y. (2001). Estimation for nonlinear structural equation system with an unspecified distribution. *Proceedings of Business and Economic Statistics Section, the Annual Meeting of the American Statistical Association* [CD-ROM].

Amemiya, Y., & Zhao, Y. (2002). Pseudo likelihood approach for nonlinear and non-normal structural equation analysis. *Business and Economic Statistics Section, the Annual Meeting of the American Statistical Association* [CD-ROM].

Anderson, T. W., & Amemiya, Y. (1988). The asymptotic normal distribution of estimators in factor analysis under general conditions. *The Annals of Statistics, 16,* 759–771.

Arminger, G., & Muthén, B. (1998). A Bayesian approach to nonlinear latent variable models using the Gibbs sampler and the Metropolis–Hastings algorithm. *Psychometrika, 63*(3), 271–300.

Bartlett, M. S. (1953). Factor analysis in psychology as a statistician sees it. In *Uppsala Symposium on Psychological Factor Analysis* [Nordisk Psykologi's Monograph Series No. 3, 23–34]. Copenhagen: Ejnar Mundsgaards, Stockholm: Almqvist & Wiksell.

Bentler, P. M. (1980). Multivariate analysis with latent variables: Causal modeling. *Annual Review of Psychology, 31,* 419–457.

Bohrnstedt, G. W., & Marwell, G. (1978). The reliability of products of two random variables In K. F. Schuessler (Ed.), *Sociological Methodology* (pp. 254–273). San Francisco: Jossey-Bass.

Bollen, K. A. (1995). Structural equation models that are nonlinear in latent variables: A least squares estimator. *Sociological Methodology,* 223–251.

Bollen, K. A. (1996). An alternative two stage least squares (2SLS) estimator for latent variable equation. *Psychometrika, 61,* 109–121.

Bollen, K. A., & Paxton, P. (1998). Interactions of latent variables in structural equation models. *Structural Equation Modeling,* 267–293.

Browne, M. W. (1984). Asymptotically distribution free methods for the analysis of covariance structures. *British Journal of Mathematical and Statistical Psychology, 37,* 62–83.

Browne, M. W., & Shapiro, A. (1988). Robustness of normal theory methods in the analysis of linear latent variate models. *British Journal of Mathematical and Statistical Psychology*, *41*, 193–208.

Busemeyer, J. R., & Jones, L. E. (1983). Analysis of multiplicative combination rules when the causal variables are measured with error. *Psychological Bulletin*, *93*, 549–562.

Carroll, R. J., Ruppert, D., & Stefanski, L. A. (1995). *Measurement error in nonlinear models*, London: Chapman & Hall.

Dempster, A. P., Laird, N. M., & Rubin, D. B. (1977). Maximum likelihood from incomplete data via the EM algorithm [with discussion]. *Journal of the Royal Statistical Society, Series B*, *39*, 1–38.

Etezadi-Amoli, J., & McDonald, R. P. (1983). A second generation nonlinear factor analysis. *Psychometrika*, *48*(3) 315–342.

Ferguson, G. A. (1941). The factorial interpretation of test difficulty. *Psychometrika*, *6*(5), 323–329.

Feucht, T. (1989). Estimating multiplicative regression terms in the presence of measurement error. *Sociological Methods and Research*, *17*(3), 257–282.

Fuller, W. A. (1980). Properties of some estimators for the errors-in-variables model. *Annals of Statistics*, *8*, 407–422.

Fuller, W. A. (1987). *Measurement error models*. New York: Wiley.

Fuller, W. A. (1998). Estimation for the nonlinear errors-in-variables model. In R. Galata & H. Küchenhoff (Eds.), *Econometrics in theory and practice* (pp. 15–21). Heidelberg, Germany: Physica-Verlag.

Gibson, W. A. (1951). *Applications of the mathematics of multiple-factor analysis to problems of latent structure analysis*. Unpublished doctoral dissertation, University of Chicago.

Gibson, W. A. (1955). Nonlinear factor analysis, single factor case. *American Psychologist* [Abstract], *10*, 438.

Gibson, W. A. (1956). Nonlinear factors in two dimensions. *American Psychologist* [Abstract], *11*, 415.

Gibson, W. A. (1959). Three multivariate models: Factor analysis, latent structure analysis, and latent profile analysis. *Psychometrika*, *24*, 229–252.

Gibson, W. A. (1960). Nonlinear factors in two dimensions. *Psychometrika 25*, (4), 381–392.

Hastie, T., & Stuetzle, W. (1989). Principal curves. *Journal of the American Statistical Association 84*(406), 502–516.

Hayduk, L. A. (1987). *Structural equation modeling with LISREL: Essentials and advances*. Baltimore: Johns Hopkins Press.

Heise, D. R. (1986). Estimating nonlinear models correcting for measurement error. *Sociological Methods and Research*, *14*, 447–472.

Honkela, A. (2004). *Bayesian algorithms for latent variable models*. Retrieved October 21, 2005, from http://www.cis.hut.fi/projects/bayes/

Jaccard, J., & Wan, C. K. (1995). Measurement error in the analysis of interaction effects between continuous predictors using multiple regression: Multiple indicator and structural equation approaches. *Psychological Bulletin*, *117*(2), 348–357.

Jaccard, J., & Wan, C. K. (1996). *LISREL approaches to interaction effects in multiple regression*. Beverly Hills, CA: Sage.

Jöreskog, K. G., & Sörbom, D. (1981). *LISREL: Analysis of linear structural relationships by the method of maximum likelihood*. Chicago, IL: National Educational Resources.

Jöreskog, K. G., & Yang, F. (1996). Non-linear structural equation models: The Kenny-Judd model with interaction effects. In G. A. Marcoulides & R. E. Schumacker (Eds.), *Advanced structural equation modeling: Issues and techniques* (pp. 57–88). Mahwah, NJ: Lawrence Erlbaum Associates.

Jöreskog, K. G., & Yang, F. (1997). Estimation of interaction models using the augmented moment matrix: Comparison of asymptotic standard errors. In W. Bandilla & F. Faulbaum (Eds.), *SoftStat '97 advances in statistical software 6* (pp. 467–478). Stuttgart, Germany: Lucius and Lucius.

Jutten, C., & Karhunen, J. (2004). Advances in blind source separation (BSS) and independent component analysis (ICA) for nonlinear mixtures. *International Journal of Neural Systems*, *14*(5), 267–292.

Kenny, D.A., & Judd, C. M. (1984). Estimating the nonlinear and interactive effects of latent variables. *Psychological Bulletin*, *96*(1), 201–210.

Klein, A., & Moosbrugger, H. (2000). Maximum likelihood estimation of latent interaction effects with the LMS method. *Psychometrika*, *65*(4), 457–474.

Klein, A., Moosbrugger, H., Schermelleh-Engel, K., & Frank, D. (1997). A new approach to the estimation of latent interaction effects in structural equation models. In W. Bandilla & F. Faulbaum (Eds.), *SoftStat '97 advances in statistical software 6* (pp. 479–486). Stuttgart, Germany: Lucius and Lucius.

Lawley, D. N., & Maxwell, A. E. (1963). *Factor analysis as a statistical method*. London: Butterworths.

Lazarsfeld, P. F. (1950). The logical and mathematical foundation of latent structure analysis. In S. A. Stouffer (Ed.), *Measurement and prediction* (pp. 362–412). Princeton: Princeton University Press.

Lee, S. Y., & Lu, B. (2003). Case-deletion diagnostics for nonlinear structural equation models. *Multivariate Behavioral Research*, *38*(3), 375–400.

Lee, S. Y., & Song, X. Y. (2003a). Maximum likelihood estimation and model comparison of nonlinear structural equation models with continuous and polytomous variables. *Computation and Statistical Data Analysis*, *44*, 125–142.

Lee, S. Y., & Song, X. Y. (2003b). Model comparison of nonlinear structural equation models with fixed covariates. *Psychometrika*, *68*(1), 27–47.

Lee, S. Y., Song, X. Y., & Lee, J. C. (2003). Maximum likelihood estimation of nonlinear structural equation models with ignorable missing data. *Journal of Educational and Behavioral Statistics*, *28*(2), 111–134.

Lee, S. Y., & Zhu, H. T. (2000). Statistical analysis of nonlinear structural equation models with continuous and polytomous data. *British Journal of Mathematical and Statistical Psychology*, *53*, 209–232.

Lee, S. Y., & Zhu, H. T. (2002). Maximum likelihood estimation of nonlinear structural equation models. *Psychometrika*, *67*(2), 189–210.

Lewin-Koh, S. C., & Amemiya, Y. (2003). Heteroscedastic factor analysis. *Biometrika*, *90*(1), 85–97.

Li, F., Harmer, P., Duncan, T., Duncan, S., Acock, A., & Boles, S. (1998). Approaches to testing interaction effects using structural equation modeling methodology. *Multivariate Behavioral Research*, *33*(1), 1–39.

Li, F. Z., Duncan T. E., & Acock, A. (2000). Modeling interaction effects in latent growth curve models. *Structural Equation Modeling*, *7*, 497–533.

Lubinski, D., & Humphreys, L. G. (1990). Assessing spurious 'moderator effects' illustrated substantively with the hypothesized 'synergistic' relation between spatial and mathematical ability. *Psychological Bulletin*, *107*, 385–393.

MacCallum, R. C., & Mar, C. M. (1995). Distinguishing between moderator and quadratic effects in multiple regression. *Psychological Bulletin*, *118*(3), 405–421.

Marsh, H. W., Wen, Z., & Hau, K. T. (2004). Structural equation models of latent interactions: Evaluation of alternative estimation strategies and indicator construction. *Psychological Methods*, *9*(3), 275–300.

McClelland, G. H., & Judd, C. M. (1993). Statistical difficulties of detecting interactions and moderator effects. *Psychological Bulletin*, 114(2), 376–390.

McDonald, R. P. (1962). A general approach to nonlinear factor analysis. *Psychometrika*, *27*(4), 397–415.

McDonald, R. P. (1965). Difficulty factors and nonlinear factor analysis, *Psychometrika*, *18*, 11–23.

McDonald, R. P. (1967a). Factor interaction in nonlinear factor analysis. *British Journal of Mathematical and Statistical Psychology*, *20*, 205–215.

McDonald, R. P. (1967b). Numerical methods for polynomial models in nonlinear factor analysis. *Psychometrika*, *32*(1), 77–112.

McDonald, R. P. (1979). The simultaneous estimation of factor loadings and scores. *British Journal of Mathematical and Statistical Psychology*, *32*, 212–228.

Meng, X. L. & Rubin, D. B. (1993). Maximum likelihood estimation via the ECM algorithm: A general framework. *Biometrika*, *80*, 267–278.

Meng, X. L., & Wong, W. H. (1996). Simulating ratios of normalizing constants via a simple identity: A theoretical exploration. *Statistic Sinica*, *6*, 831–860.

Molenaar, P. C., & Boomsma, D. I. (1987). Application of nonlinear factor analysis to genotype–environment interactions. *Behavior Genetics*, *17*(1), 71–80.

Mooijaart, A., & Bentler, P. (1986). Random polynomial factor analysis. In E. Diday, Y. Escoufier, L. Lebart, J. Pages, Y. Schektman, et al. (Eds.), *Data analysis and informatics* (Vol. 4, pp. 241–250). Amsterdam: Elsevier.

Ping, R. A. (1995). A parsimonious estimating technique for interaction and quadratic latent variables. *Journal of Marketing Research*, 32, 336–347.

Ping, R. A. (1996a). Estimating latent variable interactions and quadratics: The state of this art. *Journal of Management*, *22*, 163–183.

Ping, R. A. (1996b). Latent variable interaction and quadratic effect estimation: A two-step technique using structural equation analysis. *Psychological Bulletin*, *119*, 166–175.

Ping, R. A. (1996c). Latent variable regression: A technique for estimating interaction and quadratic coefficients. *Multivariate Behavioral Research*, *31*, 95–120.

Schumacker, R., & Marcoulides, G. (Eds). (1998). *Interaction and nonlinear effects in structural equation modeling*. Mahwah, NJ: Lawrence Erlbaum Associates.

Song, X. Y., & Lee, S. Y. (2002). A Bayesian approach for multigroup nonlinear factor analysis. *Structural Equation Modeling*, *9*(4), 523–553.

Taleb, A. (2002). A generic framework for blind source separation in structured nonlinear models. *IEEE Transactions on Signal Processing*, *50*(8), 1819–1830.

Wall, M. M., & Amemiya, Y. (2000). Estimation for polynomial structural equation models. *Journal of the American Statistician, 95*, 929–940.

Wall, M. M., & Amemiya, Y. (2001). Generalized appended product indicator procedure for nonlinear structural equation analysis. *Journal of Educational and Behavioral Statistics, 26*(1), 1–29.

Wall, M. M., & Amemiya, Y. (2003). A method of moments technique for fitting interaction effects in structural equation models. *British Journal of Mathematical and Statistical Psychology, 56*, 47–63.

Wen, Z., Marsh, H. W., & Hau, K. T. (2002). Interaction effects in growth modeling: A full model. *Structural Equation Modeling*, *9*(1), 20–39.

Wittenberg, J., & Arminger, G. (1997). Bayesian non-linear latent variable models-specification and estimation with the program system BALAM. In W. Bandilla & F. Faulbaum (Eds.), *SoftStat '97 Advances in Statistical software 6* (pp. 487–494). Stuttgart, Germany: Lucius and Lucius.

Wolter, K. M., & Fuller, W. A. (1982a). Estimation of the quadratic errors-in-variables model. *Biometrika*, *69*, 175–182.

Wolter, K. M., & Fuller, W. A. (1982b). Estimation of nonlinear errors-in-variables models. *Annals of Statistics, 10*, 539–548.

Yalcin, I., & Amemiya, Y. (1993). Fitting of a general nonlinear factor analysis model. *Proceedings of the Statistical Computing Section, the Annual Meeting of the American Statistical Association*, 92–96.

Yalcin, I., & Amemiya, Y. (1995). An algorithm for additive nonlinear factor analysis. *Proceedings of the Business and Economic Statistics Section, the Annual Meeting of the American Statistical Association*, 326–330.

Yalcin, I., & Amemiya, Y. (2001). Nonlinear factor analysis as a statistical method. *Statistical Science, 16*(3), 275–294.

Zedeck, S. (1971). Problems with the use of 'moderator' variables. *Psychological Bulletin, 76*, 295–310.

Zhu, H. T., & Lee, S. Y. (1999). Statistical analysis of nonlinear factor analysis models. *British Journal of Mathematical and Statistical Psychology, 52*, 225–242.

Contributors

Yasuo Amemiya is Manager, Statistical Analysis and Forecasting at the IBM Thomas J. Watson Research Center. He is an elected fellow of the American Statistical Association, and has served on the editorial boards of various statistical journals. His research areas include latent variable statistical analysis. Prior to joining IBM, he was a professor of Statistics at Iowa State University.

David J. Bartholomew is Emeritus Professor of Statistics in the London School of Economics and Political Science. He is a Fellow of the British Academy, a Fellow of the Institute of Mathematical Statistics, and Past President of the Royal Statistical Society. Much of his research has been on statistical problems in the social sciences and his most recent book is *Measuring Intelligence: Facts and Fallacies* (Cambridge University Press, 2004).

R. Darrell Bock is Professor Emeritus in the Department of Psychology at the University of Chicago, where he served as chairman of the Committee on Methodology and Quantitative Psychology. He is Past President of the Psychometric Society, a founding member of the Behavior Genetics Association, and a Fellow of the American Statistical Association and the Royal Statistical Society. His research interests include statistical methods and computation, item response theory, behavior genetics, and the modeling and prediction of human growth. He is author, with Lyle Jones, of *The Measurement and Prediction of Judgment and Choice, Multivariate Statistical Methods in Behavioral Research*, and, with Elsie Moore, *Advantage and Disadvantage: A Profile of American Youth*, and editor and contributor to *Multilevel Analysis of Educational Data*.

Kenneth A. Bollen is Director of the Odum Institute for Research in Social Science and the H. R. Immerwahr Distinguished Professor of Sociology at the University of North Carolina at Chapel Hill. He is the Year 2000 recipient of the Lazarsfeld Award for Methodological Contributions in Sociology. The ISI named him among the World's Most Cited Authors in the Social Sciences. He is coauthor, with P. Curran, of *Latent Curve Models: A Structural Equations Approach*, and author of *Structural Equation Models with Latent Variables*, and of over 90 papers. Dr. Bollen's primary areas of statistical research are structural equation models and latent curve models.

Michael W. Browne obtained his PhD in Statistics from the University of South Africa. He has been Chief Research Officer at the South African National Institute for Personnel Research and Professor of Statistics at the University of South Africa. He is now Professor of Psychology and Professor of Statistics at the Ohio State University. He is a former President of the South African Statistical Association, the Psychometric Society, and the Society for Multivariate Experimental Psychology (SMEP), and a recipient of the Sells Award for distinguished lifetime achievement in multivariate experimental psychology from SMEP. His research has been primarily concerned with statistical modeling of multivariate psychological data. He has made contributions on asymptotically distribution-free estimation in the analysis of moment structures, asymptotic robustness of multivariate normal theory against violation of assumptions, multiplicative models for multitrait–multimethod data, circumplex models for the investigating the personality circle, and rotational methodology for factor analysis and structured latent curve models for repeated measurements over time. His main current interests are in latent time series models and in component analysis of Q-score profiles.

Li Cai is currently a PhD student in the L. L. Thurstone Psychometric Laboratory at the University of North Carolina at Chapel Hill. He is simultaneously pursuing a Master of Science degree in statistics. His main area of interest is in estimation and inference for latent variable models, particularly computational procedures and model–data fit evaluation for latent trait models with categorical observed variables.

Robert Cudeck received his PhD from the University of Southern California and is currently a member of the Psychology Department at Ohio State University. His research activities are concerned with applications of factor analysis, structural equation models, and random coefficient models for repeated measures data in the behavioral sciences.

John L. Horn was a professor of psychology at the University of Southern California (USC), and he died in August 2006. During his years at the University, Dr. Horn was involved in graduate student education, including his training grants, courses, and graduate and undergraduate advising. Dr. Horn received his PhD in psychology from the University of Illinois. Here he studied with Sam Hammond. When he returned to the United Sates, he moved to Illinois to study with Ray Cattell. Dr. Horn's principal lines of research were on the development of human abilities over the lifespan, assessment of alcohol use and abuse, motivation, and mathematical and/or statistical methods of analysis, particularly factor analysis (invariance of, measurement of, and number of factors). During his illustrious career, Dr. Horn received a Fulbright Fellowship (Australia), a Fulbright-Hays Award (Federal Health Institute, Yugoslavia), visiting professorships at the University of California (Berkeley), University College (London) and University of Lund (Sweden), a Career Development Award (National Institutes: Aging) and both the R. B. Cattell Award for distinguished contributions by a young investigator and the S. B. Sells Award for lifetime achievements from the Society for Multivariate Experimental Psychology, in which group he was also elected President. For the past 15 years, Dr. Horn was an active member of the Data Analysis Research Network of the National Collegiate Athletic Association (NCAA). His most recent work focused on his research on "Adult Lifestyle and Intellectual Development," and his recent collaborations included a National Institute of Child Health and Human Development (NICHD) funded grant on "The Impact of Neglect on Adolescent Development" with Penelope Trickett, and Ferol Mennen of the USC School of Social Work. Chapter 11 in this volume (by Horn and McArdle) represents his last published work.

Robert I. Jennrich is Professor Emeritus in the Department of Mathematics at the University of California Los Angeles. He designed many of the components of the original BMDP statistical software system, is former Chair of the Statistical Computing Section of the American Statistical Association, a Fellow of the Institute of Mathematical Statistics, and a Fellow of the American Statistical Association. His research interests are in statistical computing, nonlinear regression, and psychometric methods. He has published a book entitled *An Introduction to Computational Statistics: Regression Analysis.*

Lyle V. Jones is Research Professor of Psychology at The University of North Carolina at Chapel Hill. Earlier he served there as Vice Chancellor and Dean of the Graduate School, Alumni Distinguished Professor, and Director of the Psychometric Laboratory. He is Past President of the Psychometric Society, the American Psychological Association's Division 5, and the Association of Graduate Schools, and is an elected fellow of the American Academy of Arts and Sciences and an elected member of the Institute of Medicine. In 2001, he was designated a lifetime national associate of the National Academies, and in 2004, he was the recipient of the Sells Award, bestowed by the Society of Multivariate Experimental Psychology for outstanding career contributions.

Karl G Jöreskog is Professor Emeritus of Multivariate Statistical Analysis at Uppsala University and Professor II at the Norwegian School of Management in Oslo, Norway. He is a past president of Psychometric Society and has received several awards for distinguished contributions in psychometrics and structural equation models. He developed the LISREL model for structural equation modeling and, together with Dag Sörbom he developed the LISREL computer program.

Robert C. MacCallum is Professor of Psychology and Director of the L. L. Thurstone Psychometric Laboratory at the University of North Carolina at Chapel Hill. He assumed these positions in 2003 following 28 years on the faculty at Ohio State University. He received his graduate training at the University of Illinois under the direction of Ledyard R. Tucker, the most prominent protégé of L. L. Thurstone. His research interests focus on methods for analysis and modeling of correlational and longitudinal data, including factor analysis, structural equation modeling, and multilevel modeling.

John J. (Jack) McArdle is currently Senior Professor of Psychology and head of the Quantitative Area at the University of Southern California. From 1984 to 2005, he was a faculty member at University of Virginia where he taught Quantitative Methods and was director of the Jefferson Psychometric Laboratory. He currently teaches classes in topics in psychometrics, multivariate analysis, and structural equation modeling. Since 2000, he has led the Advanced Training Institute on Longitudinal Modeling for the American Psychological Association. Dr. McArdle's research has been focused on age-sensitive methods for psychological and educational measurement and longitudinal data analysis, including work in factor analysis, growth curve analysis, and dynamic modeling of adult cognitive abilities. Dr. McArdle is now director of the ongoing National Growth and Change Study (NGCS), a longitudinal study of cognitive changes over age over the United States. Dr. McArdle has won the Cattell Award for Distinguished Multivariate Research (1987), was elected President of the Society of Multivariate Experimental Psychology (1993–1994), was elected President of the Federation of Behavioral, Psychological, and Cognitive Sciences (1996–1999), and was elected as the Secretary of the Council of Scientific Society Presidents (CSSP, 2000–2002). In 2002–2003, he was named Lansdowne Professor of the University of Victoria and Jacob Cohen Lecturer of Columbia University. In 2003, he was also named the Best Academic Researcher by the National Collegiate Athletic Association. In 2004 he was named a Co-PI of the HRS and in 2005 he was awarded an NIH-MERIT grant from the National Institute on Aging for his work on longitudinal-psychometric methodology.

William Meredith attended the University of Washington where he earned his PhD with Paul Horst in 1958; he also studied with Allen Edwards. After working for the Washington Pre-College Differential Guidance Program, he accepted, in 1960, a position in the Department of Psychology at the University of California at Berkeley, where he remained until his retirement in 1994. He worked with Robert Tryon at Berkeley. He is a Past President of the Psychometric Society and of the Society for Multivariate Experimental Society.

Roger E. Millsap is a Professor in the Department of Psychology at Arizona State University. He received his PhD in quantitative psychology from the University of California–Berkeley in 1983. His research interests include psychometric theory, latent variable models, and multivariate statistics. His recent published work has largely concerned the problem of detecting bias in psychological measurement, and the properties of statistical methods that are designed to detect such bias. Dr. Millsap served as Editor of *Multivariate Behavioral Research* from 1996 until 2005 and will become Editor of Psychometrika in 2007. He served as President of Division 5 (Evaluation, Measurement, and Statistics) of the American Psychological

Association during the 2004–2005 term, and is a Past President of the Society of Multivariate Experimental Psychology.

Irini Moustaki is an Associate Professor in the Statistics Department at the Athens University of Economics and Business, Greece. She is also a Research Fellow in the Statistics Department at the London School of Economics. Her research interests include latent variable models for categorical responses and mixed type responses, modeling of missing values, model diagnostics, and goodness-of-fit measures. She is an associate editor of the journals, *Computational Statistics and Data Analysis, Structural Equation Modeling and Methodology: European Journal of Research Methods for the Behavioral and Social Sciences.* She is the coauthor of the book, *The Analysis and Interpretation of Multivariate Data for Social Scientists*, published by Chapman and Hall/CRC and coeditor of the book, *Latent Variable and Latent Structure Analysis*, published by Lawrence Erlbaum Associates.

John R. Nesselroade is Hugh Scott Hamilton Professor of Psychology at the University of Virginia, where he has been since 1991. Prior to his current appointment, Dr. Nesselroade was at The Pennsylvania State University for 19 years and at West Virginia University for 5 years. He received his PhD from the University of Illinois in 1967, where he studied primarily with Raymond B. Cattell but was fortunate to take courses with the likes of Rolf Bargmann, Lloyd Humphreys, Henry Kaiser, and Ledyard Tucker, scholars who knew more than a little about the common factor model. Dr. Nesselroade is Past President of the Society of Multivariate Experimental Psychology and the Division of Adult Development and Aging (Division 20) of the American Psychological Association. His current research interests include both substantive and methodological aspects of the study of intraindividual variability and change in personality and ability over the lifespan.

Melanie M. Wall is Associate Professor in the Division of Biostatistics within the School of Public Health at the University of Minnesota. Her research interests are in statistical methods for latent variable modeling and extending traditional latent variable models (e.g., to include nonlinearities, spatial structure, and both categorical and continuous latent variables) making them more attractive to a variety of researchers. In particular, she works on applying latent variable models to answer research questions relevant for behavioral public health.

Keith F. Widaman is Professor of Psychology at the University of California, Davis. He is Past President of the Society of Multivariate Experimental Psychology (SMEP), received the Cattell Award from SMEP for outstanding early career contributions to multivariate psychology, and has twice won the Tanaka Award for best article of the year published in *Multivariate Behavioral Research*. His substantive research interests include the structure, development, and cognitive processes underlying mental abilities, the development of adaptive behavioral skills by persons with mental retardation, and the ways in which genes and environmental agents influence behavioral development within family contexts. His quantitative interests include correlation and/or regression analysis, common factor analysis, and structural equation modeling, especially factorial invariance and the analysis of multitrait–multimethod data.

Guangjian Zhang received his PhD in Quantitative Psychology from the Ohio State University in 2006, and also received a Master of Science degree in Statistics at the same university. He currently holds a postdoctoral position in psychology at Notre Dame. Prior to coming to the United States, he completed his medical qualifications in the Republic of China and was a certified medical doctor. His main interests are in dynamic factor analysis, longitudinal analysis, structural equation modeling and computing.

Author Index

Subject Index

A

Aikaike Information Criterion (AIC), 103
Alpha factor analysis, 169–173
Army Alpha, 26
Autocorrelation
    for latent variables, 274–276
    for measured variables, 273–274

B

Bayesian Information Criterion (BIC), 103
Bi-factor theory, 230

C

Censoring, 295–296
Coefficient alpha, 169
Common factors
    relation to observed variables, 10,
      153
    weak common factors, recovery of,
      161–173
Common factor model, 13–15, 35–36, 42,
    48, 101, 186, 315–318
    as an approximation, 153–189
    in multiple populations, 132–133
    as a statistical model, 13–15, 159

sources of error in, 153–154,
    160–161
Communalities, 28, 37, 40, 42, 49–50
    relationship to estimation of factor
      loadings, 191–192
    squared multiple correlations, 49
Components analysis, *see* Principal
    components
Conditional independence, 16, 20, 337
Confirmatory factor analysis, 58–62,
    99–100
    estimation in, 60
    and factorial invariance, 140–141
Congruence coefficient, 139, 165–172
Correction for attenuation, 155, 208
Correlation
    partial, 10, 48, 155
    polychoric, 71
    tetrachoric, 71
Cross-lagged model, 117
Cross-validation, 58

D

Difficulty factor, 341–342
Discrepancy functions, 102, 159, *see also*
    Estimation methods
    asymptotically distribution free,
      69–70